Visions from the Golden Land

Burma and the Art of Lacquer

Visions from the Golden Land

Burma and the art of lacquer

Ralph Isaacs and T. Richard Blurton

ART MEDIA RESOURCES

© 2000 The Trustees of the British Museum

Published by Art Media Resources, Ltd.
First published in the United States in 2000
by Art Media Resources, Ltd.
1507 South Michigan Avenue,
Chicago, Illinois, 60605
Email: info@artmediaresources.com
Web: www.artmediaresources.com

Library of Congress Cataloguing-in-Publication Data
A CIP catalog record of this book is available from
the Library of Congress

ISBN 1-878529-68-4 (Hardcover)
ISBN 1-878529-69-2 (Softcover)

First published in 2000 by British Museum Press
A division of The British Museum Company Ltd
46 Bloomsbury Street, London WC1B 3QQ

Designed by Tim Harvey
Printed and bound in England by
Balding + Mansell

Frontispiece: Detail of water bowl, cat. 70. Scenes
from the *Kusa Jataka*, with captions in palm-leaf
shaped cartouches. Prince Kusa deploys his many
talents to win back his runaway bride. At top right
he is Minister in charge of her royal father's
elephant stable, responsible for pageantry and
ceremonial. At lower centre he is seen throwing a
pot, as Minister for Ceramics. At top centre he
plays a harp in masterly fashion. However, all his
virtuosity leaves the proud princess Papawati
(centre left) unimpressed.

Contents

Preface

This Preface is divided into four parts, the first written by
Richard Blurton, and the rest by Richard Blurton and Ralph
Isaacs. These sections are
1 The Ralph and Ruth Isaacs Collection
2 Acknowledgements
3 How to use this book
4 Note to readers

1

The Ralph and Ruth Isaacs Collection

This book and the exhibition it accompanies have come about
as a result of a gift from one of the authors – Ralph Isaacs – to
the institution where the other author – Richard Blurton – is a
curator. The collection given by Ralph and Ruth Isaacs of 269
items of Burmese lacquerware covers a huge range from the
workaday to the very special, and was put together in the
early 1990s. It has transformed the holdings of the British
Museum where the collection is now housed, not only in
number of items, but more importantly in actual and potential
increase in knowledge of Burma and its culture. This is
especially important to the Museum given the lack of
knowledge of Burma amongst the general public. The Museum
is thus extremely grateful to Mr and Mrs Isaacs for the
opportunity their generous gift has provided. The collection
entered the Museum in 1998 and work on registering, storing
and studying it began the following year, based on Ralph
Isaacs' considerable manuscript record. With such a large
collection it is inevitable that this is only a first statement
about many of the items in it. Both of the authors found that
once research began, there seemed almost no limit to what
could be unearthed – so little has been studied to date, but so
much is available, not least in the records and archives in
London. This publication is made up of items from the Isaacs
Collection (about half the total), items from the existing
collections of the British Museum and items generously loaned
from other institutions. If this book encourages scholars to
pursue their interest in Burma and by their research to
question and revise what we have assembled, we shall have
fulfilled our task.

T. Richard Blurton

2

Acknowledgements

Any merit this work may claim, the authors share with
teachers, some of them established in the teaching profession,
but most recruited to the teaching role as the need arose for
help and guidance. Staff of the British Council in Rangoon
were most easily importuned for assistance in translating
Burmese inscriptions on lacquerware (often abominably spelt
and sometimes only partly legible), but nobody met with in
Burma or in Europe was immune. Informants and instructors
included university lecturers, medical doctors, librarians, a
master woodcarver and architect – not to speak of makers,
sellers and collectors of lacquerware in Pagan and the driver of
horse cart No 28. It is not the Burmese custom to refrain from
naming those who give and we give their names below. A
smaller group though must be described first as over many
years they have given unstintingly of their deep knowledge of
the literature, art and culture of Burma. For Patricia Herbert,
Sylvia Fraser-Lu, John Okell and Noel Singer we are deeply
grateful. Their scholarship and encouragement have greatly
enhanced the interest of this work and its value to future
researchers. Its deficiencies are our own.

Both authors also want to put on record their appreciation
of the staff at British Museum Press with whom we have
worked, often in difficult circumstances. Our editor Coralie
Hepburn has struggled against all the odds to ensure that the
book eventually saw the light of day and to save us from
emulating the example of Sir George Watt, curator of the
Indian Art Exhibition of 1902–3 whose catalogue (frequently
quoted by us) was issued several months after the exhibition
closed. In this she was aided by Nicola Denny, Colin Grant and
Antonia Brook. In the vexed question of the Burmese script
and its use in the chapter dealing with inscriptions, we were
dependent on Kevin Wang; our debt to him is considerable.
Earlier at the Press we were encouraged by Teresa Francis.
The designer of this book, Tim Harvey, deserves our special
thanks for producing a beautiful-looking publication in record
time.

Within the Museum we wish to make a special record of
our debt to members of the Security staff who have been
indulgent in their agreement to allow access to stores and
offices out of hours; one special occasion will long be

remembered. Richard Blurton also gratefully acknowledges Wladimir Zwalf, former colleague at the British Museum, who encouraged him, over many years, to take up the study of the Burmese collections at the Museum. Help provided at a critical moment by Dr Venetia Porter is remembered with thanks.

Funders for the exhibition, its education programme and for this volume are especially worthy of remark as finding finance for anything to do with Burma is exceptionally difficult. For help towards both the exhibition and the Education programme we are happy to credit the Burma Project (Open Society Institute, New York – Maureen Aung-Thwin and Debby Corper); further for the Education programme we thank the Paul Hamlyn Foundation (Patricia Lankester), and the Charles Wallace (Burma) Trust (David Waterhouse). For support of the exhibition we record the Missorten Foundation (Alain Missorten), Olympus (Ian Dickens), CPL, Sheldon and Barbara Kent, Sir Jeremy Isaacs, and the British Museum Friends (Sarah Carthew). For a financial contribution towards the costs of this publication we are happy to acknowledge the Green Trust at the Royal Pavilion, Art Gallery and Museums in Brighton.

Beyond these special acknowledgements, we also record our thanks to – Mrs Anna Allott (SOAS, London), Cheri Aung Khin (Bangkok), Hsaya Aung Thin (Rangoon), Erik Bentsen (UNICEF), Mrs Colleen Beresford (Tisbury), Dr Stuart Blackburn (SOAS, London), Terry Blackburn (Luton), Vicky Bowman (Brussels), Mrs Daphne Brink (Cambridge), Dr Elizabeth Dell (Brighton), Mrs Frances Franklin (Victoria and Albert Museum, London), Dr Henry Ginsburg (British Library, London), the late Sao Sai Hseng Hpa (Rangoon), U Htein Win (Rangoon), (the proprietors of) the Htun Workshop (Pagan), Dr Hu Shih-Chang (Hong Kong), Norma and Maurice Joseph (Droxford), Dr Khin May Sein (Kilmalcolm), Grace Krishnaswami (Madras), U Kyaw Zan Tha (London), the Hon. Mrs Marten (Wimbourne), Dr Maung Maung Tin (Rangoon), Daw May Kyi Win (De Kalb), Mr Alain Missorten (Brussels), Dr Elizabeth Moore (SOAS, London), U Myo Nyunt (Pagan), Mr Henry Noltie (Edinburgh), Nalini Persaud (British Library, London), Dr Jessica Rawson (Oxford), Andrew Robinson (London), Hkam Hpa Tu Sadan (Brighton), U Sein Lwin (British Council, Rangoon), Hsaya Sein Myint (Mandalay), Mrs Sarah Simpson (Brighton), Tan Bee Tin (Bognor Regis), U Thaw Kaung (Rangoon), Gillian Thida Moh (Rangoon), Daw Thin Thin Naing (Rangoon), Tom White (London), and Hsaya Win Maung 'Tampawaddy' (Ava).

For generously lending objects in their care to the exhibition and also frequently providing information, we thank the following – British Library, Oriental and India Office Collections: Annabel Teh Gallop, Beth McKillop, John Falconer and Lydia Seager; Ipswich Borough Council Museums and Galleries: David Jones and Sally Dummer; Missorten Foundation, Brussels: Alain Missorten; National Museums and Galleries on Merseyside: Louise Tythacott, Tony Eccles, Anne Fahy, Jen Kainer, and Loraine Knowles; the National Trust: Andrew Barber (East Midlands Regional Office), Paul Copestoke, Christopher Hagon, and Jill Banks (Kedleston Hall) and Sarah Hickey (London) also Mike Williams, freelance photographer; Royal Albert Memorial Museum and Art Gallery, Exeter: Len Pole; Royal Botanic Gardens at Kew (Centre for Economic Botany): Hew Prendergast and Naomi Rumball; Royal Pavilion, Art Gallery and Museums, Brighton (Green Centre for Non-Western Art): Elizabeth Dell and Caroline Cook; University of Cambridge Museum of Archaeology and Anthropology, Dr D. W. Phillipson, Dr Anita Herle and John Osbourne; Victoria and Albert Museum: Dr Deborah Swallow, Rosemary Crill, Dr John Clarke, Nicholas Barnard, Andrew Butterton, Barbara O'Connor and Miranda Percival.

Within the British Museum we record the support for the exhibition project of Dr Robert Anderson (Director) and Suzanna Taverne (Managing Director). For loans from within the Museum, we thank Dr John Mack, Dr Brian Durrans and Sara Pimpaneau (Ethnography); and Antony Griffiths, Stephen Coppel, Sheila O'Connell and Janice Reading (Prints and Drawings). The personal interest of Frank Minney (Conservation) in all matters concerned with lacquer has made his professional contribution especially valuable; we also thank David Singleton. Both the authors wish to record their very special debt to John Williams and Kevin Lovelock in the Photographic Section; much of their work was carried out to a very tight schedule and without complaint. We acknowledge with thanks the photographs commissioned from the various lending institutions; also we wish to especially thank Norma and Maurice Joseph for the generous use of photographs in the exhibition and also the photograph on p.36. The opportunity to publish the two photographs on p.22 is one for which we are very grateful to Noel Singer and to U Yu Thein (Principal, Myanmar Lacquerware Institute) and U Thaung Naing (Curator of the Lacquerware Museum).

Within the Department of Oriental Antiquities the sterling work of the Senior Museum Assistant, Sophie Sorrondegui, and Museum Assistants, Sussanah Chan, Jane Newson and Stephen Ruscoe is recalled with thanks. Steve Drury-Thurgood in the same department arranged all the loans, work that, at the beginning of the project was undertaken by Maureen Theobald. We acknowledge the generous support of the exhibition project by the Keeper, Robert Knox which resulted in his release of Richard Blurton from usual Museum duties. Also within the department we acknowledge the friendship and scholarly contribution of colleagues – Dr Sheila Canby, Dr Anne Farrer, Jessica Harrison-Hall, Justin Morris, Jane Portal, Rachel Ward and Dr Michael Willis. It is also a delight to recall the never-failing enthusiasm and charm of Mary Bagulay and

Yvonne Ashcroft. In the Design Office, it is a pleasure to mention the work of Jonathan Ould, Andrea Carr and Nicholas Newbury; the initiative taken by all of them is recalled with admiration. In the Education Department we thank especially John Reeve for perceiving the possibilities that the exhibition provided.

Finally, we put on record the names of Ruth Isaacs and Martin Williams. Only they know the extent of their contribution and we dedicate this book to them.

3
How to use this book

This publication has a dual function – initially it is a catalogue to an exhibition at the British Museum, 'Visions from the Golden Land: Burma and the art of lacquer', which runs from 8 April to 13 August 2000. Above and beyond this, we hope the book will function as a resource for those interested in the culture of Burma in general, and in lacquer in particular. To enable it to accomplish the second requirement, a few words are needed about the way in which the items have been arranged in the catalogue as the catalogue numbers, in broad outline, follow the layout of the exhibition. This layout has been determined using the following headings (the relevant catalogue numbers appear in brackets):

1   A dazzling introductory array of objects illustrating the range of magnificent objects made in Burma using lacquer (1–11).

2   The botanical recording of lacquer (12–13), the antecedents of engraved decoration in the Thai tradition (14–16) and items produced for exhibitions during the colonial period (17–18).

3   The substrates used for lacquer decoration – bamboo, cane, wood, cloth, etc. (19–27).

4   Tools for making lacquer vessels (28–9) and a sequence of plates to illustrate the way in which vessels are made and how the engraved, *yun*, decoration is executed (30).

5   Types of decoration – moulded lacquer putty, *thayo*, (31–2); inset coloured glass *hmanzi shwe cha* (33); black-and-gold, and red-and-gold decoration, *shwe zawa* (34 and 35); black-and-gold relief (36), lacquer as paint (37–8).

6   Lacquer used for sculpture – dry-lacquer (39) and on wood (40).

7   Non-figured decoration on vessels – from plain basketry (41) and its imitation (42), through to 'cloud collar' (50–2) and the 'chilli-seed' pattern (53).

8   Figured decoration on vessels – from the 'nightmare' design (54) and the 'figures and buildings' design (55) to Vessantara Jataka (69) and Kusa Jataka (70).

9   The religious sphere – Buddha images (71–7), manuscripts and folding books (78–87), offering vessels (88–98), manuscript chests, *sadaik* (99–102) and items illustrated in them (103 and 104), and equipment for the religious life (105–14).

10   The secular sphere – containers for spices, *thanahka*, medicine and cigarettes (115–20), carrying and storing water, flowers and clothes (121–5), musical instruments and the drama (126–130), betel boxes (131–2), drink and food – storage, cooking and serving, especially of rice (133–144), *lahpet* (145), miscellaneous containers (146–50), lacquer vessels of non-Burmese shape (151–4).

11   Regional variation – Kyaukka (155), Mandalay (156), Ava (157), Pagan (158–9), Prome (160), Laihka, Shan States (161), Shan States (162), Intha (163), Kentung (164–5); two Chettiar items, with Tamil inscriptions (166).

12   Inscriptions on vessels, including good wishes to buyer (167), maker's name (168–9), caption to Vessantara Jataka (170), display of calligraphy (171), donor's dedication of a manuscript (172), details of donor's gift (173), good wishes for promotion (174), captions to narrative (175), nationalist sentiment (176–7), owner's name (178–9).

13   Contemporary work (180–81, 183–5) and a vessel (182) illustrating an earlier version of (183).

The catalogue is followed by an Appendix which consists of a very imperfect list of the names and approximate dates of some lacquer makers. It is hoped that owners of signed pieces may be encouraged to record the inscriptions and to have them interpreted. Gradually in this way, gaps may be filled and a more coherent and informative account emerge of the names, style and succession of the makers.

Note to readers

Various conventions have been used in this book. For Burmese terms and names we have been guided by John Okell hoping to arrive at a consistent and sensible way of presenting the Burmese sounds. However, for the sake of simplicity, we have not used either tonal accents or hyphens. The purist may find this regrettable, but we suspect that the majority of our readers will be glad of it as those who know how to correctly pronounce the Burmese will do so with or without the marks while those who do not know will be confused by their presence. Similarly, on the occasions when we use Sanskrit terms, we do not use diacritical marks, instead adding extra letters where pronunciation in English requires it. Thus, *bhumisparshamudra*, rather than *bhumisparsamudra* with an accent on the final 's' and no following 'h'. In the area of Buddhist terms we have generally used the Sanskrit where the term is very well known (often appearing in OED), such as Gautama, Bodhisattva, *stupa*, *nirvana*. Terms which are specific to Theravada Buddhism, appear in the Pali or the Burmese

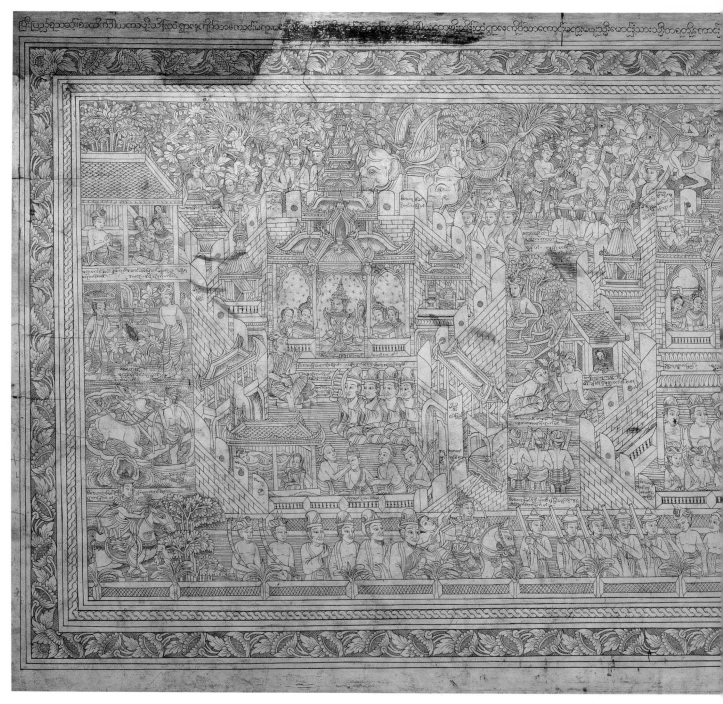

Cat. 102. Panel from a manuscript chest, *sadaik.* Burma, probably Pegu, late 18th or early 19th century.

form. There is a Glossary at the end of the book containing words in all three languages.

Each entry in the catalogue begins with basic data, including from which collection it comes. If from within the British Museum, it is prefixed with OA (Department of Oriental Antiquities, the majority), Ethno. (Department of Ethnography) or P&D (Department of Prints and Drawings). Other basic detail listed here includes dimensions where height is shown as 'H',

and diameter as 'D'; other dimensions are written out in full. Also listed here is the material of which the object is made. For the large number of vessels, this is often split bamboo, coiled or woven, but to avoid endless repetition, we have merely given 'bamboo' and where this appears it should be understood as 'split bamboo'. Whether it is coiled or woven is usually recorded in the descriptive text which follows – if it is known. In another area we have, however, allowed ourselves

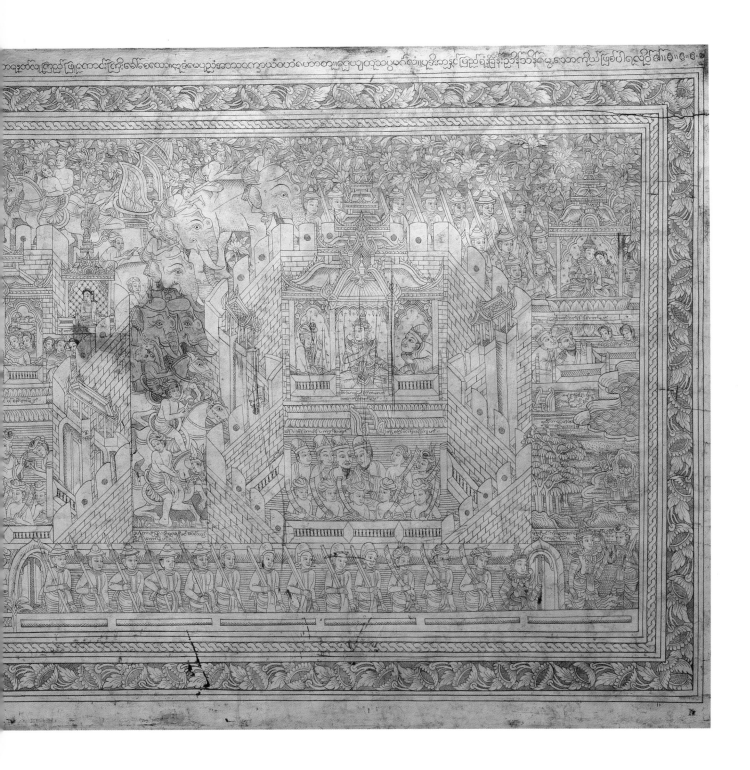

some repetition. This concerns important information concerning function of items and history. We expect that after the exhibition is over, most readers of this book will not read it from cover to cover but will use it as a reference volume, dipping into it for data on individual items. There is thus a need for a certain amount of information to be repeated – not least because for most of our readers, what we are presenting will be quite new and there will be no easy array of cultural 'hooks' on which to 'hang' it. For those stalwarts who read every word from cover to cover we ask your indulgence to us for this concession to those who have less time and stamina.

T. Richard Blurton
Ralph Isaacs

Introduction

This book is concerned with one of the major artistic traditions – lacquerwork – of a major Asian country, Burma.[1] Despite the rapid communications that mark the world today and the powerful advent of Southeast Asian economies on to the international stage, the artistic traditions of Burma – and indeed the country itself – are little known today either to the general public or to the scholarly community. This is largely explained by the fact that for much of the last fifty years Burma has been difficult to visit for long periods and, further, the Burmese government has frequently pursued a deliberate policy of self-containment and self-sufficiency, eschewing involvement with international activities. Given this situation, we are fortunate that through the subject of lacquer we are able to examine not only lacquer production and history but also many aspects of cultural life in Burma – from the rituals of Buddhism to those of chewing betel nut – for lacquer has, traditionally, been used in a huge range of activities. This book, therefore, is planned as a view of Burmese culture seen through one subject – lacquer.

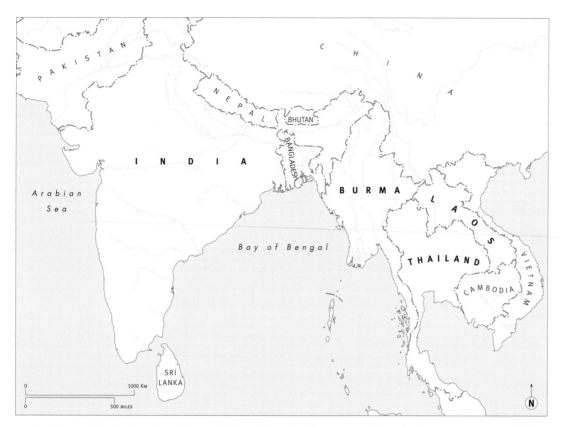

We hope that this publication and the exhibition it accompanies will in a small way add to an understanding of this important country. Faced with the general lack of knowledge about Burma, this book begins with an introduction presenting some concise information about the country, its geography, ethnic mix, history and religion. This provides a background against which the objects discussed can be better understood. Following this introduction are essays more specifically concerned with lacquer and its uses; after this comes the catalogue itself.

Burma: the country

The country of Burma is made up of several disparate geographical regions, as the current boundaries of the country are in part the result of recent colonial history. Some of these divisions also reflect the ethnic divisions that have had such a profound influence upon Burmese politics, both before and after Independence in 1948. The Burmese, who are of Tibeto-Burman stock linguistically and are almost entirely Buddhist by religion, make up the majority of the population.[2] Approximately speaking, they occupy the central, riverine sector of the country. This region is dominated by the vast Irrawaddy river,[3] which acts as the main artery of communication in central Burma. It rises in the eastern Himalayas like those other great rivers of Southeast Asia, the Salween and the Mekong. The two main headwaters of the Irrawaddy join near Myitkyina, and then flow southwards with a considerable 'kick' westwards after Bhamo, and again after Mandalay. The northern river valleys are densely forested and the source of valuable timber, while just to the north and east of Mandalay is the town of Mogok, centre of the ruby mining district; other precious stones such as sapphires, jade and amber are also mined in the north of the country. Just south of Mandalay the Chindwin enters from the northwest, and the river then runs southwards, passing on the way the oil deposits at Yenangyaung. The Irrawaddy eventually debouches into the Andaman Sea through the channels of a huge and fertile delta – this is a major rice-growing region, which in the first half

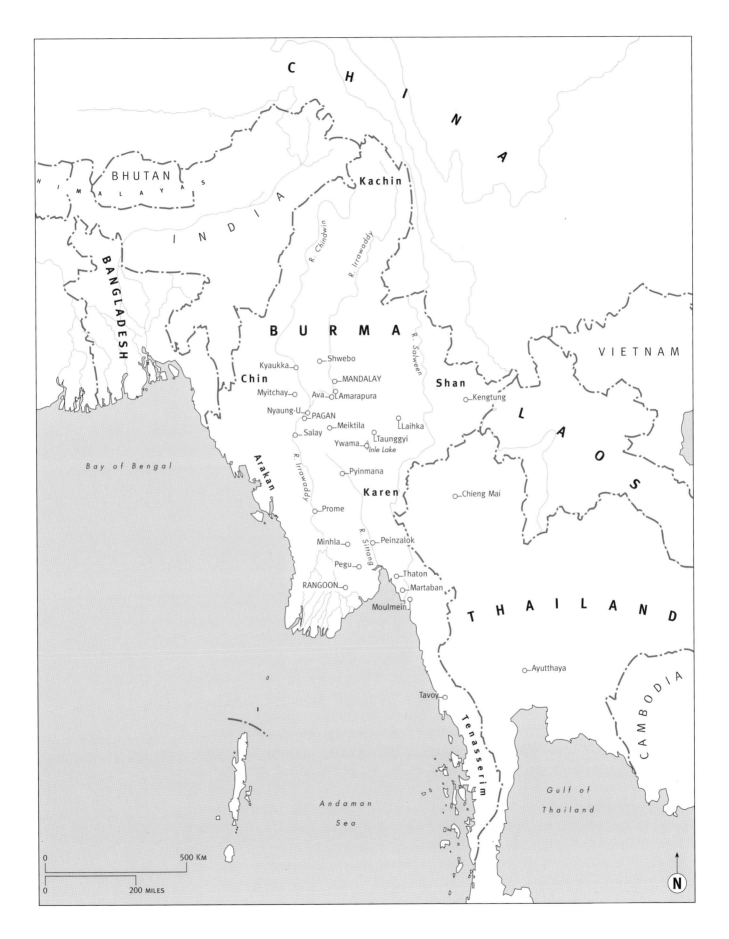

of the twentieth century enabled Burma to export large quantities of rice, as well as support its growing population. In this delta are located present-day Rangoon,[4] as well as the sixteenth-century capital of Pegu. Rangoon has historically been important as the location of the Shwe Dagon, the pagoda within which are enshrined Burma's most revered relics, hairs of Gautama the Buddha. During the colonial period it became the political, and above all, commercial centre of British Burma. Although many Burmese live today in Rangoon, the delta is historically the homeland of the Mon whose area of activity previously stretched eastwards from here around the Gulf of Martaban and into modern Thailand. Linguistically and ethnically they are related to the Khmer of Cambodia, as well as the rulers of the ancient kingdom of Dvaravati in central Thailand.[5]

Ringing this central region dominated by the Irrawaddy and its delta, are mountainous and forested areas, contiguous – east to west – with parts of modern Thailand, southwestern China, Tibet and northeastern India. These areas are, and continue to be, the seat of different ethnic groups with more or less distinctive cultures and languages, some of whose inventive uses of lacquer are described elsewhere in this book. Many of them have been in conflict with the military regime in Rangoon since independence.[6] Some of the most important, out of a very large number of disparate groups, include – from east to west – the Karen (located to the east of the Gulf of Martaban), the Shan who are ethnically close to the Thai (and found in the great eastwards extension of Burma bisected by the Salween river), the Kachin in the far north of the country, the Chin on the northwest frontier with India, and finally, in the west and separated from the Irrawaddy valley by yet further mountains, the Arakanese who have historically had close links with Bengal and who maintained an independent state until conquered by the Burmese in 1784. Arakan is also the homeland to many of Burma's Muslim population, while the Karen and Kachin states have significant Christian communities. In all these cases the difference in religion from the majority of Burmese emphasises the feeling of separateness found in these peripheral regions.

Burma: a historical sketch

The task of writing a modern English-language history of Burma, from the remote period until the present day, is still to be done. The most recent attempt was by Hall as long ago as 1950, but in many respects we are still dependent on Harvey's 1926 volume. A number of books and articles have, however, appeared more recently dealing with specific periods of Burmese history (for all these, see Bibliography).

Although Stone and Bronze Age cultures are recorded from various parts of Burma, urbanization probably did not begin until the turn of the millennium BC/AD[7] and is associated with the Pyu, a people whose main settlements were at Beikthano, and Sri Ksetra near modern Prome.[8] The Pyu were in contact with, and were clearly influenced by, the culture of southeastern India. They used both Pali (for many) and Sanskrit (for a few) of their rarely surviving inscriptions, and wrote these inscriptions in a script based on the south Indian Kadamba script. Above all, they received Buddhism from this part of India. These influences – Indian script and Indian religion – were to have a lasting effect on Burma, the profundity of which it is almost impossible to exaggerate. Lastly, and importantly within this present study devoted to lacquer, is the record in the Chinese sources that the wooden palace architecture of the Pyu was decorated with cinnabar – the brilliant red colouring agent made from mercuric sulphide.[9] In later times this colour, when used architecturally, would be applied in liquid form, suspended in lacquer sap. We cannot be certain, but it seems likely that it was during this period that lacquer was first used in Burma; also that the necessary techniques were learnt from the Chinese who had cultural and diplomatic contacts with the Pyu and who had been using lacquer in numerous contexts for at least two millennia by this date.

The Pyu cities seem to have been overwhelmed during the ninth century AD, and probably at about this time the Burmese first entered the Irrawaddy valley from the northeast; the two facts are probably connected. The greatest cultural legacy of these incoming Burmese, who settled above all in Upper Burma, was the establishment of their capital city at Pagan, the overthrow and inclusion in their empire of the Mon kingdom of Thaton,[10] and the gradual establishment of Theravada Buddhism at the expense of other schools of Buddhism that the early Burmese kings supported.[11] The eleventh and twelfth centuries saw the city of Pagan become one of the most important cities of Asia, a fact that can still be gauged from the huge array of ruined structures on the banks of the Irrawaddy to the southwest of Mandalay. Many of the kings were patrons of architecture on a spectacular scale, building hundreds of pagodas, shrines and monasteries at Pagan alone, among the most notable being the Ananda temple, which is still in use. Today one can only wonder at the economic manipulation required to support such a huge investment in activity that was economically non-productive. It was also a time of international contact – for instance with eastern India, the holy land of Buddhism, as well as with China.

We may again assume that in the Pagan period lacquer was used in architectural decoration as in Pyu times, and we can also add to this its use in sculpture. From the late Pagan period onwards, wooden sculptures were covered in red colouring carried in lacquer; examples exist both at Pagan and in museum collections around the world.[12] Finally, evidence has recently come to light of the use of lacquer in the Pagan period to cover vessels made of woven split bamboo; this is discussed further at p.22.

The Pagan period was one of political and territorial consolidation but was followed by a lengthy period in which exactly the opposite tendencies were manifest. The Pagan empire fell apart under various strains: internal, such as the huge alienation of land and wealth to the monkhood; and external, such as the advent of the armies of Kublai Khan at the gates of the city in 1287 and the slightly later overwhelming penetration into Burma of the Shans from southwestern China.[13] It was followed by a lengthy period of disintegration and confusion with separate centres of power growing up in Arakan, in the Mon delta region based on Pegu, and in central Burma under in-coming Shan kings based at Sagaing and then Ava. The kings at Pegu, most famous of whom was the pious Dhammaceti (reigned 1472–92), were eventually subdued by Burmese kings based at Toungoo, who also subsequently ruled at Pegu and then Ava. The two most famous kings of this Burmese dynasty, Tabinshweti and Bayinnaung undertook glorious, but eventually exhausting, foreign campaigns. They in their turn were deposed by Mon rebels who were countered by the first ruler of the Konbaung dynasty, Alaungpaya (reigned 1752–60), the founder of the last Burmese dynasty before British colonial rule. Once more the Burmese took centre stage and embarked on a period of expansion and international contact within southeast Asia.

The eighteenth century saw frequent diplomatic contact with both China and Thailand. The latter especially had a profound effect on the Burmese court, particularly following the Burmese sack of the Thai capital, Ayutthaya. The Burmese king, in time-honoured fashion, brought back to his capital not only political prisoners, but also captive artisans. It was this practice which was probably responsible in the late eighteenth century for the introduction into Burma of the type of engraved decoration on lacquered surfaces known as *yun*. During this period the court was based variously at Ava, Amarapura and eventually Mandalay (founded 1857).

It was also in the late eighteenth century that the first serious contact with the British occurred. As in neighbouring India, conquest was gradual, initially determined by border disputes and by trade in the time of the East India Company. Later, though, it was just as much affected by Imperial policy, especially the attempt to lessen the influence of the French. During the late eighteenth and throughout the nineteenth centuries we are fortunate in having accounts of Burma and the Burmese court from officials of the East India Company who were sent to the Burmese capital to negotiate. The records of these envoys, being contemporary accounts, are of the highest importance, even if some display the bias of their time.[14] The First Anglo-Burmese War of 1825 resulted in the cession to the British of Arakan (already contiguous with British-controlled Bengal) and Tenasserim. In 1852 the Second Anglo-Burmese War ended with Lower Burma falling to the British, and the Third War, in 1885, resulted in the fall of Mandalay, the deposition of the last Burmese kings and the annexation of Upper Burma by the British.[15] Although the subjugation of Burma took at least five further years, the whole of Burma remained part of the British Empire, with the exception of the Japanese occupation (1942–5), until Independence in 1948, when it also left the British Commonwealth. For most of the colonial period it was also ruled as part of India; only from 1937 did it have its own separate status as a colony. Freedom from colonial rule was gained under the leadership of Aung San, who tragically was assassinated in the final days before independence.

Following independence Burma forged its own system, strictly Burmese, Buddhist and socialist. This resulted in it turning its back on the rest of Southeast Asia and the area's dramatic economic changes. The craft traditions of the periphery regions of the country – Karen, Shan and Chin – have been badly disrupted for the fifty years since independence due to civil unrest. Meanwhile the tourist trade, of great importance to the same Pagan lacquer masters whose work is seen in this catalogue, has been hit by the embargo on tourism called for by opposition politicians.

Buddhism in Burma

The religion and philosophy of Buddhism was founded by a historical figure who probably lived in the sixth and late fifth centuries BC, although some scholars would place his dates slightly later. His life story is frequently illustrated in Burmese art, including items decorated with lacquer (see cat. 100 and 101). According to legend he was born as Siddhartha and brought up in the town of Kapilavastu on the borders of what is now Nepal and India. It is recorded that his birth was prefigured in a dream and that he was born, miraculously, from the right side of his mother, queen Maya. He was born into a princely family and lived in luxury until, seeing a poor man, an ill man and then a dead man, he realized that all the luxury of palace life could not protect him from these eventualities. Following this realization and in the dead of night, he left his wife and child in the palace and departed for the forest where, in time-honoured Indian fashion, he cut his hair and became a wandering ascetic. Studying with various teachers, he never found the answer to his questions about the nature of life until, alone and having abandoned all other philosophical systems, he gained Enlightenment through his own meditation seated beneath a peepul tree[16] at Gaya. He reached this point of Enlightenment having overcome the temptations and distractions of the senses, realized in physical form as the terrifying army and the seductive daughters of the demon king Mara, scenes frequently depicted in Burmese art. Following his Enlightenment, he walked to Benares where he delivered his First Sermon, just outside the city at Sarnath. In this and then many other discourses he taught a Middle Way, devoid of extremes. He said that all existence is suffering, that suffering is caused by desire, that desire can be eliminated and that this can be done by leading a life according to certain moral precepts. Practically, these moral precepts could really only be followed by those prepared to abandon all ties and become itinerant monks supported by a lay community. The ideal was thus to become a monk, and his followers quickly elevated three elements to represent the summation of their beliefs: the Buddha himself; the *dharma*, his teaching; and the *sangha*, or body of monks, who followed his teachings and taught them. These elements make up the 'Triple Gem', which all Buddhists honour or, to use the Buddhist terminology, in which all Buddhists 'take refuge'.

The Buddha accepted the Indian ideas of reincarnation and the law of *karma* – the notion that deeds committed in the present have a direct bearing on experience in the future, i.e. the law of cause and effect, both in this life and in future lives. Following his Enlightenment and First Sermon, the Buddha taught in many parts of eastern India, gathering about him many disciples who memorized his sayings which were only much later written down. On his death he entered Nirvana, or the Void, as through his attainment of Enlightenment he had escaped the tyranny of rebirth. He experienced no further rebirths because during his previous births he had accumulated sufficient merit to attain Buddhahood in his final life. Quite quickly following his death these previous existences began to be elaborated and collected in a sequence of stories, the *jataka* stories. These provided a huge reservoir for story-telling and for depiction in sculpture, painting and other arts, as can be seen especially in the art of Burma (see cat. 70, 102 and 180).

The first monks who followed the Buddha became the first members of the *sangha*, from whom those in Burma today trace their apostolic and spiritual succession. During his lifetime the Buddha taught but did not receive veneration, and it was only following his death, when his ashes were enshrined in semi-circular, solid tumuli, or stupas,[17] that a cult of the Buddha slowly developed based on the stupa as a symbol of the Nirvana, and thus the triumph, of the Buddha. The great Shwe Dagon in Rangoon is such a monument (see p. 11). Originally a small heterodox sect confined to eastern India, these doctrines spread dramatically within India during the reign of the emperor Ashoka (273–232 BC) and indeed outside India. Traditionally, the first missionary to Sri Lanka was the son of Ashoka, Mahinda. According to legend, this was also a time when missionaries were sent to Burma, though there is no historical evidence to support this.

One of the great untold narratives of South and Southeast Asia concerns the spread of Buddhism from southern India, throughout the coastal regions of Southeast Asia. Sadly, because texts do not survive, we are unlikely ever to know the elements of this extraordinary tale, though archaeology – especially in the Mon areas of Burma – might fill in a few of the shadowy details. Combining tradition and archaeological discovery, it is nevertheless clear that Buddhism arrived in Burma from important cult centres such as Amaravati and Nagarjunakonda in what is now Andhra Pradesh, in southern India. This proselytizing activity must have begun by at least the fifth century AD, though tradition records missionaries arriving in Burma during the lifetime of the Buddha himself almost a thousand years before. No surviving evidence, however, supports a date that early or before the archaeological finds from the Pyu city of Sri Ksetra such as the Maunggun gold plates (fifth century AD). These are written in a script closely related to a south Indian one and record in Pali the Buddhist creed. The evidence from Sri Ksetra also supports the introduction at this early date of both Hinayana and Mahayana schools of Buddhism.[18] Later, the Mons, from their southern cities such as Thaton, appear to have maintained contact with south India, and when Theravada doctrines triumphed there and then also in Sri Lanka, the Mons seem to have followed suit.

This also meant that they received the Buddhist canon, the *Tipitaka*,[19] in Pali, the language that by then had become adopted by the Theravada in India for their scriptures.

As already mentioned, it is clear from the archaeological evidence that the Mahayana was present in Burma during the Pyu period. Consequently it is not surprising that it is also apparent at Pagan and this can be demonstrated by wall-paintings in some of the temples, which clearly indicate the veneration of Bodhisattvas. This was doubtless linked to contact between Pagan and eastern India,[20] which was not only the Holy Land of Buddhism but also the home to the most developed of the Mahayana cults. However, it is during the Pagan period, and traditionally during the reign of Anawrahta (reigned 1044–77) following his capture of the Mon kingdom of Thaton, that the Pali canon, and monks practised in its use, were forcibly brought to Pagan; whether this introduction was actually linked to the sack of the city or to later contact is not now clear. What is certain though is that Mon civilization – writing, texts, monasticism – had a profound effect on the development of Pagan society. Slowly but inexorably, from the early Pagan period onwards, the Theravada school with its Pali canon and links to Sri Lanka gained the upper hand. In only a couple of centuries Burma became a Theravada country. Although schisms continued, indeed right to the present day, these have invariably only been concerned with matters of discipline or ritual, rather than doctrine.

While early missionary links were with south India, the decline there of Buddhism but its sturdy survival in Sri Lanka meant that this contact became increasingly important. On two occasions (1180 and 1475) monks went from Burma to Sri Lanka for re-ordination to ensure that a valid and orthodox lineage could be re-established in Burma. On one other occasion Burmese monks provided the same service for the Sri Lankan *sangha* (1071).

In all countries where Theravada Buddhism is practised, the body of monks, the *sangha*, and the discipline by which they live together in the monastery form the basis of the religious life; only rarely do monks live alone as hermits.[21] For the *sangha* to function, it depends on a supportive body of lay followers, and the importance of this is demonstrated in purely physical terms by the large number of objects produced traditionally in Burma for the offering or collecting of alms; many are seen in this volume. The system of giving is beneficial in both directions, for not only is the monk sustained by the gift (usually of food) but the donor gains merit by making the gift. Indeed, the Burmese word for monk is *hpongyi*, based on the Pali word *punna*, or merit – he both has great merit and also enables others to gain it.[22] The most severe condemnation for a monk to inflict is to refuse a gift, for this means that the layman is cut off from the possibility of gaining merit and thus of advancing towards Nirvana. Some monks live all their lives in the monastery, but much larger numbers of men in Burma live there only for a short period, in their adolescence. This has resulted in most Burmese men knowing what it is like to live in a monastery, abiding by austere rules and depending on the charity of the laity. The adolescent entrant is known as *shinbyu* and his departure from lay life – even if only for a few weeks – is elaborately marked by his family in a ceremony that recalls the abandonment by the Buddha of his life of luxury. The boy wears princely finery and tinsel in the forenoon, before his head is shaved and he assumes the garb of a novice monk. Nuns also exist in Burma, but they are few in number compared with monks and their status is low though well respected. The greatest hope for a nun is to be reborn in the next life as a man.

The function of monks who live permanently in the monastery are several. Firstly there is the injunction to find one's own salvation through study and meditation; secondly, there is the obligation to encourage the laity through preaching and example; thirdly, there is the requirement to teach. Teaching by monks was not only directed towards other monks but also to the laity, and as a result Burma has traditionally had a very high literacy rate because of this involvement of the monkhood in education. One writer in the 1940s went so far as to say, 'Education is co-extensive with Buddhism ...';[23] this has certainly been the case in Burma. The monasteries are therefore repositories of manuscripts, for the most part undecorated and engraved on palm-leaf which is then dusted with lamp black to make it legible. Some manuscripts are, however, decorated and these include those used in ordination, the *Kammavaca* manuscripts. Several are illustrated in this book, as they are traditionally written (not engraved) using an ink made of lacquer on palm-leaf, which is further decorated with lacquer using the *shwe zawa* technique (see cat. 78 and 83).

As mentioned already, monks for the most part in Burma are residential; the ancient requirement to wander has long ago been dropped. With a very large monastic population relative to the total male population (including those adolescents temporarily monks, and those who have retired to the monastery once their secular lives are complete), it is not surprising that monastery buildings are found throughout the country. Many, traditionally, were of wood and these were frequently decorated with gilding. The use of gold leaf as a means of indicating sanctity has a very long history in Burma, and a very frequent act of merit is the contribution to the re-gilding of a sacred structure, such as a pagoda. The gilding of both stucco and wooden architectural elements is effected by first applying a layer of lacquer; some elements were also decorated with red lacquer, cinnabar suspended in lacquer sap.[24]

Finally, although no Burman would deny that Burma is a Buddhist country, it is necessary to briefly discuss a cult that runs parallel to, but is separate from Buddhism – that of the *nats*. These are often local spirits of the place – the house, or a tree or another natural feature – who are invoked for protection or immediate help. Some scholars see them as the last vestiges of pre-Buddhist religion, though some of these figures are associated with historical events or specific cities. Many are also associated with violence, themselves having frequently come to a tragic end. They also have their own wild *pwe,* or ceremonial performances, characterized by the consumption of large quantities of alcohol and the breaking down of gender barriers.[25] In many ways they represent the exact antithesis of the sublime qualities of Buddhism and in this clearly provide a mostly harmless outlet. Although there are countless of these godlings, there are thirty-six major *nats*, with a thirty-seventh represented by the Indian god Indra (known in Burma as 'Thagya'). In their veneration of these spirit deities the Burmese are no different from inhabitants of other Buddhist countries where the indigenous religious system has often been incorporated into Buddhism as long as it was subsidiary and was only concerned with daily life and not with the great questions of the human condition. This is how the situation is today in Burma, with the cults of the *nats* accepted, even at Buddhist pagodas, though usually outside, or below, the pagoda itself, and usually separate from the monastery.[26] Nothing seriously interferes with the law of the Buddha in Burma, even today.

1 Burma is today also known as Myanmar. We have continued to use the old name because the name Myanmar is associated with the present regime and because Burma is the name by which the great majority of our readers will know the country.
2 Exact figures are difficult to obtain as there has been no complete census since 1931, firstly because of the interruption of the Second World War, and secondly because of civil unrest since independence in 1948.
3 Also now renamed Ayeyarwaddy.
4 Also known today as Yangon.
5 The Burmese used to know the Mon as Talaings.
6 For further information on this subject, see Donkers and Nijhuis 1996; Smith 1991.
7 The prehistoric and early historic sequence in Burma is still very unclear. For references to the prehistoric material, as well as much of what follows concerning the Pagan period, see Aung-Thwin 1985. A few examples of both stone and bronze axes from these early cultures are in the collections of the British Museum.
8 Although these are the best known, other sites such as Halin, Binnaka and Winka have now been recorded. For a recent overview of Pyu art, see Guy 1999: 13–28. For an exhaustive survey of the evidence concerning the Pyu, see Stargardt 1990.
9 See Luce 1937.

10 Known also by the Indian name of Sudhammavati.

11 Aung-Thwin 1985: 23, says of the amalgamation of cultural influences at the time of the second great Pagan king, Kyanzittha (1084–1111), 'One word best describes the demands of his age as well as the age itself – syncretism. It was an age characterized by Burman military rule, Pyu traditions, Mon culture, and Theravadin spirit.' For a brief history of Buddhism in Burma, see pp. 16–19.

12 Luce 1970, vol. 3, pls 421–2. An example in the British Museum with the registration number 1981.6-11.1 is on permanent display in the Sir Joseph Hotung Gallery, Room 33 (case 45).

13 The arrival of the Shans repeated a process noted before – invading hordes entering the fertile plain of the Irrawaddy from the northeast; compare the arrival of the Burmese themselves and before probably, that of the Pyu.

14 The names of Symes, Cox, Crawfurd, Burney and Yule spring to mind among some of the most important of these visitors to the court of the Burmese king. Their descriptive writings on Burma were continued during the colonial period by enthusiasts such as Scott (aka Shway Yoe). For all these, see the Bibliography.

15 See Stewart 1972.

16 This became known hence forward as the Bodhi tree, the tree of Enlightenment; its reputed descendant still survives at Bodh Gaya in the modern Indian state of Bihar and cuttings have been taken all over the Buddhist world. The leaf of this tree is one of the most frequently seen motifs in the art of Buddhism.

17 In Burmese, *zaydi*; these structures were called pagodas by the British.

18 In the centuries following the death of the Buddha divisions developed within the *sangha*. Some of these schisms related to doctrine, others to monastic discipline. By the early centuries AD two basic branches of Buddhism began to diverge and are known today as the Hinayana and the Mahayana. The former probably kept closest to the teachings of the Buddha, avoiding as far as possible notions of the divinity of the Buddha. Buddhism as a philosophy, rather than a religion with gods who are worshipped, is much stronger in the Hinayana than it is in the Mahayana. In the Mahayana the importance of compassion is emphasized above all else, as well as the realization that, if Nirvana was possible for everyone, there were those both behind and indeed ahead of us on the notional ladder. From this realization developed the idea that almost at the most developed point were Compassionate Beings, close to Buddhahood, who could be invoked by devotees for aid in this world. The Buddha himself was beyond reach because he had entered Nirvana and had left the round of rebirths, but the Compassionate Beings, known as Bodhisattvas, were approachable and could help ordinary mortals. Indeed, their help could ensure that eventually everyone reached Buddhahood – and not necessarily just by the austere route of mental practice that the Hinayana preached. These two different emphases on the teachings of the Buddha resulted in the two schools (and their many smaller sub-sects) that today still dominate Buddhism. Because of the history of mission, Buddhism in northern India and then further north (Tibet, China, Korea, Mongolia and Japan) is Mahayana (despite the fact that the earliest Mahayana ideas were developed in south India), while the Buddhism of Sri Lanka and most of Southeast Asia – including Burma – is today Hinayana. Of the once many Hinayana schools, only that known as the Theravada (Sanskrit, *Sthaviravada*, 'the Doctrine of the Elders') survives. This is practised in Burma.

19 *Tipitaka*, literally 'three baskets', refers to the three sections of the Buddhist canon: the sayings of the Budhha, *Sutta*; the monastic discipline, *Vinaya*; the philosophical discourses, *Abhidhamma*.

20 The links were close enough for a king of the Pagan dynasty to sponsor the restoration of the Mahabodhi temple at Bodh Gaya – the shrine marking the place where the Buddha gained Enlightenment – in the eleventh century. The presence of temples at Pagan with towers modelled on that of the Mahabodhi temple is yet further evidence for this link with the Bengal/Bihar region of India. A similar reliance on eastern India is also very evident in the wall-painting traditions at Pagan.

21 One of the present authors remembers meeting one such solitary, at Pagan. His meditation on the transience of human life consisted in the daily contemplation of a collection of scores of human skulls piled up in his cell.

22 See Bechert 1984: 155–6.

23 Mya Sein, Ma 1943: p. 20.

24 See Yule 1858: 165.

25 For the nat *pwe*, see Rodrigues 1992 and Brac de la Perrière 1992.

26 For further information on the *nats*, see Temple 1906.

The History of Lacquer

The pre-colonial period

It is not known when lacquer was first used in Burma. The earliest written record of its use in Burma survives in a Chinese text describing the Pyu, the first urbanized inhabitants of Burma.[1] This source, however, refers to its application in a sophisticated palace setting, and we should assume – although we cannot prove it – that the use of the sap of the lacquer tree as a waterproof coating for vessels among non-urban, forest-dwelling populations long predates this record. It seems logical to suppose that, before it was applied to palace decoration in the complicated form the Chinese text describes, it was used in the forest from which the raw materials came: to collect the sap and coat a basket vessel with it is much easier than using it to decorate palace architecture. The search for organic remains, however, which has become such an important part of archaeological investigation elsewhere in the world, has not yet been undertaken in Burma, where there has been very little archaeological work in the last fifty years. Consequently, water-logged deposits, which are the obvious place to search for the remains of lacquered vessels from the first millennium AD – or earlier – have not yet been sought out. Contact between Burma and China may also be relevant in searching for the origins of lacquer use in Burma, as lacquer has been employed in China since at least the Neolithic period; certainly, by the time they recorded the use of cinnabar by the Pyu to decorate palace architecture,[2] lacquer had already had a very long history in China.

For the Pagan period the evidence was until recently confused. In 1919 A.P. Morris, quoting a personal communication from the archaeological researcher U Tin at Pagan, wrote 'The [lacquer] industry was brought from the Yun State [in northern Thailand] to Thaton and thence reached Pagan in 1058 AD. The tube of lacquer work exhibited[3] is dated 1274 AD, and was discovered in the Mingala Pagoda at Pagan.' Morris then goes on to comment: 'The reference is to the yellow circular box of teak which has been painted with thitsi and yellow ochre.' It is assumed that U Tin's assertion of the transfer of the craft from Thaton to Pagan was based on the idea that the sack of Thaton by Anawrahta and his forcible relocation of population to Pagan also included the relocation of lacquerworkers. There is no certain evidence to substantiate this assumption.[4] Although the idea of lacquered vessels being available at Pagan during this period is not in itself impossible, this reference to a specific vessel in Morris's article is unfortunately the only direct record we have: there is no photograph or drawing of the vessel and it has long since disappeared. Thus any opportunity for this claim to be verified has been lost; further, the few bald words that the vessel 'was found in the Mingala Pagoda' give us no chance to assess whether it was found in a relic deposit dating from the foundation of the pagoda or was part of a later deposit. The date that Morris gives for the vessel – 1274 – is presumably based on the (assumed) notion that it belonged to an original deposit, but we are not told; it could just as well come from an inscription on the vessel.[5]

Overall, this reference is frustrating, and it has been doubted by several recent writers, including Singer.[6] However, very recently it has been possible to review this information

afresh, as through the generous activities of Noel Singer and fellow-scholars in Pagan – U Yu Thein, Principal of the Myanmar Lacquerware Institute, and U Thaung Naing, Curator of the Lacquerware Museum – it is now possible to publish photographs (see above) of fragments of lacquered basketry vessels that have a very good chance of being dated to the thirteenth century. They have been excavated from a deposit in the Laymyethna temple at Minnanthu in Pagan. This is dated by foundation inscriptions to the first quarter of the thirteenth century.[7] We understand that these lacquer fragments and the rest of the material buried with them are all of a piece chronologically, and of the Pagan period; further, that they are of a brown colour.[8] What the photographs show clearly is the intact bases of at least five cups, as well as many fragments presumably of the walls of the vessels. The spiral form of woven split bamboo basketry is clearly apparent, as is the lacquer coating sitting on top of the basketry. Here we have a much better standard of evidence than Morris was able to provide. Carbon-14 dating of some of these fragments would answer the question categorically as to the Pagan period usage of lacquer, but the situation is a great deal more certain now than it was. This also corroborates the sculptural evidence, for from the Pagan period onwards sculptures of the Buddha made of wood are known to have been covered with a layer of red lacquer – that is cinnabar (the red colouring agent) mixed with lacquer sap. Examples are recorded by Luce at Pagan itself,[9] while others have periodically appeared on the art market.[10]

Information on the development of lacquer techniques in Burma is scant in the late medieval period, and it is not until the series of wars between Burma and Thailand in the sixteenth to eighteenth centuries that references appear once more in the literature. Harvey, a twentieth-century historian, mentions the forcible transfer of artisans from northern Thailand to Burma, including 'from Chiengmai … her famous lacquer workers'; he goes on to say, 'it is probably these who introduced into Burma the finer sort of lacquerware called *yun*, the name of the Yun or Lao Shan tribes around Chiengmai.'[11] Later, following the sack of Ayutthaya in 1767, artisans were similarly transported back to Burma and it now seems certain that the tradition of engraved work which we know today as *yun* and which is the mainstay of Pagan was introduced to Burma at that time (see photograph on p. 36). The new evidence from Pagan described above shows that plainly lacquered wares were in use, and probably made in Burma from the thirteenth century onwards. However, the later evidence suggests that decorative techniques such as engraved, *yun* work and probably also the black and gold,

Fragments of lacquered basketry vessels recovered from the Laymyethna temple, Pagan. Thirteenth century.

shwe zawa method were introduced only gradually during the later periods as a consequence of warfare with Thailand and the capture of craftsmen.

The use of lacquer vessels in diplomacy

Singer has shown the way in which the sumptuary laws of the Burmese court affected the way lacquer vessels were made and used.[12] This hierarchical treatment of objects is also evident from the use made by the Burmese of lacquer vessels in diplomacy.[13] In the eighteenth and nineteenth centuries it is clearly seen in the relations between Burma and China where a system of exchanged gifts every ten years developed.[14] Records survive for gifts during the reign of king Mindon and gifts were assembled and sent from the Golden Palace in Mandalay in 1874. In these last days of independence, after the British acquisition of Arakan and Lower Burma, the country was land-locked and closely watched by the British who were ever-worried by the intentions of the French in nearby Indo-China and the possibility of a trade route overland between Burma and China. In these circumstances an embassy from the Burmese to the Chinese court was of great interest to the British and it is for this reason that records of the accompanying gifts survive. The size of the gift naturally reflected the balance in relations between the two countries.

The composition of the gift and its value followed precedent and included gold and silver leaf, jade boulders, live elephants and pictures of white elephants – and lacquerware. From the list obtained by British intelligence we know every item. First in the list are 'wooden *oks* (trays), gilt and covered with mosaic work' and 'ditto gilt and ornamented with lacquerware designs' – a pair of each. It is not clear whether these objects were covered salvers, *kalat*, but the finish of the first was clearly relief decoration, with gilt and glass inlay, *hmanzi shwe cha*, while the second was relief work, *thayo*, without glass inlay. The next items were '2 *yunto* coloured engraved *oks*' and '2 ditto with high legs'. These must have been *yun* engraved, and very probably a pair each of *hsun ok* of the round globular sort and of the tall spire-lidded sort. Last, and of special note because the size is indicated, come '4 *yunto oks, 2 seiks* in capacity' and '50 *yunto oks, 2 salis* in capacity.' These are clearly two different sizes of *yun* vessels.

From the internal volume we can deduce the external measurements more accurately if we make the reasonable assumption that all the boxes were cylindrical. However, it is necessary to work out the metric equivalent of the old Burmese measurements, the *seik* and the *sali*. Before proposing an answer to this question of absolute volume, however, it is interesting to note that the next ten-yearly gift, sent by the last king of the Konbaung dynasty, Thibaw, in 1884 to his imperial brother in Peking, included under the heading of lacquerware, '4 "number 4 size" ornamented boxes' and '50 "number 5 size" ornamented boxes'. We can safely assume that the capacity of a 'number 4 size' box was 2 *seiks* and that of a 'number 5 size' box was 2 *salis*. Precedent demands constancy, and no doubt king Thibaw's ministers ensured that the 1884 gift was no more and no less than his father king Mindon had sent ten years earlier. Any fluctuation might have given the wrong impression to the Chinese, and also have excited conjecture among British spies. King Thibaw had the same adviser as his father: U Kaung (1821–1908), the Kin Wun Mingyi minister, who was an astute diplomat and a remarkable survivor.

Traditional Burmese measures were listed by Scott in 1882,[15] after the 1874 gift but before that of 1884. The equivalents in British Imperial bushels, and in metric volume, are given for the standard units of 'Burma Proper'. The capacity of the small and large gift boxes would have been approximately 1 litre and 18 litres respectively. The smaller boxes would have had thinner walls than the large ones. Most Burmese cylindrical boxes of the period have a diameter a little greater than their height, in the ratio of 11:10. Shan boxes are often proportionately broader. Burmese cylindrical boxes of fine construction and 1 litre capacity would have measured about 10 centimetres in diameter and 9 in height. Large boxes of 18 litres capacity would have been roughly 30 centimetres in diameter and 27 centimetres in height. Curiously, betel-boxes of late nineteenth-century age are rarely as large as the 'Number 4 size' boxes in the royal gift, while small betel-boxes are rarely as small as those king Mindon and king Thibaw sent to the Chinese emperor. Possibly special sizes distinguished these imperial presents.

For the British period there is as yet no evidence for the continuing use of lacquer vessels as items of royal exchange. However, among objects given to or acquired by Lord Curzon during his viceregal visit in 1901 were a number of fine lacquer objects (see cat. 100 and 161), and it is possible that in these exquisite items there is a remnant of the old idea of lacquer vessels as items fit for diplomatic gifts. Although the royal collections in Britain contain items of lacquerware, mostly with *shwe zawa* decoration, neither the documentation nor the style of them indicates a diplomatic context. It is also possible that the drum illustrated and described at cat. 126, which was acquired at the Delhi Durbar in 1911, may be viewed in this light, but here there is no documentation to go with it; we can only speculate.

The European encounter with Burmese lacquer

There is little in the botanical department which can escape the activity and skill of Dr Wallich.[16]

Although lacquer was known to travellers, traders and diplomats from Europe by the seventeenth century,[17] the first scientific record of the Burmese lacquer tree and the use made of lacquer sap in Burma are to be found in the work of Nathaniel Wallich (1786–1854). By birth a Dane and by training a medical doctor, Wallich is renowned today as a botanist, eminent in plant collecting and categorization. Arriving in India in 1807, he settled at Serampore, the Danish enclave in Bengal. Following the annexation of Serampore by the East India Company, he joined the service of the Company and in Calcutta he became part of that memorable group of men who, in the late eighteenth and early nineteenth century, responded so readily to the intellectual challenges of India and the neighbouring lands. The names of William Jones, James Prinsep, Colin Mackenzie and Stamford Raffles spring to mind, though their achievements are perhaps better known today to the general public than is Wallich's. This is certainly so in Europe but in India the memory of his work is still fresh and the two hundredth anniversary of his birth was celebrated there recently.[18] For most of his official life Wallich was based in Calcutta, but he visited parts of South and Southeast Asia as far apart as Singapore and Kumaon in the western foothills of the Himalayas in search of plants.[19] In 1826–7 he visited Burma as part of the East India Company mission from Calcutta to the court of king Bagyidaw (reigned 1819–37) at Ava. This embassy was headed by John Crawfurd and was sent with the purpose of putting into effect the agreements enshrined in the Treaty of Yandabo which brought the First Anglo-Burmese War to a close. Crawfurd was not successful in his diplomacy, but, as he himself says:

> I had also the great advantage of the society of Dr Wallich, Superintendent of the
> Government Botanical Garden at Calcutta, deputed to accompany me for the purpose of
> examining and reporting upon the resources of the forests of Pegu and Ava, as well as of
> those of our recently acquired possessions to the south of the Saluen [Salween] river.[20]

The economic concerns expressed in this quotation are typical of the background that lay behind so much of the scientific work carried out by the servants of the East India Company. Elsewhere in the same volume Crawfurd describes the valuable teak forests he and Wallich inspected on their river journey up the Irrawaddy to Ava. Wallich's description of and interest in the lacquer tree must, at least partly, be viewed in the same light.

As Superintendent of the Botanic Garden at Calcutta, Wallich had succeeded William Roxburgh (temporarily in 1815 and then permanently in 1817) and worked with William Carey of Serampore on the publication of Roxburgh's *Flora Indica*. His visit to Burma was concerned with plant collecting and recording, but it was unfortunately followed by a breakdown in his health, obliging him to return to England to convalesce. However, while there, he was able to see his greatest work, *Plantae Asiaticae Rariores*, through the press.[21] This was published in three volumes in 1830, 1831 and 1832 and includes the first scientific listing and illustration of the lacquer tree.[22] He subsequently returned to India where he continued to record plants and to send dried specimens to botanical gardens in Europe, above all to the Royal Botanic Gardens at Kew.[23] He finally left India for London in 1847, dying in 1854 at a house in Gower Street in Bloomsbury not far from the British Museum.

In *Plantae Asiaticae Rariores* (p. 10) he describes his visit to Burma as follows: 'I ascended the Irrawadi as far as Ava, and visited the mountains in the neighbourhood of that capital and proceeded afterwards to the lately acquired territories on the coasts of Martaban and Tenasserim.' These latter were 'lately acquired' following the Treaty of Yandabo with the result that, until this date, little botanical work had been conducted there. He saw the lacquer tree first at Prome in Lower Burma and at Martaban, where it was in fruit, in March 1827. He says 'They [the trees] were loaded with bunches of red, nearly ripe fruit, but were not very large; few only exceeding thirty feet in height, with a short trunk measuring not more than four or five feet in circumference.' Later again he recorded it inland from Moulmein in the valley of the Salween River, where he felt that the trees 'were of greater dimensions than [those seen at Martaban]; one of them being forty feet in height, with a stem twelve feet long and eleven in girth at four feet above the ground.' Although he didn't himself go to Tavoy, he records that it grew that far south as an assistant brought him a fruit-bearing specimen. He noted also that it sheds its leaves in November and is naked until May after which it flowers and then fruits.[24] Further, 'During the rainy season, which lasts for five months, from the middle of May until the end of October, it is in full foliage. Every part of it abounds in a thick and viscid greyish-brown fluid, which turns black soon after coming in contact with the external air.' In his desire for empirically valid information Wallich even tasted it – apparently without ill-effect – though he does record that in the *Edinburgh Journal of Science* for 1828 (pp. 96–100) there is information on 'its deleterious effects on the human frame'. Burney (see p. 27) also speaks of the side effects of working with lacquer sap and mentions the proverb that he translates as 'Varnish is a witness; it affects a man not true; to a true man it matters not.'

In the entry for the tree in *Plantae Asiaticae Rariores* Wallich identified the Burmese tree as the same as, though smaller, than a variety called the *Kheu*, which had by then already been described as growing in the forests of both Manipur and Sylhet.[25] He goes on to say:

It follows, hence, that the tree has a very wide geographical range, extending from Munipur (in latitude 25 degrees N and longitude 94 degrees E) to Tavoy (in latitude 14 degrees, longitude 97 degrees). The valley of Kubbu, which has been ascertained by actual survey, made by Lieutenant Pemberton, to be only five hundred feet above the plains of India, is distant two hundred miles from the nearest sea shore. The tree there attains its greatest size, and I believe it becomes smaller as it approaches the sea on the coast of Tenasserim, where it grows in comparatively low situations.

He then meticulously describes the method of collecting the lacquer sap, which is slightly different to the one recorded at Ava by Burney:[26]

> short joints of a thin sort of bamboo, sharpened at one end like a writing pen, and shut up at the other, are inserted in a slanting direction into wounds, made through the bark of the tree and principal boughs, and left there for twenty-four or forty-eight hours, after which they are removed, and their contents, which rarely exceed a quarter of an ounce, emptied into a basket made of bamboo or rattan previously varnished over. As many as a hundred bamboos are sometimes seen sticking into a single trunk during the collecting season, which lasts as long as the tree is destitute of leaves, namely from January until April;[27] and they are renewed as long as the juice will flow. A good tree is reckoned to produce from 1&1/2 to 2, 3 or even 4 Viss annually, a Viss being equal to about 3&1/2 avoirdupois. In its pure state it is sold at Prome at the rate of one Tical, or 2s 6d the Viss. At Martaban, where everything was dear when I was there, the drug was retailed at 2 madras rupees per Viss; it was an inferior quality, and mixed with sesamum oil; an adulteration which is often practised.

The description of gathering the sap almost certainly refers to the region around Prome and perhaps indicates the extent of tree-cover then extant. Shway Yoe writing in the 1880s does not mention any particular part where the tree grows better than elsewhere, but in Burma today lacquer sap comes primarily from the Shan States, according to lacquerworkers at Pagan, the main centre of contemporary lacquer production (see pp. 31ff). Crawfurd also suggests that the Shan region was the place to get the best lacquer sap.[28] However, Wallich writing at the same time as Crawfurd, says:

> In the neighbourhood of Prome a considerable quantity of varnish is extracted from the tree; but very little is obtained at Martaban, owing, as I was told, to the poverty of the soil, and partly also to the circumstances of there being none of the people in that part whose business it is to perform the process.

Although Wallich does not have any very precise information about the method of production of lacquer vessels, he notes that

> At a village close to Pagam on the Irrawadi, called Gnaunee [this is the village known today as Nyaung-U, to the immediate northwest of Pagan] this sort of manufacture is carried on very extensively and to great perfection...[29]

He records correctly that

> the most essential as well as difficult part of the operation consists in the process of drying, which must be effected in a very slow and gradual manner: for which purpose the articles are placed in damp and cool subterraneous vaults...[30]

He also relates the way in which the lacquer sap is used as a size for gilding,

> nothing more being required than to besmear the surface thinly with the varnish, and then immediately to apply the gold leaf.

Further,

> If it is considered how very extensively that art is practised by the Burma nation, it being among their most frequent acts of devotion and piety to contribute to the gilding of their numerous religious edifices and idols, it will be evident that a great quantity of the drug [i.e. lacquer] must be consumed for that purpose alone. Finally, the beautiful Pali writing of the religious order of the Burmas on ivory, palm-leaves, or metal, is entirely done with this varnish, in its native and pure state [see cat. 78 (ivory), 79–81 and 83 (palm-leaf)].

It was as a result of this visit to Burma that Wallich established the tree in its own genus and published it as *Melanorrhœa usitatissima* (later, mistakenly, changed to *usitata)*.[31] Back in

Calcutta he grew some 500 plants, and managed to bring one back to Kew; sadly there is now no living descendant there. Also in Calcutta he had prepared the two drawings of the tree that accompany the textual description. They are both signed by the Indian artist Vishnupersaud and show 'a branch with leaves' (Plate XI) and 'a naked fruit-bearing branch a little before maturity' (Plate XII; see cat. 12). At the bottom of the latter illustration there are also six details, including a whole fruit, the same sectioned and the seed, as was the usual format. The original drawings are still held in the Library at Kew.[32] The work of Vishnupersaud was apparently rated highly, as Wallich had taken him on his tour of Nepal as well as Burma and he was also lent to Royle at the Botanic Garden in Saharanpur.

Wallich was not, however, alone in his interest in Burma, which through military and commercial activity was now opening up to British colonial power. One of the terms of the Treaty of Yandabo was that a 'resident' should be stationed at Ava and the most important incumbent of this post was the second resident, Henry Burney (1792–1845).[33] Burney was keenly interested in the country in which he served and quickly mastered Burmese, thus enabling him to communicate at the court. The success he had at Ava was surely founded on the three years he spent in Tavoy as deputy commissioner following the cession of this part of southern Burma to the British at the end of the First Anglo-Burmese War. He reached Ava in 1830 and served there until the change of government in 1837 and the accession of king Tharrawaddy. He is remembered today for his diplomatic skill while in the Burmese capital, the magnificent *parabaiks* in the British Library that still bear his name – and most importantly in the present circumstances – his description, the first in any Western language, of the way in which lacquer vessels were made. Here, unlike Wallich, he elucidated the whole process by arranging for craftsmen to make some vessels for him, while he watched and recorded them. Among much other contemporary information about lacquer production, he says specifically that

> The first and by far the best articles, are brought from the Shan countries – *Shan-pyee-ga*; and *Lè-gya*, Dr Buchanan's Lækhia, a Shan province situate to the S. E. of Ava, is the principal place of manufacture. The Shan ware may be distinguished by the lightness and elegance of the manufactures, and the superior brilliancy of the varnish and colours.

This, like many of his other writings on Burma, appeared initially in the *Journal of the Asiatic Society of Bengal*.[34]

It is interesting to note that the embassy to which Wallich was attached brought to an end the First Anglo-Burmese War, and that it was as a result of this war that the first major Burmese artefacts entered the collections of the British Museum. Captain Frederick Marryat (1792–1848) who served in the war gave two outstanding Burmese objects, now in the Museum, as well as fine manuscripts, which eventually entered the collections of what is now the British Library.[35] He also displayed other Burmese objects in the rooms of the Asiatic Society in London, thus bringing Burmese artefacts to the attention of a wider public.[36] He was also involved, along with another officer, Colonel Miles, in a display of Burmese objects, including what is described as 'The Rath; or, Burmese Imperial State Carriage and Throne, studded with 20,000 precious stones … as drawn by elephants at the Egyptian Hall, Piccadilly'.[37] This exhibition included items which, still today, are of the type used to indicate the individual character of Burmese culture: a gong circle, a harp, a xylophone, a bell, two lacquered boxes,[38] and a 'Burmese cabinet', the description of which makes it clear that this was a manuscript chest, a *sadaik*. According to his war record, Marryat served in or near Rangoon, and we can therefore be fairly certain that his gifts originated in that part of the country.[39] Thus, as a result of the First Anglo-Burmese War and through the very different

activities of men such as Wallich, Burney and Marryat, Burma and its unique culture –
including that of lacquer – began to be known in Europe.

Following the political changes consequent on the First Anglo-Burmese war, the situation
remained static for twenty years. At the very end of that period in far-off London, and perhaps
marking the ever-increasing confidence of the British in their colonial mission, the idea of the
Great Exhibition was conceived, and in 1851 this immense trade fair, representing the whole
world, was assembled in Hyde Park. One of the most important elements of the British
contribution was that prepared by the East India Company. In the preparations for this
massive undertaking, committees were set up in each of the Presidencies of India. British
Burma – at that time still just Arakan and Tenasserim – was administered then as part of
Bengal, so on the Calcutta committee list we find Arakan represented by Captain A.P. Phayre[40]
and Tenasserim by Major A. Bogle. The exhibition was to consist of four major categories:
(1) raw materials, (2) machinery and mechanical inventions, (3) manufactures, and (4)
sculpture and plastic art. Although dwarfed among the massive array of thousands of exhibits,
lacquer from Burma found a place in categories 1 and 3. The official catalogue for the
exhibition itself gives a list of 'Vegetable Substances used in Manufactures', which is
subdivided into a number of different lists, among which was one headed 'Gum and Resin
Series'. In this we find 'Thetsee (*Melanorrhoea usitata*), used as lacquer, from Arracan [*sic*]', as
well as 'Thenatthu, coating to paper umbrellas and varnish, for manufacture of papier mache'.
How these items were displayed is not clear from the catalogue, but samples, perhaps in
bottles, seem likely.

Under manufactures there are two entries. One of these comprises an entire collection of
Burmese musical instruments, which are illustrated (p. 912/IV). They are described as 'Musical
instruments, model of a tsigu wigu, and one complete, &c., from Moulmein'[41] and 'Tsoung, or
harp, tin box containing cymbals, model of a harp, patala, patma, or Burmese drum, cymbals
used in religious ceremonies, &c., from Moulmein'. Most of these would have used lacquer in
their decoration.[42] The final and perhaps most intriguing entry concerned with lacquer merely
states 'Shan lacquered boxes – Mr. W. Norris'. There is no further information concerning
these boxes which, if they had been illustrated, would provide important chronological
information. There may have been other lacquered items exhibited, but the bald descriptions
now make it difficult to be certain: for instance, 'An assortment of Burmah boxes, from the
Tenasserim Province.' No materials are given but it is likely they were lacquered, whether they
were made of wood or of basketry.[43] Various items of sculpture as well as models were also
shown and it is probable that these too were made using lacquer. No record has yet been
found of a specific public reaction to these items, though the general reaction to the Indian
exhibits was highly favourable. Sparling mentions that the 'Indian section appeared to many
as "a fresh well of art"'.[44]

The fate of most of these objects is difficult to determine, though a few items from the
Indian section were acquired directly by the South Kensington Museum (now the Victoria and
Albert Museum) following the closure of the Exhibition.[45] Of the Burmese lacquer items, only
the musical instruments can be followed – though but briefly – after 1851. The following year,
during early June, the auctioneers Hoggartt, Norton and Trist put under the hammer items
from the Indian section of the Exhibition. These included the musical instruments. On page
107 of the catalogue for the sale are listed the harp, gilt and inlaid with 'garnets' (probably
red glass and presumably decorated in the *hmanzi shwe cha* technique); a '*myacgyoung*' in
the form of an alligator; a *pattala*, or xylophone; a collection of gongs, '*kyay gout*', with a
carved and painted case (probably the gongs and the case would have had lacquer

decoration); a different collection of gongs, '*kyay wygn*', also in a case; and a *tharran*, described as 'a small Burmese violin'.[46] There is, sadly, no record of who bought them. The model musical instruments may well be those now in the Swiss Cottage at Osborne House, the Isle of Wight seat of Queen Victoria and Prince Albert. The Prince Consort had been the moving spirit behind the Great Exhibition.

Once begun, the idea of exhibitions became popular. For almost one hundred years after the Great Exhibition international expositions, exhibitions and fairs flourished. They were also exported to various of the colonies including India, where at Delhi in 1902, during the viceroyalty of Curzon and in the year following his visit to Burma, lacquerwares of considerable variety were displayed.[47] They were also popular in Europe, and in the 1900 Exposition Universelle in Paris we know that Burmese lacquered basketry vessels were displayed, as one was acquired from the exhibition for the ethnographic collections of the British Museum.[48] In Britain international exhibitions were frequently linked to notions of Empire and several of them, such as the Indian and Colonial Exhibition of 1886, and the British Empire Exhibition of 1924 at Wembley, make this clear from their names alone.[49] The 1924 exhibition included a Burmese palace [read 'pavilion'], incongruously set up in drab north-west London, and a troupe of Burmese dancers. Among the objects displayed were lacquer vessels decorated in the *shwe zawa* technique, at least one of which was then acquired by the Imperial Institute in South Kensington. When the institute was disbanded, the vessel was acquired by Liverpool Museum and is now displayed in this exhibition (cat. 34).

1 See note 9 on p. 20 for this text.

2 It is assumed that the mention of cinnabar implies the use of lacquer as an agent to carry it. This is the exact use made of it in architecture in later periods.

3 The Morris 1919 publication is the text of a lecture given to the Burma Research Society to accompany an exhibition, and it is this to which Morris refers here.

4 The validity of the lists of craftsmen who were transferred which appears in the *Glass Palace Chronicle* has been doubted, not least because the chronicle was written centuries after the events described.

5 Fraser-Lu 1985: 3 says it was 'marked with a date equivalent to AD 1274'.

6 Singer 1996 and, following him, Blurton 1999.

7 The inscriptions are listed in Pichard 1993: 248–52, 407.

8 Personal communication from Noel Singer, who has seen the items, and through whose intervention it was possible to secure the photographs (they are reproduced here courtesy of U Yu Thein and U Thaung Naing in Pagan and Noel Singer in the UK). The authors are very grateful to Noel Singer and to those who assisted him in Burma.

9 Luce 1970: vol. 3, pls 421–2.

10 For example in *Burmese Art and its Influences*, exhibition catalogue for Beurdeley and Matthews & Co., London 1981, cat. 26.

11 Harvey 1967: 166

12 Singer 1996: 94.

13 Richly decorated lacquer vessels had a high status and were used in diplomacy even before the Burmese themselves made such vessels. The Kalyani inscription at Pegu records that coloured lacquer betel-boxes were among the gifts sent by king Dhammaceti to the monks of Sri Lanka in 1475. Note that they were from Chiengmai in a foreign country; they were not Burmese. For the bi-lingual inscription (Pali and Middle Mon), see Taw Sein Ko 1893: 11–53.

14 The last formal treaty between China and Burma, signed on 13 December 1769, merely stipulated 'an exchange of affectionate letters in gold every ten years'. The Chinese regarded this as indicating a tributary status, while the Burmese saw it as defining equal and fraternal relations. This ill-defined situation caused the British some concern after the fall of Mandalay. See Stewart 1972: 145ff.

15 Scott 1906.

16 Crawfurd 1834: 148.

17 Some of the earliest accounts are difficult to interpret due to the free use of the word lacquer – sometimes it refers to stick-lac, lac or shellac made from the stick-lac insect and an important Burmese product in the early modern period, and on other occasions to lacquer, made from the sap of the lacquer tree.

18 In 1986 a monument to Wallich was unveiled in the Botanic Gardens on the banks of the Hooghlyi at Calcutta.

19 For full biographical details of Wallich, see *Dictionary of National Biography*, vol LIX, ed. Lee, Sidney 1899. See also the Preface to Wallich's own *Plantae Asiaticae Rariores*, London 1830–32, cat. 12. For a portrait, see cat. 13; for his involvement with the founding of the Botanic Garden at Singapore, see Barley 1998: 21.

20 Crawfurd 1834: 2.

21 This was also when he sat for his portrait, painted by Lucas – see cat. 13.

22 The description, in botanical style, is in Latin (p. 10); this is followed by discussion (in English) and two illustrations. See cat. 12.

23 See Desmond 1995: 103, 141, etc. Wallich's first deposit of botanical specimens for Kew was in 1817. The *Dictionary of National Biography*, op. cit., p.135, tells of him returning to London in 1828 with 'some eight thousand specimens of plants, duplicates of which were widely distributed to both public and private collections.' The non-duplicates entered the East India Company Museum where he listed them as *A Numerical List of Dried Specimens of Plants in the East India Company's Museum, collected under the Superintendence of Dr. Wallich*, London 1828. He enumerates 9,148 items in this list.

24 He seems to contradict himself here, as earlier he says that the tree fruits in March. It is possible that the plants fruit earlier or later depending on the height above sea level, and latitude. See note 27 for a similar confusion.

25 In lists of exhibits prepared for the Great Exhibition in London, twenty years later, lacquer sap is listed as coming from Assam. See J.F. Royle, *Papers referring to the proposed contributions from India to the Industrial Exhibition of 1851*, London 1851 (consulted at the National Art Library, Victoria and Albert Museum, London).

26 See Burney 1832.

27 Again there is some confusion here, as there was with the date for the fruiting of the tree – see note 24. Wallich implies that the collecting season is between January and April, whereas Burney: 1832 (see below) says that the sap is not of good quality if it is 'collected from the tree when it is in fructification; which, they say, occurs during the three months of January, February and March.' Scott (as Shway Yoe) 1882 agrees, 'The sap may be collected at all times, except when the fruit is on the trees, from Pyatho to Tabaung – the first three months of the English year. Then it is thin and does not produce such a brilliant polish.' Fraser-Lu 1985: 7 follows Shway Yoe. Perhaps a negative has, mistakenly, dropped out of Wallich's text.

28 Crawfurd 1834: 210.

29 For discussion of Nyaung-U, see cat. 159.

30 See chapter on techniques of production, pp. 31ff.

31 All items previously known as *Melanorrhœa* are now reclassified as *Gluta*. See Mabberley 1997.

32 We acknowledge the assistance of Henry Noltie for this information. These two drawings are among the 1,200 botanical drawings which Wallich records (1832: 10) as 'executed under my direction by Indian artists, at the Calcutta Garden, and on my various journeys'. Six more natural history drawings made for Wallich in Burma now survive in the British Library – see Archer 1962: 41 and 91.

33 For the details of his life and career, see Hall 1974 and Desai 1939. For Burney and his collection of *parabaik*, see Herbert 1989. For the greatest of the Burney *parabaik*, see Herbert 1993.

34 See Burney 1832. The lacquer items produced for, and recorded in this article, he sent to the museum of the Asiatic Society, in Calcutta. They survived there and were listed in 1849. See *Catalogue of Curiosities...*

35 For examples of this Marryat material in both institutions, see cat. 72 and 83.

36 See the unpublished journal of the Reverend John Skinner for 1 June 1827 – see British Library Add. Ms. 33697.

37 Anon. (printed by James Bullock at Whitefriars), London 1826, pp. 21–32. This very interesting document is probably the first catalogue for a Burmese exhibition. It is remarkable for its even tone and general lack of triumphalism. In this we may see the hand of Marryat whose recorded views of the Burmese include much admiration. What became of the throne and the state chariot, both of which are illustrated, is unknown.

38 These are described as 'elegant in their construction, and well adapted to their purpose. They also use red boxes somewhat similar to these, for their *betel*, a nut of which they are very fond; and for *cheroots*, or segars [sic], with which they regale themselves. The women smoke as well as the men.' Ibid., p. 28.

39 From May to September 1824 Marryat was the senior naval officeer in Rangoon, 'and in February 1825 he had the naval command of an expedition up the Bassein river, which occupied Bassein and seized the Burmese magazines.' He was back in England by the beginning of 1826 (*Dictionary of National Biography*, vol. XXXVI, ed. Sidney Lee, London 1893, pp. 201–3.

40 For Phayre's later career, see cat. 84.

41 The comic 'tsigu wigu' presumably represents a typographic mistake for 'tsign wign', the instrument we know as 'hsaing waing'. Later on they have more correctly spelt the instrument today spelt 'kyi waing' as 'kyay wygn'.

42 For late nineteenth- or early twentieth-century examples of a drum, *pattala* and harp, see cat. 126–8.

43 In the list of objects submitted to the exhibition from Calcutta we read of object '2768. Burmah Boxes (an assortment,) made of bamboo in the Tenasserim Provinces' (*Catalogue of East India Productions Collected in the presidency of Bengal and forwarded to the Exhibition of Works of Art and Industry to be held in London in 1851* – see note 46 for London location). It is likely that these were the items listed so baldly in the exhibition catalogue. Any vessel made of bamboo in Burma, almost by definition, must have been lacquered.

44 Sparling 1982: 35.

45 Guy and Swallow 1990: 222, 223.

46 *A Catalogue of the Highly Important and by far the greater Portion of the Valuable and Interesting Collection as Exhibited by the Honourable the East India Company at the Great Exhibition in 1851...* This and the other documents relating to the Great Exhibition were consulted by the author at the National Art Library at the Victoria and Albert Museum where expert guidance was provided by Elizabeth James, which is gratefully acknowledged.

47 For the Indian Art Exhibition at Delhi, see cat. 17 and Watt 1904.

48 This is a tiered container for holding snacks from Shwebo District, reg. no. Ethnography 1901.6-5.20. It is similar in shape and function to cat. 149.

49 For the phenomena of international exhibitions, see Greenhalgh 1988.

Techniques of Production

Many of the techniques of lacquer production have, in their broad outline, been listed and described in the literature. These earlier records include work by the pioneer Henry Burney who in the early 1830s, in the aftermath of the First Anglo-Burmese War, was stationed at Ava as the Resident of the East India Company at the Burmese Court. In fine empirical fashion he ordered a set of vessels, the production of which he then recorded as they were made.[1] At the beginning of the twentieth century A.P. Morris, writing in the *Journal of the Burma Research Society*, also brought together much useful information dealing with varying aspects of production, including lacquer sap, the development of the craft of making lacquer vessels, the production and designs of 'Pagan ware' (i.e. vessels decorated with engraved patterns), moulded work, the use of lacquer in architecture and the future prospects of lacquer in Burma.[2] In more recent years Fraser-Lu has notably collated a great deal of dispersed information, adding new data along with photographs of the various processes.[3] Finally, one of the present authors has made further contributions by using field records and examples of lacquer vessels in the British Museum.[4]

Given this situation, it seems unnecessary to repeat information that is readily available elsewhere, and more profitable instead to present a report which, for the most part, was gathered during a visit to Pagan in October 1995, when both a video film[5] and a written record were made at the Htun Lacquer Workshop in New Pagan.[6] This illustrates the technique as practised today in the town that in the late twentieth century is the most important lacquer-producing centre in Burma; many of the processes are the same as those recorded 170 years ago, but other features have inevitably changed. Although some of the production there is of wooden trays, screens and tables, the chief output is of vessels, and it is that which was recorded. Further, the decoration of lacquer items at Pagan is dominated by the technique known as *yun*. This Burmese word means both 'lacquer' in general as well as specifically 'the form of decoration where a surface is engraved and colour is then added'. This word appears frequently throughout the rest of this volume, almost always in the specific sense.

First of all, though, what is lacquer? All the very varied uses of lacquer are based ultimately on the remarkable properties of the resin of a tree common in much of Southeast Asia, *Gluta usitata*.[7] The tree is found in a number of different parts of Burma and was probably even more widespread in the days before

Cans of raw, uncoloured lacquer ready for use.

forest clearance than it is today.[8] The resin is harvested from the tree by tapping, in the same manner as rubber. When tapped, the sap is straw-coloured but quickly turns a glossy black. Morris describes the gathering of the sap, as follows:

> The usual method of tapping is to make two deep notches to form a V. The notches are eight to ten inches long, and about two inches deep. At the base of the V, small bamboo cups are placed, with an edge stuck into a small horizontal cut just at the base of the V, in such a way that the oil which exudes from the V-shaped notch flows into the cup.[9]

He then goes on to describe how often the tapping can be done and also that it apparently has no deleterious effect on the health of the tree. Unlike rubber, lacquer has never been grown under plantation conditions, but gathered, haphazardly, in the forest.[10] Given the obsession which the British had with harnessing the natural products of the countries they controlled during the days of Empire, this is rather surprising and must reflect the lack of serviceable uses which the colonial administrators could find for the material.[11] In Burma, though, there has never been any lack of uses for this versatile resin.

One of the remarkable features of lacquer sap is that it can be used as a coating on many different surfaces. Examples seen in this publication include split bamboo, wood, cane, palm-leaf, metal and leather. When applied to a surface, lacquer both waterproofs and heatproofs the object; it can carry colour and has adhesive properties; when mixed with powder, it can be moulded or sculpted; and it makes the substrate rigid. In addition, it is insect and bacteria resistant and, if thin enough, retains its flexibility; it is also a natural polymer. Thus, from a functional point of view it is very attractive. There are some disadvantages, but they are few compared to the many advantages: prolonged exposure to the raw sap for those in the lacquer workshops can cause a blistering rash (this seems to affect people differentially),[12] and, as an organic material, lacquer is subject to decay in humid and damp conditions. Further, as it forms a hard surface when dry, it is liable to crack if mistreated. Once broken, it is difficult to repair without the break being obvious. It is true, though, that until recently there were itinerant craftsmen who mended vessels, especially domestic ones where the importance of maintaining decorative integrity was less. Several of the functional items illustrated in this volume have been repaired.

For vessels – always the major product for lacquer application in Burma[13] – the other main raw material is bamboo, split into thin strips.[14] The bamboo used in Pagan today comes from the Chin State, to the north and west of Pagan, and is transported to the workshops by river, first down the Chindwin and then down the Irrawaddy.[15] The hollow lengths of bamboo are cut into shorter lengths, each length being the space between the nodes in the bamboo. These lengths are then turned on end and split further into strips. Each strip is shaved to make it smooth and the remnants of the node are chopped off. These strips are still too thick to be useful for making coiled basketry so, having tipped the end of the strip in oil to make it pliable, the worker skilfully makes a series of cuts

Strips of bamboo for coiling, with small part-complete vessels nearby; one is very similar to cat. 19.

Right: Coiling of the separate elements of large vessels.

Far right: The two main elements of a large coiled flower vase; they will be joined prior to lacquering (see cat. 181 for two complete examples).

The substrate of a lacquer cup being woven on a spindle from split bamboo (uprights pointing towards viewer) and horse-hair (being threaded between the uprights). On the mat in the foreground, to left, a spindle, a finished woven cup prior to lacquering, and loose horse-hair.

in the top. This is then held firmly in the toes and each cut is pulled on, towards the worker, producing a thin, pliable length of split bamboo for either coiling or weaving.

Most vessels such as vases, offering vessels (*hsun ok*), bowls (except the small ones) and plates are made of coiled, rather than woven split bamboo, though in most workshops in New Pagan today both skills are to be found.[16] The coiled vessels are made as follows. A strip of split bamboo is cut to make the correct length for the bottom of the wall of the vessel (the base is a separately coiled circular element which is joined to the walls later). A V-shaped cut is made in each end of the strip, at the top of one end and the bottom of the other. These can then be 'hooked' on to each other, thus holding this first element in the vessel in place; here and at other crucial parts of the construction, the strips may be tied in place with a small length of cotton. The next strip of split bamboo is then pushed against the 'hook', on the inside, slightly above the first round strip; it is then coiled upwards. The whole structure is built up by the repetition of this process.

Other vessels, such as small cups (made in very large numbers today in Pagan) and bowls, are woven on wooden mandrels (see cat. 29) set on a spindle. Before being woven on the mandrel, the strips that will form the uprights and the base of the vessel are laid out across each other, and the base of the vessel is woven. When this is completed, the uprights are then bent up and the framework of the cup can be put on the mandrel; the base is held in place by a circular piece of wood with a point, which penetrates the centre of the bowl and passes through into a hole in the mandrel. The strips of bamboo used for these small cups and bowls are very thin and made especially soft by being boiled first in water. In most instances these finely split strips of bamboo make up both the uprights and the pieces woven in between, but in a few cases horsehair is used for the woven element instead of bamboo (see p. 33, photo. below right; and cat. 20). This produces an extremely pliable vessel where the lips of the bowl can be pressed together without causing any damage to the vessel (see cat. 21), as is famously and repeatedly demonstrated to visitors. This technique is much more time-consuming than making the vessels only of bamboo; it also requires special skills. Consequently, the horsehair cups and bowls are more expensive and are mostly produced by one or two skilled workers only.[17]

Next the interior of these small vessels is covered with *thayo*, a paste made of lacquer sap mixed with ash (other accounts of lacquer production mention that clay is sometimes used as the mixer). This application is done with the fingers. The use of this paste ensures that the interstices of the basketry are filled and that the surface can be made smooth; indeed, most of the sequence up until engraving for decoration is a repetition of covering with *thayo*, drying, smoothing and re-lacquering. The number of times this is done determines the quality of the finished article. Once the first application is complete, the vessel must be dried in a cellar in dark and humid conditions for at least a week. It is for this reason that all lacquer workshops have a cellar, *taik*, where the lacquerwares – in many different stages of production – can be stored away from direct sunlight and in humid conditions. The cellar is lined with wooden shelves on which the wares are stacked, and is entered by a trap-door. Because of the humidity requirement for curing the lacquer, the few months of the dry season are not suitable for making lacquer vessels. Once the vessel has dried it is brought out for the exterior of the vessel to be covered in lacquer paste. This is done by placing the bowl back on a mandrel, but this time attached to a bow-operated lathe (see below left and cat. 28c). This is activated and a piece of coconut husk, acting as a brush and dripping with lacquer paste, is held by the craftsman against the spinning bowl, thus coating the exterior.[18] Once more the vessel returns to the cellar for a further week of drying.

Once dry, the vessel is brought back to the workshop where it is mounted again on the lathe to smooth the outer surface where the lacquer paste has penetrated into the basketry. This is done by holding a blade against the bowl as it revolves (see below right). This coarsely

Below left: Bow-operated lathe ready for use, with mandrel on viewer's left and bow to right. On the ground to left is a stone slab on which smoothing materials are ground.

Below right: Lathe in use. The operator holds a blade against the rough interior of the vessel scraping away the excess *thayo*. Where it has been smoothed, the yellowish colour of the basketry is visible.

evens out the surface. The metal blade is right-angled in shape (see cat. 28a, second from top) and is mounted on a wooden handle; the blade is periodically sharpened on a slab of abrasive sandstone to which a little water has been added. To enable different-sized bowls to be smoothed, there are several different-sized mandrels that can be fitted on to the lathe.

In the next stage the lacquer paste, *thayo*, is finer, being made of lacquer sap, *thit si*, mixed with the pounded ash of cow bones. This makes a smoother paste than the earlier one. Once more the vessel is attached to the lathe and the *thayo* is added using the fingers – and with considerable skill. A cloth is used to smooth away any finger marks, and when the bowl is removed from the mandrel, the operator wears a little pointed cover over his thumb, so as to avoid any fingerprints on the tacky surface. Again it returns to the cellar for drying. As before, the next phase after drying is one of smoothing on the lathe, but this time, instead of the relatively coarse blade held against the revolving bowl, a stone is placed against it, followed by a handful of basketry shavings, which further refines the smoothing.[19] After this there are a series of applications of raw lacquer (i.e. no longer mixed with ash or other thickening agent) to build up an increasingly smooth surface, both inside and out. Each time lacquer is applied, the vessel has to return to the cellar for drying. The greater the number of applications at this point, the finer the end product – and the more expensive it will be, not only because more lacquer is used but because it takes longer to make.[20]

At this point some vessels will have applications of lacquer sap to which red colouring has been added. Traditionally this colour – the most distinctive and brilliant of the colours used for Burmese lacquer – was produced by adding powdered mercuric sulphide, cinnabar, to the lacquer sap; this mixture is known in Burma as *hinthabada*. Today other colouring agents, such as ochre or even red paint, are used, as *hinthabada* is expensive and has to be imported from China.[21] The mixture is

added by hand on top of a richly glossy black lacquer surface. Again the vessel is returned to the cellar for drying and when ready comes out for its final polishing before engraving. The polishing is done on the lathe with a cloth using teak ash, which is ground up on a palette with a little water. After this it is washed. These two actions – polishing and washing – produce a dull

surface which is required for the next major process: the engraving of the pattern.

The vessel is structurally complete and now only lacks its decoration. In Pagan most vessels are decorated in a number of different colours on a single-coloured background; the most common colours for the designs are red, green and yellow (blue is found less frequently) and the backgrounds are usually red or black.[22] This style of decoration is based on the principle that, when the smoothed surface of the vessel is engraved with a design and then covered in a mixture of lacquer and a colouring agent, the mixture will adhere where the design has been engraved but will not adhere – and can be wiped away – where it is not engraved. It follows that, if a multi-coloured design is planned, all that part of the design that is to be of one colour will need to be engraved at the same time, and that those parts that will be a different colour must be left unengraved; any part that is engraved will take colour when the colour-charged lacquer is applied.

Thus the first element in this sequence of decoration is for the design for one colour to be laid out by someone who has mastered the variety of different styles and motifs. The designer does this using a small engraving tool (see cat. 28 for two examples), with a mixture of free-hand and compass technique.[23] The stylus is held in the right hand and is pushed across the surface to be engraved with the left thumb.[24] As the point moves across the surface, it scratches down to the basketry beneath, leaving coils of debris which the engraver clears away as he works. The majority of the design is done free-hand and seemingly entirely from memory. There are apparently no pattern books, nor is it necessary for the design to be measured out first; it is all arranged by eye. The work with the compass is restricted to concentric lines, usually around the edge of the main design at the top or on the base. The designer often undertakes the

Yun technique – a betel box is engraved for the application of colour. Note the way the tool is held in the right hand and pushed with the left thumb.

engraving of the more complicated elements, while younger, less-experienced workers fill in much of the detail – and in this style there is usually plenty of detailwork. At the Htun Workshop today, as elsewhere in Pagan, designs are gathered from a variety of sources, including murals that range from the twelfth century to the more recent nineteenth-century examples of the Kon-baung dynasty.[25]

If the expensive *hinthabada* is used, it is prepared as follows. First it is weighed out and then a little water is added. After leaving it for a short period, any remaining water is pressed off and a pestle that has been dipped in peanut oil is used to mix it. Once the mixture is fully crushed, the lacquer sap, *thit si* is added, along with a little more peanut oil.[26] This mixture is applied to the outside of the vessel using a swatch of cotton threads, and then rubbed into the engraved surfaces using a handful of vegetable debris,[27] which presses the *hinthabada* mixture into the engraved surfaces. When finished, the vessel is once again returned to the cellar to dry for between seven and ten days, after which it is mounted on the lathe and rubbed with a handful of wet rice-husks. This removes the red colouring from the surface, except where it is embedded in the engraved design. The bowl is left to dry in the sun and then put back in the cellar for a further week. When it comes out, the surface is matt from the polishing with the wet rice-husks and is ready to be engraved again – but for another colour.

At the Htun Workshop the next colour to be engraved is green, which is done according to the same principle as before but with different details, including the use of glue as well as lacquer. The glue is made by dissolving lumps of resin from the acacia, or *htanaung*, tree in water,[28] and the mixture is then strained through a cloth. The vessel is covered with the glue, and the part of the design that is to be green is engraved using a small engraving tool, which is sharpened, as required, on a small sandstone slab. Next the cup is mounted on the mandrel and *thit si* is rubbed over the outer surface. This is then wiped off, but where it has settled in the engraved design, it remains so that when the green colouring powder is rubbed on to the surface of the vessel, the *thit si* acts as an adhesive and the green colour remains.[29] The vessel is then returned to the cellar for drying for a further seven days. This whole process is done a second time, and when finally dry, it is taken from the cellar and washed, using shavings from the lathe. The water removes the glue and the green colour from everywhere except where the design has been engraved. It is returned for a final session in the cellar where it hardens; for the best quality it should stay there for at least ten days. The last process, before it goes to the sale room next door, is to polish it on the lathe.

A similar sequence was recorded for the addition of yellow, starting with an application of the acacia tree glue, followed by engraving, in the instance recorded, with a ruler and a pin mounted in a wooden handle to create a series of straight lines (see cat. 28, bottom). Yellow was certainly a secondary colour in this instance, reserved for the decorative borders. The main free-hand design was produced in red and green. This is followed by the same sequence of covering with plain black lacquer, wiping it clean, then adding the yellow powder – all of this accompanied by repeated periods of drying in the cellar. In this instance the final polishing was recorded in detail. After the vessel comes from the cellar for the last time, it is polished not only with powder made from teak charcoal, which has been wetted before it is powdered, but also with powder ground from lumps of fossilized wood.[30] This is then washed off with wet and then dry cloths before a final buffing with the hands.

The above observations are concerned almost entirely with the preparation of the exterior of the vessel. The interior is rarely decorated, except perhaps for some concentric rings around the rim and red colouring. When colouring with red, the inner surface is first of all rubbed with emery paper and then cleaned with a cloth and water. *Thit si* is applied to the inside and the vessel is then placed back in the cellar for seven days to dry. This work has to be done in sunlight to ensure that any excess water in the *thit si* can evaporate. After the period of drying, the red *hinthabada* is applied, as usual, by hand. Again this operation has to be done in direct sunlight because of the *thit si* in the *hinthabada*,[31] which means that the months of the monsoon, June–September, are not good for this stage in the process, as the cloud cover is often great. Usually a team of several men sit together and colour the interiors of a large number of vessels, all at one sitting. The first man roughly applies the *hinthabada* and then sets it in the sun for five minutes or so to ensure a good colour. Next two men work in the *hinthabada*, and the fourth one finally smooths it, making certain that there are no inclusions. After each stage of this process the vessel is put in the sun as after the first stage. Then, of course, it needs to go back to the cellar for final drying before it is quickly dusted off and sent to the shop for sale.

A small amount of gold marbled work is made at the workshops in New Pagan, but this technique has only been introduced from Japan within the last few decades. It remains to be seen whether it will become popular.[32]

Apart from *yun* engraving, the other main technique practised at Pagan today is the black and gold, *shwe zawa* method of decoration. This work was witnessed at the Htun Workshop in 1995. It is clear from examples with known dates of purchase that this technique has been used at Pagan for much of the twentieth century,[33] though in the nineteenth century it was more connected with Prome, and especially, at the end of that century, with Hsaya Pa.[34]

Shwe zawa technique – the design which will remain glossy black on this tray is painted on in an orpiment/gum mixture.

At Pagan today this technique begins with placing a quantity of resin of the neem tree in water, which by the next day has formed a viscous glue. This is then strained through a cloth and mixed with the yellow colouring agent, which in the past would certainly have been orpiment (arsenic trisulphide).[35] Based on the principle that where the gum/orpiment mixture is painted on, the gold leaf will not adhere, the technique is usually applied to items that have been prepared with a very high-gloss black surface, thus providing a contrast between the black and the gold.

The design on the plate recorded at the Htun Workshop was a mythical lion, *chinthe*, at the centre with leaf borders at the rim. The outlines of these are drawn in – free-hand for the *chinthe* and with a compass for the border – using the yellow colour/gum mixture. This means that at the end of the process the outlines will remain black. Details within the design, such as the coat of the *chinthe* and the interior of the leaves in the border, are then engraved. The rest of the plate is dusted with a powder made from pulverized petrified wood, and then the whole of the plate other than the area already drawn in outline (the *chinthe* and the border) is covered with the orpiment and gum mixture. The interior of the *chinthe* and of the leaves of the border are thus the only part left black, as it were 'in negative'. The yellow mixture quickly dries and the plate is again covered with a dusting of the pulverized fossil wood. A layer of lacquer or varnish is applied,[36] and the plate is wiped clean; the sheets of Mandalay gold leaf are then pressed on to the area which has had the yellow/gum mixture applied to it.[37] The gold leaf is peeled off its distinctive paper backing and pressed into place using a

Shwe zawa technique – the lid of a pumpkin box is washed to clear away the orpiment/gum mixture leaving the gold leaf decoration (see cat. 183 for a large pumpkin box of this type).

cotton swab that has had a little oil added to it. Any gold that does not adhere is caught up in the oily cotton and is then cleaned by someone who will recycle the gold leaf. Once all the gold leaf is pressed into place, the plate is set aside in the cellar to dry. Before it has become hard, it is brought out and carefully cleaned in a bowl of water. The water quickly becomes brilliantly yellow from the orpiment/gum mixture, which soon comes away from the surface of the plate, leaving the gold leaf attached to the reserved surface, in this case the *chinthe* and the leaf border.

This completes the record of the work carried out in the Htun Lacquer Workshop in New Pagan in October 1995. On the evidence of that visit, by far the most numerous objects being made in the workshop were basketry vessels decorated with the engraved, *yun* technique in red, green and yellow, with some blue. Certain items of furniture were also seen in the workshop: circular and octagonal tables (the latter a design imported from northern India during the colonial period), chests, and screens. There was no sign of any relief-moulded work, though on a previous visit to Pagan a mould for pressing out repeating *thayo* elements was seen (see cat. 31 for such a mould). Such work has clearly been done there in the past, despite the prominence today of the *yun* technique. The main market for the wares produced was the tourist trade – buses of visitors to Pagan regularly stopped at the premises during the making of this record – and, despite the political turmoil in the country, there appears to be a sufficiently steady stream of visitors to enable this workshop, and others at Pagan, to continue in business. Generally, however, centres of lacquer production in Burma are now few because of the greater reliance on metal and plastic vessels for domestic use, though while the whole of Southeast Asia remains a tourist destination, it seems likely that the lacquerware traditions of Pagan will continue.

1 Burney 1832.

2 Morris 1919.

3 Fraser-Lu 1985 (new edition forthcoming); also Fraser-Lu 1994: 221–51.

4 Blurton 1999: 103–16. Some authors have also completely incorrectly described the production of engraved, *yun* lacquer vessels, such as Talbot Kelly 1905: 180 and Yule 1858: 157 and 197–8 (the former probably drawing on the latter, whose quality of information is usually dependable). Even the redoubtable Scott, writing under his nom-de-plume Shway Yoe (1882: 277–8), fails to describe the technique correctly. The mistake common to all three writers was the assumption that the pattern is exposed on the surface of a vessel by smoothing down through a layer of lacquer to the previously laid-on design. They entirely misunderstood the purpose of the engraving, as is described here.

5 Made by U Htein Win of Rangoon.

6 New Pagan is the settlement to which all the lacquer workers of Pagan were forcibly moved by the government in 1990; it is located to the south of Myinkaba village, close to the Lawkananda pagoda.

The Htun Lacquer Workshop (G/1, Khanlaung Quarter, New Pagan) is, like most lacquer establishments in Pagan, made up of two separate elements: workshops and a sales area. The latter also has facilities for potential buyers to be provided with refreshments. The pressure of non-Burmese tourists in Pagan has had an effect on the industry. Those items not sold in Pagan itself are transported to Rangoon, while large quantities are also exported to parts of Southeast Asia with high tourist exposure, such as Bangkok. This tourist market is countered by a decrease in sales to Burmese, as vessels made of mass-produced metal and plastic force lacquer out of the market, especially for domestic vessels.

This lacquer workshop was founded about seventy years ago by the grandparents of the present proprietor. It only opened in New Pagan, however, in 1991. One of the workers who has been there for fifteen years trained at the Lacquer School for eight years (for the Lacquer School at Pagan, see Fraser-Lu 1986), having started there at the age of thirteen. Some of the designs used at Htun are those developed at the school, while others have been invented 'in house'.

7 Previously known as *Melanorrhoea usitata* or *usitatissima*.

8 Nathaniel Wallich in 1828 mentions seeing it near Prome and later at Martaban, as well as in the Salween valley; in *The Imperial Gazetteer* (1908) under 'Pegu, District' (vol. XX, p. 90) there is mention of the *thitsi* tree '... among trees which have a marketable value' (whether for the wood or the sap is not indicated). Morris, in 1919, says: 'The bulk of the present supplies [of lacquer sap] come from Katha and the Shan States and it is estimated that the total output is about 200 tons a year.' Certainly the Shan States was the source for the lacquer used at the Htun Workshop in Pagan in 1995, which cost then 7,500 *kyat* for a box of 10 *viss*; they used approximately fifty boxes of this size per year. In addition to specific locations in the southern Shan States (Momeik, Loilem, Kengtung and Lawsawk), Fraser-Lu (1985: 8) also refers to Katha in the Sagaing District and Bhamo in Kachin State as sources for raw lacquer. She also mentions areas where second quality lacquer comes from. Morris 1919: 1 defines the tree as a 'fine upstanding tree found particularly in the drier forests of the province up to 3,500 feet'.

9 See p. 26 for Wallich's slightly different method of collecting the sap.

10 Morris has something to say on this subject: 'Bad methods of tapping threaten the future supplies, and the question of preserving the tree and regulating tapping is under consideration. At present the right to tap trees is subject to forest licences, but there is no attempt to ensure scientific and safe methods.' Morris 1919: 2. So far as we know, there never was any attempt to regulate tapping.

11 Burney in 1832 (p. 180) did make several suggestions, such as for 'ladies' square work boxes, and gentlemen's hats'. A recent acquisition in the British Museum is of exactly such a ladies' sewing box, with internal tray (OA 2000.2–3.1). It was used by a British teaching/missionary family based in Burma between 1915 and 1940, and bears an inscription with the maker's name, Hsaya Ba. Burney also suggested several more industrial uses for lacquer such as the waterproofing of boats and rigging, as well as caulking: ' I applied a coat of it [lacquer], in the absence of paint, to the sides of some gun-boats, and found the material cheaper and more durable than paint.' Burney, delightfully, was not prepared merely to speculate but was keen to experiment. See cat. 153, 157 and 174 for examples of vessels made of lacquer but in European shapes.

12 Again Burney (1832: 170) is one of the first to record this effect, though see also the *Edinburgh Journal of Science*, 1828, 96–100, for an even earlier mention.

13 For the techniques of lacquer use other than for vessels, see the relevant entries in this catalogue, e.g. for the method of making dry-lacquer sculpture, see cat. 39; for items decorated with gilded and moulded lacquer paste, see cat. 33.

14 Traditionally bamboo had an almost universal usage in Burma. Yule (1858) speaks of 'the all-useful bamboo' and (p. 153) lists forty different usages of bamboo, including 'cooking pots…, clothes-boxes, pan-boxes, dinner trays…', all of which are illustrated in this volume.

15 According to the 1912 *Burma Gazetteer: Lower Chindwin District, Upper Burma*, under the entries for the two villages of Kyaukka North and South, both important centres of manufacture of lacquer vessels even today, 'The variety of bamboo used is the *tinwa*, which is imported from the Upper Chindwin, the quality which renders it suitable being its pliancy.' This is no doubt the same today.

16 Although not recorded at the Htun Lacquer Workshop, other investigators mention that preparation of the basketry substrates is farmed out. This would certainly make sense as huge quantities of these frames were stored in the Htun workshop, probably more than could be produced within the workshop itself. A common sight on the road to New Pagan is groups of people, on foot or bicycle, carrying enormous numbers of ready-woven basketry shapes for betel-boxes. Further, the author saw no evidence of matting being woven in the workshop, and amounts of this will have been used for items such as large trays.

17 At the Htun Lacquer Workshop the specialist in this technique was Win Ma Aye. From personal observation, it is usually women who do both types of weaving on the mandrel – with plain bamboo and with bamboo and horse-hair.

18 The author was pleased to discover, several years after this fieldwork, that Burney records exactly the same utensil in use in 1832 (p. 170): 'Generally, to save the hand, the first coat is applied with a rude brush made of the husk of the cocoa-nut.'

19 In the example witnessed, the shavings used were those produced from the previous work on the lathe.

20 Morris mentions that the very finest wares may have as many as twenty-six different applications. He goes on to say that as a result these vessels may take up to six months to produce and are consequently more expensive (Morris 1919: 6). At the Htun Workshop the finest wares may take up to eight months to produce. In nearby Myinkaba, at the workshop of U Aung Myin, items of *yun*-decorated wooden furniture, such as chests of drawers or screens (see cat. 180) may take up to two years to complete. The unengraved wares made in Kyaukka (black outside and red inside, see cat. 155) take less time: 'Each article requires from two-and-a-half to three months to complete.' See *Burma Gazetteer: Lower Chindwin District, Upper Burma*, Rangoon 1912, p. 125.

21 At the Htun Workshop they go to Rangoon to buy both cinnabar and orpiment.

22 Burney (1832: 172) records that the Pagan wares were noted for being decorated in red and green.

23 At the Htun Workshop the designer was Kyaw Kyaw.

24 Exactly the same arrangement is recorded by Burney at Ava in 1832 (p. 173).

25 See cat. 184 for a design copied from Pagan murals.

26 Fraser-Lu 1985: 13 mentions the use of *shanzi*, or tung oil, 'which comes from a tree in the Shan States (*Aleurites* spp.)'. Morris 1919: 3 & 6 mentions the same *shanzi* oil. Presumably the two oils have the same function in the mixing of the *hinthabada*. It may be that peanut oil is easier and cheaper to acquire today. Burney in 1832 says that *shanzi* oil comes from the tree *Dipterocarpus turbinatus*.

27 At the Htun Workshop they used the outer wrappers from maize cobs.

28 In this context it is perhaps no coincidence that the inscription on cat. 155 from Kyaukka mentions the workshop of lacquer-master U Htun as at 'Acacia Grove'. The acacia is the source of the glue known in the West as 'gum arabic'.

29 In the past green colour would be made from a mixture of the mineral dye, orpiment (arsenic trisulphide), and the botanical dye, indigo. Today, we suspect that a mass-produced chemical colour is used and Fraser-Lu, writing in 1985, records the (then) current use of house-paint.

30 This unusual material is easily found in and around Pagan. Burney 1832: 170–71 says that the tree is called 'en-gyen', that it is *Ficus religiosa*, and that the powder is termed 'en-gyen kyouk-tshowe amhoun.'

31 Compare Burney 1832: 178: 'The workmen seem to prefer always to use the varnish in the sun.'

32 See cat. 59 for a typical example of this work.

33 For a cup decorated with a *shwe zawa* design which was acquired in 1920 at Nyaung U, close to Pagan, see cat. 159.

34 For mention of this master craftsman, see Watt 1904 (he won a commendation at the Indian Art Exhibition at Delhi in 1902/3) and Morris 1919.

35 The author did see some of this at the Htun Workshops where it is undoubtedly sometimes used. However, it is unlikely to be used every time yellow is required; that used for the *shwe zawa* work witnessed for this record was exceptionally bright and looked rather like poster paint. It is apparently imported from China.

36 Traditionally this would certainly have been lacquer, but today it is called 'furniture polish'; Fraser-Lu 1985: 23 says 'lacquer or varnish'.

37 For the preparation of gold leaf of this type, see Keretsky 1991.

Inscriptions on Lacquerware

Inscriptions: added value

The appeal of any well-crafted object lies partly in its beauty and fitness for its purpose. Inscriptions added by the maker or owner can greatly enhance an important part of its appeal: the power to convey something of the way of life of the men and women who made and used it. When it was made and first changed hands, an inscribed object formed a message between members of a cultural group with a language and much else in common. Properly interpreted, the inscriptions offer us a means of tapping this dialogue and learning directly from real people about the beliefs and values they shared in a distinct culture separated from ours in space and time.

Inscriptions on Burmese lacquer are seldom formal, and often engagingly lively. Most frequent are the names of maker, owner or donor. A maker keen to sell his wares always gives his address, often asserts the quality of his products and cites, if he can, in support of his claims the awards he has won for his craftsmanship. Frequently he finds space for good wishes for the health and prosperity of the buyer and users. Catchy advertising 'jingles' may also enliven the lacquer surface. A few buyers commission important pieces and have their names conspicuously inscribed by the maker, but most purchasers take the article home and add their name to it, usually daubed on the underside. Donors to monasteries, almost always couples, take care to record their names and their deed of merit on the object donated.

The story scenes depicted on lacquerware are so well known and loved by all Burmese as hardly to need the captions that the lacquer master provides. All the main actors may be labelled and the key incidents described, so that a single piece may have several dozen captions. Even the familiar signs of the zodiac and the eight planets that govern the days of the Burmese week may each be given its name.

Less frequent, but all the more welcome, are inscriptions recording the date a piece was finished. Sometimes, too, the maker adds his asking price. These and all the various inscriptions on lacquerware, from rare lengthy dedications in elaborate calligraphic script to a pair of letters on the underside of a betel-box, have something to tell us about real people living in a fascinating culture.

Regional variety

Donors had for centuries recorded their names and deed of merit on objects such as bronze bells, but also on the lacquered surface of teak manuscript chests. But it was only in the first years of the twentieth century that lacquer makers began to sign their work, and Pagan was the obvious place for this innovation. The scribing needle used for the traditional *yun*, engraved decoration was an ideal writing instrument. Where Pagan led, other centres followed. At Kyaukka plain black, red or brown wares were the rule, *yun* the exception. But by the end of the first decade of the twentieth century Kyaukka makers had taken up the graving tool and were putting their names on their best work. In Ava, the lacquer masters followed suit, using the same tool. In Kentung in the far east of the Shan States lacquer vessels were decorated in relief with tiny strands of lacquer putty, *thayo*, stuck on in floral scrolls, and gilded. When Kentung makers took to signing their wares, the signatures were painstakingly formed in raised *thayo* lettering, and gilded (cat. 169). But it was at Pagan that makers' inscriptions waxed most voluble and varied.

Makers' signatures

Early pieces of Burmese lacquerware are unsigned. Bowls and boxes in the Victoria and Albert and the Pitt Rivers museums certainly date from the mid-nineteenth century. Probably the earliest surviving masterpiece of *yun* lacquer in Britain, and indeed earlier than any currently in Burma, is the wonderful *bi it*, or toiletries box, of Ma Nu the Sorceress in the collection of Noel F. Singer, which he dates convincingly to the 1830s. It is profusely decorated in *yun*, but not signed.[1] A large panel in gold leaf work (*shwe zawa*) now in the British Museum (cat. 102) dates from the late eighteenth or early nineteenth century and once formed part of a manuscript chest (*sadaik*). The scenes depicted are from the *Mahosadha Jataka*: the future Buddha is the wise Young Judge. There are no less than fifty captions naming the locations, protagonists and incidents. Along the top border a long inscription names the couple from Po Thein Tan village who donated the chest and probably also a whole library of palm-leaf manuscripts to a monastery as an act of merit. Like all similar inscriptions, this one names the donors who commissioned the work but not the artist who created it.[2] It was certainly not illiteracy that precluded signature. The very idea can never have crossed the mind of the master, and if anyone had suggested it he would have been shocked at the presumption.

British Imperial rule soon changed this after Burma became a Province of British India in 1886. Great exhibitions of the arts and crafts were organized to feed designs and materials and techniques to the factories of Birmingham, Leeds, Manchester and Glasgow. In 1902–3 an Exhibition of 'Indian Art Manufactures' in Delhi assembled a vast array of craft work from many parts of the Indian Empire. The Director of the Exhibition and author of the official catalogue, Sir George Watt had enlisted the help of every Provincial government, and travelled widely himself seeking out the finest examples well in advance of the opening of the exhibition. In the catalogue Sir George notes that he personally visited 'the rather inaccessible village of Pagan' accompanied by the sub-Divisional Officer, Mr E. Dawson, who 'acted as his interpreter in studying this industry and in selecting the samples now shown in the Exhibition'.[3] So British officials spoke directly to the lacquer makers in their own workshops, viewed and assessed their best work, and earmarked pieces for Delhi. They must also have explained that craftsmen whose work was judged worthy of a prize would receive a medal (gold, silver or bronze) or a certificate of commendation, as well as an appropriate sum of money – provided of course the name of the maker was readily known. To ensure this, each piece must be accompanied by the maker's name affixed as closely as possible. We may reasonably assume that the suggestion was made, either by the British officials or by the maker, that this could best be done by using the scribing tool of the *yun* artist to engrave the name of the maker on the lacquer piece. Since Sir George Watt and Mr Dawson were selecting ready-made pieces, the maker's name could not be added to

Letter tube signed and dated 'year 64' (1902) by Hsaya Nyunt (cat. 18).

the decorated surface, but on most pieces it could very easily have been engraved on the base or underside.

Just such a signature appears on the base of a small letter canister of fine workmanship ဆရာညွန့် ၆၄ခု (cat. 18) which the maker Hsaya Nyunt has also dated to the Burmese year '64 or 1264, equivalent to 1902. A commendation for lacquered betel-boxes was awarded to 'Saya Nyain of Pagan', probably the same craftsman. An actual prize certificate (cat. 17) has survived despite insect damage. It was awarded to 'Maung Nyun of Pagan' for 'lacquerwork executed in the Artisans' Gallery' at the Delhi Exhibition of Indian Art Manufacturers. This prize certificate and the letter canister were obtained in Pagan some ninety years after the exhibition. The present writer knows of no earlier dated and signed lacquer piece, but has seen in a private collection one other piece bearing a date equivalent to 1902, a fine betel-box by Hsaya Kyawt Hmu. This bears an intriguing inscription:

ကိုကြော့မှူးလုပ် အစ်ဖြစ်သိ
အပိုတ် ငွေ၂၀ဖြစ်သို့
လက်ဟောင် အကောင်စုံ
၁၂၆၄ခု ဝါခေါင်လ္လွန် ၁၀ရက်

'This box was made by Ko Kyawt Hmu in the year 1264 [and finished] on the 10th day of the waning moon of [the month of] Wagaung. It is priced at 20 silver [rupees].' This was an extraordinary price, so high that it suggests something unusual was afoot in Pagan in August 1902. Perhaps the recent search by high officials of the British government for excellent specimens of lacquerware had inflated prices.

A small cup (cat. 60) with scenes from a stage play has six captions in small script but no maker's signature. Drawing, colouring and lettering closely resemble those of the letter canister signed by Hsaya Nyunt. If this cup is indeed by his hand, it would date from before 1902. Once a lacquer master had won prizes, he not only signed his work but mentioned his awards, medals, prizes and certificates. Admirers of his work were potential customers. Thus a flat betel-box of early twentieth-century date in a private collection is inscribed: လက်မှတ်ယ ဆရာညွန့်မှ 'Made by Prize certificate holder Hsaya Nyunt'. The decorative scheme for standard vessels, such as cylindrical betel-boxes and water bowls, was modified to allocate spaces for the maker's name, and his titles if any. Narrow friezes at the top edge and foot of a betel-box held pairs of cartouches shaped like miniature palm-leaf manuscripts. The mark of authenticity was now also a marketing mechanism. In a typical betel-box (OA 1998.7–23.75) the cartouches in the top frieze read,

ပုဂံမြို့ တန်းကြီးရပ် ဆရာထူးမွန်
ရှေးယွန်း စပယ်ရှယ် မင်္ဂလာအစ်

'Pagan Town, Tan Kyi Ward, Hsaya Htu's product; special ceremonial box of old-style lacquer', and those in the lower frieze add,

အဘိုးတန် အကောင်းဆုံး
အမျိုးမွန် လက်ဟောင်း

'Superior quality, the very best genuine traditional workmanship'.

Neither the box bearing these inscriptions nor any other lacquer piece is the product of a single hand. Division of labour is the rule within a lacquer workshop, or *taik*, and the basketry foundations, which are ready-woven to common shapes and sizes, are bought in from producer family groups outside. The term *taik* means any brick building and includes the walled yard enclosing the huts and thatch shelters where the dozens of workers practise their craft, and most important of all the deep cool humid underground cellar where the wet lacquerware is carefully stored to set after every stage of manufacture. So a piece ဆရာမောင် တိုက်တွက် မှ / က / ဖြစ် 'from the *taik* of *Hsaya* x' is a product of his workshop, from his cellar, and need not be by his hand. In his report for the year 1930 on the Pagan Lacquer School, the colonial Government's Superintendent of Cottage Industry refers to the *taik hsayas* as 'capitalists of this industry'.

The title *hsaya* can indeed mean artist or master craftsman, but it also means teacher, and also simply boss. Originally a *yun hsaya* (master of the art of lacquer decoration) and *taik hsaya* (owner and master of a workshop) may have been synonymous. But as production grew the *hsaya* could set his hand to only some of the last stages of *yun* decoration. His role would have taken on quality control, the training and supervision of the other *yun* engravers, instructing them in his personal versions of traditional designs, and perhaps in cautious innovations.

A few pieces bear the signature of the lacquer craftsman (*yun hsaya*) who engraved the decoration, as well as the name of the workshop owner (*taik hsaya*). A fine flat betel-box (cat. 168) has unusually elaborate *yun* work in pink on black by ယွန်းဆရာ မောင်စန်အေး *yun hsaya* Maung San Aye, who has inscribed his signature in fancy script on the side of the box, while the underside is clearly labelled,

(၁) (ပုဂံမြို့မ) (1)
ပြည်စုရပ်တောင်ပိုင်နေသာ
ပဋ္ဌမ ယွန်းဆရာမောင်ဝကြီး

'From the workshop of the well-known (lit. 'first') lacquer master Hsaya Maung Wa Kyi of South Pyizu Ward, Pagan'. A rectangular tray (cat. 170) with scenes from the Vessantara Jataka is inscribed on the upper surface,

ပုဂံမြို့ဈေးပိုင်းရပ်=ဆရာကိုအေးဖေတိုက်က မြမ္မာပြည် = ဖြစ်သော=ကာဖီစပွဲ အကောင်း

'This fine coffee table is from the workshop of Hsaya Ko Aye Hpay of Bazaar Ward, Pagan, Burma' and on the underside,

ဘထက်=မြမ္မာပြည်=ပုဂံမြို့=ဈေးပိုင်းရပ်မှာ လုပ်ပါသည်= ယွမ်းတည်အချော "၁"

'This first-class lacquer piece is the work of Ba Htet, Bazaar Ward, Pagan, Burma'.

But these are exceptional: the vast majority of 'signed' pieces name the workshop owner and location. Only one piece is known where the *hsaya* explicitly acknowledges the teamwork that goes to make every article of *yun* lacquerware and which is normally taken for granted. On a matt green betel-box in a private collection the maker's inscription reads: ၆ဦးအဖွဲ့ ဆရာကျော်တိုက်မှ 'Product of the workshop of Hsaya Kyaw and his team of 6 craftsmen'.

Many lacquer workshops nowadays are owned and run jointly by married couples, but it is rare for a couple to put both names on their product. A fine water-bowl made in Sale near Pagan (cat. 62) is signed quite unequivocally: စီမန်လုပ်ကိုင်သူ=ဆရာဘမမအောင် 'The craftsmen who made this article are Hsaya Ba and Ma Ma Aung.' Many *yun* engravers are young women or girls, and this was also the case at the turn of the century when Sir George Watt visited Pagan workshops to select outstanding pieces for the 1902–3 Delhi Exhibition. A woman artist, Ma Gyan of Mandalay, won a commendation 'for a lacquered teapot', and Sir George ranked a round box by Ma Kyan Yi as a 'chief exhibit'. Perhaps this woman artist was from Pagan. Certainly a flat betel-box in the British Museum collection and another in the Liverpool Museum dating from the mid-twentieth century are ပုဂံမြို့မှန်ကြို့=မညွန့်တိုက် 'from the workshop of Ma Nyunt of Hman Gyo Ward, Pagan'. A set of tea-plates also in the Liverpool Museum are signed by a woman lacquer artist styling herself,

ဆရာမ မမသစ် အမုံ
ပုဂံမြို့မ ရှီးတန်းရပ်

'*Hsayama* – female master-craftsman Ma Ma Thit of lacquer industry quarter, Pagan.'

Lacquer masters often prefix their name with the title *pahtama*, literally 'first'. Burmese names are few, and in government offices it is common to find an official with a plastic name-badge reading 'U Maung Maung 23', which means that at least twenty-two of his colleagues in the same department have the same name. But the honorific *pahtama* rather conveys that the business is well established, well known and the original workshop of that name. No *hsaya* ever style himself as 'The Second Hsaya Sein'!

Trademarks
Particularly successful workshops invented their own brand or trademarks, which were clearly modelled on the British and foreign trademarks for familiar goods, though not registered and legally protected. Such devices are usually found in a roundel on the top of the lid of a betel-box, and consist of a sketch of the chosen bird or beast with lettering around it naming the brand and the workshop master using it. Examples from the period before the Second World War are ကျားတံဆိပ် ဆရာထပ် 'Hsaya Htat's Tiger Brand' (cat. 7), and Hsaya Pyant used the same name, for nobody had exclusive rights to the popular tiger; ကျေးတံဆိပ် ဆရာလှိုင် ပေါက္ကံပြည်စု 'Hsaya Hlaing's Parrot Brand'; 'First Hsaya Min's Hawk Brand' (cat. 64); and the distinctive colours and drawing style of သိန်းတံဆိပ် ပဋ္ဌမဆရာမင်ဆန်တန်းရပ် 'First Hsaya Ban's Peacock' or ဒေါင်းမင်း 'Royal Peacock Brand' (cat. 167). In the post-war period ရွှေလရောင် ဆရာကြည်မြင်ကပါတောင်ရပ် U Ba Kyi's workshop in the South Ward of Myinkaba village produced 'Golden Moonlight Lacquerware'. More recently the term 'enterprise' (*lut ngan*) has gained currency, and a number of workshops use this term without naming the owners or lacquer artists. Thus the ရွှေလိပ်မင်း ရှီးရာယွန်းထည်လုပ်ငန်း ပုဂံမြို့သစ် 'Royal Golden Turtle Traditional Lacquerware Enterprise of Pagan New Town' dates from 1991 after the enforced removal from Pagan of all its inhabitants to a bleak dry hillside several miles distant. Between Pagan and Nyaung-U, at Wet-Kyi-In, is the ပစ်တိုင်းထောင် ယွန်းထည်လုပ်ငန်း ဝက်ကြီးအင် 'Everstand Doll Lacquerware Enterprise', which uses as its device the *Pyittaing Daung* doll, bottom heavy on a rounded base, and hard to upset. The Burmese-to-English Dictionary gives the charming if dated English terms, 'billiken or tumbling Kelly', and also the figurative meaning (apt these days in Burma), 'a person inured to life's vicissitudes'.

In other lacquer-producing centres makers followed Pagan and signed their wares.

Kyaukka, a large village near Monywa and the Chindwin river, made mostly plain black or red wares, sturdy and durable. The best, such as the round *ok khwet*, or offering bowl (cat. 155), achieve balanced proportions and a sober dignity. The maker, Hsaya Ko Htun Aye, signs his name and workshop ထနောင်းဝန်းတိုက်ဆရာ ကိုထွန်းအေး 'Acacia Tree Circle' in an inconspicuous roundel on the base, using a *yun* engraving tool and red colour for his signature.

In Ava many makers appended the words 'Number One' to their name: The large basin (cat. 157) is by အင်းဝမြို့ ယွန်းတန်းရပ် တိုက်ဆရာ မောင်စ ၁ နံပါတ် 'Lacquer Master Maung Za, Number One'. The word for 'number' used in this phrase is a Burmese transliteration of the English word, so the expression must have been a slang term equivalent to 'top notch' or to the 'super' or 'fab' of more recent years.

In Kentung, in the far south east of the Shan State near the border with China, lacquer masters worked in a very distinct tradition. Singer has traced the development of a simple basket shape into the *ko kaw tee*, or ceremonial gift basket, decorated in elaborate low relief patterns built up from thin strands of *thayo* putty.[4] This is a mixture of liquid lacquer and finely sifted ash, which can be rolled into tiny 'worms' and used to form floral scrolling, and also lettering. Singer credits a British official, Mr Gahan, resident in Kentung at the turn of the century, with encouraging the lacquer workers to make improvements in their wares.[5] Mr Gahan may also have suggested that the lacquer masters should sign their best pieces, for almost all surviving *ko kaw tees* are in fact signed, and in Burmese not Shan script. Two distinct means are used for these signatures: early pieces have the lettering formed in relief from small strands of *thayo*, while later pieces usually use the *shwe zawa* technique, black writing on gold leaf.

An early *ko kaw tee* (cat. 169) has a large circular medallion on the base with raised lettering in *thayo*, the whole gilded:

ရှမ်းပြည်တောင်ပိုင်း ကျိုင်းတုံမြို့
အာလောဂဆရာ လုပ်ပါသည်
နတော်လှ္ဆုပ် ၁၂ရက်ပြီး

'In Kentung in the Southern Shan State Ah Law Ga Hsaya finished this on the 12th day of the waning moon of the month of Natdaw'. Tantalizingly, this beautiful inscription omits

Two types of signature by Kentung lacquer masters on ceremonial baskets, *ko kaw tee*. The circular medallion (cat. 169) has lettering in raised *thayo*, while the rectangular cartouche is worked in *shwe zawa* gold leaf (cat. 165).

the year, but we may safely date it to the first decade of the twentieth century.

The second way of signing *ko kaw tees* is less laborious. On the base of the basket a cartouche, usually rectangular, is formed: sometimes the border is in raised *thayo*. Within this frame, while the black lacquer coat is still tacky, the inscription is written in water-soluble ink. Next gold leaf is stuck all over the cartouche. When the lacquer has set hard, the area is gently washed and the gold leaf over the water-soluble 'ink' is removed. An elegant *ko kaw tee* by Hsaya Tay Ya (cat. 165) is signed in this way and dated 1936:

ကျိုင်းတုံမြို့
ဆရာ တေယ
၁၂၉၈ ခု

One family in Kentung claiming descent from Hsaya Tay Ya have in recent years revived the craft and are now producing *ko kaw tees* of acceptable quality. One example in the British Museum is inscribed:

ကျိုင်းတုံမြို့
၁၃၅၂ ခုနှစ်
ခွမ်မွန်းရွာ
ဦးမှုလိန္ဒာနန်းပုတ်
ပြုလုပ်သည်

'Kentung Town, Year 1352 [1990], Köng Möng Village; U Mu Leinda and Nan Pouk Pyu made this.' Lacquer makers in Prome used a seal to impress their signature, and a large red *hsun gwet* (cat. 160) is signed:

ပြည်မြို့
ဆွာဖြူ

'Prome Town, Hsaya Hpyu'.

Seal-impressed signature of Hsaya Hpyu of Prome on a *hsun gwet* (cat. 160).

Addresses of makers and retailers

Pagan makers regularly put their address on their wares, usually simply the word or quarter in which their *taik* was to be found, as an aid to buyers visiting Pagan:

ပုဂံမြို့ဈေးရပ်/ဆရာရုံးတိုက်တွက်

'Product of Hsaya Yon's Workshop, Market Ward, Pagan';

မြင်းကပါတောင်ရပ် ဆရာကြည်

'Product of Hsaya Kyi, South Ward, Myinkaba Village'.

Occasionally the number of the building or walled plot is added. Hsaya Tha Shein, who won both a bronze medal and a commendation at Delhi in 1902, styled himself 'Prizewinner' and gave his address as:

> မြန်မာနိုင်ငံတော် အထက်ပိုင်းပုဂံမြို့တွင်းတိုက်စုအရပ်။
> တိုက်နံပါ် – ၁၀၂ – ဦးသာရှိန်တိုက်ဖြစ်သော

'Myanmar Country, Upper Region, Pagan Town, Taik No 102 Lacquer Works Ward Pagan'.

Wholesale and retail purchasers, their agents and friends had no difficulty dealing with Pagan lacquer producers. The frequent steamers of the Irrawaddy Flotilla Company carried millions of passengers annually and their purchases. There were also 'Bazaar' steamers which carried hundreds of market stalls selling produce to villagers at every riverbank stop, and between stops.[6] Many Pagan producers must have had a standing arrangement with wholesalers in nearby Nyaung-U, but some dealt directly with retailers in Rangoon or Mandalay.[7] A betel-box in a private collection was inscribed ၆ဦး အဖွဲ့ ဆရာကျော် တိုက်မှံ 'made by Hsaya Kyaw and his 6-man team' for sale by,

> မန္တလေးမြို့ဘုရားကြီးမြောက်မုတ်
> ဦးမြိုယွန်းကုံသည်

'U Myo, lacquer trader at the north entrance to the Great Pagoda in Mandalay City'.

Lacquerware producers in Ava, the ancient capital and rather a backwater after the foundation of Mandalay in 1859, regularly added the name and address of their retailer in Rangoon. A large basin (cat. 157) made by အင်းဝမြို့ယွန်းတန်းရပ်တိုက်ဆရာမောင်ဇ ၁နံပါတ် 'Number One Hsaya Maung Za of Ava' also bears the name of the retail outlet: ရန်ကုန်မြို့ ကုန်ဈေးတန်း ဦးမောင်ကလေး 'U Maung Galay, Commercial Trade District, Rangoon City'. And a brown bowl made by ဦးမှင်ကုမ္ပဏီ ကိုင်မာရပ် အင်းဝမြို့ 'U Hmin Company, Kaing Ma Ward, Ava' could be purchased from မကျော့ရင် နံပါတ်၇၃ ၁၄လမ်း ရန်ကုန်မြို့ 'Ma Kyaw Yin of 73, 14th Street, Rangoon'. One enterprising Rangoon merchant seems to have ordered from Pagan high quality horsehair boxes without the maker's name but inscribed with an insistently commercial message: ရန်ကုန်မြို့ ၂၅လမ်း ဝါဆိုတန်း တိုက်နံပါတ်၃၅ ကိုတိပ်ဂွမ်း မကျော့ရင် တိုက်ဆိုင်မှာ ယွန်းကုန် အမြိုးမြိုး ရနိုင်ပါသည်။ 'In Rangoon City, at No. 35 Cotton Dyers' Yard on 25th Street, Ko Teik Gwan and Ma Kyawt Yin's important shop stocks a wide range of lacquerwares.' (OA 1998.7–23.223)

Makers' claims of quality

A signed piece with the address of the maker was in itself an advertisement for his wares. But the smooth surface of a lacquered box or tray offered fine spaces which producers were quick to exploit for promotional messages. Pithy phrases fitted into the cartouches in the shape of palm-leaf manuscripts impressed on customers the quality of the wares, the authenticity of the materials and the superior workmanship, as proved by the awards and distinctions which the lacquer master had won. Some of these claims are general, others quite specific.

Makers' awards in shows and exhibitions were a matter of pride and a marketing feature. A master who had won a certificate or medal made sure his customers knew of it, adding to his name such titles as လက်မှတ်ရ / ဆုရ / ပဌမဆုရ / ဆုတံဆိပ်ရ 'certificate holder', 'prize winner', 'first prize winner' or 'prize medal holder'. In Burma it is normal practice for authors and craftsmen to include in their pen-name or signature the name of a better-known relative. Typical is the signature on a betel-box in a collection in Singapore: ဆရာထပ်သား မောင်ဘချို 'Hsaya Htat's son Maung Ba Chon'. A young man in Kyaukka with no distinction of his own as yet, was determined to utilize the reflected glory of his famous elder brother:

အန့်ပွဲတွင် နာမည်ကျော်ခဲ့
လက်မှတ်ရ
ထနောင်းဝန်းတိုက်ဆရာ
ဦးထွန်းဧညီ ဦးထွန်းပေါ်

'Famed for awards won in exhibitions of "Wonders of Art and Nature" the lacquer master of the Acacia Circle workshop, U Htun Aye – his younger brother U Tun Paw.'[8]

Sometimes it was not enough merely to mention his distinctions: the lacquer master had also to convince the sceptical customer: လက်မှတ်ပြနိုင်သည် 'Award certificates can be produced for inspection.' One piece in the Victoria and Albert Museum has a somewhat aggressive claim: သက်သေခံ 'Evidence of awards can be proved in court.'

The most frequent phrases claiming general quality are the rhyming pairs: လက်ဟောင်းအကောင်း *Let-haung, a-kaung*, literally 'old hand is best', i.e. reputable craftsmanship; and အဘိုးတန် အမျိုးမှန် *a-botan, a-myo hman*, 'valuable, genuine'. Often both are combined in the jingle:

အဘိုးတန် အကောင်း
အမျိုးမှန် လက်ဟောင်း

a-bo-tan a-kaung
a-myo hman let haung.

These pairs neatly fill the cartouches at the foot of the standard cylindrical betel-box. Other claims abound, အကောင်းဆုံး / အချော့ဆုံးဘဲ / ရွှန်းထီပေါ်ပြင် 'Best of all', 'Most superior', 'Simply the finest' and even more high-flown အတုမရှိ / မင်္ဂလာယွန်း / စပယ်ရှယ် / ယွန်းညွန့် 'incomparable', 'unbeatable' and 'special festive ware'. After the deposition in 1886 by the British of the last Burmese king, it soon became possible for Pagan lacquer masters to claim with impunity: စားတော်ဝင်အခံ 'This box is fit for a King's table', 'This bowl is of royal quality'. More specific claims emphasize the authenticity of materials and techniques: ရှေးယွန်း / ရိုးရာယွန်း 'Old-style traditional lacquerware', မြင်းမီးခွက်မှန် 'This bowl is of genuine horse-hair', အဆင်ငါးမျိုးရှိယွန်း 'Five layers [i.e. five colours] *yun* ware', သားရိုးမှံ 'Real thayo lacquerware', အမြိုးမှံ ကျွန်းသစ်တာ 'This box is of real teak'. Or they tell the customer the superiority of the article in use: အခိုင် / အင်မတ် ခိုင်ခန့်ပါသည် 'durable and long-lasting', ရေနွေးခံသော 'resistant to damage by hot water', နေ့ရှိန်ရေစိမ်မကျိုးခန် 'will not spoil if left in the sun or left to soak in water'. One rhyming jingle on a betel-box in a private collection points out how well made the box and lid are, and how neatly the deep cover fits the box:

တင်လိုက်လျှင်သက် မှတ်လျှင်တက်

'Just put the lid on – down it slides.
Puff [at the side] and up it rides.'

A circular inscription on the base of a lidded dish for sweetmeats or pickled tea leaf (OA 1998.7–23.96) epitomizes the enthusiasm of the maker for his own product: စိမ်သော – သားရိုးမှံ – အထူးစပါယ်ရှယ် – အနိုင် 'Created in genuine *thayo* of exceptional truly special quality by Maung Waing of Central Ward, Myinkaba Village, and guaranteed durable.' Hsaya To, the maker of a splendid teak box in a private collection warns: နောင်ကို သီလိုအထည် ယနိုင်ခဲပါသည်။ အမြိုးမှံ 'In future pieces of this fine quality will be hard to find.'

The *yun* artist Hsaya Maung signs the base of an elaborate teak casket (in a private collection) with verses of his own composition arranged round a self-portrait. He reclines on a couch dressed in Burmese finery except for his footwear: English lace-up shoes of brogue type and knitted stockings. He holds a cheroot and looks the perfect dandy, of about 1910. In his enthusiasm for his own skills as a lacquer master, he violates some of the rules of his chosen verse-form, the *taydat*:9

ရေးစပ်သည့် တေးထပ် –

ယွမ်းသေတ္တာ ပြုသမှုတုမရဲ့ညိုစံ
ရှုဆရှ် ကဝိကျဲသည်
မကဲသံ အကဲ
ငါးထပ်ယွန်း ဆက်ခါသော်တည်
သက်ယာကျော် သုံးပိုမလဲ့။

ဆေးမှင်စုံမ်းအင်းစွဲရှ်
ရင်တနဲ တန်ချည်
မင်းကုသ ဇာတ်တော်ခင်းပါလို့
မှတ်နောာ်တသင်း မယွင်းစေပို့ အညို
ရှုလိုက်တိုင်း မောာင်မသီသည်
ရောာင်အဆီ လုပ်တော်ရှ်
မြကျောက်သို့ သွင်ပမာ
ဆရာမောင် သေတ္တာကိုင်သူမ်းသူ အဆွေမော်မှာ
အသရေတော် ကြီးစေပို့လေး။
                ဆရာမောင်

Taydat verses of my own composition

This box I've laboured to create
Is a pure joy to contemplate.
Another like it can't be found
However much you look around.

Just look how the engraving's done:
Five colours laid in one by one
So skilfully that you can feel
A surface smooth as polished steel.

Its joints are made so tight and strong
This box will last a lifetime long
And will remain in use, I vow,
A century or more from now.

With graving point and full palette
I've delicately drawn a set
Of pictures from the Kusa Zat –
And, by the way, you'll notice that
I've strictly kept the story line
(Not stuck inventions in of mine)

And every scene a blaze of colour
Like brilliant gemstones – not one duller.

This box of Hsaya Maung's will bring
Its owners joy in everything:
Praise for their taste, and admiration.
It will enhance their reputation.

Hsaya Maung

50

Makers' good wishes to buyers

As if all this were not enough to tempt a customer, the maker included for no extra charge effusive good wishes, which targeted the buyer but extended to all users who would see and handle the article, especially the betel-box which was passed round the conversational group. The standard pair of phrases expressing good wishes happens to rhyme in English as well as in Burmese: ကျွမ္မာပါစေ / ချမ်းသာပါစေ 'Wishing you health', 'Wishing you wealth'. Other sentiments appropriately found on betel-boxes include မိတ်ဆွေတိုးများ 'May you have many friends', မင်္ဂလာတိုးကျပါစေ 'May you meet with auspiciousness/luck', မေတ္တာ / သစ္စါ 'Loving kindness (*myitta*) and fidelity (*thissa*)', သည်အထိကို ယသောသူများ ကုသိုကောင်းဆိုသည် 'Those fortunate enough to own this will gain merit', ဝယ်သူမင်းများ အသက်ရှည်စေသား 'May the honourable owner enjoy long life', အာရုဝန် သုခံပလန် 'Long life, good looks, joy and strength'. Much more worldly is the emphasis on material good fortune: စီးပွားတိုးကျပါစေ 'May your business prosper', ရတနာမိုးရွာပါစေ 'May treasures shower down on you', သိန်းထီပေါက်ပါစေ 'May the owners win a prize in the 100,000 Rupees lottery'; and shrewdly on a gun box made for a police inspector (cat. 174): ရာထူးတိုးတက် / ဘေးကင်းဘ၁စေ 'May you be free from danger', 'May you gain promotion in your career'.

Rhymes abound in Burmese, and a large rectangular tray (170) offered the maker plenty of space for this effusion:

"၁"ကျွန်နုပ်မောင်အေးဖေ =
မေတ္တာရေကြောင့် = ဝယ်သူသုံးသူတို့များ
မင်္ဂလာတိုးကျ၍= ရတနာမိုးရွာစေ။

'I Maung Aye Hpay, who made this tray
With all my heart and soul I pray
That those who buy and use it may
Meet more auspiciousness each day
And treasure rain down in their way!'

Such sentiments of goodwill, good fortune and auspiciousness were also conveyed by the choice of story scenes depicted on the *yun* box or bowl. These will be discussed later: first, a few examples of owners' marks.

Owners' names

Many lacquer articles are marked with the name of the owner. Grand pieces may be commissioned complete with the owner's name, which in rare cases may form part of the decorative scheme.

A fruit bowl (cat. 171) made in Pagan for a couple living just across the Irrawaddy river has a horseshoe-shaped inscription in flowery script repeated three times between

Detail of bowl (cat. 171). The couple who owned this bowl had their name and address repeated three times in fancy script and integrated the arc-shaped inscription into the design.

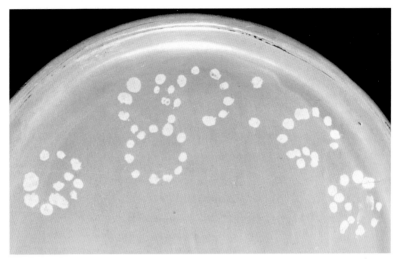

hintha birds, but no maker's name: မြစ်ချေမြို့ နောင်းကုံးရပ် ဦးအုံးစိန် ဒေါ်ဟွန်းရဲ့ သုံးစွဲရန် 'Made for use by U Ohn Sein and Daw Lun Yone of Danaung Lon (Acacia Tree Circle) Ward of Myitchay Town'. But such calligraphy is exceptional. More often the makers will be asked to add the buyer's name in a cartouche left blank for the purpose on a finished article. On a large water bowl commissioned by Ma Hla Hpyu (cat. 70) မလှဖြူ ခွက်ကြီး အညွန့် ခြောကိုင်း her name takes up more space than does that of the maker Hsaya Kaing of Pagan. In contrast, the maker of a round tray (OA 1998.7–23.113), Hsaya Min, uses up all the cartouches on the rim of the upper surface,

မြန်မာနိုင်ငံတော် အထက်ပိုင်း ပုဂံမြို့
ရှုံးတန်းရပ် ဆရာမင်း ကိုက်ထွက်

leaving only a small roundel on the bottom of the tray ဆားပွဲဦးဖိုရိုက်သုံးရန် for the owner U Hpo Yaik.

Most often the buyer takes the article home and adds his or her name wherever space can be found, usually on the bottom of the base. Such inscriptions are invisible in use but serve readily to tell the owner's vessel among others. This is very useful after a *hsun*, a meal offered to the local monks. Devout Burmese ladies invite monks to eat their one meal of the day at their home on special days in the religious calendar or to mark a family occasion. The host family start cooking before dawn, for the meal must be over by noon. The more numerous the monks fed, the greater the merit for all the donors and helpers, including of course those who lend their trays, bowls and cups. Clearing up after the *hsun* means returning the many similar vessels to the families who lent them, so a name on the base is useful. Ma Aye has impressed hers into the cover of her food dish (cat. 179) ωc while the red lacquer was still wet. Liquid lacquer bonds best to lacquer. It was readily available, and this is the paint used by many owners for adding their name to a bought piece.

In Rangoon streets before the Second World War, lacquer repair men carrying two bamboo tubes suspended from a yoke would call out: 'Fix your lacquer, black or red!' Housewives with flaking or worn trays or bowls would call the repairman up the stairs, and with a practised bare hand he would stroke on the new wet gleaming coat to set hard in a few days. Small children had to be taught not to touch the glossy surface meanwhile. My teacher of Burmese told me that as a child he learnt this lesson the sticky way.[10]

Owners' marks. Left: (detail cat. 179) Ma Aye impressed her name in wet lacquer. Right: (detail cat. 178) Ma Hpwa May used her candy pink nail varnish.

Ma Sein Pu မစိန်ပု painted her name on her rice measure (OA 1998.7–23.254), Daw Kyan Bon ဒေါ်ကျမ်းဘုံ on her water bowl, and the prudent Daw Thein daubed her name ဒေါ်သိန်း not only on the base of her betel-box but also on the bottom of each of its two internal trays (OA 1998.7–23.254, OA 1998.7–23.92, OA 1998.7–23.107). Ma Hpwa May မဖွားမေ, however, used her nail varnish and brush to write her name in candy pink dots on the set of toffee brown soup bowls (cat. 178) အင်းဝမြို့ယပ်တန်း ဦးဘိုးရာ made by lacquer master U Hpo Ya in Ava in the 1930s. Some owners used a pin or needle to peck their names in separate dots.

Indian owners of Burmese lacquerware added their name in their own script. 'Madras lacquer' is a term used for lacquer taken back to Tamil Nadu by Chettiar families. Owners' names in Tamil script can be found on such pieces (cat. 166). One Chettiar betel-box in the British Museum (OA 1998.6–13.3) is decorated in the *za yun* 'lace' pattern and has the Burmese inscription ပုဂံမြို့ တန်းပြိုးရပ် ဦးကြီးတိုက်ထွက်, 'made by U Kyi of Tanbyo Ward in Pagan'. He used the chequered pattern to form the lettering of his signature and added the wish, 'May the buyer be a rich man'. The new owner may indeed have been well-off.

Gifts and donations

Many visitors to Pagan bought gifts for friends. But some inscriptions from colonial times use formal language and show marked regard for rank and status. One young lady who chose from her father's stock a gift for a lady friend, perhaps on her marriage, was careful to include in the inscription the colonial title of her friend's father. A flat black betel-box in a private collection bears the legend:

ပုဂံမြို့ = ရိုးတန်းရပ်
ယွန်းကုံသည် = ဆရာစိန်၏သွီး
မဝေါတင်တို့က
မန္တလေးမြို့ =
သစ်တောဝန်မင်း ဦးကျော် ATM
သွီးမခင်မြသုံးရန်
ရေးယွမ်းဗုဒ္ဒံ

'This traditionally crafted flat betel-box is the gift of Ma Waw Tin, daughter of Lacquer Merchant Hsaya Sein of Pagan Town, Lacquer Works Quarter, to Ma Khin Mya, daughter of Chief Forestry Officer U Kyaw, A.T.M., of Mandalay Town.' A wide-mouthed spittoon in black lacquer (in the same private collection)[11] was a gift to a social superior, as the inscription shows: ပစေတာ်ကတော်ကြီး သုံးတော်မုရဲ ထွေးခံ 'This spittoon is for the esteemed use of the lady consort of the Sub-Divisional Inspector.' The maker adds အတုမရဲ အခြောယွန်းထည် "1" 'Lacquerware of unbeatable quality, Class "1"', which one suspects was more than could be said for the rank of the recipient's husband.

Traditional Burmese Buddhists regarded a material surplus as an opportunity to donate and thus to gain merit. Many purchasers bought articles as donations to monasteries. Such donations could be on a grand scale. A large gold-leaf (*shwe zawa*) panel (cat. 102) of late eighteenth- or early nineteenth-century date probably formed part of a splendid manuscript chest, donated with a full set of manuscripts. The scenes depicted from the *Mahaummaga Jataka*, known to the Burmese as the *Mahosadha* after the Bodhisattva as the Wise Young Judge, have no less than fifty captions naming characters, locations and incidents. The donors' inscription is well preserved except for its opening phrases, which may have included the date. Nowhere on this wonderful panel does the name of the lacquer artist appear:

[ပြီးပြည့်စုံသည်။ စာတိုက်ဒါယကာ ဖိုးသိန်းတံရွာနေ ကိုဝ်သာကောင်းမရား]

မင်ချယ်လယ်ရှိပြီးပြည့်စုံသည်။ စာတိုက်ဒါယကာ ဖိုးသိန်းတံရွာနေ ကိုဝ်ဘကောင်းမရား မဖူး သွီးမောင်နှံ
သားသွီးတစုတို့ ကောင်းမှုနံပွာန်ဆု။ သာဓုနတ်လူ ကြည်ဖြူကောင်းကြီး ခေါ်စေသော။ ကျွံဒံမေပုည် အာသဝက္ကယံ
ဝပ်ဟောတု။ ဇေယျတု သမ္ပမင်္ဂလံ။ ပုဒံအာနှင် ပြည်စုံခြန်းည်နံ သိန်မွေသောကိုယ် ဖြစ်ပါရလိုဝ်၏။

... has been completed. The lacquerwork has been completed by the wife of library donor
Ko Tha Kaung of Po Thein Tan village. This deed of merit is done by library donor Ko Tha
Kaung of Po Thein Tan village, his wife Ma Pu, daughter and all their family with the aim
of attaining Nirvana. We share the merit with all celestial and human beings and may this

Opposite and above: details of betel-box cat. 167. The large displaying peacock on the top of the lid (opposite) is the maker's trade mark or brand name. Above this, at the edge of the cover, the buyer had his name added, as donor of the box to a monastery. In the upper frieze on the side of the lid, two cartouches (above left and right) contain the name of the donor's spouse and her partner in merit. The maker uses the two cartouches at the foot of the box to claim supreme quality for his wares.

good deed cause them to call out in approval 'Well done' [*thadu*]. May we, on account of our deeds of merit, attain Nirvana where all defilements are extinct. May we obtain the celestial eye by which we can see the cycle of rebirth, the destiny of beings and the process of the extinction of all defilements.[12]

So owner becomes donor, and names are recorded with the deed of merit in an inscription on the lacquer betel-box, bowl or cup. Donors' inscriptions are conspicuous: not for Burmese Buddhists charity by stealth. The merit of the deed is shared by all whose attention can be attracted so that they can call out *thadu* ('Well done')!

About eighty years ago a young couple planned to donate a betel-box to the monks of a monastery. In Pyizu Quarter of Pagan they visited the workshop of Hsaya Ban ပဝ္စမ ဆရာဘန်း to select a box in his distinctive ဒေါင်းတံဆိပ် 'Royal Peacock Brand' (cat. 167). The colours and designs of this brand were so fashionable that they attracted imitators, so Hsaya Ban took to including his own guarantee in the inscription: ဒေါင်းမင်း တံဆိပ်စစ် 'This is the real thing, the genuine article'. Furthermore, Hsaya Ban claimed, it was ယွန်းထံပေါ်ပြင် အချောဆုံးတဲ့ 'the ultimate in lacquerware, simply the finest there is'. Impressed, the young couple ordered their names to be added to record their meritorious deed ကံပန္ ကိုဘိုးချိုမ် မက်ဘ ကောင်းမှု. The young man, proud of his situation with a modern commercial firm, styled himself 'Company Ko Hpo Gyon'. The young lady who shared his life and prospects, and of course the present deed of merit, was Ma Kaba, whose name can be rendered as 'Miss World'. The maker of the box has inscribed his wishes for them (or any purchaser): ကျွမ္ဘာစေ ချမ်းသာစေ မေတ္တာ သစ္စါ 'May you enjoy health, wealth, loving kindness and loyalty.'

A typical inscription is found on a pretty betel-box (OA 1998.7–23.56) by Hsaya Tha

55

ဆရာသာတိုက်မှ in a pattern which seems confined to such donated articles. It was

ဘုရားတကာ ဦးကျုံပေါ
ဘုရားအမ မယ်ဆိုင်
ကောင်းမှုန်ဗွာန်ဆု

'presented by Pagoda Founder U Chon Paw and his spouse Pagoda sponsor Meh Hsaing, as their deed of merit, seeking Nirvana'. Another betel-box (cat. 58) of the same 'Pagan Age' pattern was made by U Thet Shay in the month of *Wazo* (July), 1963, as a gift to the senior monks of the Eastern Park Monastery. Most unusually, the monastery's formal title – it is named after a Buddhist site in northern India – is given in Pali ပုဗ္ဗါရုံ = အမိက = သံဃိက = သုံးစွဲရန်. A much more modest donation is a small drinking cup, perhaps but not strictly in accordance with the rules of monastic life, for the inscription is personal to a particular monk,

ဆွာတော်ဦးတုပ်သုံးရံ
မောင်ထွန်း

'For the use of Senior Monk U Tut'. The donor, Maung Htun, may have been a relative.

A fine large red *hsun ok* in the British Museum (cat. 160), made in Prome by Hsaya Pyu, was gifted to a monastery by the family of ကွယ်လွန်သူ ဦးလျှုံဝင်းရို ကောင်းမှု the deceased U Hliang Win Yi as his final deed of merit. Presumably the monks had come to the family home for *hsun zin* (offering of food for seven days from the day of a person's death) and to chant suttas at the request of the bereaved family. The name suggests Chinese descent.

Also funerary is a small oval black lacquer tray, a funeral salver (cat. 173), which has particularly interesting inscriptions. On the upper surface two scratched inscriptions

အင်းဝမြို့ ယပ်တန်းရပ် ဦးဘိုးရာ

လေပျော်ဘွယ်ကြီးရှာ ကိုဘိုးခင်း
ဖေါးကျင်သားသွီးတစု ကောင်းမှု
နတ်လူသာရ ခေါ်စေသော်

inform us that the tray was made in Ava in the Fan Makers Quarter by Lacquer Master U Hpo Ya. It was presented to the village of Bwe Kyin by Ko Bo Khin and his family, who invite *nats* and humans to applaud their deed of merit by calling out *thadu*. Such trays were used to carry cooked food to the burial ground, ostensibly to provide sustenance to the deceased, but in fact consumed by indigent cemetery dwellers. The trays would not have been kept in a house but in the village monastery. Most curiously, a short additional inscription on the underside of the tray has been pecked with a pin into the lacquer surface မင်းလန်းမသာဘန်း, and states that this funeral salver is for the 'royal' street of the village. We can reasonably guess that the monastery lay helper had other trays perhaps donated by the same donors, and allocated each tray for use when deaths occurred in different parts of the village.

The elaborately decorated manuscripts known as *Kammawaca* are invariably donated to a monastery, often by the family of a monk to mark his ordination after many years of novitiate. The text is an anthology of *Vinaya* rules for monastic life. The leaves are lacquered on a substrate usually of cloth, but in the past copper or even ivory was used. The script employed

is a form of archaic Pali lettering called 'tamarind seed' and the ink used by the scribe is thick lacquer (examples are cat. 10, 78, 80, 172). Donors' dedications appear in twentieth-century examples, not on the leaves themselves but on the inner surface of the wooden board cover, and (at much greater length) on the specially woven binding tape used to hold the set of leaves neatly together in their protective silk or cotton sleeve bag.

Two *Kammavaca* MSS (cat. 10 and 172) in the Isaacs collection were donated in the same year 1929, by separate donor families and in contrasting family situations. One (cat. 10) has the touching inscription:

၁၂၉၁ခုနှစ်။။ နတ္တော်လ။။ ပိန်းဇလုပ်မြို့။။ ဦးမြတ်ထွန်းအောင်၏ဇနီး။။ သွီးမမခင်။။ မသန်းတို့၏ မွေးသမိခင်။။ ဒေါ်ဒေါ်လှ၏အရိုးကို မွေစေတီအဖြစ် ကိုးကွယ်လျူ့ဒါန်း ပူဇော်သည် ကောင်းမှုသာဓု

'Dated 1291, month of *Nadaw* [December 1929]. This is the work of merit of the wife of U Myat Htun Aung and her two daughters Ma Ma Khin and Ma Than, all of Peinzalok town. We make reverent offering of this sacred text, made with the bone ash relics of our dearly beloved mother and grandmother Daw Daw Hla. May this deed of merit meet approval and calls of *thadu*!'

It seems that the bereaved husband and daughters gave a quantity of the ashes of their mother and grandmother to a lacquer master to be sifted, mixed with raw liquid lacquer (*thit si*) and smeared on the cloth foundation of the leaves of the manuscript.[13] The other *Kammavaca* MS (cat. 172) was donated in very different mood. The text of the donation inscription inside the manuscript cover tells us:

၁၂၉၁ခု။။ မင်းလှမြို့။။ မိုးသုံးညှုတန်း။။ ဦးရွှေခွန်း ဒေါ်ထား။။ တို့၏သွီး မမြရီ၏ ခင်ပွန်း။။ မောင်မိတ်တို့ကောင်းမှု နတ်လှ သာဓုခေါ်စေသော်

'In 1929 in Minhla Township, Mo Nyo Quarter, U Shwe Dun, his wife Daw Hta, their daughter Ma Mya Yi, and son-in-law Maung Po Meik, did this deed of merit. May *nats* and humans call out *thadu*!' But the matching woven binding tape in this case (cat. 172) has a much longer dedication which reveals the immediate context of the donation:

＿＿၏၊ သိချားမိတရာ၊ ခင်းအဂ်ါနှင့်၊ ပညာစုံညီ၊ မမြရီဟူ၊ ရှင်မိုက်ဟုန်း၊ ခေါ်တုန်ကြောင်းဟိတ်၊ မောင်ဘိုးမိတ်တည်း၊ ခပ်နှိုပ်သည္ဒာ၊ ခင်ပွန်လ္လ္ဘတို၊ ရင်မှာပေါက်ဘွား၊ မြေးမအားမှု၊ ထူးခြားရောင်ကွန့်၊ မသိမ်းညွှန့်တို၊ ပွင့်တွန်းသာသွ္လာ၊ စောသတ္တာ၏၊ အဏာမိန့်မြွက်၊ ဓမ္မစက်ကိုးဖြာ၊ ကမ္မဝါကို ＿＿

'...Their beautiful and intelligent daughter Ma Mya Yi and her husband Maung Po Meik have bestowed on her parents U Shwe Dun and Daw Hta a lovely baby granddaughter Ma Thein Nyunt. Inspired with an impulse to donate, they have commissioned the writing of this *Kammawaca* manuscript...' So in grief donate and in joy donate.

The Burmese zodiac and the eight planets

Favourite patterns for *yun* ware, especially betel-boxes, are the twelve signs of the zodiac or 'twelve seasons', *t'seh hnit yathi*, and the eight planets, *gyo shit myo*, one for each of the eight days of the Burmese week – eight because Wednesday is divided into forenoon and afternoon. Often the twelve signs of the zodiac are depicted around the deep lid of the box, while the eight planets are arranged in a ring on the top of the lid. Apart from their inexhaustible decorative value, the eight planets have a social function, since the birthday animal of owner, family friends or guest is bound to be among those depicted. The box therefore offers a general welcome to all who give and receive its contents.

A large betel-box made in Kyaukka by Hsaya Ko Aung Hpay (OA 1998.7–23.115) has the planets on the side of the cover, together with the name of the planet which is also the name of the day. The script enhances the decorative effect. Occasionally the *yun* artist writes more than a single word, but a box (cat. 130), probably by Hsaya Nyunt, has inscriptions that run riot. In a narrow frieze round the top of the side of the box all twelve signs are drawn, each followed by a long phrase such as တန်ယူလ ဆုပ်ယွတ်ရာသည္၊ ဝါဆိုလ ပဇွန်လိုရာည္၊ [sic] 'The sign of the goat is right for the month of *Tagu* [April]' or 'For the month of *Wazo* [July] the prawn is correct', written in lettering barely 2 mm high. Having completed this virtuoso feat, the lacquer master must have turned the box on his lap to engrave an identical sequence in the narrow frieze at the foot of the box with the result that all the tiny zodiac signs and minute script are upside down. He must have been rather eccentric, for his spelling is so idiosyncratic that no less than ten of the twelve months are spelt differently on the upper and lower friezes.

Story scenes and captions

Tales and legends, sacred or secular are ideal subjects for the stylus of the *yun* artist. Trays, bowls, cups and betel-boxes provide a fine canvas, and the cylindrical vessels even allow a sequence of several episodes.

After the British annexation of Upper Burma in 1885 Pagan lacquer makers experienced increasing demand for wooden chests in the shape of European travelling-boxes or secretaires. These offered the *yun* artist five oblong surfaces – six including the base or the inner surface of the lid – for decoration. A chest acquired around 1902 by Lord Curzon (cat. 175) is densely covered with scenes from the legends of the Pagan heroes, Anawrahta and Kyanzittha, with no less than fifty captions naming characters, places and heroic feats. The five surfaces have a broad border, a total of well over 3 metres, all of it filled with floral scrolling and tiny birds. Nowhere does the maker sign his name. In complete contrast are the captions on a chest of very similar shape made by Hsaya To in 1911 and now in a private collection. There are twelve captions of which only two name the characters depicted – the brother princes, Arittha and Pola Janaka. The remaining ten cartouches are used by the maker to give his name and address and to proclaim the quality of the article – ဆေး ၅ မျိုး / အမြိုးမုံ ကျွန်သစ်တော / အင်မတံ နိုင်ခန့်ပါသည် 'five-colour lacquer', 'real teak', 'sturdy and durable' – and to offer good wishes to the buyer – သိန်းထီပေါက်ပါစေ / ယသောသူများ ကုသိုဆိုသည် 'may you win a prize in the lottery', 'users may acquire merit'. Hsaya To ends with the warning နောင်ကို သိလိုအထည် ယနိုင်ခဲပါသည် 'In future an article of this quality will be hard to find'.

The stories most often found on betel-boxes, those dispensers of generous hospitality, are the *jataka* legends of former lives of the Buddha, especially the last ten 'Great Jatakas' and the last of all, the *Vessantara Jataka*, which is by far the favourite. The Bodhisattva is born as a prince whose generosity is unbounded. Having given away all his kingdom's treasure, even the royal white elephant, he is obliged to abdicate, and sets off in his coach to become a forest hermit. On the road he gives away coach and horses, and completes the journey on foot. The climax comes when a cruel and scheming brahmin Jujaka receives the prince's two children as a gift, despite their mother Maddi's efforts to intervene. She is frustrated by spirit beasts conjured up by the evil brahmin. This all provides rich material for the lacquer artist and seller, which buyer and users can admire. While Vessantara is the Buddhist model of perfect generosity, Maddi, his gentle wife, is one of the four paragons of womanhood (*taw lay wa*), dutifully sharing the trials and tribulations of her husband after his untrammelled charity brought about his abdication.

Another much loved *jataka* is the Maha Ummaga Jataka in which the Bodhisattva is a wise young judge, Mahodhata. Each case he resolves is known by all Burmese. Parts of this story are depicted in *shwe zawa* gold leaf and black line on a fine early-nineteeth century panel from a *sadaik* manuscript chest (cat. 102).

A legendary adventure of the great hero Kyanzittha is depicted on a large *yun* screen by Hsaya Sein 'holder of a first-class prize certificate', which is now in the V&A (IS 78-1990). The episode chosen (elucidated by Noel F. Singer)[14] is Kyanzittha's mission to the Mon capital Pegu to fetch the princess Manisanda 'as a gift of gratitude' for the powerful king Anawrahta (1044–70) of Pagan. Kyanzittha, however, ကျွန်ရစ်သား ရွှေချုပ်ကို ဖွင့်သောအခမ်း 'opens the gilded screen' protecting the princess, and when နော်ရထာမင်းစော မဏိစန္ဒာကို စစ်ဆေး မေးမြန်းနေသော အခမ်း 'king Anawrahta questions Manisanda' he discovers she is pregnant by Kyanzittha.

A large *yun* bowl (cat. 61) freely depicts a further expedition of the legendary heroes of Pagan, king Anawrahta's eleventh-century quest to Yunnan in western China for the Sacred Tooth Relic of the Buddha.[15] Opposite sides of the bowl show the Yunnanese and Burmese palaces. Fans, hats and a bug-eyed lion-dog identify the Chinese, and the tiered roofs and royal umbrellas mark the Burmese. Captions label the places and name the heroes; အဖိုးတံခွက်ပေ / စွယ်တော်ပြိ / ကျေးစန္ဒီ a 'cup of great value'; the Land of the Sacred Tooth; and the great bronze image worshipped by the Yunnanese, the '*Kyi Sandi*'. Despite striking this fearsome idol, Anawrahta failed to secure the Sacred Tooth relic and returned to Pagan with a replica that he enshrined in the Shwezigon Pagoda.

Cylindrical betel-boxes and round water bowls used in Burmese households offer curved surfaces and good dramatic potential. A skilful *yun* artist can pack in several incidents from a well-loved story, a few appearing together as the vessel is turned round in the hands of the admirer. A water bowl made for Ma Hla Hpyu by Hsaya Kaing of Pagan (cat. 70) depicts

Detail of water bowl
(cat. 70) with scenes
from the *Kusa Jataka*.
The four captions
name (top, left and
right) Prince Kusa and
Papawati. The Queen
Mother (lower right) is
mounted on an
elephant, and (lower
left) 'They set out to
seek Papawati'.

scenes from the *Kusa Jataka*, the story of the beautiful and fiery princess Papawati. She is tricked into marrying the ugly prince Kusa disguised as his handsome brother, but runs away to her father's house. Kusa follows her and adopts various tricks to win her back. In one he becomes Minister of Pots and makes a wonderful vase for Papawati, which she smashes. The lacquer artist has scattered among the tiny figures no less than twenty-five captions all in minuscule lettering and most of them very short: (ပဗ္ဗဝတီ) (မယ်တော်) (မင်းကုသ) (စတော်ဝန်) (ဆင်ဝန်အိန်) (အိုဝန်အိန်) 'Papawati', 'The Queen Mother', 'King Kusa', 'House of the Minister of Cuisine', 'House of the Minister of Elephants'.

Such captions, naming a character or location, are very common. But longer captions also occur, summing up a key incident in a story with a single sentence: နော်ရထာမင်း ဗျတ္တရစ်ပစ်ပေးဟန် 'King Anawrahta throws a spear at Byatta' (betel-box, OA 1998.7–23.75); ဒေဝဒမင်းသား စောင်းကျိုးကိုဖြတ်ခဲ 'Prince Devada cuts the harp strings' (letter canister, cat. 18); ဘီလူးမနှင့်သူငယ်အမိတို့ မပော် တရားစီရင်ဟဲ 'Mahothata's judgement in the case of the Ogress and the (true) mother of the baby is put into execution' (water bowl, V&A); ကုသမင်း ဆင်ချေးချွင့်ပေါဲ 'Prince Kusa flings elephant dung' (teak box, private collection). The cartouches containing these captions are as a rule subordinate to the story narrated. But occasionally the script takes over and rambles on and on: မယ်မတ်ဒီ မြိုင်ခရီးက အဖျံ ဆင်ချသေ့ ကျားများဆီးသည်ဟု ဆိုလိုသည် 'As Queen Maddi returns through the forest, her path is blocked by the [wizard's] Elephant, Chinthé and Tiger, so the story goes' (betel-box lid, OA 1998.7–23.134).

The *Ramayana* cannot be condensed to fit on a betel-box, but the figures of prince Rama, his wife Sita, and Rama's brother Lakshmana are popular. They appear on a particularly fine betel-box (cat. 65) by Hsaya Thu of Taikkun (Lacquer Works Trade) Ward Pagan, and on an oval tray (OA 1998.7–23.189) by Hsaya Pyay of Pyizu Ward.

Contents

It is rare for an inscription on a container to show the contents, but a small bottle in the shape of a gourd (cat. 120) from Ywama on the Inle lake in Shan State is an exception. Scratched on the black lacquered surface are the words ဆေးဝါ ပရိတ်ရောဂါ ဘဝင် 'yellow medicine for the plague Ba Win', and deep inside the little bottle traces of a yellowish substance remain. U Ba Win was the healer (*hsay hsaya*) who made up and sold the medicine. Perhaps his patient survived the plague, and the cure. In 1939, when plague broke out at Pagan, two teachers and a student died at the Lacquer School.

Politics

Life in colonial Burma was not all Indian summer. Several years of resistance and of 'pacification' followed the 1885 annexation of Burma as a province of the Indian Empire. Though enforced order and stability was appreciated by many Burmese, resentment at foreign rule was also widespread. What rankled most were the lumping of Burma with India, the massive Indian immigration to feed the fast-growing economy, and the resultant marginalization of the Burmese themselves.

The period between the two World Wars saw a series of nationalist movements campaigning against British rule. Aung San Suu Kyi describes the 1920s as 'the *wunthanu* era: *wunthanu* signifies the preservation of one's lineage and as used during the 1920s it denoted patriotism in the form of a preference for traditional values and the eschewal of things foreign. The influence of the *swadeshi* movement of India was clearly discernible.'[16] Two lacquer trays bear, on the underside, an appeal to the patriotic purchaser to buy Burmese, locally produced rather than imported British goods. One (cat. 177) has a ringing call:

ဝံသာနုသာရကွံသော အမျိုးကိုစေါ ်ရှောင့်ပါသဖြင့် သုံးစွဲတော်မူကျပါမျည် အကြောင်းကို စါ၌ငွေမေါင်း ခပ်လိုက်ပါသိ။

'The silver gong is struck to proclaim that using this product will safeguard the race and the national identity.' A very similar appeal is inscribed on the underside of a tray seen at the Asian Arts Museum in San Francisco USA: ဝံသာနု ယက္ကံထော အမြိုးေစာင့်ယှောက် သဖြင့် ဝယ်ယူတော်မူကျပါ 'You are urged to buy this and so preserve the lineage and national spirit of our people.' But the maker adds a further marketing point: ရေ၌နွေးခံ လင်ဘန်း 'This tray is resistant to hot water.'

The mild constitutional reforms conceded by the British to India in 1920 following the recommendations of the Montagu Mission were not extended to Burma until after school boycotts and other protests. When diarchy finally reached Burma it was too little, too late. Aung San Suu Kyi records the next phase:

> The implementation of these reforms entailed elections to the legislative council and this led to a split in the GCBA (General Council of Buddhist Associations) over the question of whether or not its members should stand for election. The next decade would find the Burmese divided between the supporters of diarchy and the adherents of the alternative system, Home Rule.[17]

The political message on a betel-box (cat. 176) ပုဂံမြို့ တန်းကြီးရပ် ဆရာကျွန်းမှမှန် made by Hsaya Kyon of Tangyi Ward Pagan dates it to this period, the early 1920s. The top of the lid bears a 'Mother Burma' figure with a peacock helmet and a peacock, the national bird, at her knee. She is a kind of anti-Britannia, and she holds a staff with a banner carrying a strange device. It is not easy to read since the lettering is Burmese but spells out English words ဟုမ္မရှရမည်။ 'Home Rule will be achieved' or 'Home Rule will be ours'. Above this banner the lacquer artist has started to engrave in English capitals the letters 'HOME' but has stopped, leaving only

Detail of tray (cat. 177). The matting foundation of the tray shows through the black lacquer. The patriotic nationalist inscription is not signed.

Detail of the lid of a betel-box (cat. 176). At the time this box was made in the mid-1920s it was illegal to form a Home Rule Association.

'HO'. Perhaps the purchaser wanted no English lettering on his betel-box. This was after all the time when women stopped wearing combs of tortoise-shell because the words *leik* (tortoise) and *ingaleik* (English) sounded similar!

In 1924 the government declared Home Rule associations illegal. So did a police anti-sedition unit under Eric Blair (the future George Orwell, who served in the Burma police) intervene? We shall never know. The Hsaya San peasant revolt of 1930/31 followed, and was bloodily suppressed. Maurice Collis looking back on the errors of colonial rule, in 1938 wrote:

> It seemed to me that during our occupation of Burma we had done two things there, which we ought not to have done. In spite of declarations to the contrary we had placed

English interests first, and we had treated the Burmans not as fellow creatures, but as inferior beings.[18]

1 Singer 1996: 91–101.

2 See Prunner 1966, fig.14.

3 Watt 1903: 218–25.

4 Singer 1991: 154–8.

5 Ibid.

6 See McCrae and Prentice 1978: 174–5.

7 Before the Second world War a visitor to Pagan was advised: 'To see the work done and learn about it, go to the Government [Lacquer] School, not in the village at all; but to buy, go to Nyaungu, or the Arakan pagoda at Mandalay, or the Scott Market in Rangoon. The makers work here [at Pagan] to order only, and keep no stocks...' (Raven-Hart 1939: 71)

8 This inscription appears on a tiffin carrier illustrated in Fraser Lu 1985: 118, figs 135 and 136.

9 I am grateful to U Kyaw Zan Tha for this information and for help in translation. The *taydat* was a popular verse form from late Konbaung times to late in the colonial period. It reached its zenith with U Ponnya, 1812–67). It is not very demanding.

10 Personal communication, Hsaya Aung Thin.

11 That of Cherie Aung Khin of Elephant House, Bangkok and Rangoon, whose generous assistance with research is gratefully acknowledged.

12 I am grateful to Patricia Herbert for transcribing and translating this inscription.

13 Shway Yoe (1989: 588) describes in 1882 how after the embers of the funeral pyre of a senior monk have cooled, 'the monastic brethren search for any pieces of bones that may remain... Sometimes in the case of a particularly saintly man, they are pounded down, mixed into a paste with thitsi, and moulded into an image of the Buddha...'

14 Personal communication.

15 The story depicted is that narrated in *The Glass Palace Chronicle*, pt IV: 80–82, paras 133–4. I am grateful to Noel Singer for pointing this out and providing the reference.

16 Aung San Suu Kyi 1991: 143.

17 Ibid.

18 Collis 1938: 221.

The Betel Habit and Betel-Box

To appreciate Burmese lacquerware and to understand Burmese culture, some acquaintance with the betel habit is essential.[1] In the past every household had at least one cylindrical lacquer betel-box to hold all the ingredients of the little leaf-wrapped packets which are stowed between cheek and teeth and slowly savoured. Betel was offered and consumed by men and women in everyday social intercourse, and featured in every special occasion and in every ceremony. Betel had a role in courtship and was produced in courts of law to be consumed by litigants settling their differences. It also appeared in the reception of diplomatic envoys at the Royal Palace. Even a prisoner condemned to death was given betel before his execution.

The betel-chewing habit, universally enjoyed in Southeast Asia for many centuries, is now fast receding before the aggressively marketed cigarette, which looks more sophisticated and is certainly more addictive and injurious to health. Betel chewing is not suited to the restless hurry of modern life; it is meant to be indulged 'in a leisurely and relaxed manner'.[2] Betel eating or chewing is really neither eating nor chewing: rather it is sucking a quid stowed in the side of the mouth and moved with the tongue now and then to be squeezed between the teeth. Sir J.G. Scott, whose definitive work on Burmese life appeared under the pen-name Shway Yoe in 1882, warns 'the experimenting Briton' of the nasty consequences of outright mastication: 'having all the interstices between the teeth choked up with little fragments of the nut'.[3]

Ingredients

The betel quid or packet has three essential ingredients, which come as a boon and blessing to men, women and monks in Burma: the leaf, the lime and the nut. Although the term 'betel' is used indiscriminately for the habit, the packet and the nut, the nut itself is the fruit of the areca palm (*Areca catechu*) not the betel vine. The leaf of the betel pepper vine (*Piper betle*) is glossy dark green and broad, with a long stalk and point. Topped and tailed, it forms the wrapping of the parcel.

The lime is slaked lime (calcium hydroxide) made by burning limestone or mollusc shells, and pounding and sifting the powder before adding water. It is usually left white but turns a pretty salmon pink if a little turmeric is added. It is smeared thinly on the betel leaf. Street sellers of betel quids keep their lime in a round glazed pot, but in the household betel-box it is kept in a little oval box of brass or copper, *hton bu*. Formerly, silver lime boxes were not rare. Indeed most Burmese used to own a personal portable lime box. Brownrigg notes the wide currency in the Southeast Asian region of stories of poisoned betel, the poison usually contained in the lime paste: 'For this reason etiquette requires the traveller to accept leaf and nut from those he meets but to carry his own lime-box.'[4]

The areca nut may be used fresh or bought cured. It is cut in half and again into small slivers using a special tool with a blade of iron or steel, *kun hnyat*. To make up a simple betel quid, the betel leaf is smeared with lime, and the slivers of areca nut are wrapped in the leaf, which is then deftly rolled to form a neat green packet. A huge range of optional extra ingredients exist, most of them spices which abound in the Southeast Asian region. Singly or in chosen combinations, these subtly alter the aroma and flavour. Prunner concludes admiringly that 'betel chewing is far from a primitive custom, since it uses highly differentiated ingredients made up in individual recipes to the taste of each connoisseur'.[5] Indeed the betel quid is less like the mass-produced cigarette and more like wine.

In recent centuries tobacco leaf has become by far the most important of the additional ingredients, almost a fourth basic. Of the others, cutch resin (from *Acacia catechu*) is the most frequent. In Shway Yoe's day (1882) 'a little morsel of cutch and tobacco' was the standard additive. The others most used in Burma are aniseed, cardamom, liquorice and citrus peel. A clove adds to the aroma and can also be stuck into the rolled betel leaf packet to pin it closed.

Betel chewers' mild euphoria is an effect of the areca nut's main alkaloid, arecoline, which works on the parasympathetic nervous system, inducing relaxation. It also stimulates copious salivation, reduces appetite and increases thirst. Arecoline turns saliva bright red, and also reddens the mouth, lips and teeth. The latter may eventually turn black. Arecoline reacts with the lime and is hydrolized into another alkaloid, arecaidine. These two alkaloids, with the essential oil of the betel leaf, are responsible for the euphoric effects of chewing. The alkaline nature of the quid explains its role as a digestive; betel is nature's Alka-Seltzer.[6]

Betel also comforts and sustains. The British anthropologist, Tom Harrison, found that when he was worn out after an hour's hard climbing in Sarawak, a few minutes of betel chewing sent him shooting up again, the stuff sending waves of energy through his body. Several medical experts have concluded that: 'The ... feeling of well-being, good humour and ... increased capacity for activity provide a typical picture... Taken as a whole, the ill consequences of betel are relatively so trifling that we might wish that the devotees of other substances of the same kind experienced as little inconvenience.' But the incidence of mouth cancer is high in some areas where betel chewing is widespread.[7]

Social and ceremonial use

The feeling of well-being experienced by users accounts for the universal popularity of the betel habit in Burma. In all gatherings of friends, in receiving visitors, betel was synonymous with goodwill, hospitality, geniality and social enjoyment. Every household had a betel-box, however battered.

Betel was embedded in social convention and in court ceremony. No less than seven variously shaped betel receptacles, all of gold, formed part of the formal regalia of Burmese kings of the Konbaung dynasty.[8] Europeans visiting courts in Southeast Asia had therefore to come to terms with a practice that they found was central to the etiquette of the royal courts.[9] As well as complying with this convention when visiting native rulers, the Dutch soon employed the same etiquette when receiving envoys. The Council of the Indies permitted the purchase of an official betel set for use by the Governor-General. British Imperial officials seem not to have followed the Dutch lead, but an old photograph of the staff of the Rangoon Office of the Irrawaddy Flotilla Company shows that large lacquer betel-boxes were part of the furniture of head office.[10]

Betel quids were tokens of favour in village courtship and in royal courts in Burma. Daw Khin Myo Chit (1988) tells of an audience given by the queen consort of a Burmese king to an English merchant, who brought her gifts. She gave him in token of thanks a betel quid from her personal royal gem-set bowl. The Englishman thanked her, but put the quid in his trouser pocket. The court ladies tittered. He was fortunate not to have been remotely eligible for the much higher favour of a ready-chewed mass of scarlet pulp straight from the mouth of the royal donor!

Daw Khin Myo Chit also recalls how in the 1920s and 1930s, before imported lipstick had penetrated to small-town Burma, girls were handed a betel quid each to chew before dressing-up occasions to ensure their lips were ruby-red and attractive to young men. In earlier days betel played a key role in courtship customs. Marriageable girls sat at their spindles in a special loggia to entertain visiting groups of young men with jokes and riddles. As another group of young bachelors came along, the first group left. The girl had plenty of time to make her choice, which she signalled by giving the young man of her preference a betel quid made with her own hands. The other young men then knew they must seek elsewhere.

Today in Burma every little boy enters into his Buddhist inheritance in a ceremony called *shinbyu*. He wears princely tinsel, then puts off this finery to have his head shaven, and adopts yellow-brown robes. For a few days he will live in a monastery as a little monk. The traditional family procession that carries the young boy to the pagoda in his hired tinsel is led by the prettiest girl the family can recruit, and she carries an elaborately decorated betel-box, gilded and set with coloured glass. Often nowadays it is hired for the occasion together with the young initiate's princely gear. The expression 'bearer of the betel-box' has come to mean a very pretty girl or a village belle.

In many other ceremonies and social occasions in Burmese life the betel-box has a key role. It also provides a fine smooth surface for the *yun* lacquer artist to practise his skills. The patterns and pictures depicted on the top and sides of the tall cover are always relevant to the social context in which the box is used.

Inside the betel-box

First and foremost is the function of the box as a container of all the requisites of the betel users. A box of household size is about 20 cm in diameter and a little less in height. To see

The deep cover or lid (on the left of the picture) fits closely over the box (behind, to the right). Two trays fit inside: a deep one (leaning against the box); and a shallow one, which here holds a lime box. A betel cutter, too large for the tray, is also shown.

how the contents are arranged inside, the lid must be lifted off, but that is not easily done. The deep cover fits so close as to be almost airtight, and reaches almost to the base of the box. This keeps the contents fresh, protects the interior from dust and insects and prevents desiccation of the betel leaf deep inside.

Directly beneath the lid, in the upper of two internal trays, are four little cups or baskets of lacquer or brass or silver, a small oval brass or copper box, and perhaps also a small nut cutter, *kun hnyat*. In the baskets (cat. 115) are the ingredients for chewing: areca nuts, cutch resin, aniseed, cloves and liquorice. The brass box, *hton bu*, holds lime, white or pink. Lifting out the upper tray exposes the lower, which holds tobacco leaves. Below this second tray is the deep main box, with neat piles of fresh green betel leaves. The whole box, less the deep lid, can pass from friend to friend so each can make up his own quid. The empty lid of a fine betel-box might be passed round separately to be admired by friends already chewing or waiting to roll their quid.

Western reactions to betel

The formidable manager of the Irrawaddy Flotilla Company, Mr George Swann, pictured in the office photo with betel-boxes mentioned above, probably never chewed betel but his fellow Scotsman, Sir J.G. Scott, certainly did. Scott arrived in Burma in 1876, and barely three years later published under the pen-name of Shway Yoe, or Mr Golden Elephant, an encyclopaedic survey of Burmese customs, *The Burman: His Life and Notions* (1882). Scott advised caution 'the first time you make a trial with the lime and cutch. The latter especially is very astringent.' But Scott did not acquire the habit, the 'unlovely practice' of chewing betel. That august person George Nathaniel Curzon showed keen interest in the habit during his travels in Indo-China many years before he came to Burma as Viceroy of India, but it would be hard, and wrong, to imagine him with a betel quid in his mouth. He noted in French Indo-China that 'the habitual and universal solace of both sexes ... the areca nut and betel ... is rarely absent from the mouth of man or woman' and wrongly attributed to the prevalence of betel the absence of 'that agreeable mark of salutation', kissing: 'Lips so tainted could hardly embrace.'[11]

Many Europeans visiting Southeast Asia were appalled by the blood red mouths and black teeth. But the Portuguese, who had to live long years among betel users in sixteenth-century India, adopted the habit, as described by van Linschoten:[12] the women 'have the like custome of eating these Bettele leaves, so that if they were but one day without eating their Bettele, they persuade themselves they could not live' and the men 'by the common outcome of their wives eating of Bettele, doe likewise use it'. It was the spitting that disgusted the nineteenth-century British in Burma. The Burman, wrote Scott, 'has none of the delicacy with regard to a spittoon which characterises the American, and these articles require to be of a very considerable size'.[13] Spittoons were indoor or veranda furniture; out of doors betel chewers spat. Victorian society looked down on spitting. Expectoration was an offence against hygiene, and worse, against gentility. The rule was: gentlemen who expectorate cannot 'expect to rate' as gentlemen. In British India spitting also marked a racial divide. The famous limerick recording the most unappealing conduct of the old man of Darjeeling omits the colour of the resultant stain on the ceiling: it would have been scarlet.

Betel chewers produce a copious flow of bright red saliva, which leaves its mark everywhere in South and Southeast Asia and has done so for thousands of years. A *jataka* story of a previous life of the Buddha tells how a rich and idle king awoke in his forest pavilion to find his many wives had left his side to go strolling in the forest. He followed angrily and came upon them gathered reverently round the ascetic hermit Kshanti Vadin. In a fit of fury the king drew his sword and cut the patient future Buddha limb from limb. This no doubt stained the ground red with blood, but it was by following other red stains that the cruel king had been able to track down his wives 'who had traced out in their juvenile wantonness a path marked by posies of flowers and the red dye of betel on the ground'.[14]

Burmese women of all ranks and all ages chewed betel as much as their menfolk. Monks were no exception, indeed 'the most persistent chewers of betel. Smoking is prohibited, but nothing is said against betel, and it is considered a great stimulator of the meditative faculties'.[15] Betel-boxes were donated to monasteries in Burma as deeds of merit (cat. 58). But in early twentieth-century Ceylon the zealous lay reformer Anagarika, striving to rehabilitate the vocation of the Sasana, looked on the habit with disdain. He accepted Christian criticism of the selfishness of some monks, and excoriated indolent and ignorant monks who 'exist only to fill their spittoons'.[16]

Spittoons were in general use in polite society, and those in Mandalay Palace were of gold. The mild and devout King Mindon selected a fine spittoon of royal quality in solid gold as a gift sent in 1872 to the Queen Empress Victoria, who thanked him graciously for the flower vase. A black lacquer spittoon in the collection of Cherie Aung Khin is inscribed: 'This unbeatable top quality Class 1 spittoon is for the esteemed use of the lady consort of the Sub-Divisional Inspector'.

Targeted spitting as an act of political protest is recorded by Orwell.[17] When the colonial regime in Burma was deeply unpopular, an Englishwoman walking through the bazaar might find that her white dress had been splashed with betel juice. During Orwell's years with the Burma Police (1922–7), an arm of the Indian Imperial Police, Hsaya Kyon of Pagan made a betel-box (cat. 176) with a sharply political theme. It shows a proud Mother Burma figure, a sort of anti-Britannia, wearing a peacock helmet and with that bird (ex-royal but still the national beast) nestled against her side. She holds a spear with a pennant and a message. Written in Burmese letters, it uses the English expression for its key political term: 'Home Rule will be achieved'. Above this the *yun* engraver has started to write in English capital letters the words 'HOME RULE', but has inexplicably stopped after 'HO'. Why, we shall never know, nor whether the fiercely nationalist resentment of the box's owner against British Imperial rule remained bottled-up or got spat out.

1 A full and entertaining account of 'the art of Betel chewing' is in Khin Myo Chit 1988: 37–47. The variety of practice in other lands in the region is treated in Rooney 1993.
2 Khin Myo Chit 1988.
3 Shway Yoe 1989: 71–2.
4 Brownrigg 1991: 29.
5 Prunner 1966: 54.
6 Brownrigg 1991: 22.
7 Brownrigg 1991: 23.
8 Temple 1902.
9 Brownrigg 1991: 26.
10 McCrae 1990: 25, pl. 14.
11 Curzon 1893: 193–218 (quoted in Rooney 1993: 6).
12 John Huyghen van Linschoten, a Dutch traveller to the East in the late-sixteenth century. Quoted in Rooney 1993: 5.
13 Shway Yoe 1989: 71.
14 Conze 1959: 28.
15 Shway Zoe 1989: 71–2.
16 Gombrich 1988: 192.
17 Orwell 1951.

Catalogue

1

Pair of offering vessels, *hsun ok*

Burma, Mandalay, mid-19th century
Bamboo, lacquer, coloured glass, gold leaf; also
gilded metal sheet and wood
(a) H 116 cm, D 60 cm; (b) H 119 cm, D 56 cm
OA 1994.11-16.1 & 2, Brooke Sewell Fund

The making of offerings to the monkhood is one of the important injunctions on the laity in a Buddhist society. Further, through giving, lay Buddhists accumulate merit and in this way ensure better prospects in their next lives. Giving, therefore, benefits both parties; indeed the argument can be made that the benefit to the giver is greater than to the receiver.

Given this background, it is not surprising that the ritual of giving in Burma has substantial accoutrements, one of the most obvious being the *hsun ok*, lidded vessels with an internal tray for carrying offerings to the monastery or for displaying the offerings there on either side of a Buddha image. These two examples are of a size and quality that sets them aside from other examples,[1] and this, coupled with their history, suggests they may have come from a royal monastic establishment in Mandalay, in the years immediately after the Third Anglo-Burmese War (1885).[2] They are known to have been acquired in Burma, probably in Mandalay, by 1895, only ten years after the end of hostilities. The purchaser was an Englishman, Herbert Allcroft, whose round-the-world trip took him to Burma in the winter months of 1894/5. From Rangoon he went up to Mandalay, of which he wrote in his diary extensively where he recorded that in the bazaar 'there is not a single Burmese article that cannot be bought there. We spent some time there and went through it from end to end and then Mr Dale took us to Mr Beaton's curio store.[3] He has a most interesting collection and his house is crammed.' Many items were purchased by Allcroft to be shipped back to the family seat at Stokesay Court in Shropshire,[4] where they remained until 1994 when the contents of the house was sold at auction.[5]

The decoration is a *tour de force* of the *hmanzi shwe cha* style, where relief modelling is built up on the lacquered surface of the coiled basketry. Although the majority of the decoration is of floral and abstract design, prancing animals (probably mythical lions) made of *thayo* lacquer putty can be seen chasing through the scrollwork in the bands that run around the belly of the vessel on both sides of the opening. The intricacy and depth of the design reveals a sure hand practised in this technique. Mandalay has been the centre for this type of work certainly from the second half of the nineteenth century and continues to the present.[6] This, along with the fact that Allcroft is known to have visited Mandalay, corroborates the suggestion that these two vessels were made there.

The spired lid of the vessel, so reminiscent of the soaring outline of the Burmese pagoda, bears a *hintha* bird set into it.[7] Internally, the basketry, including the single surviving tray, is decorated with brilliant-red lacquer.

1 Many are illustrated here, for example cat. 89–96.
2 The use of all-over gilding may also indicate a royal origin for these vessels. 'In the days of the Kon-baung kings, sumptuary laws decreed that objects with gilded decoration were reserved for religious and royal use.' (Fraser-Lu 1985: 88)
3 This must surely be the shop of Felice Beato. For Beato, see Singer 1998: 96–107.
4 Another Burmese item from Allcroft's collection is cat. 33. There is some doubt, however, as to whether it was purchased in Mandalay or some years later at the Delhi Durbar.
5 See Sotheby's sale catalogue for 29 September to 1 October 1994, lot no. 701.
6 See Fraser-Lu 1985: 31–2.
7 The intimate connection between royalty and this bird, variously described as a swan or a brahminy goose (Burney even described it as a peacock), has been commented on by Yule in 1858 (see Yule 1858: 85). Yule also mentions the ancient name for Pegu, Hanthawadi (Pali, Hansavati, 'city of the Hansa').

2

Pair of wooden door panels, *tagaywet*
Burma (perhaps southern Burma), 20th century
Wood, lacquer, gold leaf and paint; H 170 cm, W 38 cm
OA 1994. 5-18. 1 & 2, gift of Ian Macdonald, Esq.

The architecture of Burma is dominated by the ready availability of fine hard woods with the result that the majority of domestic and monastic buildings were traditionally built of wood.

These two door panels of gilded and lacquered wood depict guardian figures in a rude but lively style, and probably came from a monastic building. Such panels are often seen at the entrance to the central monastery building with the main Buddha image, reached from the elevated veranda that invariably ran around the outside of the main building.[8] The two figures stand on full-blown lotus blossoms, which emphasize their religious status; they are minor guardian deities. Lacquer is used here not only for decoration but for preservation of the wood, as lacquer is a water-proofing and insect-proofing agent; when surfaces are gilded, it also acts as a size for the gold leaf.

The dating of wooden sculpture from Burma is still very much in its infancy, but a forthcoming volume on wooden monastic architecture will help clarify the situation.[9] Two other examples of such door panels are in the Victoria and Albert Museum.[10]

8 The way in which such panels functioned can be seen in Ferrars 1901: 3, pl. 7, or in Courtauld 1984: 32.
9 Fraser-Lu, forthcoming.
10 Reg. nos IS 82 and 83-1954. See Lowry 1974: 42.

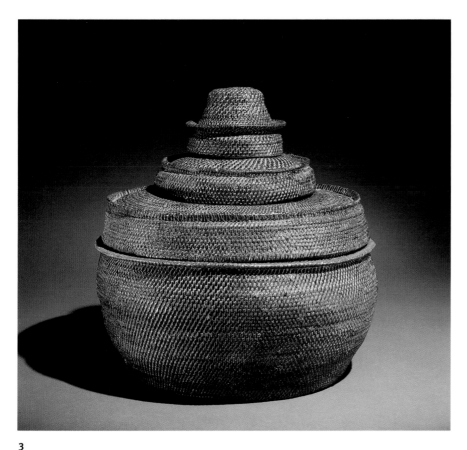

3

4. Offering vessel, *hsun ok*

Burma, late 19th century
Wood, lacquer; H 75 cm, D 37.5 cm
OA 1992.7-28.2

Unlike the previous offering vessel made of basketry, this example is of wood, which has then been covered with red lacquer – *hinthabada*, or cinnabar mixed with lacquer sap. The swelling urn-like element set halfway up the spire is a distinctive feature of this style of offering vessel. Despite the classic beauty of this type, its region both of manufacture and of use is not certain. A recently published example is described as being from the Shan States, but this seems unlikely.[13] More probable is the provenance of Pagan given by Fraser-Lu,[14] despite the lack of *yun* decoration, the hall-mark of that centre. She also perceptively remarks on the way in which, with use, the red of the lacquer becomes differentially smoothed away, leaving, as she describes it drawing on Japanese

3
Offering vessel, *hsun gwet*
Burma, perhaps Meiktila,[11] mid-20th century
Cane, lacquer; H 37.5 cm, D 37 cm
OA 1998.7-23.132, gift of Mr and Mrs R. Isaacs

This understated but elegant vessel illustrates the basic building blocks for almost all lacquered containers. An armature is created on which the subsequent lacquer decoration will be set. Here the armature is readily apparent, and the complete vessel – as is usual with Burmese offering vessels – consists of a sequence of stacking elements, from largest (at the base) to smallest (at the top). The five parts of this vessel (this number includes an internal tray, not visible from the outside) are made of woven cane basketry, which is clearly seen under the coating of dark red-brown lacquer decorated with contrasting brighter red on the rim of the main bowl.[12] The subtle decorative scheme is deliberate

for it would have been simple to cover and conceal the basketry, filling all the interstices with *thayo* and then smoothing the surface. Instead the lightly stained basketry is the main, and satisfying, decorative pattern.

Such vessels were owned by a family and used for taking *hsun*, offerings, of cooked food to the monks of the local monastery. The deep bowl of the vessel held the cooked rice, the upper trays perhaps a curry, and the uppermost part of the vessel reverses to form a cup.

11 This provenance is based on the example illustrated in Fraser-Lu 1985: 88. No reference is, however, given there for this suggestion, and no other information on Meiktila as a lacquer centre is known to the present authors.
12 Baskets, made either of cane or split bamboo (woven or coiled) are, in Burma, the most common receptacle and are the basis for almost all other vessels. This surely explains the marvellously organic quality of Burmese containers, a quality that has in recent decades become highly admired in the West.

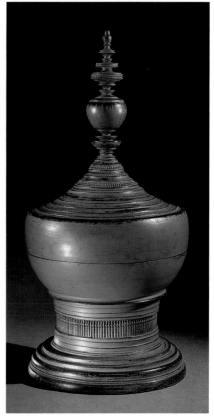

4

lacquer terminology, 'a most pleasing negoro effect'.

Two further features are worth mentioning here: the two registers of laid-on decoration just below the spire, which are made of strips of *thayo* fashioned in a stone mould;[15] and the small series of wooden balusters, each one carved separately and then lacquered, which make up the lower part of the pedestal to the vessel. Much time has gone into producing this fine old vessel.

The authors M. and B. Ferrars writing before 1901 illustrate (pl. 47) a *hsun ok* being carried to the monastery (on the head) and describe it as follows: 'The food, which is the best of its kind, is brought every morning by the daughters and young children of the supporter ... An ornamented vessel is used, having a tall finial to the cover (*ot* [= *ok*]).'[16]

13 Di Crocco 1998: 170.
14 Fraser-Lu 1985: 90, pl. 94.
15 For one of these stone moulds, see cat. 31.
16 Ferrars 1901: 22–3 and pl. 47.

5
Lion sculpture, *chinthe yok*
Burma, late 19th/early 20th century
Wood, lacquer, gold; H 58 cm, L 47 cm, W 15 cm
National Trust, Curzon Collection at Kedleston Hall, Derbyshire, no. 647

In Burma wooden sculpture is frequently gilded using lacquer as a size. In this mythical Burmese lion, *chinthe*, the carving is typical of the Konbaung dynasty, though Lord Curzon acquired it during his Viceregal visit in 1901, sixteen years after the British forces entered Mandalay and deposed Thibaw.

Singer[17] has described the carved and gilded figures associated with the thrones of the palace, and this account draws copiously on his. All nine thrones were shaped like high hourglass towers, and niches in the top, waist and base held the figures which identified each throne. There were two lion thrones and one each lily, bee, peacock, deer, *hintha*, elephant and conch. Four large lions stood in pairs at the front corners of the throne. Sixteen small ones sat in the niches, like those in the shrine, cat. 71. Nine medium-sized lion figures were ranged away from the throne, facing it, in a single row alternating with eight *thungedaw*, gilded wooden figures of naked male children, like those on the end panels of the metallophone, cat. 127.

Two of the lion figures are now in England, a large one in the Pitt Rivers Museum, Oxford, and a medium one in a private collection; both are illustrated by Singer. Like the Curzon lion, they stand on a plinth with chamfered corners. The Curzon beast has its claws peaceably sheathed, whereas those of the Pitt Rivers figure are unsheathed. Curzon's lion has eyes of red glass. Its body is decorated with flower heads and a large flower on the chest. These differences are evidence that Curzon's lion was new when acquired in 1901, and was not from Mandalay Palace. Today, only one of the nine thrones of the Palace survives, in the National Museum in Rangoon.

Chinthe in brick and stucco flank the steps to pagodas throughout Burma, some 20 metres tall.[18]

17 Singer 1988: 94–102.
18 For drawings of *chinthe*, see Aye Myint 1993: 111–16.

5

6

Sculpture of a *nat*, the evil Mara, *Man nat yok*

Burma, from the palace at Mandalay, second half of the 19th century
Wood, lacquer, gold, paint; H 71 cm, W 36 cm
OA 1937.1-12.1, gift of Miss W. Carey

Magnificently gilt and coloured, this wooden sculpture well illustrates the quality of some nineteenth-century Burmese sculpture.[19] The record of its gift, along with another image from the same donor,[20] indicates that the sculptures came originally from the place at Mandalay, the seat of the last two kings of independent Burma, Mindon (1853–78) and Thibaw (1878–85).

The gesture of the figure – the two hands clenched on the knees – marks him out as being non-Buddhist, and it seems likely that this is an Indian deity whose shrine was located in the palace as part of the inherited accoutrement of royal power that had descended in the Burmese polity, along with other ancient Indian elements such as brahmins as court officials and the use of Indian law codes (for the Indian law codes in Burma, see cat. 84 and 85). Intriguingly, the number 15 in Burmese numerals can still be seen on the base of the lotus throne, suggesting the way in which sculptors worked in the palace workshops, carving from designs recorded in folding books, *parabaik*. Indeed, Singer has convincingly linked this image and the other one in the same group with a *parabaik* in the British Library whose title he translates as 'Illustrations of objects in daily use in the Golden Palace'.[21] This *parabaik* contains paintings of Indian deities who were enshrined in the Mandalay palace. Number 15 in this sequence, the last, is named either 'Si-tra-bali' or 'Man'.[22] Man or Mara is illustrated three times in Temple's *Thirty-Seven Nats* where he is described as 'Man Nat, Mara, the Evil

Principle'. Mara is the demon who, in the Life Story of the Buddha, summons warriors and seductive maidens to distract the Buddha during his meditation. This scene culminates in the Buddha calling on the Earth Goddess to witness that his merit accumulated in previous lives is sufficient for Enlightenment. The inclusion of the evil Mara among the images in the palace shrine was presumably to ensure that the evil principle was deflected through propitiation. Singer notes that, according to the Konbaungset Chronicle: 'Once a year at Thadingyut [October] "fifteen days after the new moon", the fifteen images were propitiated with great ceremony.'[23] He goes on to say: 'In 1862, when Phayre and his entourage were visiting the Palace, they were allowed to witness the rituals performed by the court brahmins, mediums and guardians of the shrine.'

The figure is shown cross-legged on a roughly triangular double-lotus throne, which is fully gilded. He wears a fine lower garment, similar to a modern *longyi* (the Burmese sarong), decorated with yellow spirals on green, and red flowers on black; this has an extravagant outflowing of material between the knees. His upper body is also clothed and on his chest and shoulders lies a fine golden cope. He wears a tiered crown, the only part of his apparel that has a parallel in the iconography of a Buddha image.

19 The authors are most grateful to Noel Singer for his help in understanding this important sculpture.
20 The registration number of the second figure is 1937.1-12.2. It is a multi-headed figure swathed in a snake and riding on a bull. This must be Shiva riding on his bull mount, Nandi.
21 British Library, Oriental and India Office Collections, Burmese MS no. 199, 'Shwe-nan-let-thon-pon'.
22 Nay Myo Pan-chi 1993.
23 Personal communication.

7

7
Betel-box, *kun it*
Burma, Pagan, workshop of Hsaya Htat, second quarter of the 20th century
Bamboo, lacquer; H 25.8 cm, D 27.0 cm
OA 1998.7-23.4, gift of Mr and Mrs R. Isaacs

Cylindrical betel-boxes of this colour and pattern have been popular for hundreds of years. This box, a fine example of the type, was made by Hsaya Htat of Pagan (see cat. 9 for a further example of his work). His name appears on the centre of the base of the box together with his 'trade mark', a tiger, in a roundel on the top of the cover. The sides of the deep cover are left free for the pattern, the *kunan kanbyat*, or 'Yunnan semicircle'.[24] This has many variants but is seen here in its classic form, drawn free-hand with a very fine needle-point, a tool that gives

its name to such delicate work – *tont-yun*. The pattern still continues in use today in the lacquer workshops of Pagan.

The bright red colour derives from cinnabar (mercuric sulphide) powder mixed with raw lacquer sap. The vessel is not, however, in a single colour: minute dotting with yellow orpiment (arsenic trisulphide), scarcely visible to the eye, has the effect of heightening the shade to the brilliant vermilion.

The deep box holds the betel-vine leaves, the lower of the two internal trays tobacco leaf and the upper tray the spices and lime to make up the chewing quid with the sliced areca nut.

24 For other examples of this pattern, see cat. 49 and 63. The use of Yunnan in the name presumably indicates the origin of this design, though no research has yet indicated this categorically.

8

Bowl, *khwet*

Burma, probably Pagan, early 20th century
Bamboo, lacquer; H 17.3 cm, D 20.5 cm
Liverpool Museum, National Museums and Galleries
on Merseyside, 50.4.158

Black and gold *shwe zawa* lacquer work
has been made in Pagan since early last
century. However, at the end of the
nineteenth century the technique was
the speciality of the town of Prome,
where Hsaya Pa was renowned for his
work.[25] The Liverpool collections are
especially strong in *shwe zawa* vessels
(see cat. 34 and 35), and some are
connected with a body known as the
Hita Co-Operative Society. At least one
was acquired at the time of the 1924
British Empire Exhibition at Wembley.
This bowl is likely to have been made
specially for exhibition and thus never
used. This would certainly explain its
fine condition.

The interior of the vessel is left gloss
black, the effect produced through the
application of fine lacquer sap. The
exterior of this fine bowl, in dramatic
contrast, is decorated with scrolls of the
variety known as *chu pan*, a standard
decorative motif in the *shwe zawa*
technique.

Probably the most famous of the
Southeast Asian lacquer traditions is the
black and gold work executed in
Thailand.[26] This has been especially

developed for furniture of the type seen
in this exhibition only in cat. 102. It is
almost certain that the technique of
working in this way entered Burma
along with captive craftsmen following
the sack of Ayutthaya in 1767.[27] In
Burma, however, the technique was
used on vessels rather than
architecture.

25 He won Third Prize with Bronze Medal at the
Indian Art Exhibition at Delhi in 1902/3 for a gilt
lacquered tray. See Watt 1904: 204.
26 Bangkok, National Museum 1987: 84–7.
27 See also pp. 22–3.

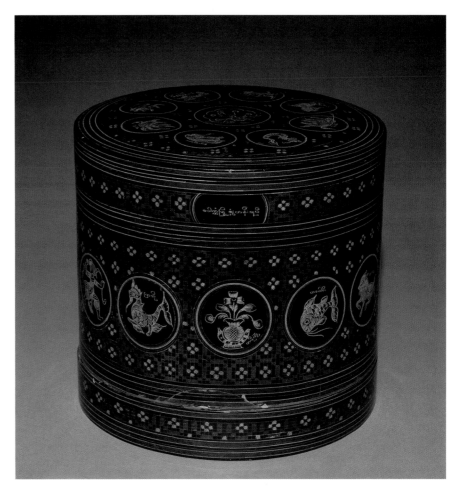

9

9

Betel-box, *kun it*

Burma, Pagan, workshop of Hsaya Htat, mid-20th
century
Bamboo, lacquer; H 24.4 cm, D 26.6 cm
OA 1998.7-23.119, gift of Mr and Mrs R. Isaacs

The colour-filled *yun* decoration of this
fine betel-box from the workshops of
Hsaya Htat of Pagan combines two
traditional patterns. The background
uses the *za yun* 'netting' in dark green
and yellow on black.[28] Two sets of
medallions are placed against this: one
on the sides of the deep cover depicts
the twelve figures of the zodiac, or
yathi yok, each with the name of its
month; while the other, in a ring on the
top of the lid, depicts the eight planets,
which are also the signs of the days of
the Burmese week, or *gyo shit myo*.[29]
Both days of the week and signs of the

8

10

zodiac are named in Burmese. The zodiac signs are ram, bull, *kinnara* (bird-man), crab, lion, maiden, pair of scales, scorpion, archer, *makara* (sea-monster), water-pot, fish. The animals of the days of the week are tiger (Monday), lion (Tuesday), tusked elephant (Wednesday forenoon), tuskless elephant (Wednesday midday to midnight), rat (Thursday), guinea-pig (Friday), snake (Saturday) and *galon*[30] (Sunday). The eight days of the week appear again, but this time unnamed, around the drum of the vessel that is covered by the lid.

The signature of the master of the lacquer workshop, Hsaya Htat, appears in the frieze at the top of the sides of the cover. For another example from this atelier, see cat. 7.

28 For another example of *za yun*, see cat. 48.
29 In the Burmese system there are traditionally eight planets, each of which is linked with one of the days of the week; Wednesday is assigned two planets, one from midnight to midday and the other from midday to midnight. See Shway Yoe 1882, ch. 1.
30 The animal known as *pu* in Burmese and representing Friday and the planet Venus cannot be a true guinea-pig, which is exclusively American. It may originally have been a hamster, which occurs in the far north of Burma, in the ancestral lands of the Burmans. We are grateful to Ann Searight for this suggestion. *Galon* is Burmese for the Indian *garuda*, half-man, half-hawk.

10

***Kammavaca* manuscript**[31]

Burma, 1929
Cloth, lacquer, gold leaf: L 58 cm, H 13.9 cm
OA 1998.7-23.172, gift of Mr and Mrs R. Isaacs

This is a *Kammavaca* manuscript, a selection of texts from the *Vinaya* that provided rules of conduct for monks in the Burmese monastic system.[32] Manuscripts such as this are commissioned by donors for presentation to a monastery on the occasion of the ordination of a monk. *Kammavaca* manuscripts are also used in other ceremonies: at the *Kahtein* ceremony before building a house and in the *thein hnok* ritual when people are not sure if the land they are building on has in the past been the site of a *thein*, or prayer hall. The term *thein hnok* means 'erasing the trace of a *thein*'.[33]

Many different materials may be used as the substrate for the leaves of a manuscript, the most expensive being ivory or precious metal.[34] This leaf has a foundation of cloth, stiffened with many coats of lacquer, but still flexible.[35] The final coat of pure filtered lacquer is part gilded in the *shwe zawa* gold leaf technique at the ends of each leaf and between the lines of script. The language is Pali, as for all the Buddhist canon, but the special script is Burmese. Used almost exclusively for *Kammavaca* manuscripts, it is known as 'tamarind seed', *magyi zi*, from the resemblance of the letters to the dark brown, glossy seeds of the tree. The ink is boiled and filtered raw lacquer mixed with a little red cinnabar to give the raised lettering a dark brown colouring (without the addition of the red cinnabar it would be black). Tamarind-seed script is difficult to read, and a monk holding a Kammawaca leaf, but actually reading from a printed book held up by an assistant, is the subject of a photograph taken in 1900.[36]

The manuscript of which this leaf is part was donated in 1929 by the widower U Myat Htun Aung of Peinzalok[37] and his two daughters, and an inscription on the inner surface of the wooden cover states that the bone relics of his deceased wife Daw Daw Hla 'have been enshrined in [this] reliquary pagoda for worship'. Some of her ashes would have been mixed with liquid lacquer and used to make this manuscript, which is the reliquary pagoda (*damma zaydi*) and in a way the *Tipitaka* itself. Each time the manuscript was used merit would accrue to the donors whether alive or dead.[38]

11

31 *Kammavaca* is the Pali for a set of monastic rules drawn from the *Vinaya*; the Burmese word is *Kammawasa*.
32 For further discussion of the *Vinaya* and the *Kammavaca* texts, see cat. 79–83. See also Zwalf 1985: 172, cat. 240.
33 I am grateful to Daw Thin Thin Naing for this information.
34 See cat. 78 for an ivory leaf from a *Kammavaca* manuscript.
35 See also cat. 172.
36 See Ferrars 1900: 21 and pl. 48.
37 Peinzalok is a village between Nyaunglaybin and Yedashay on the Rangoon–Mandalay railway, 120 km north of Rangoon.
38 Daw Thin Thin Naing, personal communication. Shway Yoe (1989: 588) describes how bone fragments were collected from the pyre of a saintly monk to be pounded down, mixed with *thitsi*, and moulded into an image of the Buddha.

11

Offering vessel, *hsun ok*

Burma, perhaps Mandalay, mid-19th century
Bamboo, wood, lacquer, gold leaf, glass inlay; H 56 cm, D 36 cm
The Green Centre for Non-Western Art at the Royal Pavilion, Libraries and Museums, Brighton and Hove, no. 505255

The base of this attractive vessel is quite conventional. It consists of a bowl integral with its stand and foot, built of coiled split bamboo lacquered red inside and decorated on the outside with green and white spangles of glass set in *thayo*, and gilded. The cover or lid is made of the same materials, but modelled in the form of a crested bird, possibly a *karaweik*, or legendary

Burmese crane, its tail held high. The stand has two bands of *thayo* moulded relief work, a narrow one round the foot and a broader one round the waist. The latter represents *put lon*, the small balusters of turned wood that once served to support a separate tray or bowl. On the broad bevel of the foot is a row of fish-scales, rendered in glass inlay and gilt. The same motif decorates the bowl itself, but since this forms the lower part of the body of the bird, feathers would be a more apt name than fish-scales; certainly both overlap producing a similar pattern.

The lid or cover, also lacquered red inside, presents the artist working in the *hmanzi shwe cha* technique (relief gilt and glass-inlaid lacquer) with opportunities that he has confidently seized, creating a satisfying portrayal of a bird. The neck and breast are scaled using the same pattern as on the lower bowl. The wings and tail with longer and stouter feathers form one sweeping curve. On the back of the neck are two ridges or 'collars', typical of the rendering in Burmese art of the mythical *karaweik*. The head has a curved and swept-back crest, and a stout beak, probably of solid lacquer putty and entirely gilded. The eyes are beads of crimson glass. The whole artistic creation has a fine balance and dignity, and avoids absurdity. Although the shape of the lid is very unusual,[39] the function of such gilt and glass-inlaid vessels is not in doubt: it was invariably devotional. They were used to hold donations of food or other articles and offered to monks or set, usually in pairs, before the principal Buddha image in a shrine.

Gilt and glass-inlaid reliefwork in lacquer was a speciality of Mandalay, and this vessel was probably made there.[40] However, if this is correct, it must have been made only a few years after the foundation of Mandalay by king Mindon in 1857, since by 1870 this

12

vessel was in Brighton. With other fine gilt and glass-inlaid *hsun ok*, two of which are of Shan form, they were presented by Mr Willett to the Brighton Museum in 1902.

39 The only other known comparable example is in the Andreino Collection. See Mazzeo, Donatella (ed.) 1998: 54, cat. 58.
40 See Watt 1904: 222–4, 'Section 3. Mandalay Moulded Lacquer', where the modelling, gilding and inlaying with glass of lacquer putty, is described. The writer speaks of a whole street in the city being given over to this work.

12

Plantae Asiaticae Rariores

By Nathaniel Wallich, published in London, 1830–32; H 54.5 cm, W (open) 76.5 cm
Courtesy British Library Board x.765 and x.766

Wallich was the Superintendent of the East India Company's Botanic Garden in Calcutta, and his three-volume work contains the fruits of his visit to Burma in 1826–7 on behalf of the Company. He made this visit accompanying the embassy lead by John Crawfurd who attempted to negotiate with the Burmese government of king Bagyidaw at Ava.

These volumes are of importance as they contain the first scientific classification and description of the lacquer tree and coloured plates of it both in bloom and in leaf. Shown here is the plate depicting the flowers of the tree, the original drawing having been done by the Indian artist Vishnupersaud whose name is shown at bottom left. In three and a half pages of text following the two plates Wallich first gives a formal description of the tree in Latin, naming it *Melanorrhoea usitata*,[41] and then in the next two and a half pages describes the habitat of the tree.

41 Now known as *Gluta usitata*.

13

Mezzotint of Nathaniel Wallich (1786–1854)

By John Lucas, published in London, 1833; H 35.5 cm, W 28 cm
P&D 1915.2-16.46

It is significant that this portrait print of Wallich was published in 1833, as the previous year had seen the appearance of the last part of Wallich's monumental work, *Plantae Asiaticae Rariores* (see cat. 12). Indeed, the oil painting on which the print is based was painted the previous year and exhibited at the Royal Academy exhibition (no. 233 in the RA catalogue). Wallich was clearly

13

14

15

well enough known as a result of his publication and the presentation of new botanical information from his visit to Burma for a portrait print of him to be produced for sale.

The oil painting of Wallich was executed by John Lucas (1807–74) and Lucas was also the engraver and publisher of the print as his address is given on the lettering below;[42] he is recorded elsewhere as both a painter and an engraver. The lettering at the base of the image says that the print is based on 'a portrait [now] in the possession of Major-General Hardwicke [and] is dedicated by permission to the Linnean Society by their obedient servant, John Lucas'.[43] The link with the Linnean Society is relevant as Wallich was already a Fellow at this time, and following his final return to England in 1847, he became Vice-President of the Linnean Society, often chairing their meetings.[44]

42 'No 20 Charles Street, Middlesex Hospital.'
43 We are grateful to Stephen Coppel, BM Department of Prints and Drawings, for his help with this entry.
44 *Dictionary of National Biography*, vol. LIX, ed. S. Lee, London 1899, pp. 135–6.

14–16. Three Thai vessels

14. Offering stand, *phan* (Thai)
Thailand, probably Chiang Mai, early 20th century
Bamboo, lacquer; H 23.5 cm, D 32.5 cm
OA 1996.5-1.65

15. Betel-box, *hip maak* (Thai)
Thailand, probably Chiang Mai, 19th century
Bamboo, lacquer; H 19.4 cm, D 23.2 cm
OA 1998.7-23.153, gift of Mr and Mrs R. Isaacs

16. Bowl
Thailand, probably from Chiang Mai, early 20th century
Bamboo, lacquer; H 19 cm, D 35 cm
OA 1994.5-30.1, gift of Martin Williams and T. Richard Blurton, in memory of Damian Doran (1959–93)

The engraved decoration and dark-red-on-black colouring of these three vessels is typical of the style associated with the northern Thai city of Chiang Mai.[45] Although none of them is probably more than a hundred and fifty years old, they represent a tradition which, it is believed, was influential in the development of lacquer work in Burma – above all the *yun* type of decoration. The designs on these vessels are all versions of the floral pattern that in Burma, where it has

been widely copied, was known as *zin me*, literally Chiang Mai. The copying of this motif is doubtless a further example – along with so much else in the cultural field such as elements of theatre, dance and music – of Thai influence on Burmese culture following on from the spate of cross-border wars that culminated in the devastating sack by the Burmese of the Thai capital, Ayutthaya, in 1767. Craftsmen were repeatedly brought back to Burma from Thailand as booty and, unsurprisingly, introduced their techniques and styles to Burmese craftsmen.[46] The style of *zin me* on lacquer vessels was, in somewhat more pacific conditions, re-introduced in the 1920s at the Government School in Pagan, together with the pearly-grey colour then fashionable in Thailand, although it never proved very popular.[47]

The decoration on the betel-box is far and away the finest of the three with a mass of swirling lotus flower heads depicted in minute detail at a tiny scale. It is likely to be the earliest of the three vessels with a date in the nineteenth century; the stand and the bowl are probably early twentieth

16

century in date. The design on the bowl, while coarser and now darker, also includes figures which rise up from open lotus flowers with hands raised in the gesture of adoration, entirely suitable for a vessel for offerings to the Buddha, or the monkhood. Bowls of this type would usually have had a small stand in which the flat base of the vessel would have sat.[48] The stand, also for offerings and functionally cognate with the Burmese *hsun ok*,[49] uses a more regular version of the *zin me* design.

Just as elsewhere in Southeast Asia, the betel habit in Thailand is well established and the paraphernalia of this activity is well represented in Thai material culture.[50]

45 To date, most art-historical investigation on Thai lacquer has concentrated on the traditions of black and gold work (the equivalent of the Burmese *shwe zawa*). For this, see Bhirasri 1995.
46 Fraser-Lu (1985: 47) says that the *zin me* pattern was introduced from northern Thailand 'about the mid-nineteenth century', but does not give a reference. It seems that the turbulent years of cultural exchange of the eighteenth century were a more likely time for the transference of the pattern than the more stable years of the

nineteenth century. For an example of similar influence from Thailand, in the introduction of theatrical versions of the *Ramayana* story, see cat. 65; for the use of mother-of-pearl inlay, in the Thai fashion, for Burmese manuscripts, see cat. 82.
47 Fraser-Lu 1985: 50, pl. 22, for a grey-coloured *zin me* betel-box.
48 See Pothisoonthorn and Vorasart 1981: 50.
49 All three vessels have their direct and obvious counterparts among the Burmese shapes.
50 For betel-cutters in Thailand, see Brownrigg 1991: 95–8. For general information on betel in Thailand, see also pp. 38–9, 46 and 132. For betel in Thailand, see also Reichart and Philipsen 1996.

17
Prize certificate, *let hmat*
India, probably Delhi, 1902–3
Paper; H 57 cm, W 45 cm
OA 1998.7-23.199, gift of Mr and Mrs R. Isaacs

This certificate states that 'Maung Nyun [*sic*] of Pagan' was awarded a commendation for lacquerware at the Indian Art Exhibition held at Delhi in 1902–3. The catalogue of the exhibition,[51] which was not published until after its closure, lists among winners of prizes and certificates a 'Saya Nyain [*sic*] of Pagan', who was commended for lacquered betel-

boxes.[52] The exhibition held in Delhi included examples of Burmese artwork as well as items from all over the Indian subcontinent because until 1937 Burma was administered as an integral part of British India; Burmese art was thus subsumed within Indian art. Exhibitions such as this, both in the colonies and in Britain, displayed and promoted arts that were considered useful and capable of 'development' under colonial tutelage; the catalogue is full of judgmental values about the quality of the work displayed.[53] Objects were chosen by the Director and Assistant-Director of the exhibition and shown close to items from all over the Indian Empire. Awards and commendations were given, so the catalogue says, to denote 'art merit'. Later it says 'when a certificate of being "Commended" has been given, the goods so distinguished should be viewed as possessing distinct artistic merit over many others.'

Cat. 18 is a small letter canister dated 1902 and signed by the maker Hsaya Nyunt, evidently the correct name of the craftsman whose work was commended, since both the letter tube and the certificate were in the possession of a descendant of Hsaya Nyunt when obtained in 1992. The intervening years have seen the effects on the certificate of damp and insects.

17

51 Watt 1904.
52 Ibid: 224.
53 On p. 221 of the catalogue we read: 'The patterns used by the Pagan workers are over-burdened. There is an entire absence of any knowledge in the value of spacing or of contrasts.'

19

18

Letter canister, *sa dauk*

Burma, Pagan, made by Hsaya Nyunt, 1902
Bamboo, lacquer; H 19.5 cm, D 7.6 cm
OA 1998.7-23.130, gift of Mr and Mrs R. Isaacs

The maker of this small letter canister, Hsaya Nyunt, has signed his work on the base and also dated it 'Year 64' or 1264 in the Burmese era, equivalent to 1902 (see photo. p. 42). Hsaya Nyunt won a commendation for lacquered betel-boxes at the Indian Art Exhibition in Delhi in 1902–3. His certificate,

cat. 17, and this letter canister were obtained in Pagan from one of Hsaya Nyunt's descendants.

The very fine *yun* work in orange, pink and green on black depicts in two friezes scenes from a Burmese legend, that of prince Devada and Gothila the master harpist, with captions written in minuscule letters. Although Sir George Watt makes no mention in the Delhi catalogue specifically to Hsaya Nyunt, he records his visit to 'the rather inaccessible village of Pagan'[54] and that he made his choice of objects for the exhibition while he was there.

A lacquer master whose work had been awarded a prize or commendation usually adopted a title such as 'prize-winner' or 'certificate holder', prefixing it to his name, e.g. 'Medal winner Hsaya Maung'. So, pieces signed by the same master without such a prefix probably date from the years before he won the award. It is sometimes possible to recognize the palette and style of drawing of individual *yun* masters. Cat. 60 and 130 may be confidently attributed to Hsaya Nyunt, even though

unsigned; the size of the engraved scenes, the minute script of the captions, as well as specific features such as the palm trees that bend over in the same distinctive way, indicate a definite style. If these pieces are indeed by his hand, they would date from before 1902 as there is no mention of him being a 'prize-winner'. A shallow betel-box in the *za yun* netting pattern in silver or black, in a private collection and signed 'made by award certificate holder Hsaya Nyunt', can thus be dated with confidence 'after 1902'.

54 Watt 1904: 221.

19

Armature for small lidded vessel

Burma, New Pagan, G/1 Khanlaung Quarter, Htun Handicrafts, late 20th century
Bamboo, lacquer; H 11 cm, D 9 cm
OA 1996.5-1.37

This illustrates the main building block on which most Burmese lacquered vessels are constructed – split bamboo. This is coiled with one level carefully

20

overlapping the next, and with the end of one length of bamboo notched and hooked on to the beginning of the next strip. In this example the vessel has not been completed to show the means of production, but it has been lightly glued, the next stage in the process of manufacture. This helps hold the structure solid while the layers of lacquer paste are applied.[55]

The address for this lacquer workshop is in New Pagan, to which the entire population of Old Pagan and its lacquer workshops were forcibly removed in 1990.

[55] See also the sequence, cat. 30 a–i.

20
Armature for a cup with flexible sides
Burma, New Pagan, Royal Golden Tortoise workshop, late 20th century
Bamboo, horsehair
OA 1991.10-23.24

As in the previous example, this illustrates a substrate used in the preparation of a lacquer vessel, in this case a cup. Here, there is the added interest of the extreme flexibility of the armature as the woven part is made of horsehair, not split bamboo. This results in a vessel that is so flexible – even after it has been fully lacquered – that the sides can be bent in close to one another, sometimes even touching.

Produced to much acclaim for tourists today, this technique was already well established when Burney, in his pioneering study, commented upon it, in 1832.[56]

[56] Burney 1832: 172.

21
Bowl, *khwet*
Burma, New Pagan, Royal Golden Tortoise workshop, 1991
Bamboo, horsehair, lacquer; D 127 mm, H 108 mm
1998.7-23.123, gift of Mr & Mrs R. Isaacs

An inscription on the base of this cup or bowl gives the manufacturer and date. It was made in 1991 in the workshops of the 'Royal Golden Tortoise Traditional Burmese Lacquerware Enterprise' in Pagan 'New Town'.

The foundation is a mixture of fine bamboo splints and horsehair, the latter forming the weft of the basketry (see left). This creates a thin-walled, flexible and lightweight finished article even after several coats of lacquer. The *yun* decoration shows buildings and figures (Burmese *let taik let kya*), which the lacquer artist Hsaya Win is consciously reviving after decades of disuse. His effort is rather stiff and stilted compared with cat. 55 made perhaps sixty years earlier, and the colours are dull. The interior, bottom of the base and background colour of the whole piece are all a brownish terracotta, the traditional vermilion having all but disappeared since the price of cinnabar has risen beyond the reach of lacquer makers and their customers.

21

22

Offering vessel, *hsun ok*
Burma, early 20th century
Bamboo, lacquer; H 19.5 cm, D 13.5 cm
OA 1998.7-23.20, gift of Mr and Mrs R. Isaacs

This little *hsun ok* of tightly woven, split bamboo basketry is made in only three parts, including an internal tray. The bowl and integral foot have five sharp ridges woven in one piece with the main body of the vessel. The lid has a spire and ends in a knob decorated with a small point as a finial. The whole article has been lacquered sufficiently to harden the basketry without concealing the weave and the skill of the basket-maker.

23

Such miniature vessels were not made merely as decorative examples of the skills of the craftsman (or craftswoman). They were used in the domestic shrine or 'Buddha shelf', *hpayazin*, on the auspicious east wall of the house, where they were set before an image or images of the Buddha.

23

Dish with cover, *ok*
Burma, probably from either Meiktila or Pyinmana, mid-20th century
Cane basketry, lacquered; H 5 cm, D 16.3 cm
OA 1998.7-23.244, gift of Mr and Mrs R. Isaacs

Both the dish and the lid are made of coarse basketry, which has then been thickly covered in red lacquer inside and out. The basketry on the inside has been previously smeared with *thayo* to fill in the interstices and produce a smooth surface. The basketry on the outside has been deliberately left prominent so that the weave becomes the decorative pattern. This piece is similar to two larger, deep bowls in the British Museum, also made of thickly red lacquered cane basketry, which bear inscriptions on the base in raised *thayo* giving the names of the makers, Hsaya Kyi and Hsaya Kyaw.[57] All three vessels

22

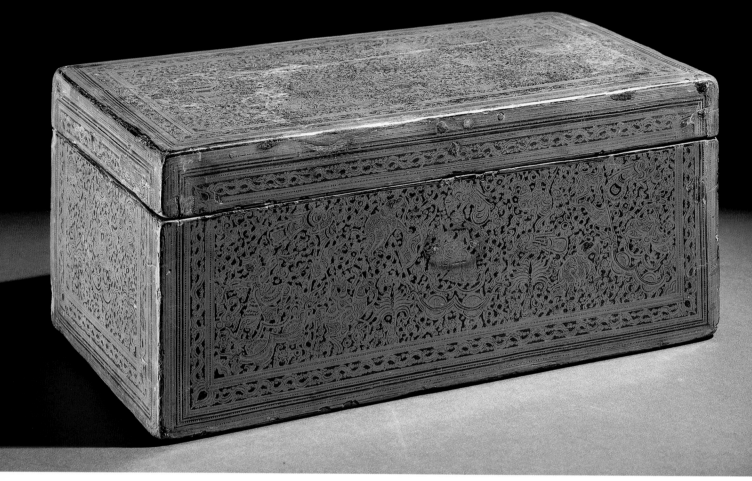

24

are very close to two in the Museum of Archaeology and Anthropology in Cambridge, which were purchased new in Pyinmana.

A dish such as this would have been used to hold the pungent pickled tea-leaf, *lahpet*. In Burmese society the taking of *lahpet* follows a meal and accompanies conversation.[58]

57 BM reg. nos OA 1991.10-23.95 and 1992.7-28.1 respectively. See also cat. 166.
58 For another *lahpet* tray, see cat. 145.

24
Wooden coffer, *yun thitta*
Burma, Pagan. 19th century, perhaps before 1850[59]
Wood, metal hinges, lacquer; H 16.5 cm, W 22 cm, L 39 cm
OA 1996.5-1.52

After bamboo basketry, wood is the most common of the substrates used in lacquer production. Wooden boxes of all sizes have been produced using lacquer as well as much more complicated wooden objects such as sculpture, furniture and musical instruments.[60]

The *yun* decoration is fine and densely spread over the surfaces of the box. The compact nature of the decoration, in green, red and black lacquer, includes horsemen, palace towers, elephants, chariots and trees. A narrative is certainly suggested but it is quite unclear today what that is, not least because there are no captions. This lack, as also the lack of any name of the workshop, certainly implies a nineteenth-century date, as does the very denseness of the patterning, a feature that colonial administrators tried hard to 'better'. The Burmese aesthetic – certainly of the nineteenth century – seems to have preferred the wild,

gyrating over-all type of design, which is very much in opposition to designs such as the twentieth-century *nandwin* variety. Interestingly, the box on loan to this exhibition from the National Trust at Kedleston (*c.*1900, cat. 175) is equally covered with engraved designs, also of heroic scenes, but here, although there is still no name of the workshop, there are identifying captions. This current box seems to be an earlier version of that type.

59 I am indebted to Noel Singer for his suggestions on the date of this object.
60 See cat. 72–7 for sculpture, cat. 99–103 for items of furniture and cat. 126–8 for musical instruments.

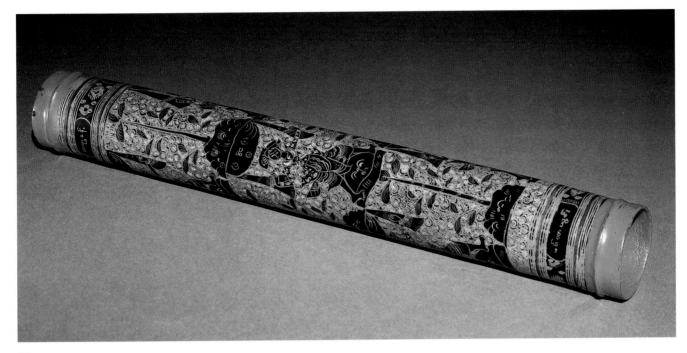

25

25

Letter tube, *sa dauk*

Burma, Pagan, workshop of Hsaya Hkant, mid-20th century

Cloth, lacquer; L 42 cm (incomplete), D 5.5 cm

OA 1998. 7-23. 152, gift of Mr and Mrs R. Isaacs

The cylinder is formed of cloth stiffened with lacquer and rolled to form a tube. A 'seam' glued with lacquer runs along the inside. Caps that closed the ends of the tube are missing. The *yun* decoration consists of figures and trees against a background of pink and yellow hatching. In a pair of cartouches at each end the maker Hsaya Hkant uses the title 'prize medal winner'[61] and claims that this letter or certificate canister is authentic ceremonial lacquerware. Such cylinders were used to hold letters to or from senior monks or secular officials and documents such as university degree certificates.

61 For the use of such titles, see cat. 18.

26

Box in the shape of a chicken, *kyet pon ok*

Burma, mid-20th century

Palm-nut shell, bamboo, wood, lacquer; H 21.5 cm, L 13.5 cm

OA 1998.7-23.198, gift of Mr and Mrs R. Isaacs

A nut of the toddy palm or palmyra palm (*Borassus flabellifer*) split in half lengthwise forms the body of the box. The head and feet are made of a core of wood built up with *thayo*, and the base is a disc of coiled bamboo. The exterior has been thickly lacquered in red, and the interior is lacquered brown. Such boxes held lumps of palm sugar or other sweets, and are a visual pleasure with their complex external shape and smooth, uncomplicated interior.

An orange-lacquered ladle or drinking cup (cat. 27) is another article made from a nutshell, but in this case a coconut shell.

27

Cup or ladle, *hmok*

Burma, early 20th century

Coconut shell, wood, lacquer; L 24 cm, D (bowl) 7.5 cm

OA 1998.7-23.247, gift of Mr and Mrs R. Isaacs

The cup is cut from a coconut shell and fixed to a wooden handle. Both are lacquered orange. This utensil has several uses: in the home it can serve as a ladle or as a cup to scoop up drinking water from an earthen water-cooler; but it can also form part of the equipment of a public drinking-water shelf, or *yay gyan zin*. These are set up in the shade of a banyan tree at the

26

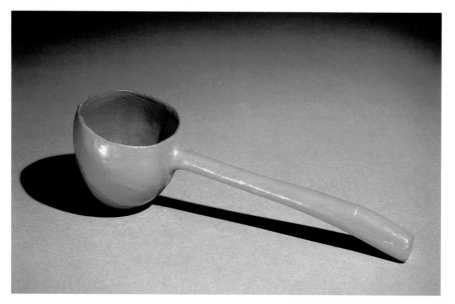

27

(28a, second from bottom); a device for engraving parallel lines (28a, bottom); and most remarkably a bow-operated lathe, *put knon* (28c), complete with mandrel and bow. This lathe was used to smooth vessels following the application of *thayo* and also to polish them later in the sequence. Such lathes are still in use today. For all these tools and their use, see further pp. 31–40.

63 The tool and orpiment shown here are located inside the box with this number; see cat. 50.

29. Mandrel for weaving lacquer cups
Burma, 19th century
Wood with vessel of bamboo; H 15.5 cm, D 10.5 cm
Centre for Economic Botany, Royal Botanic Gardens, Kew, no. 61957

Most vessels decorated with lacquer are initially made of woven split bamboo or, the larger ones, of rattan. If a small vessel with a flat base or lid is required, it is easiest to weave this substrate on a wooden form that will support the uprights of thin split bamboo, holding them flat and in place while the weaving is completed. The

roadside for thirsty passers-by, and are donated as a deed of merit. The other element of these typical acts of charity are porous earthenware pots which keep the water cool by evaporation.[62]

Another practical article made from a lacquered nutshell is the chicken-shaped sweet-meat box, cat. 26.

62 For an early illustration of both a water shelf with earthenware vessels and a coconut-shell drinking cup, see pl. 13 of Yule 1968, a print from a photograph by Linnaeus Tripe entitled 'Waterpots for the traveller's refreshment, a Burmese charity'. Captain Tripe, probably the first photographer in Burma, accompanied the embassy to Ava, under the command of Arthur Phayre. His photographs, recorded on waxed paper negatives, are of great historic importance; they are in the collections of the Royal Photographic Society in Bath.

28
Tools and materials used in making lacquer vessels
Burma, probably all from Pagan, 19th and early 20th century
Wood, metal, orpiment; 28a (top to bottom) L 23 cm, 13 cm, 16.4 cm, 50 cm, 28 cm; 28b 3 x 3 cm, L 14.5 cm; 28c L 74 cm, W 24 cm, H 39 cm
28a/c Museum of Archaeology and Anthropology, University of Cambridge, gift of Dr O. Samson Clarke, 38.365, 366, 367, 368, 369 and 370; 28b Royal Botanic Garden, Kew, no. 67713[63]

All these items are used in the

production of lacquer vessels. They include a knife (28a, top) for cutting and preparing the strips of bamboo that are coiled and woven together to make the vessels; a blade (28a, second from top) for scraping the surface of roughly lacquered vessels on a lathe; two double-ended engraving tools (middle of 28a; and 28b, below, from Kew; dividers for marking concentric circles

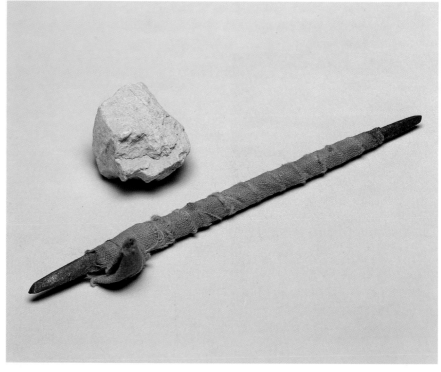

28b

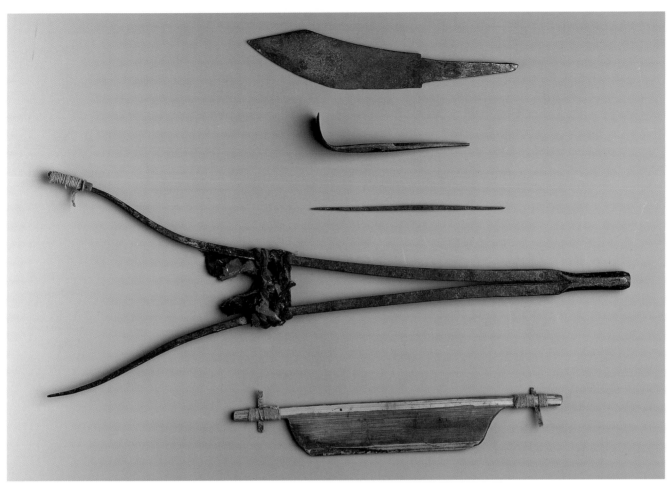

28a

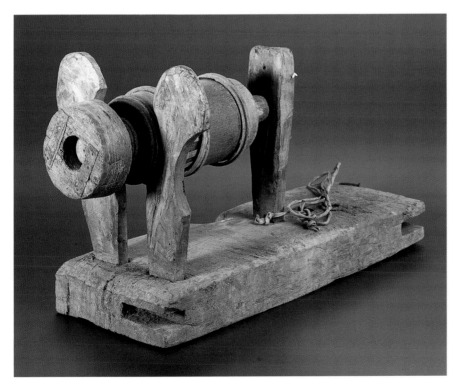

28c

woven base is further anchored by a plug with a spike on it. The spike penetrates the centre of the base and is held in a hole in the base of the form, thus securing it. This wooden form is linked to a spindle and set on a frame that holds it steady (see photo. p. 33).

This piece from the Centre for Economic Botany at Kew is one of a large group otherwise made up of small betel-boxes, all in various stages of

29

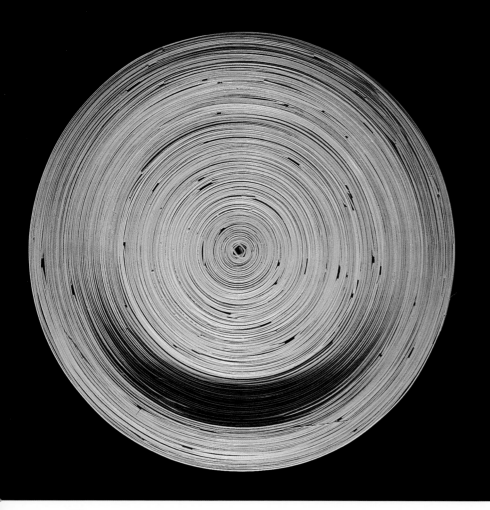

30a

production and decoration, illustrating the stages of vessel manufacture. Although there is no surviving documentary evidence, it is likely that this group came from the India Museum, along with the tool and the orpiment (see cat. 28b), and was part of a display in the museum that showed all the processes of making lacquer vessels. This would be in keeping with the policy of the East India Company: 'As a commercial body, responsible to its shareholders, the East India Company encouraged its officials in India [read 'Burma'] to identify plants with economic potential.'[64] The India Museum was disbanded in 1880, with the majority of its collections divided between the British Museum and the South Kensington Museum; a smaller portion, concerned with botany and botanical illustrations, went to Kew.[65]

64 Desmond 1995: 123.
65 Desmond 1982.

30

Nine plates illustrating the *yun* process
Burma, Pagan, late 20th century
Bamboo, lacquer; (a) & (c–i) D 26 cm, depth 3 cm;
(b) L 26 cm, W 22 cm, depth 2 cm
OA 2000.3-30.4-12

These nine plates – eight of which are all from the same production – illustrate the technique of *yun* decoration as it is practised today in Pagan, the centre of this type of work. It is assumed – and the eyewitness account of Burney confirms this[66] – that this is how the technique was carried out from the time that it was introduced into Burma.

a) The process begins with a plain, undecorated plate made of split bamboo strips that have been coiled and overlapped to produce the circular plate. This is covered with a thin coat of lacquer which helps hold the bamboo strips in place.

b) All the interstices of the coiled plate

30b

30c

30e

30d

30f

30g

are completely filled in with rough *thayo*, as illustrated on this oval plate (not from the same production as the others). For circular vessels the roughness of the putty coating can be removed by the use of a lathe (see p. 34), and once it has been smoothed, further layers of *thayo* are applied, each one less rough. After each application of lacquer – and this applies to every application from here until the end of the process – the vessel must dry in dark and humid conditions. All lacquer workshops need a cellar on the premises to provide the necessary conditions for drying between each coating.

c) Once the correct thickness and fineness of finish have been achieved, the plate is coated with layers of refined lacquer. Again, between each coating there will be drying in the cellar, followed later by smoothing on the lathe. If a plain black glossy finish is required, this plate can be the end product. However, if the fully engraved, *yun* decoration – for which Pagan is famous – is desired, the next time-consuming steps need to be accomplished.

d) The basic quadrants and circles of the complex design are drawn out using a pen and a compass. Next the design that will appear in the first colour – here red – is engraved free-hand on to the surface, the only guide being the compass-marked lines in pen. In this example the outlines of the overall pattern have been engraved, and in one place the minute background etchings have also been scratched on to the surface of the plate. This needs to be done all over the vessel, so that both the strong lines of the design as well as the finer background lines take the red colouring in the next phase.

e) Here the plate is shown after it has been fully engraved for the red colouring and after the whole plate has then been covered in a mixture of lacquer sap and cinnabar, *hinthabada*. When this mixture is rubbed on to the vessel, the red colouring takes where

30h

30i

the surface has been roughened by the engraving; where it is only in contact with the plain black lacquered surface, it does not adhere and can be wiped away. As in all the other phases where lacquer has been applied, the plate will need to be dried again in the cellar and then polished once more, probably now by hand and only with a fine powder.
f–g) The engraving to take the next colour is completed, and the colouring process, as outlined for red in the previous stage, is now carried out for green. Traditionally, green would be a mixture of orpiment (yellow)[67] and indigo (blue) added to lacquer sap, though today chemical colours are also sometimes used. Here two examples of green colouring are shown: a brilliant version and one after polishing.
h) With the engraving for each new colour, the complex design is built up. The last in the sequence is yellow, traditionally made from orpiment. Here again the plate will need to be laid aside in the cellar to dry before the next stage in the process can take place.
i) Once dry after completion of the yellow stage, the plate is polished and is ready for sale.

Such wares are sold today at Pagan itself and in the major cities – in Rangoon especially at Scott Market.[68]

66 See Burney 1832.
67 For an example of orpiment, see cat. 28b.
68 Also known today as Bogyoke ('General') Market, after (General) Aung San, the leader who brought Burma to independence.

31

31

Carved stone for moulding lacquer putty, *thayo, ponzangwet*

Burma, 19th century or earlier
Fine-grained stone; L 28 cm, depth 7 cm, W 5 cm
Centre for Economic Botany, Royal Botanic Gardens, Kew, no. 61961

Three of the four sides of this mould are carved with designs; two of the faces have repeating motifs. All of these are familiar from the relief decoration found on a wide range of vessels, many seen in this exhibition and book. Such stone moulds are especially useful when a design is to be used in a continuous strip. *Thayo* can be pressed into the mould and then lifted out. Next, using further lacquer as an adhesive, the strip of decoration can be applied to the exterior of a vessel. A frequent application is on the columnar base of an offering vessel (see cat. 89).

This example was registered at Kew in 1889 having been transferred from the museum of the India Office, which closed in 1880.[69] This information provides a terminus for it, but its age when acquired is unknown. This technique is mentioned by Watt who describes its use in Mandalay at the turn of the century;[70] the present authors have seen such stone moulds still used in Pagan.

[69] It came with a large quantity of other material including polishing stones, finished and unfinished vessels, and vermilion (all of which can still be identified), as well as a manuscript chest, *sadaik*.
[70] Watt 1904: 223-4.

32

Offering vessel, *ok khwet*

Burma, possibly Prome, first half of the 20th century
Bamboo, lacquer; H 28.5 cm, D 38.5 cm
OA 1998.7-23.41, gift of Mr and Mrs R. Isaacs

This vessel consists of four parts excluding the now missing finial which would have been in the form of a shallow cup.[71] The main bowl stands on eight short feet and has numerous vertical ribs. The relief decoration around the rim of the bowl and around each of the upper trays consists of strips of moulded *thayo* pressed into a stone mould previously dusted with ash.[72] This is then lifted out in strips, cut to size and stuck in place on the still tacky lacquer surface of the vessel. When the whole is dry, further coats of red lacquer complete the piece. There are two basic designs used in the *thayo* bands on this vessel: a hanging triangular motif, like the one known in Burmese as *kya hmauk* (used for six of the seven bands), and the wave-like scroll motif, *acheik chu pan*.

The suggestion that this vessel may have been made in Prome is based on its similarity, both in shape and decoration, to cat. 160, which has the seal-like inscription impressed on the base in raised *thayo* lettering, 'Pyay Town, Hsaya Pyu.' Pyay in Burmese is the town the British knew as Prome. Two other food containers, both in a private collection, are decorated with moulded low-relief motifs and also signed, one of them with 'Hsaya Po, produce of Pyay Town' and the other with 'Pyay Town, Hsaya Pyu'.

[71] See cat. 3 for a vessel with the cup-finial in place.
[72] See cat. 31 for a stone mould made to prepare strips of this repeating decoration.

32

33
Table, *sabweh*
Burma, probably Mandalay, late 19th century
Wood, ferrous metal sheet, lacquer, gold leaf, white
paint, coloured glass spangles, prisms and globes;
H 73 cm, D 64 cm
OA 1994.11-16.3, Brooke Sewell Fund

This item of *bizarrerie* demonstrates the
extreme possibilities of lacquer and

wood. It shares a previous owner with a
pair of *hsun ok* (cat. 1) and was
auctioned in the same sale at Stokesay
Court, Shropshire, in 1994.[73] It was
acquired by Herbert and Margaret
Allcroft in 1902 in Delhi.[74] In this
important respect it is unlike the two
hsun ok, cat. 1, which were almost
certainly purchased in Mandalay during

Herbert Allcroft's visit to that city in
1895. The Durbar held by Curzon in
1902 to celebrate the accession of
Edward VII as King-Emperor included an
exhibition of art from the whole of
British India, which at this date included
Burma.[75] There was a series of sale
galleries in the exhibition, including one
devoted to Burma.[76] Although we

cannot be certain, it is likely that the Allcrofts bought this wonderful table at the exhibition. Indeed, they will have found there wares from Felice Beato, the dealer in photographs[77] and furniture whose shop Herbert Allcroft had visited in Mandalay in 1895 (see cat. 1). The 1904 catalogue for the Delhi exhibition informs us that the 'numerous articles of furniture and fittings are all specially selected to exemplify the best features of Burmese art, many of which have been contributed by Messrs. Beato and Co. of Rangoon and Mandalay'.[78] The Stokesay archives record that the Allcrofts paid 75 rupees for the table.[79]

The table is primarily of wood and is made up of a circular base and a circular top held apart by a central baluster with swellings and mouldings, around which are three figured groups separated by three rearing sea-monsters, *nagas*. Almost every surface is lacquered and gilded as well as being decorated with coloured glass spangles and prisms. Perhaps the most unusual elements are the table-top, and the supports of figures and *nagas*.

The top surface of the table is densely decorated in high relief with figures and animals made of *thayo*, set with coloured glass. In the centre is a turbaned figure riding an elephant and holding a goad. Around this central tondo is a band of scrolling set with floral decoration with alternating prisms and globes of coloured glass. Beyond this is a register of lion-like animals set within lobed cartouches. There are four animals in total, grouped so that each one faces one of the others. Immediately around the lions are open lotus blossoms on stalks, while beyond are more formal floral patterns. At the edge is a band of twisted rope set with white and green glass spangles. Attached to the edge of the table is a fringe of cut metal which is periodically pinched out to form a point.[80]

The Burmese decorative repertoire includes many motifs of Indian origin, and the *naga* is one of these.[81] However, like so many of these motifs, they have become completely 'Burmanized' since they were first introduced from the subcontinent in the first millennium AD. In this instance the body of the beast forms an almost complete circuit, with the forepaws and feet on the base, the body kicked up above the head and the multiple-pointed tail hanging down, high above the head. It is thus the upthrust body that supports the table-top.

In between each *naga* is a group of two male figures with white painted faces: a kneeling and bracing male figure with double pigtails down the back and, balanced on his shoulders, a crowned figure dressed in court costume. This costume includes stiff wing-like projections between the legs and hanging from the waistband, which in real life would have been held up by bamboo but which are here made of sheet metal so that they stand proud of the body. These upper figures have outstretched arms, as if to support the table-top, although they in fact do not reach that far.

The function of such an item is difficult to determine as it would always have been completely impractical to have placed anything on the table-top; the relief decoration would have got in the way. We can only imagine that its use was solely as a decorative feature, something to be admired and wondered at, a true demonstration of the skills of the *thayo* artist.

73 Sotheby's sale catalogue of 29 September to 1 October 1994 at Stokesay Court, Shropshire, lot no. 702.
74 'A Trip to the Delhi Durbar, Burmah, Ceylon, 1902–3', MS at Stokesay Court.
75 For the Delhi Durbar, see Metcalf 1994: 196–8.
76 Watt 1904: 6–7.
77 Photographs by Beato, his 'Military Portraits from the Indian Mutiny' of 1857, were in the collection at Stokesay. See Sotheby's sale catalogue in note 73 above, lot 1478.

78 Watt 1904: 6–7. Beato also won a prize at Delhi for a 'collection of lacquered work of Burma' (Watt 1904: 224).
79 See note 73.
80 This sheet metal is clearly ferrous, since, when it entered the British Museum, parts of it were rusty.
81 For the *naga* motif in Burmese art, see Aye Myint 1993: 95, 122–5.

34
Circular box, *it*

Burma, probably Pagan, but exported from Mandalay, before 1923
Bamboo, gold leaf, lacquer; H 5.6 cm, D 11 cm
National Museums and Galleries on Merseyside (Liverpool Museum), 50.4.126

The collections in Liverpool are particularly strong on vessels illustrating the *shwe zawa* technique of black-and-gold lacquer decoration (see also cat. 35 and 67). This box is typical of objects in the group not only in its standard of execution but also in that it shares a similar history. It was exported, and perhaps made by members of the Hita Co-operative Society, whose offices were in Mandalay. It was subsequently shown at the British Industries Fair in 1923 in London and acquired by the Imperial Institute, South Kensington. When the Institute was disbanded in 1950, its collections were dispersed and this example of 1920s *shwe zawa* work found its way to Liverpool Museum.

On the lid of the box is an unidentified scene of a man and a woman in a forest setting, while around the edges of the box are hunters

34

chasing mythical animals. Considering the proximity in date, it is useful to compare this box with the cup bought at Nyaung-U in 1920 (cat. 159).

35
Cosmetic box, *thanahka bu*
Burma, Pagan, mid-20th century
Bamboo, cotton netting, lacquer, gold leaf; H 9.1 cm, D 9.1 cm
National Museums and Galleries on Merseyside (Liverpool Museum), 50.4.204

This cylindrical box has a deep and close-set cover, and a unique internal fitting consisting of a tray made of netting like a sieve or strainer. This stays high so that the contents of the netting tray are kept close to the lid and easy to remove for use. Although the box has never been used, and there are therefore no traces of the substance it was designed for, it seems reasonable to surmise that it was meant to hold cosmetic powder, and a puff for applying this to the skin.

The whole box is lacquered red inside and out, and the exterior is decorated in the *shwe zawa* gold leaf technique, here unusually executed with red lacquer rather than the more usual black.[82] The main frieze around the walls of the cover is in the classic *chupan* design of fernlike spiral whorls of

36

foliage. Very narrow friezes at the upper edge of the cover and round the foot of the box echo this pattern. The circular top of the lid affords a fine area for the craftsman to employ the same *chu pan* design.

Liverpool Museum records indicate that this box was bought at the shop of Mah Kyi, 545–50 Scott Market, Rangoon.

82 Red and gold *shwe zawa* is most commonly seen on manuscript coverboards: see cat. 79a. For black and gold *shwe zawa* vessels, see cat. 159 and 183.

36
Bowl, *ko kaw tee*
Burma, Kentung, Shan States, made by Hsaya Maung Htun about 1930
Bamboo, lacquer, gold leaf; H 11.7 cm, D 17.2 cm
OA 1998.7-23.158, gift of Mr and Mrs R. Isaacs

Elaborately decorated bowls of this type are called *ko kaw tee* in Kentung, their place of manufacture in the far eastern part of the southern Shan States. This

town was the capital of the small state of the same name.[83] Noel Singer, whose many publications on lacquer and other aspects of Burmese art have been immensely influential, has traced the development of this distinctive vessel from a mere domestic receptacle like a rice-measure to the purely ornamental object of the early twentieth century.[84]

This example was made by Hsaya Maung Htun who has signed his name on the base and added the month, *Pyatho* (January), but not the year, which was probably around 1930. It exhibits the full range of high-relief decoration: four panels on the sides with tribal couples, male followed by female and some carrying musical instruments; four roundels at the corners, each with a lively cockerel; and crows, wings outstretched, to decorate the feet of the bowl. All the modelling is executed in *thayo* rolled out into suitable morsels to build up the figures. As each piece is laid in position, it sticks fast to the tacky lacquer surface,

35

37

and further pieces can be stuck in place with a dab of lacquer as glue. Gold leaf is applied before the lacquer has set hard.[85]

83 In the 1930s when this vessel was made, the town of Kentung had a population of 5,508 (Burma Government of 1944: 85).
84 Singer 1991: 154–8. For another published example, see Fraser-Lu 1985: 126, fig. 150.
85 For other examples, see cat. 136, 165 (unfigured) and 169 (figured).

37
Tray on stand, *kalat*
Burma, Shan States, Inle Lake, Ywama, early to mid-20th century
Wood, lacquer; H 26.5 cm, D 42 cm
OA 2000.3-30.1

Handsome vessels made of wood and decorated with strikingly bold designs are a feature of the Intha people who live around Inle Lake.[86] They tend to use neither the *yun* technique nor the

thayo sculpting technique but instead apply lacquer as paint, either on wood or on basketry. This sturdy stand is made of three separate elements: the upper circular tray, the series of turned pegs and the ring base. The convention of such a stand is widespread throughout Burma,[87] but here it has a regional flavour on account of its distinctive decorative scheme. The ground colour of the interior is black on

38

which the red pattern has been painted with one of the favourite designs of the region – a spiral hooked motif. This tray on a stand functions as a small table for dishes from which food is taken communally.

There is no greater indication of the way in which collecting tastes have changed than these Intha wares. To the late-twentieth-century eye the sense of design seems so sure and strong and yet there are no examples of this type of decorated vessel in the early collections of the British Museum.

86 For other examples of work from Inle Lake, see cat. 38 and 163.
87 For the taller plate on stand, see cat. 141.

38
Betel-box, *kun it*
Burma, Shan States, Inle Lake, Ywama, mid-20th century
Bamboo, wood, lacquer; 28 cm square
OA 1998.7-23.218, gift of Mr and Mrs R. Isaacs

The Intha people live around the Inle Lake in the Shan States. They speak a dialect of Burmese said to be related to the speech of Tavoy far to the south in the Tenasserim peninsula, and may be descended from a population relocated hundreds of years ago. Their decorative art is quite distinct and shows affinities with northern Thailand. Unlike all Burmese betel-boxes, which are cylindrical, the Intha box is square. It is made of fine split bamboo basketry, raised on a light wooden base of decorative fretwork. There is one internal tray. The inside is lacquered with very fine lacquer mixed with a

trace of red to give a dark treacle brown. The outside is lacquered black, and the decoration painted on in scarlet. It consists of a variety of motifs, hooks, diamonds, zigzag and wavy lines.

An inscription painted in red lacquer on the base of the box and repeated on the base of the tray is in English lettering, not Burmese. The name of the maker (or possibly of the owner) is Ko Hteik. It is followed by the words 'YEMA LE QU', which could be Yaymaleh Quarter, part of the large village Ywama, where lacquer is still made today.

39
The Buddha, *manbaya*
Burma, probably from Lower Burma, 18th century
Lacquer, gold leaf, wood; H 54.6 cm, W 41 cm
OA 1872.7-1.2, Bridge Collection

The dry-lacquer technique of sculpture production has an ancient history in Asia. In China texts dating to as early as the fourth century AD refer to its use. By the Tang period (AD 705–907) there are quite specific descriptions of sculptures that are hollow and made of lacquer, though it is only much later, in the Yuan period that there is a definite description of the technique of production.[88] There seems no doubt that it was a Chinese invention, which later spread both eastwards to Korea and Japan, and south to Burma.

When it was first practised in Burma is unknown. The sculptures of Shin Arahan and Kyanzittha in the Ananda pagoda at Pagan, which Luce believed to be of dry lacquer and of the eleventh century, are now generally thought not to have been made using this technique. Apparently they are made of sandstone, the outer surface of which has been lacquered.[89] Despite this, there is no reason historically why the technique could not have spread to Burma some time in the first millennium AD. From the Chinese sources it is clear

that there were diplomatic links between the Pyu of Lower Burma and the Chinese court in the first decades of the ninth century, and the Pyu probably knew of the use of lacquer at least in an architectural context at that time.[90]

Although we do not know for certain when the dry-lacquer technique was first practised in Burma, it is clear that it was certainly well established in the eighteenth century but had died out by the mid-twentieth century. It is today an almost completely lost technique.[91] The earliest example that can be dated by inscription is from Butalin in the Lower Chindwin District; this bears a date equivalent to 10 September 1765.[92]

While dry-lacquer images of the Buddha were doubtless made in a number of different places in Burma, a description of the method of production is recorded in the Burma Gazetteer for the Shwebo Distict.[93] A core image is made of clay, which is moulded by hand and by metal instruments. This is then covered with a wash of straw ash and water, on top of which is laid a putty made of lacquer sap mixed with teak sawdust. This can be moulded with tools to make the detailed parts of the sculpture, the end result depending entirely on the skill of the sculptor who, certainly in Shwebo, only undertook this work in his spare time. Once the fully sculpted image has been made and has then dried, the inner core of clay can be removed. Where the clay remains, in the arms or in the head, the lacquer skin can be cut, the clay dug out and then the cut sealed again with *thayo*. Finally, the image is covered with a refined lacquer mixture, polished and then gilded. Williamson calls these images *manbaya*, and tells how most of these dry-lacquer sculptures from the Shwebo District, were sold in the Shan States (not in lowland Burma) and were often carried there one within the other. A life-size image, he says, sells for rupees 60–70.[94]

This sculpture depicts the Buddha seated cross-legged with his left hand in the meditation pose of *dhyanamudra* and his right hand in the popular position of 'calling the Earth goddess to witness', *bhumisparshamudra* (with the fingers touching the ground). He sits enthroned on a stylized double-lotus plinth – small darts pointing both up and down act as lotus petals; below are pendent triangular elements articulated with lines and dots. The plinth is supported around the base with a wooden frame suggesting the way in which other dry-lacquer sculptures, all too often broken at this point, would have been set. On the reverse of this plinth is a black lacquered space, ungilded but outlined in red. This remains blank but if another dry-lacquer sculpture from the Bridge Collection is a good comparison, this space was reserved for a painted inscription, giving dedicatory information. Along with other dry-lacquer sculptures in this publication,[95] the folds of the drapery below the knees are stylized, here into simple '3' and reverse '3' shapes. The hair is formed of small points made of *thayo*;[96] the *ushnisha* (the cranial bump on Buddha images signifying spiritual attainment) is broken. The elongated ear-lobes rest on the shoulders.

On the base is painted the number '115'. This style of numbering indicates that the sculpture belonged to John Bridge who bought a large part of the collection of Major-General Charles Stuart in 1830.[97] Stuart died in Calcutta in 1828, so it is possible that this Burmese sculpture, along with other Burmese items in his very large collection,[98] were acquired by him in the final years of his life. In the immediate aftermath of the First Anglo-Burmese War a great variety of items left Burma and would have been easily available in Calcutta, the home base for many of the troops involved in the war. One other intriguing possibility exists

and that is that Stuart came by his Burmese objects as a result of postings in Chittagong; he was there in the years 1816–19.[99] However, the complete lack of any Arakanese objects and the generally mainstream Burmese nature of the items, militates against this explanation.

88 We are grateful to Dr Hu of Hong Kong for references to the Chinese sources for dry-lacquer sculpture. See especially Fernald 1927: 286; Lee King-Tsi and Hu Shih-Chang 1996: 34.

89 See Luce 1970: 126. He records that during the Second World War Griswold and U Lu Pe Win discovered that the two sculptures were hollow and made of lacquer. Although there has been no published refutation, the present authors understand that this claim has been examined in less turbulent times and that the two sculptures, although externally lacquered, are actually made of sandstone (Noel Singer, personal communication).

90 See Luce 1937: 250.

91 The only exception known to the authors is provided by a husband and wife team of sculptors living in North Okkalapa, Rangoon: U Thaung Htun and Daw San Yi. They make portrait busts of the famous using the dry-lacquer technique. The old practice of making Buddha images in this way does, however, seem to be extinct.

92 For this and related material, see Fraser-Lu 1994: 244.

93 See Williamson 1929: 128–9. What follows is based on Williamson's description.

94 Williamson also records the production in this district of a wide variety of lacquer vessels, reminding us that although today we think of only one or two lacquerware centres, other than the pre-eminent Pagan, earlier in this century lacquer was produced in many different places in Burma. We are only now beginning to work out the distinct features of the individual centres.

95 See especially cat. 72 and 73.

96 Again, note the similar form at cat. 72 and 73.

97 See Willis 1997: 252–5.

98 For another example, see cat. 113. Yet further items are to be found in the collections of the British Museum.

99 I am grateful to Anne Casile for this information, which she has put together from Stuart's military record in the India Office Library (British Library) – *Bengal Military Establishment Annual Statement*, India Office Military Department Records (L/MIL/8/9-35).

40

The Buddha crowned, *minwut hpaya*

Burma, perhaps from the southeast, (?)18th or first
half of the 19th century
Wood, lacquer, gold leaf; H 69.2 cm, W 25 cm
OA 5856 (Christy Collection)

Wooden sculpture in Burma has
traditionally been finished with lacquer,
both as a colouring agent and as a size
for taking gold leaf, with which almost
all sculptures of the Buddha are
decorated. This striking example
illustrates these features.

This Buddha image, along with the
equally impressive example of cat. 76,
represents a distinct aesthetic in
Burmese images of the Buddha. The
emphasis here is not on serenity and
calm, but on making a powerful and
direct impression. Here is sculpture that
can be immediately understood by a
viewer already conversant with the work
of sculptors of our own day.

The Buddha is depicted seated and
with his right hand in the ever-popular
gesture of *bhumisparshamudra*; his left
hand rests, palm upwards, in his lap.
The right hand is prominently marked
with the addition of large rings at the
very beginning of the fingers, almost on
the knuckle. He is fully robed in royal
style with a mass of jewellery on his
chest and with large tubular ear-plugs.
The costume is further set off by large
cuffs and pointed epaulettes. These
accoutrements, together with the tiered
crown, indicate that this is a type of
image of the Buddha known to the
Burmese by the name Jambupati, the
name of a proud king whom the
Buddha humbled by magically
appearing to him resplendent as a
world-emperor, enthroned in a
magnificent palace.[100]

This sculpture is recorded in the
British Museum as being part of the
Christy Collection. Henry Christy left his
collection of ethnographic material to
the Museum on his death in 1865; he
also left five thousand pounds for the

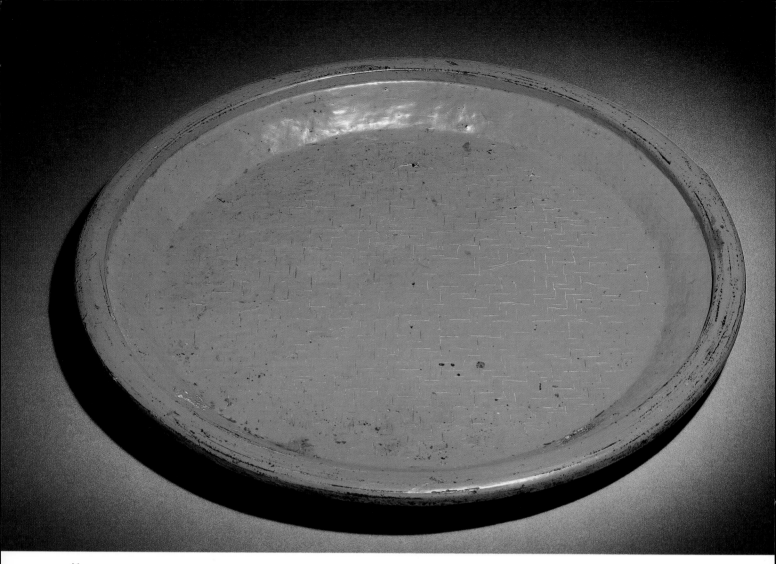

41

continuing acquisition of ethnographic material. Unfortunately, the documentation of the collection is sparse and it is unclear whether an item belonged to Christy before his death or was acquired using his bequest. Further, some items from the Christy Collection were used as 'swaps' to acquire items from other collections, and these new additions were then listed as 'Christy Collection', with the result that it is now very difficult to trace specific objects.[101] Hence the uncertainty of date ascribed above.

On the matter of date and provenance a recent publication has illustrated and described similar, though considerably less fine sculptures as being about seventeenth century in date and from the Kaw Gun Cave.[102] Unfortunately, no reference is given for

either of these assertions, but another example has been published in a number of the *Burmese Art Newsletter* from Denison University, which also gives a provenance from Moulmein and shows many similarities – five-tiered crown, ear-plugs, epaulettes, etc.[103] The date is given as late seventeenth or early eighteenth century. Final dating of this type will probably depend on fieldwork.

100 For further information on the story of Jambupati, see cat. 75.
101 Information in this paragraph is drawn from King 1997. A preliminary search in the Museum's archive has not produced any further information.
102 See Inglis 1998: 138, fig 2.
103 *Burmese Art Newsletter*, vol. 14, no. 1 (May 1983).

41
Tray, *byat*
Burma, mid-20th century
Bamboo, lacquer; D 46.5 cm
OA 1998.7-23.62, gift of Mr and Mrs R. Isaacs

The tray is formed of a circular piece cut from a length of matting woven from flat strips of split bamboo. It is supported below by a frame of bamboo slats radiating like spokes from centre to rim and attached with a cement of coarse *thayo* (raw liquid lacquer mixed with sawdust). A thin coat of raw lacquer applied to the tray has dried black, while the upper surface has also had a few coats of red lacquer, leaving the bamboo matting clearly visible beneath. This simple but satisfying object is of a type which, until recently, would have been present in almost

42

box probably derive from the narrow hoops of natural shiny yellow bamboo, which are still used to decorate some vessels in the Intha region of the Shan States (cat. 89).

every household in Burma.

There are signs of wood-boring insect damage, which is rare in lacquered articles.

42
Betel-box, *kun it*
Burma, the Shan States, early 20th century
Bamboo, lacquer; H 13 cm, D 14.2 cm
OA 1998.7-23.54, gift of Mr and Mrs R. Isaacs

This vessel is of special interest because it appears to demonstrate a sequence of decorating the exterior of vessels, starting with undecorated basketry, moving on to plain lacquer and then coming to lacquer-engraved design that imitates basketry. The dark green and dark red colouring of the sides of this box has been obtained by dense hatching in black over the green and red. The hatching appears on the base of the box and on the underside of the two internal trays, and the pattern of vertical and horizontal lines seems to echo that of the fine basketry that lies beneath a coat of lacquer. If this is true, the *yun* artist would be using his engraving tool to reproduce patterns that predate the *yun* craft.

Similarly, the fine yellow bands above and below the broad bands of dark green on the top and front of the

43
Offering vessel, *hsun ok*
Burma, Shan States, Inle Lake, late 19th century
Bamboo, lacquer; H 65 cm, D 38.5 cm
OA 1998.7-23.240, gift of Mr and Mrs R. Isaacs

This vessel of coiled bamboo has a finial knob of turned wood; all of it is lacquered in red. The complex shape is known as 'pagoda-form' (*zaydi pon*) and

43

is a speciality of the Intha lacquer masters who work in or near Ywama on the Inle Lake.[104] The resemblance to the Burmese Buddhist stupa can be seen in the profile of the cover of the vessel. The decorative bands on the lid, waist and foot of the vessel are of two quite distinct types and of different materials. Some are moulded in low relief in *thayo*. The pattern in the two broadest bands derives from the serried pegs or balusters of turned wood, *put lon*, which in the eighteenth and nineteenth centuries were part of a separate stand (*kalat*) for placing the offerings themselves on or for placing separate offering vessels on (the two vessels were eventually amalgamated into the *hsun ok* found today). These little pegs can be seen, free-standing and still made of wood, in the waist or stem of vessels which are themselves of turned wood (see cat. 4).

There are no fewer than twenty-seven narrow hoops of bamboo on this vessel, plain or notched and the notches filled with red lacquer – an extremely time-consuming process. The highest can be seen at the join of the finial knob at the top of the lid, and the lowest, low on the foot. Each was cut to size and stuck in place on the still tacky lacquer surface.

104 The beautiful and romantic Inle Lake running almost due south from near Taung-gyi, is the centre around which the Intha people are settled (see cat. 38 for their link with Tavoy). The town of Ywama, situated in a side bay on the west side of the lake, is the main town of the area. The landscape around the lake has been much photographed and published, e.g. Courtauld 1985.

44
Jar with lid, *bu*
Burma, probably from the Shan States, 19th century
Bamboo, lacquer, metal eyelets; H 16.7 cm,
D 11.7 cm
OA 1998.7-23.238, gift of Mr and Mrs R. Isaacs

This vessel of woven bamboo basketry lacquered red, has a very unusual

44

shape.[105] It is decorated with *yun* patterns embellished with silver, which has now oxidized black, as well as with hoops or rings of bare bamboo. Of these hoops, some are plain glossy golden yellow, as seen just above the foot of the vessel, while others are notched to form rope-like patterns. Two stout metal eyelets are set into the shoulder of the vessel to hold a carrying cord. The use of silver in the decoration of this jar suggests Laihka or another Shan centre as its place of manufacture.[106] Its function is a matter for conjecture, but it may perhaps have held sweetmeats.

105 See Fraser-Lu 1994: 21 for a ceramic vessel of this shape.
106 See cat. 90 and 161 for the argument which links the use of silver with Laihka.

45
Betel-box, *kun it*
Burma, Pagan, late 19th or early 20th century
Bamboo, lacquer; H 19.0 cm, D 22.0 cm
OA 1998.7-23.5, gift of Mr and Mrs R. Isaacs

This well-used betel-box is decorated in a *yun* pattern known as *myin mo*, a name that derives from Mount Meru, the centre of the cosmos in the Indian system of beliefs used by the Burmese, and refers to the stepped shape of the panels or frames. The lines of these frames stand out clearly from the background, but the figures within are drawn so as to be almost submerged in the overall scrollwork; this is a deliberate conceit. This convention allows the *yun* artist scope for considerable playful skill, but was not appreciated by several British observers and officials who found it perverse and irritating.[107] They preferred clearly delineated figures, strongly detached from the background, and found the overall infill fussy and over-elaborate. Above and below the main frieze are borders, including narrow bands that are chequered in imitation of notched bands of bamboo (cat. 43 and 94) and are surely an older form of decoration than the *yun* technique.

The figures within the frames on the sides of the cover are the twelve signs of the Burmese zodiac, while the eight planets or days of the week are drawn

47

in the radial panels on the top of the lid.[108] These two sequences – zodiac and days of the week – are frequently combined on betel-boxes in this way.

107 See cat. 17, note 53, for a typical British response to this type of patterning.
108 For these two motifs, see cat. 9, 49 and 63.

46

46
Betel-box, *kun it*
Burma, Karen, mid-20th century
Bamboo, palm leaf, lacquer; H 8.4 cm, D 10.2 cm
OA 1998. 7-23. 138, gift of Mr and Mrs R. Isaacs

This box and its two internal trays are made of bamboo basketry, rather coarse and heavily lacquered black. The sole decoration consists of three broad

hoops cut from the smooth mid-rib of the leaf of the palmyra or toddy palm (*Borassus flabellifer*). These have been glued in place with lacquer so as to stand up slightly above the black surface and form bands of white at the top rim and bottom edge of the cover and at the foot of the box.

The Karen people commonly decorate their betel-boxes with white or yellow bands but usually scored or notched. This example, though unusual, is very probably of Karen manufacture. The Karen are one of the non-Burman groups who have, since independence in 1948, been in almost constant disagreement with the central government in Rangoon. Although they are spread quite widely, their heartland is approximately the area bounded on the south by the Gulf of Martaban and the Burma-Thailand border and on the north by the town of Loikaw and the southern Shan States. The lower reaches of the Salween river run through much of the Karen region before finally debouching at Moulmein.

47
Betel-box, *kun it*
Burma, Pagan, workshop of Hsaya Sein, *c*.1930
Bamboo, horsehair, lacquer; H 11.5 cm, D 12.8 cm
OA 1998.7-23.55, gift of Mr and Mrs R. Isaacs

This thin-walled box probably has a basketry foundation of split bamboo uprights, with horsehair woven between. This would account for its light weight. The distinctive orange-vermilion colour of the lacquer is achieved by minute yellow dotting all over the cinnabar red. The maker Hsaya Sein has left the sides of the cover clear of other decoration, and has signed the piece on the bottom of the base. The only other decoration is a roundel on the top of the cover, in which a masked dancer wearing a dragon headdress carries a banner with the inscription 'Health and Wealth'.

Inside, the colour is bright cinnabar red, and the two internal trays are finely made. On the bottom they have an extraordinary number of fine concentric black lines, and a central medallion with a very old all-over design which imitates basketry, the original substrate of most lacquered articles in Burma.[109] The interior of one of the trays is deeply pitted from the chemical action of some acid seed or salt – a very unusual form of damage to lacquer which is resistant to most substances.

[109] For another example where *yun* designs imitate basketry, see cat. 42.

48

48
Betel-box, *kun it*
Burma, Pagan, made by Hsaya Htway, mid-20th century
Bamboo, lacquer; H 16.7 cm, D 22.5 cm
1998.7-23.70, gift of Mr and Mrs R. Isaacs

This betel-box has a slightly tiered lid, an unusual feature.[110] It is decorated in the *za yun* pattern, literally netting or chequerwork. Here the chequers form rosettes like lace, and this variant of the *za yun* pattern may have been derived from imported textiles, possibly Scottish.[111] It survives in unusually good condition and shows few signs of wear, a fact perhaps connected with the fact that it was acquired in Penang, in northern Malaysia.

The name of the maker Hsaya Htway appears on the base.

[110] Among the many betel-boxes in the Isaacs Collection, there is only one other with this type of domed lid and this was also made by Hsaya Htway; it has the registration number, 1998.7-23.38. This distinctive type of lid was perhaps the speciality of his workshop.
[111] See Swain 1982. Scottish activity in Burma during the colonial period was considerable, with the Irrawaddy Flotilla Company being but their best-known undertaking; see McRae 1990.

49
Betel-box, *kun it*
Burma, Pagan, first half of 20th century
Bamboo, lacquer; H 11.6 cm, D 21 cm
OA 1998.7-23.78, gift of Mr and Mrs R. Isaacs

The *kunan kanbyat* pattern (or Yunnan semicircles) on this flat or shallow betel-box provides the frames for the very popular design, *yathi yok*, or signs of the zodiac.[112] As usual on cylindrical betel-boxes, the zodiac signs for the twelve months of the year appear around the sides of the box, while the eight planets or days of the Burmese week, *gyo shit myo*, are arranged radially on the circular lid within the frames of the *kunan kanbyat* pattern. The figures are integrated with the background and neither fully detached nor deliberately submerged. An unusual colour combination of yellow, pink and green with very little black has been chosen for this box.

112 For a classic example of the *kunan kanbyat* design, see cat. 7; for the signs of the zodiac and the eight planets, see cat. 9.

49

50

Betel-box, *kun it*

Burma, probably Pagan, mid-19th century (definitely pre-1855)
Bamboo, lacquer; H 18 cm, D 22 cm
Royal Botanic Gardens, Kew, no. 67713 (India Museum number '4378' on the base)

Although now missing its trays, this beautiful betel-box illustrates the sensitive use of one of the standard patterns in the *yun* repertoire, the 'cloud collar' pattern.[113] The colours used are yellow and red. In this example each element of the 'cloud collar' repeating pattern is internally decorated with a motif that imitates basketry, a feature enhanced by the yellow lacquer used for this motif. The 'cloud collar' design appears on all the outer-facing parts of the vessel – the top and sides of the lid, the drum and the base – but there is a subtle grading of the decoration throughout. Thus, the exterior of the drum has the most uncomplicated design; this is followed by the design on the base with a still uncomplicated but fine pattern. Meanwhile the exterior of the lid has all of this plus pattern work inside each of the cloud elements, while the top of the lid displays a veritable *tour de force* of

50

51

51
Betel-box, *kun it*
Burma, Shan States, early 20th century
Bamboo, lacquer; H 15 cm, D 19.2 cm
OA 1998.7-23.140, gift of Mr and Mrs R. Isaacs

Both the cover and the base of this box are slightly domed, a feature often seen on betel-boxes from the Shan States.[118] This one is decorated with an elaborate 'Chinese cloud-collar' design in red, black and yellow.[119] Black lines edged with yellow form designs like clover-leaves within which tiny figures – human and animal – are drawn. These are so small as to be virtually hidden. The animal is a deer, while the human appears to be a female dancer. The same pattern combination is used round the sides of the cover, in a frieze set between bands of red lacquer, grooved and inset with very narrow hoops of bare bamboo, once golden but now darkened with age. There is a frieze of four-footed animals, strongly stylized, around the sides of the box, below the cover. The base has been badly damaged, and crudely mended with gritty lacquer and sawdust.

The art traditions of the minority groups of the Union of Burma, such as the Shan, have hardly been studied or published. Examples such as this box are thus of some interest. The neglect of scholars has largely been because of difficulty of access to these more remote parts over the last fifty years. This box was acquired in one part of the Shan States which has been more readily accessible, the region around Inle Lake, south of Taunggyi, at the market at Ywama, on the west side of the lake. There is no suggestion, however, that the box is necessarily from this region – indeed, it is certainly not the work of the local Intha people, whose lacquer work with its dependence on painted, rather than engraved decoration, is much more closely allied to that of northern Thailand.[120]

swirling and interlocking pattern. This is *yun* work of considerable quality.

The East India Company set up its own India Museum in 1801 and acquired all manner of material until it was disbanded in 1880. Its collecting policy was to some extent influenced by the Great Exhibition of 1851 and the French International Exhibition of 1855; as a result, some of its holdings were of an antiquarian nature, while other parts were economic and included samples of products from the regions with which the company traded.[114] In 1880 when the museum was disbanded, the collections were divided between the British Museum, the South Kensington Museum (later the Victoria and Albert Museum) and the Royal Botanic Gardens at Kew. Each institution appointed a representative to negotiate the division.[115] Items relevant to the collections at Kew included wood samples as well as objects made using

natural products. Although there is no published record of what existed in the old India Museum, record slips exist at the Victoria and Albert Museum that do list the collections. Under the number 4378, which appears on the base of this box, is an entry that records 'four round flat-top boxes of bamboo'.[116] Also, it records that it was acquired by the India Museum in 1855.[117] This box, unusually for any item of nineteenth-century Burmese lacquer, can be given an approximately secure date.

113 For other examples, see cat. 51 and 52 and for discussion of the 'cloud collar' design, see Rawson 1984: 132–8.
114 See Desmond 1995.
115 For documentation, see Willis 1997: 257.
116 A further betel-box, handsomely decorated with the *kunan kanbyat* design, still survives at Kew and bears the same India Museum number, 4378. The remaining two can no longer be identified.
117 I am indebted to Dr Michael Willis (BM) and Dr Graham Parlett (V&A) for this information.

118 Two examples can be seen in Singer 1996: 100.
119 For other examples, see cat. 50 and 52, also the large *bi it*, cat. 125.
120 For Intha examples, see cat. 37, 38 and 163; for those from northern Thailand, see Warren and Tettoni 1994: 74.

52

Miniature cylindrical box, *thanahka bu*
Burma, Pagan, late 19th/early 20th century
Bamboo, lacquer; H 5.3 cm, D 5.8 cm
OA 1998.7-23.7, gift of Mr and Mrs R. Isaacs

Made in imitation of a betel-box, with a deep cover and two internal trays, this little box has never been used for betel ingredients and was not intended for such use. It may have been used for face powder (*thanahka*) or other cosmetics.[121] Or perhaps it was only a toy. Some very similar 'model betel-boxes' even had a tiny copper or brass lime-box to fit into the upper tray – clearly a plaything.[122]

The bright cinnabar red and green design is the 'Chinese cloud-collar' pattern, and not only covers the lid and side of the box, but even appears on the bottom of the box and on the bottom of each of the two little trays. It is a rare pattern on Pagan *yun* betel-boxes, but nineteenth-century use for it can determined from its appearance on the betel-box now in the collections at Kew (cat. 50). Further, the large *bi it*, or ladies toiletries box, in the Department

52

53

of Ethnography of the British Museum (cat. 125) is not a recent acquisition and is surely of late nineteenth-century date.[123]

121 *Thanahka* is a preparation made from the ground bark of a tree. It is worn, usually, on the cheeks in pale yellow circles, to ensure fresh and unwrinkled skin. Most young women wear it (occasionally young men wear it, too), and to have a box to carry the small piece of wood, or the powder produced from it, would be entirely normal. Young Burmese belles are often photographed wearing this distinctively Burmese make-up.
122 See Ferrars 1900: 9, where children are shown playing with miniature boxes.
123 Fraser-Lu 1985: 139 suggests late nineteenth century.

53

Box with domed lid, *it*
Burma, probably Pagan, 19th century
Bamboo, lacquer; H 13.2 cm, D (at base) 11.4 cm
OA 1998.7-23.226, gift of Mr and Mrs R. Isaacs

The flared foot and stepped and domed lid of this box give it an unusual profile. It has two internal trays like conventional cylindrical betel-boxes and traces of both lime and of *thanahka* cosmetic powder are visible in the interior. This suggests that, even if originally used for betel, it was later used as a cosmetic box.

The *yun* decoration is rich and

varied. On the broadest step of the lid is the yellow flecking of the chili-seed, *nga yok si* pattern. Meanwhile the drum of the cover uses the *pabwa yok let* design, that is tiny figures of riders mounted on horses and practically submerged in the floral scrolling of the background. The top of the dome of the lid bears a bird sketched in bold strokes, and in the deeply hollowed bottom of the base in a roundel is a dancing figure holding a scarf and a sword.

The shape and decoration of this vessel – let alone the lack of any inscription – suggests considerable age, and the signs of wear on the keels and ridges support this.

54

54
Betel-box, *kun it*
Burma, Pagan, late 19th or early 20th century
Bamboo, lacquer; H 14.5 cm, D 16.7 cm
OA 1998.7-23.53, gift of Mr and Mrs R. Isaacs

The *yun* work on this betel-box is exceptionally fine. Though the lid has suffered severe damage and been crudely repaired, the sides and base of the box and even the underside of each of the two internal trays are decorated in a masterly style. There is no signature, which strongly suggests a date before 1900.

The pattern on the cover and sides of the box is the *yok let pagya*, a design consisting of a dense crowd of tiny figures in a background of green hatching. All the beasts, birds, humans and celestial beings are in vigorous movement and interlock as it were in a jigsaw. The friezes packed with these figures are bordered above and below with bands of yellow, which are dotted and hatched to represent the notched bamboo strips that decorated lacquer vessels long before the advent of *yun* engraving (see cat. 45 for imitation notched bamboo and cat. 43 and 94 for actual notched bamboo).

For the circular spaces on the base of the box and on the underside of each of the two tight-fitting internal trays, the *yun* artist has employed a different decorative scheme: scenes from the Indian epic the *Ramayana*.[124] The base of the deeper tray (see opposite) shows Lakshmana with his bow setting off to aid his brother Rama. He leaves Sita ill-protected from the ogre Ravana, menacing at the right of the picture. Overhead, the bird Jatayu waits to inform Rama when Sita is seized and carried off by the ogre. At Sita's feet is a snake, perhaps indicating the line drawn by Lakshmana within which Sita would have remained safe.

124 For the *Ramayana* in Burma, see U Thein Han and U Khin Zaw 1976: 137–54; also Singer 1989: 90–103. See also cat. 65 for other references to the *Ramayana* in both Burma and Thailand.

55
Cup, *khwet*
Burma, Pagan, 19th century
Bamboo, lacquer; H 8.3 cm, D 9 cm
OA 1974.2-26.85, gift of Sir Harry and Lady Garner

Cups of all shapes and sizes are produced at Pagan,[125] and this example demonstrates a fine degree of *yun* work of considerable liveliness. The interior has a plain covering of deep red 'pigeon-blood' lacquer (where this is cracked the woven basketry is visible). The background colour of the exterior is, unusually, brown while the engraved decoration is in yellow, red and – again unusually – blue (this is only visible today in the interior of the body of the horses).

The main register of decoration is set between smaller bands, which include concentric yellow lines, engraved with a

54 (base of inner tray)

compass. These imitate strips of bare bamboo set into the lacquer surface, a style that is assumed to be earlier than the engraved technique. The main register sports engraved decoration using the 'figures and buildings', *let taik let kya* design, which is made up of a repeating pattern (here shown four times) of a woman in a building with, in front, a man on horseback.[126] Sylvia Fraser-Lu has suggested that the figures in this type of design are characters from the *Ramayana*, and this may be so.[127] On this cup, however, the figures are so stylized and apparently so similar to each other that this interesting link is now difficult to substantiate. She has also traced this design to the Ava period (eighteenth and early nineteenth century) which would certainly accord with the assumed date of this cup.[128] On the base of this example are engraved and coloured designs – further rows of concentric circles, imitation basketry and geometric pattern.

This cup came to the British Museum

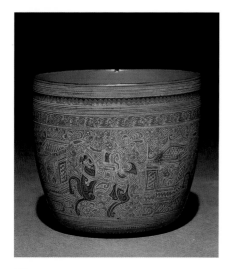

55

from the collection of Sir Harry and
Lady Garner in 1974 and was first
published, as cat. 188, in the catalogue
that accompanied the exhibition of their
collection in the Museum in 1973.[129]
Garner also published it in his later
1979 volume.[130] Today we have a better
understanding of the method of
production of these wares than is found
in Garner's books, but we are still, for
the most part, in that position he
poignantly described in 1973 when he
wrote that 'the problems of tracing the
origins of lacquer manufacture in South
East Asia are formidable'.[131]

125 For other examples, see cat. 143 and 144.
126 For a contemporary rendition of this design,
see cat. 21.
127 For the *Ramayana* in Burma, see cat. 65.
128 Fraser-Lu 1985: 40.
129 See Garner 1973: 19 and pl. 80, no. 188. Their
main interest was in Chinese and other Far Eastern
traditions of lacquer. Indeed, of the 190 examples
illustrated in the 1973 catalogue, only three are
described as being from South East Asia. One is
this cup, one is a small offering bowl on a stand
from Thailand – and the third is actually from Sindh
in western India and is decorated with lac, not
lacquer. All three of these are now in the British
Museum.
130 Garner 1979, ch. 14 and pl. 211.
131 Garner 1973: 19.

56

56
Betel-box, *kun it*
Burma, Pagan, workshop of Hsaya Kyon in the
Yundan ward, early 20th century
Bamboo, lacquer; H 26 cm, D 26.5 cm
OL 11-275, courtesy of the Missorten Foundation

The top of this betel-box has been
decorated with the signs of the Eight
Days of the Week and, around the
sides, with the zodiac signs of the
twelve months of the year. As a
background to these major designs, a
floral *kanok* motif was selected for the
top, while the zodiac signs are framed
with *nagalein* motifs – frames made up
of eight snakes, *naga*, creating a
window effect.[132] The *naga* motif is very

common throughout Burma and is
found in every branch of decorative art.

The Burmese calendar is derived
from that of India, probably arriving
along with Buddhism in the middle of
the first millennium AD. A calendar
system is essential in a Buddhist
country because of the need to
accurately determine the start of the
rainy season, during which, traditionally,
Buddhist monks are forbidden to travel
due to concerns about killing animal life
underfoot. The Burmese system of
astronomy consists essentially of lunar
months that need to be regularly
adjusted to the solar year.[133]

According to popular Buddhist belief,

the current world consists of three regions: the upper region inhabited by the *nats*,[134] the middle one by human beings, and the lower one by those who are punished. In the centre of the middle region rises Mount Meru around which turns the sun remaining a full month in each of the twelve zodiacal houses.[135] There are three seasons – hot, rainy and cold – and each one has four months. The beginning of the new year starts in the middle of the hot season with the month of *Tagu*, corresponding to April, when the water festival, *Thingyan*, is celebrated. The Burmese signs of the zodiac are mostly those known in the Western system.

In order to avoid confusion, the lacquer designer has given the name of each day with the corresponding sign, as he has also with the months. The signs for the months, though these do not correspond exactly, are goat for April, ox for May, *kinnara* (half-bird, half-human) for June, shrimp for July, lion for August, a figure holding a rice plant for September, a figure holding scales for October, scorpion for November, archer for December, *makara* (water monster) for January, water-pot for February and a fish for March.

132 Many variations of these *nagalein*, or intertwined snakes, can be seen in the caves of Hpowindaung. See also Aye Myint 1993: 124–5.
133 See Soni 1955: 4–17. On the verge of independence Soni proposed adjustments to the solar year which were 23 minutes and 50 seconds out of line with the rest of the world.
134 For the important part that the cult of the non-Buddhist spirit figures, or *nats*, have in Burma, see Temple 1906; for the *nat pwe*, see Rodrigues 1992.
135 See Htoon Chan 1905: 17.

Alain Missorten

57
Betel-box, *kun it*
Burma, probably Pagan, mid-19th century
Bamboo, lacquer; H 25 cm, D 29.7 cm
OA 1998.7-23.108, gift of Mr and Mrs R. Isaacs

This large betel-box of coiled and woven split bamboo is thick-walled and heavy. Part of the weight is due to the flared foot and concave profile of the deep cover, features that are not seen in boxes made after the mid-nineteenth century.[136] The *yun* decoration in red, yellow and green on black is elaborate and dense. The basic pattern is *gwin-shet* ('twisted field') frames, of which there are twenty-eight around the sides of the cover, twenty-nine round the walls of the box, and eighteen – radially arranged – on the circular top of the lid. The base, and the bottom of each of the two internal trays, are also decorated.[137]

The tall narrow frames on the sides of the box and cover are filled with elongated and stylized dancing figures, with long-tailed birds or with floral garlands. On the top of the lid dancing figures alternate with floral scrolls. On the base four tall dancers hold ribbons, and on the bottom of each of the internal trays is a large and boldly stylized bird.

This old box has seen a century's use and consequently much repair, some of it quite recent. However, the liveliness of the free-hand engraving of the *yun* artist can still be appreciated.

136 See Singer 1996: 94: 'All the boxes have a flared tiered base lacquered red; such distinct features were to disappear by the second half of the nineteenth century.'
137 See Fraser-Lu 1985: 39, fig. 9, for an example of a vessel in the Pagan Lacquer Museum with the *gwin-shet* pattern, which is believed to be late eighteenth or early nineteenth century in date.

57

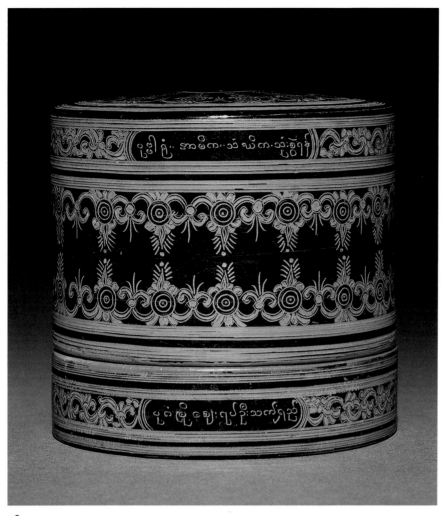

58

58
Betel-box, *kun it*
Burma, Pagan, made by U Thet Shay in the Market Ward, 1963
Bamboo, lacquer; H 11.8 cm, D 12.7 cm
OA 1998.7-23.196, gift of Mr and Mrs R. Isaacs

The pattern used by the lacquer master U Thet Shay to decorate the outside of this betel-box is derived from the stucco swags which survive on the exterior walls and doorways of the eleventh- to thirteenth-century temples at Pagan.[138] Nowadays this pattern is called *bagan khit*, 'Pagan Age', as are several other quite different designs which only share with this one the fact that they are copied or adapted from the stucco or mural-painted decoration of Pagan temples.[139] *Yun* lacquer-workers have

lived among the extensive ruins of Pagan for at least the last 150 years, which has provided them with access to a huge repertoire of motifs. However, the consciously deliberate copying of motifs as seen on this vessel is something that is a product of this century and surely unlikely to have occurred before the establishment of the Government Lacquer School in 1924.[140]

This specific design seems always to have been used with the same colour scheme of pink on black, and exclusively on vessels intended for donation to monasteries.[141] The inscriptions on the lower base of this box give the name of the maker, U Thet Shay, that his workshop was in the

Market Ward of Pagan and (unusually) record the month, Waso (July), in the Burmese calendar, when the article was finished in 1963.[142] The cartouches at the top rim of the cover state that the box is for use by the principal monks of a monastery whose Pali name, Pubbayon Amika Thangika, can be rendered as 'Eastern Park Monastery'. This inscription, in Burmese letters, provides a rare occurrence on a lacquer vessel of the Pali language, which only appears here because of the link with a monastery.[143]

138 For a clear illustration of these stucco swags at Pagan, see Strachan 1989: 99, fig. 90, where an example at the thirteenth-century Hti-lo-min-lo pagoda is shown; earlier examples from the eleventh- or twelfth-century Kyauk-ku-ohn-min pagoda are illustrated in ibid: 51, fig. 39. For drawings of four of these different types of swags, see Fraser-Lu 1984: 53, fig. 10; she also provides the Burmese term for the swags, *bilu* [ogre]-*pan-shwei*. The device of garlands that descend from the open mouth of a monster is a direct transposition to Burma from India of the *kirttimukha* motif, an ancient architectural device of Indian temple decoration.
139 For other examples, see cat. 184.
140 See Fraser-Lu 1985: 116.
141 There are two other inscribed examples in the Isaacs collection: OA 1998.7-23.56 and 86.
142 For the Burmese calendar, see Shway Yoe 1882, ch. LIX.
143 For manuscripts written in Pali, using a lacquer ink, see cat. 78–83.

59
Flat cylindrical box, *it*
Burma, New Pagan, G/1 Khanlaung Quarter, Htun Handicrafts, 1990s
Bamboo, lacquer, 'gold' powder; H 4.5 cm, D 16 cm
OA 1996.5-1.44

This small box is an example of a recent development in lacquerworking at Pagan. The armature is built up in the usual way of coiled split bamboo. In this instance the interior has been lacquered reddish-brown and the exterior black. Gold powder in solution has then been applied to the outer surfaces followed by a further layer of brown lacquer. This is 'feathered' both up and down and side to side to produce the pattern. This type of box, although now made primarily for the tourist trade, would originally have been used for snacks.

This decorative technique was introduced to Pagan workshops by U Tin Aye, head of the Government Lacquer School. Prior to his appointment, he was sent to Japan where he learnt this method, which has thus been named *Japan yun*.[144]

[144] For the Government Lacquer School, see Fraser-Lu 1986.

60
Cup, *khwet*

Burma, Pagan, possibly by Hsaya Nyunt, pre-1902
Bamboo, lacquer; H 9.5 cm, D 11.8 cm
OA 1998.7-23.193, gift of Mr and Mrs R. Isaacs

The decoration on this cup depicts scenes from the story of Maung Hpo Thi and the beautiful Shwe Nagi. This was very popular as a stage play around 1910 and became known, in a process identified by Noel Singer, merely by the names of these characters, so that the original title of the play was omitted.[145] The captions to the story scenes on this cup include the 'Taunghpila' location, a hill near Sagaing where the famous monk Tipitakalankara (1578–1650) had a monastery.[146] In fact, he was known as the Taunghpila Hsayadaw.[147] In 1634 he rediscovered the long-abandoned and then ruined Shwesettaw Pagoda, where were enshrined the Footprints of the Buddha; this was located in the foothills of the Arakan Yoma Mountains, west of Minbu.[148] Singer is convinced that the original title of the play was *Shwesettaw Thamaing*, 'History of the Pagoda of the Buddha's Footprints'. A play of this title was printed in Rangoon in 1881.[149] A monk, attended by a lay brother and a pupil, pays a visit to the palace. A princess falls in love with the pupil. Hearing of this, the king quarrels with the monk, both of them using angry words. Later the pupil is executed on the king's orders. The lay brother then sings a dirge for the dead pupil. Singer casts the Taunghpila Hsayadaw as the monk, Maung Hpo Thi as his pupil, and Shwe Nagi as the princess.[150] On the cup further captions label Maung Hpo Thi, Shwe Nagi, a corpse and Kundinnya (the youngest of the first five disciples of the Buddha).

Although this cup bears no maker's signature, it strongly resembles the work of Hsaya Nyunt, who won a commendation at the Indian Art Exhibition in Delhi in 1902–3.[151] A letter canister (cat. 18) by Hsaya Nyunt is dated 1902 and his certificate (cat. 17) has also survived. If this unsigned cup is indeed by his hand, it must date from before 1902 because he appears to have signed his work after this date. The stage play depicted would perhaps still have retained its original title of *Shwesettaw Thamaing*, but the scenes

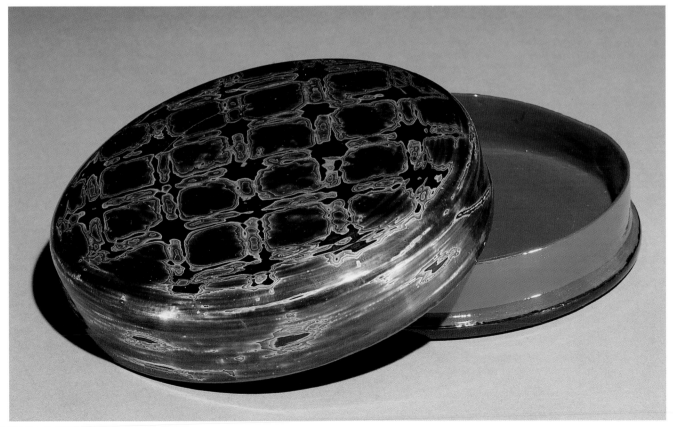

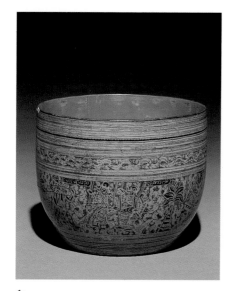

chosen reflect the popularity of the hero and the heroine.

145 Personal communication.
146 For Tipitakalamkara, see Bode 1909: 53–4.
147 Hsayadaw means head monk, abbot, senior cleric.
148 The continuing popularity of the cult of the Buddha Footprint, *Buddhapad*, at the Shwesettaw Pagoda is indicated by popular prints produced for sale to pilgrims visiting the shrine. Examples exist in the collections of the British Museum (OA 1996.5-7.01 to 04, gift of Mr and Mrs R. Isaacs).
149 Kan Gyi 1881.
150 Singer adduces evidence from Pok Ni 1952.
151 For the exhibition, see Watt 1904.

60

61

Large bowl, *khwet gyi*

Burma, Pagan, early 20th century
Bamboo, lacquer; H 20.9 cm, D 36.3 cm
OA 1998.7-23.205, gift of Mr and Mrs R. Isaacs

The wide shallow shape, large size and rolled rim of this bowl are unlike ordinary domestic vessels. It may have been made for display rather than use. It is magnificently decorated in the *yun* technique using the broad gouge point (*shauk*), not the needle-point (*tont*). The colours used are green, pink, orange and red on black. The scenes depicted in a broad frieze round the bowl are all from a historical legend of early Pagan: the

62

62

Water bowl, *yay khwet gyi*
Burma, Salay, made by Hsaya Ba and Daw Ma Ma
(husband and wife team), c.1930
Bamboo, lacquer; H 23.4 cm, D 28.3 cm
Displayed in the British Museum exhibition
'Collecting the 20th Century' in 1991
OA 1991.10-23.66

This handsome bowl beautifully illustrates in its main register the *yun* design which has become one of the most popular in the twentieth century, the *nandwin* 'king at court' design. This places royal figures in front of a backdrop of spired wooden palace buildings with, in this instance, a fortification wall behind. On this bowl the design is further added to by situating some of the palace scenes within one of the most popular of the *Mahajataka* (the Ten Last Jatakas) – the *Mahosadha Jataka*.[154] This is indicated by a series of captions written within the decoration. The main court of the king is shown twice, once on each side of the bowl. He is depicted centrally, beneath the tallest spire, and with courtiers around him on either side, half-sitting and half-lying in the manner demanded by palace etiquette.

The development of the *nandwin* pattern is interesting as it appears to have had a part-political and part-nostalgic function. In the days of British rule the palace of the old kings at Mandalay must have been a potent symbol, both as an icon of glory past, as well as an image of a non-colonial future to come. Given this meaning, it is ironic that this design is one of those that most clearly demonstrates the effect of the British aesthetic on local crafts. Gone is the dense submersion of figures in a swirling mass of pattern that was so associated with earlier wares and was seen as confusing by the colonial administrators.[155] Here the figures do not impinge on one another and there is even an element of perspective: it is legible to the Western eye and is surely a product of exercises

expedition of king Anawrahta and the four heroes to Gandalarit (Yunnan in western China) to secure the Sacred Tooth Relic of the Buddha.[152] Only partly successful, Anawrahta had to be content with a jade Buddha image which had come into contact with the Tooth and which he enshrined in the great Shwezigon Pagoda in the late eleventh century.

The life and legendary deeds of Anawrahta, the first great king of Pagan, have become a major source for Burmese literature, theatre and dance. On opposite sides of the bowl, two palaces are depicted. The Burmese has tiered *pyathat* roofs and umbrellas, and is captioned 'Great Land of Pagan'. The Chinese 'Land of the Sacred Tooth' has different architecture, hats, fans and a bug-eyed lion-dog. It also has the 'Kyi Sandi', the great copper image 'so large that four men with joined hands might

embrace it, and worshipped by the Utibwa and the whole country' says *The Glass Palace Chronicle*.[153] The four mounted heroes of Pagan are named in captions on the bowl: Nyaung-U Bee, Maung Lon, Maung Dway and king Kyanzittha. The last was to usurp the throne after Anawrahta's death and to complete the Shwezigon Pagoda.

More difficult are captions naming 'a cup of great value' and 'the great master's own work'. These do not fit the legend and could be a sly addition of the master who made this bowl.

152 A number of body relics of the Buddha are venerated in Burma, including hairs (Shwe Dagon, Rangoon: for the legend, see Win Pe 1972, ch. 2) and teeth. However, the most famous of the tooth relics in the Buddhist world is enshrined at Kandy in Sri Lanka. The possession by the Sri Lankan kings of this relic was a constant source of envy to the kings of Burma.
153 *Glass Palace Chronicle* 1922: 80–82.

such as the Delhi art exhibition of 1902 (see cat. 17 and 18) and the establishment of European-style art schools.

Of great interest is the provenance of this bowl. There is no other known example in the British Museum collection of work from Salay, some 100 km south from Pagan on the Irrawaddy. However, in 1870, Talboys Wheeler recorded lacquer workshops there:

> We arrived at the lively town of Sillay-myo, famous for its manufacture of boxes, drinking cups, and small trays painted and varnished red inside, and curiously ornamented with nondescript gold coloured figures outside. Captain Bacon kindly bought me three boxes with trays[156] for about eight rupees. In Rangoon or Calcutta they would have cost at least three times the price. The varnish and workmanship are very superior. My Bengallee servant bought some quaint black and red drinking cups for a few annas.[157]

Salay was an important town in the Pagan period, as the presence there of twelfth-century pagodas demonstrates. However, the discovery of oil nearby (at Chauk) in the 1930s, and the transference there of the district headquarters, precipitated a decline including probably the closure of the lacquer workshops; there are certainly none there today. (For the oil industry here, see Khim Maung Gyi 1989.)

Bowls of this type are for holding the domestic supply of water; a plate with a cup or dipper would have rested on top. Such items were also often presented as gifts to the monastery.

154 For further information on this previous life story of the Buddha, see cat. 102.
155 For examples, see cat. 24 and next entry.
156 Presumably betel-boxes
157 Talboys Wheeler 1871: 27.

63

63
Betel-box, *kun it*
Burma, Pagan, late 19th century
Bamboo, lacquer; H 8.8 cm, D 9.6 cm
OA 1998.7-23.228, gift of Mr and Mrs R. Isaacs

Over a background of 'chili-seed' yellow flecking on red the *kunan kanbyat* pattern (or Yunnan semicircles) is boldly drawn in black to form frames that are separated by vertical rows of little circles also strongly drawn in black.

There are eight of these frames on the top of the cover, accommodating the eight planets or days of the Burmese week (*gyo shit myo*), and twelve frames around the sides of the cover hold the zodiac figures for the months of the year. Each beast or human figure is drawn in lines much finer than the frame that contains it, so that the figures almost merge into the background. This playful device is a popular convention in the art of the Burmese *yun* lacquer master and reveals his skill. But it irritated the British at the turn of the twentieth century, who advocated clear outline drawing of figures, detached from the background (see previous entry).

64
Betel-box, *kun it*
Burma, Pagan, workshop of Hsaya Min in Sandan Ward, mid-20th century
Bamboo, lacquer; H 13.1 cm, D 23.7 cm
OA 1998.7-23.112, gift of Mr and Mrs R. Isaacs

The pattern of *yun* decoration is the *yathi*, twelve figures of the zodiac and eight planets or days of the week

64

(Burmese divide Wednesday into forenoon and afternoon, to allocate a day to each point of the compass). Using an extremely simple colour scheme, pink on black, the *yun* artist in the workshop of Hsaya Min has drawn around the sides of the box, against a background of bold foliage scrolls, twelve roundels or medallions for the figures of the zodiac, one for each month. On the circular top of the lid eight medallions ranged around a central peacock (symbol of the sun) accommodate the eight planetary beasts (*gyo shit myo*) and their names, which are also the names of the days. On the bottom of the base is a perching bird, wings outstretched and above it the Burmese for Hawk Brand.

65
Betel-box, *kun it*
Burma, Pagan, Taikkon Ward, workshop of Hsaya Thu, early 20th century
Bamboo, lacquer; H 211 cm, D 23.1 cm
OA 1998.7-23.166, gift of Mr and Mrs R. Isaacs

This box is decorated with scenes from the Indian epic, the *Ramayana*. The design has been engraved with a fine point and filled with colour – red, green and yellow on a black ground. The top of the lid shows prince Rama setting off, bow in hand, in pursuit of the golden deer and leaving his wife Sita in the care of his brother Lakshmana. The *yun* artist follows the convention of the drama and gives the deer the headdress of an ogress to reveal her actual nature beneath the disguise.[158] Round the drum of the cover two further scenes are depicted, each twice, but furnished with different captions: 'The great prince Rama;' 'Bewitched he follows Kambi through the forest;' 'Lakshmana (Lekkhana) guards his sister-in-law;' 'Ma Kambi assumes the shape of a deer and runs off.'[159]

In two cartouches in the frieze at the top of the lid the maker Hsaya Thu of

65

Taikkon Ward, Pagan, signs his name, and in two cartouches in the frieze on the sides of the base are the standard sentiments, 'Established, reputable work is best' and 'May the buyer be wealthy'.

Rama, as an *avatara*, or incarnation, of the Indian deity Vishnu, was known in Burma as far back as the Pagan period (1044–1287), as is clear from stone sculpture which survives in the Nat-hlaung temple at Pagan itself, where figures of Balarama, Rama and Parashurama are located; these are dated to the eleventh century.[160] A painted tondo, one of a sequence, in the Abeyadana temple at Pagan shows Rama riding on Hanuman. The conjunction of the two more clearly indicates a knowledge of Rama as the

hero of the epic, as well as Rama as *avatara*.[161] As an element in *jataka* stories,[162] the *Ramayana* is reported among the 'long' sequence of the stories depicted on terracotta plaques at the Petleik pagodas also at Pagan. They are allotted a similar date.[163]

However, the much greater popularity of Rama as the hero of the *Ramayana* (as opposed to him merely as an *avatara* of Vishnu) seems to date from the Konbaung period (1752–1885). This was almost certainly due to the contact between the court cultures of Burma and Thailand following the sack by the Burmese king Hsinbyushin of the Thai capital Ayutthaya in 1767. It seems likely that both members of the Thai royal family, as well as players and

66

musicians – all of them captive at the Burmese capital Ava – introduced the Thai theatrical version of the *Ramayana*[164] to the Burmese court.[165] This proved hugely popular and from court circles it spread out into the general population via the vibrant traditions of Burmese theatre.[166] Given this background in the Burmese drama, it is not surprising that on this betel-box the theatrical convention of mask-wearing is maintained.

158 For a similar depiction, see Fraser-Lu 1994, pl. 229.

159 In the Indian original it is Marica, the uncle of Ravana who disguises himself as the Golden Deer. Why in the Burmese version there is a change of sex is unclear.

160 For the Nat-hlaung temple at Pagan, see Luce 1969, vol. I: 219–22; vol. II: 92–4; vol. III, pls 143–9.

161 See Luce 1969, vol. I: 326; vol. II: 109; and vol. III, pl. 219. In the plate description in vol. II Luce is cautious about the identification of the monkey-riding figure as Rama on Hanuman.

162 For *jataka* stories, see p. 17.

163 See Thein Han and Khin Zaw 1976: 137–54. For the Sinhalese listing with the now common numbering of 547 and the ?earlier version of 550, see Luce 1969, vol. I: 262. For illustrations of many of the terracotta plaques at the two Hpet-leik pagodas, see Luce 1969, vol. II: 80–87 and vol. III, pls 97–118; for the pagoda itself, see vol. II: 79–80 and vol. III, pls 94-6.

164 For the *Ramayana* in Thailand, see Cadet 1975.

The importance of the Rama story can be gauged by the naming of the capital of the Thai state itself after the city of Rama, Ayodhya (in Thai, Ayutthaya).

165 See Singer 1989: 90–103.

166 For the Burmese theatre, see Singer 1995.

66

Clothes box, *bi it*

Burma, Mandalay, mid-20th century
Bamboo, lacquer, glass: H 30 cm, W 40 cm
OA 1998.7-23.33, gift of Mr and Mrs R. Isaacs

This box is of unusual size and elaboration, though of a common shape. It is made of bamboo basketry, thickly lacquered red and encrusted outside with *thayo* relief decoration, which is inlaid with glass and originally gilded, though only a few traces of gilding remain. The *thayo* has an orange-red colour that imparts a warm glow to the very thin gold leaf of the gilding. Most articles decorated in *thayo hmanzi shwe cha* (see cat. 10) are for devotional use, but this box is secular in purpose and iconography.

The four scenes on the cover and four on the box corners are from the *Ramayana*, and form a sequence with a moral. The cover illustrates successively prince Rama with his wife Sita; Rama and Sita seeing the golden deer, and Sita begging Rama to catch it for her; Rama drawing three lines with his bow and warning Sita to stay within them for protection; Rama in pursuit of the golden deer. The four scenes on the corners of the box show Sita and her brother-in-law Lakshmana, a decorous distance apart; Sita persuading Lakshmana to go to the assistance of Rama, whose cries for help she hears; Lakshmana drawing three lines with his bow and urging Sita not to cross them while he goes to his brother's aid; and the *balu* ogre, disguised as a hermit (with bowl) unable to cross the magic lines but coaxing Sita to cross them and, as soon as she does so, casting off his disguise to seize her and carry her off.

This box for silk skirts (*htamein*) was perhaps a gift from a well-to-do husband to his wife, and the chosen scenes a warning to the lady not to stray or disobey!

67
Rectangular box, *yun thitta*
Burma, Pagan, mid-20th century
Wood, lacquer, gold leaf; L 22 cm, H 11 cm
National Museums and Galleries on Merseyside
(Liverpool Museum), 50.4.162

This rectangular wooden box has a bevelled lid and is lacquered black

67

inside and out. The exterior surfaces, lid and four sides are all decorated in the *shwe zawa* gold leaf technique.[167] The draughtsmanship is both assured and delicate and of excellent quality. Since the box has never been used and has been carefully looked after, this type of decoration – so often impaired through wear – can be seen in pristine condition.

Each of the long sides of the box has a design known in Burmese as *balu pan gaik*, 'demon disgorging garlands', which derives from eleventh-century stucco decoration on temples at Pagan; ultimately, its origins are Indian.[168] Here the ogre has an unterrifying grin and a full set of teeth. The foliage is very boldly drawn. On the rectangular field offered by the top of the lid the *shwe zawa* artist has rendered an episode from the popular Indian epic, the *Ramayana*.[169] The scene is set around the hut of Rama and Sita in the mountains. Prince Rama is shown pursuing the Golden Deer through the

forest.[170] His brother Lakshmana is seen at top left hastening to his aid. His precious wife Sita steps over the protective lines that Lakshmana has drawn to protect her, and warned her to stay within. She holds her bowl from which to give alms to the mendicant (lower left), since this is her duty. Alas, the mendicant is none other than the demon-king of Lanka, Ravana, in disguise, who will seize her and carry her off to be his wife.

167 For a description of this technique, see pp. 38–9; for other examples, see cat. 8 and 69.
168 For references and bibliography to this subject, see cat. 58.
169 For the *Ramayana* in Burma and its use to decorate lacquer vessels, see cat. 65.
170 In the Burmese version of the story it is not Marica (male) but Ma Kanbi (female) who takes the disguise of the Golden Deer.

68

Thanbula is to sell the ring and thus ensure that they both have a comfortable life. Many years later Thanbula visits Kyanzittha, who had by this time become king of Pagan, and she introduces the king to his firstborn son, Rajakumar.[173] King Kyanzittha had long since forgotten his adventure with Thanbula and, in an effort to make up to both of them, he makes Rajakumar a prince and gives him a domain with thirty villages. This story is well loved in Burma as it demonstrates the good character of prince Rajakumar: he bore no grudges against his father, despite having been deprived of the title of crown prince.[174]

This box is unusual not only because it bears Hsaya Pyant's proud inscription, 'especially well-made, authentic and truly the best lacquerware', but also because he has 'signed' it with his brand mark – a tiger – on the top of the cover, and on the underside of the two internal trays.

171 For this story, see Bharadwaja 1959: 17.
172 Another, though slightly damaged, example of this type is in the collections of the British Museum: OA 1999.3-1.6.
173 The name, in Pali, means 'son of the king'.
174 We learn of the death of Kyanzittha from the Mya-zedi Inscription at Pagan; this was set up by Rajakumar in 1113. The inscription on each of the four sides of the stele is in a different language: Pali, Mon, Pyu and Burmese. See Lubeigt 1998: 216.

Alain Missorten

68

Betel-box, *kun it*

Burma, Pagan, workshop of Hsaya Pyant in the Taikkon ward, early 20th century
Bamboo, lacquer; H 24.5 cm, D 26 cm
OL 7-18, courtesy of the Missorten Foundation

The scene chosen for the decoration on the top cover of this fine betel-box suggests that the story of king Kyanzittha and prince Rajakumar will be illustrated on the rest of the box.[171] The lacquermaster goes on to do this by means of the convention of four 'windows' set into the side wall of the cover. Each scalloped cartouche shows one of the scenes from the story, and is framed by a scrolling floral design. Only two colours – orange and black – are used. The artist creates the effect of the viewer looking in at the scenes through the frames. The *yun* technique is used throughout.[172]

'King Kyanzittha and Prince Rajakumar' is one of the many legends of Pagan. The story is as follows. When Kyanzittha was still a soldier, and a bachelor, he had a brief affair with Thanbula, the niece of a famous hermit with whom he took shelter. By the time Kyanzittha has to move on, Thanbula is pregnant and as a keepsake he gives her his ring. He tells her that if the child is a boy, she is to bring it to him showing the ring; if the baby is a girl,

69

Flat betel-box, *kun it*

Burma, Prome, *c.*1900
Bamboo, lacquer, gold leaf; H 11 cm, D 21 cm
National Trust, Curzon Collection at Kedleston Hall, Derbyshire, no. 427

The foundation of coiled split bamboo for this lacquer and gilt cylindrical box is unusually thick and heavy. The interior and bottom of the box are red but the decoration around the sides and on the top of the lid is in the *shwe zawa* technique, in gold leaf and black line.

Around the side of the cover is a narrow frieze of floral design made up of large flower heads. A much deeper frieze runs around the sides of the box with a lobed wave-line over foliage, flowers and charmingly rendered birds. The main scope for the *shwe zawa* artist, however, is offered by the top surface of the cover, and he has filled it in masterly fashion with the key scene from the *Vessantara Jataka*, the last in the series of 547 stories of the previous existences of the Buddha.[175] In the story the Bodhisattva is the prince Vessantara, whose boundless generosity culminates in giving away his own two children to the cruel and greedy brahmin, Jujaka. Prince Vessantara is shown here in his mountain hermitage pouring water on the hands of Jujaka, thereby sealing the agreement. A large kite-shaped cartouche contains the caption to this scene:[176] 'Prince

Vessantara's son and daughter, Kanhajina and Jali, are given into the hands of the great brahmin, Jujaka.'

There is no other inscription and thus no maker's signature, but the box could be by the hand of Hsaya Pa of Prome who won a Third Prize and Bronze Medal for his gilt lacquered tray at the 1902 Indian Art Exhibition at Delhi.[177] Hsaya Pa of Prome was certainly renowned for *shwe zawa* work. Curzon was viceroy during the 1902 exhibition and took a keen (and some say an acquisitive) interest in quality craftwork. He may indeed have acquired the box in Delhi from Mr Felice Beato,[178] or equally during his viceregal visit to Burma in 1901. A label (not in Curzon's hand) beside the box in the Indian Museum at Kedleston describes it – confusingly – as 'Box and cover of gilt and lacquered wicker-work. From Prome. Burmese. (Shan States).'

Unfortunately, Prome is about 120 miles north of Rangoon and nowhere near the Shan States.

This box is similar in shape to betel-boxes of the shallow or flat type (see cat. 49 and 64), but has clearly been made and decorated purely as an art object, to be admired rather than used.

175 See Cowell 1985, vol. VI: 246–305.
176 Distinctive kite-shaped inscription cartouches, while not confined to *shwe zawa* work, are also seen on the harp, cat. 128.
177 See Watt 1904: 224.
178 For Beato, see cat. 1 and Singer 1998.

70
Water bowl, *yay khwet gyi*
Burma, Pagan, made by Hsaya Kaing, early 20th century
Bamboo, lacquer; H 19 cm, D 24 cm
OA 1998.7-23.2, gift of Mr and Mrs R. Isaacs

The *yun* decoration on this water bowl is in four colours: red, yellow, green and black. The scenes depicted in a deep frieze around the sides of the bowl are from the *Kusa Jataka* (for the *jatakas*, see p. 17). This *jataka* is no. 531 of the series of 547 tales of the previous lives of Gautama, the Buddha.[179] The story tells of the beautiful princess Papawati who, married by a ruse to the ugly prince Kusa, then runs back to her father's house. Kusa follows and tries many tricks to win her back. As chief potter, he throws a superb pot for her, but she smashes it; as master chef, he cooks her ambrosial dishes, but she rejects them.[180] These scenes depicted on the vessel are interspersed with no fewer than twenty-five captions on small palm-leaf shaped cartouches which name the characters, the scenes and the action. These captions effectively form part of the overall pattern.

The bowl was commissioned from the lacquer master by a lady, Ma Hla Hpyu, and four short cartouches set in a frieze of beasts and birds around the top of the bowl's sides declare that it is

69

70 (see frontispiece for a detail)

Ma Hla Hpyu's finest quality great bowl, made by Hsaya Kaing.

179 The *Kusa Jataka* is in Cowell 1895, vol. V: 141–64.
180 Although not depicted here, the eventual outcome is a happy one with the prince and princess living happily ever after.

71
Shrine, *hpaya khan*

Burma, probably from Mandalay, possibly the Royal Palace,181 mid-19th century
Wood, lacquer, gold, coloured and mirror glass, metal sheet, textile, palm leaf
Victoria and Albert Museum, IS 11-1969

This is one of the most important items of Burmese architectural art to survive outside Burma. It demonstrates several of the uses of lacquer illustrated in this publication: lacquer used to gild wood;

lacquer putty, *thayo*, used as a sculpting medium; lacquer used as a cement to hold coloured glass; lacquer used in the black-and-gold, *shwe zawa* technique; and lacquer charged with cinnabar to provide a brilliant red for the interiors of vessels as well as a contrast to the gold of most of the rest of the shrine. These methods of lacquer use are all combined here to produce an object that impresses immediately with its grandeur. It is made up of many parts: the Buddha image seated high up in the centre of the shrine; the gilded wooden shrine surrounding the image; the double-waisted throne, *palin*, on which the shrine is set; two betel-boxes with *hintha* covers and a figure holding a lamp, all sitting on a lower moulded base: and, set around the base, two

couches with figures of Sariputta and Moggallana, two vases for flowers, two bowls for offerings, two domed containers and a manuscript box with the manuscript in it.

The Buddha image is shown as a king with royal costume, marked particularly by the winged projections at knee, upper arm and shoulder level as well as by the *salwe*, the insignia of crossing bands over the chest.182 He is depicted with his right hand in the posture of 'calling the Earth Goddess to witness', *bhumisparshamudra*; the left hand is held flat, palm upwards in the lap. The central niche of the shrine is surrounded by a mass of carved and gilded woodwork, which sums up all that is remarkable about Burmese wood-carving.183 The most distinctive feature of nineteenth- and early twentieth-century work is the depth created by overlapping scrolls and floral elements. Nestling within these features, one on either side of the recessed niche, are small figures of celestials, honouring the Buddha. The mass of frothy scrollwork descends both around the central shrine and down over the first and second plinth. Its topmost part is a tiered umbrella, similar to the finial on a pagoda, the *hti*. Smaller umbrellas rise, lower down, above the side-panels of scrollwork.

Woodwork of this exuberant type has survived in Burma, but fire has taken a terrible toll. For instance, the platform of the Shwe Dagon pagoda was a mass of wooden buildings, many decorated with such tracery, especially around entranceways where it hung down in festoons filled with figured scenes.184 The fire that swept over the platform in 1931 destroyed twenty-one such structures, many of which, in the subsequent reconstruction, were replaced by decorative elements executed in cut metal, rather than the riskier wood. Elsewhere in Burma fine tracery work can still be seen at the Shwezigon Pagoda at Pagan, as well as

in the few surviving wooden monasteries in Mandalay; cut metal, however, is now much commoner.

The double-waisted throne with its mass of gilding, *thayo* work and inset glass spangles is clearly related typologically to the royal throne known from the palace at Mandalay and recorded by visitors such as Yule and Phayre.[185] Further royal associations can be inferred from the lower part of the double-waisted throne which is supported on small figures of lions; these are located in niches around the base and recall the Lion Throne of the Burmese kings. The presence of these lions, along with the magnificent quality of the entire structure and the history that is attached to it, has suggested to Lowry that the shrine was from the palace itself at Mandalay.[186] Further, on the platform are placed, to right and left, two stands holding betel-boxes with lids in the form of *hintha* birds (the Indian *hamsa*), a motif also associated with royalty. These are certainly very fine examples of an otherwise known type. Both the stands and the boxes are decorated in the *hmanzi shwe cha* technique.

Between the two boxes is a male figure, of wood and cut metal, lacquered and gilt. He holds up a lamp of European design. Lowry has suggested that this is either one of the Indian deities Brahma or Indra (Sakka), both of whom have a part in the life-story of the Buddha, or perhaps merely an unidentified *nat*.[187] Whoever it is, the striking use of a contemporary European feature within this otherwise very traditional Burmese design is remarkable but not unharmonious. The lowermost platform is again decorated with *hmanzi shwe cha* designs, and terminates in a magnificent outflowing of billowing elements supported by *garuda* figures crouching below.

Placed at the base of the shrine, in an arrangement the precise details of which are no longer known, are an array of objects, the most important of which are two couches, *tha lun*, made of lacquered and gilt wood and sheet metal. On each of these sit a monk, also of lacquered and gilt wood. These are the foremost disciples of the Buddha: Sariputta to his right and Moggallana to his left. They are depicted in typical Burmese monastic guise and in positions of eager listening (Sariputta) and adoration (Moggallana). The couches on which they sit, with their mattresses of red lacquer, are miniature versions of items often presented to monasteries.[188] This type of couch is, iconographically, also very similar to the type on which the Buddha is frequently shown at the moment of his entry into Nirvana. The couch is supported by legs shaped like lions, which kick their legs in the air in a similar way to the *nagas* that support the table from Stokesay Court (see cat. 33), a conceit frequently found in Burmese art of this period.

Also associated with the shrine are a group of vessels: two flower vases with handles in the form of rearing mythical animals and of the type normally placed on either side of or on an altar associated with a Buddha shrine (see cat. 181 for two modern examples); two vessels with domed covers, probably for holding offerings and decorated with free-standing figures which are perhaps to be taken as *nats* or *zaw gyi* (wizards); and two open-mouthed vessels decorated in the *shwe zawa* technique, also probably for offerings and decorated with cartouches of *nat* figures. The final element of this ensemble is a manuscript box complete with palm-leaf manuscript and wooden cover boards, and decorated in the red *shwe zawa* technique, the whole wrapped in a yellow cloth.

The history of this extraordinary group of Burmese objects is of some interest. As mentioned already (note 181), it was acquired by Lt.-Col. Raikes during the Third Anglo-Burmese War. However, following his career in Burma, Raikes retired to Porlock in Somerset and at his death left a large collection of Burmese objects to the Bristol City Museum and Art Gallery, including this shrine. For many years it was on display there, but in the mid-1960s it was sold, along with other items from the collection and in the wake of serious damage to the museum building during the Second World War. For a time it was in the hands of auctioneers before it was finally acquired by the Victoria and Albert Museum in 1969.[189] Given this 'prehistory', there must be an element of doubt as to whether all the loose items now presented with the main shrine originally belonged with it.

181 John Lowry says of the shrine (1972: 117), 'It was originally acquired by an army officer, Lt.-Col. F.D. Raikes, CIE (1848–1915); he took part in the final stages of the third Burmese war, which culminated in the capture of Mandalay in 1885. Raikes collected the group after the fall of the capital; about the turn of the century he brought it to this country, where it has remained ever since. According to documentation left by Raikes, the shrine came from the royal palace at Mandalay.'
182 For a discussion of the Buddha in the royal or 'Jambupati' form, see cat. 75.
183 This style was especially highly regarded during the colonial period. Watt's catalogue (1904) of the 1902 Indian Art Exhibition in Delhi illustrates a number of examples: see pp. 135ff. Four prizes for different items of Burmese woodwork were awarded at the exhibition and are listed in the catalogue, p. 139. For a discussion of Burmese woodwork, see Tilly 1903 and Fraser-Lu 1994, ch. 3.
184 See Win Pe 1972: 6 and 7.
185 Yule (1858: 82) says: 'This [the royal throne] was in character exactly like the more adorned seats of Gautama in the temples, and like that from which the High Pongyi preaches.'
186 Lowry 1974: 1. This discussion of the shrine, along with Lowry 1972 are the two main places of publication of this object to date.
187 Lowry 1974: 4.
188 See Fraser-Lu 1994: 101 for a photograph of one such couch.
189 I am grateful to Peter Hardie, formerly Curator of Oriental Art at Bristol City Museum and Art Gallery, for this information.

72

The Buddha, *manbaya*

Burma, probably Lower Burma, late 18th/early 19th century
Lacquer, gold leaf, shell inlay, wood; H 180 cm, W (at base) 123 cm
1826.2-11.1, gift of Captain F. Marryat

Hollow lacquer sculptures of this size are most unusual, especially in collections outside Burma.[190] The sculpture has a remarkable history as it has been in the British Museum since immediately after the First Anglo-Burmese War of 1825. Captain Marryat, who donated the sculpture to the Museum,[191] took part in the war, most of which was fought in Lower Burma (hence the suggested provenance for the sculpture). In later years he wrote a number of books, including a volume of reminiscences of his time in Burma. However, there is no record of this extraordinary image in those writings,[192] and by the time he displayed his other Burmese antiquities to the public in 1827,[193] this image was already in old Montagu House, the building that functioned as the museum prior to construction of the present building in the 1830s and 1840s. In that first building the sculpture was to be seen on the main staircase, close to the giraffes! It is described in the Museum's *Book of Presents* as 'A Colossal Figure of Gaudma, a Burmese deity from Rangoon'.[194] It is difficult to assess the importance of the provenance provided here as anything brought out of Burma after the campaign would have come 'from Rangoon'. In recent years it has been substantially conserved, and filled cracks in the dry lacquer are visible in many places.

The Buddha is depicted in the lotus position with his left hand in the posture of meditation. The right hand, however, instead of being in the usual earth-touching posture, *bhumisparshamudra*, so common in Burmese sculpture of the Buddha,[195] holds a small fruit or seed between the

72

thumb and the first fingers as if offering it to those who approach. There has been some discussion as to the meaning of this iconography, and in connection with another sculpture

where the Buddha holds a similar fruit, Zwalf has drawn attention to the fact that the myrobalan fruit has medicinal properties, that the 'Buddha as healer is an old and widespread concept...' and

129

that 'the "historical" Buddha is also recorded as having received a myrobalan fruit from the god Indra after the Enlightenment'.[196] The way in which the fruit appears as if being proffered to the devotee inclines the present authors to the first explanation, but there is no categoric evidence to support this.

The hands, and the less visible feet, are very large, a distinctive feature that should provide a clue as to date and region of manufacture, but presently does not. The robe, which covers the left shoulder but leaves the right bare, is scalloped along the edge where it lies directly on the chest, as well as more extravagantly where the end of the robe falls from the shoulder down towards the navel; the same design is seen where the robe falls down the back.[197] This wave design is picked up again where the robe falls below the knees and across the base. Again, these features are highly distinctive and should be diagnostic. Beneath on the plinth is a running scroll of leaves and full-blown blossoms. Below again is a row of small lotus petals. Four holes, two at the front and two at the back, puncture the plinth. These perhaps testify to the way in which the image was brought from Burma to England in 1825. The lower part of the plinth has been restored in recent years to enable the sculpture to be exhibited. The carved and lacquered wooden base, *palin*, was made for the sculpture in Mandalay in 1994.

Finally, the face with its withdrawn downward gaze is framed by the large ears and highly elongated lobes, the ends of which rest on the wide shoulders. The hair is made up of many tiny points modelled in *thayo*, while above rises the tall wooden *ushnisha*. These features of the hair and the *ushnisha* again recall the image in the Victoria and Albert Museum.[198] A thin band separates the hair from the face, a feature that becomes developed during the late nineteenth century, frequently being set with pieces of coloured glass.

190 The opportunity to publish another image of similar size here – cat. 73 – is remarkable. It is surely significant that both these dry-lacquer Buddha images were donated to the two museums concerned – British Museum and Exeter Museum – immediately following the First Anglo-Burmese War, in 1826 and 1827, respectively. The conclusion that they came from the same place in Burma is a tempting one. For the technique of dry-lacquer sculpture, see cat. 39.
191 Other items he gave include the large stone print of the Buddha's foot, 1826.2-11.2. A manuscript that also once belonged to him and is now in the British Library can be seen at cat. 83.
192 See Marryat 1840.
193 See Skinner's Journal.
194 I am grateful to Chris Date in the Archives Department for this reference. 'Gaudma' refers to Gautama, the Buddha.
195 For this more usual iconography, see cat. 73–6.
196 See Zwalf 1985: 165.
197 The scalloped edge to the robe is also seen in a smaller dry-lacquer Buddha image in the Victoria and Albert Museum (IS 21 & A-1970) illustrated in Lowry 1974: 17. It is dated 'Possibly 17th century', though without any corroborative information.
198 See note 197.

73
The Buddha, *hpaya*

Burma, probably from Lower Burma, late 18th/early 19th century
Lacquer, gold leaf, wood; H 143 cm, W ??
Exeter City Museums and Art Gallery, E321, given by Captain Truscott

Serenity, meditation and power are the attributes of the Buddha that are projected in this hollow lacquer image. The Buddha is depicted seated with the soles of the feet visible in his lap, with his left hand held in the posture of meditation, *dhyanamudra*, and the right in the commanding and frequently seen posture of *bhumisparshamudra*; the fingers are exaggeratedly long. The robe on the chest is plain except for the stole-like end that falls from the shoulder as if bisecting the body; it is, however, undecorated. Only over the crossed legs and beneath is the viewer more conscious of the rippling drapery. The face is approximately triangular reflecting the last remnants of the medieval style developed at Pagan where this was such a distinctive feature. The eyebrows are stylized and make an almost 'L'-shaped outline. Meanwhile, the decorated fillet between the forehead and the hairline, such a feature of the later Mandalay period (see cat. 77), is not yet prominent. Around the base is written, in English, 'Sitting Budh or Buddha. A Burmese Idol', presumably added after it reached Exeter.

This sculpture is clearly linked to that in the previous entry. Both were presented to the individual institutions by naval captains immediately after the First Anglo-Burmese War (cat. 72 in 1826 and this one in 1827), and for cat. 72 there is a good record of the donor's involvement in the war. For the Exeter sculpture, the history is less certain as there is no record of a Captain Truscott in the war, though there was a man of this name in the East India Company Army at the time – and he was both born and buried in Devon. We know from other collections, such as the Stuart Collection,[199] that Burmese artefacts were available in India at the beginning of the nineteenth century, so there may be no contradiction in assigning the acquisition of this Buddha image to the Truscott known from Devon.

The sculptures have many stylistic features in common. They are both made of hollow lacquer that has been coloured the same deep maroon and further decorated with gold leaf, now very fugitive. Both figures have very large hands; this is especially noticeable in the left hands held in *dhyanamudra*, which are almost identical. Also strikingly similar are the tall *ushnisha*, which are not only both made of wood and thus made separately, but also have the same shape. The drapery over and below the knees on the Exeter example is more realistic than in the British Museum example, but in both

74

The Buddha

Burma, perhaps central Upper Burma, probably 18th century

Lacquer, cloth, gold leaf; H 55.8 cm

OA 1880-250

The Buddha is depicted in that most typical Burmese way, seated in the lotus position, *padmasana*, with his right hand in the posture of *bhumisparshamudra*. The left hand is held in the lap, with palm upwards in the posture of meditation, *dhyanamudra*. His robe is shown covering his left shoulder with a lightly decorated edge hanging down the torso, while the right shoulder is left bare. This is the 'southern style' of wearing the robe, known throughout Burma and inherited from the practice of ancient Sri Lanka and southern India. The curls of the hair are indicated by rows of points, and this, as well as the fillet bound around the forehead, gives the whole hair arrangement the look of a close-fitting cap. Although the *ushnisha* is depicted in the way associated with the Mandalay period (1855–85), the fillet at the hairline is not yet the elaborate version found in the nineteenth century. Similarly, the end of his robe, hanging down over his chest, is not the cascade of billowing textile associated with the Mandalay Buddha images (see cat. 77), but is more restrained. Also the way in which the volume of the body, though not its details, remains clearly visible due to the robe's lack of pleating and decoration – such features of nineteenth-century depictions of the Buddha – links this serene image with the work of the earlier Pagan period.[200]

The technique of making dry-lacquer Buddha images was well known from the eighteenth to the first half of the twentieth centuries, and probably much earlier; for a discussion of this history, see cat. 39.

there is a dependence on pattern-making at the expense of realism. Study of these features, along with fieldwork in Burma, should eventually enable art historians to locate better the place of production of these images. However, at present we can only speculate using the fact of the British presence in Lower Burma during the First Anglo-Burmese War, and the proximity of that to the period when the images were donated.

199 See cat. 39 and 113 and Willis 1997. I am grateful to Mr L. Pole of Exeter Museum for information on this sculpture.

200 For instance, see Zwalf 1985: 161–2, cat. 222.

75
The Buddha, *minwut hpaya*
Burma, 18th or 19th century
Lacquer, cloth(?), wood, gold leaf and coloured
glass spangles; H 82.5 cm, W 30 cm
OA 1919.7-17.1

This type of Buddha image – crowned
and dressed in royal costume –
represents a special Southeast Asian
development of the iconography of the
Buddha. This was nowhere more
popular than in Burma especially in the
eighteenth and nineteenth centuries. In
this hollow dry-lacquer sculpture
decorated with gold leaf,[201] the Buddha
is shown not in monastic robes but in
Burmese royal costume with its mass of
winged elements at the knees, cuffs,
elbows, shoulders and crown, and
distinctively with the chains of office,
salwe,[202] crossing over the chest. The
Buddha is shown as a king.

Several elements have probably
combined to produce this type,
including the eastern Indian icon of the
crowned Buddha, which was understood
in Mahayana Buddhism to represent a
cosmic lord, and the royal ancestry of
prince Siddhartha. Crowned images of
the Buddha are known from Pagan
where the influence of Bengal and non-
Theravada Buddhism was clearly
substantial.[203] However, although such
elements may be part of the
background of this image, the
foreground must be taken by the
legend of Jambupati, whose name has
become attached to these Burmese
crowned images. This legend is
unknown in India, but records the
humbling of a boastful king, Jambupati,
by the Buddha. The story tells how the
Buddha has Jambupati brought before
him having first transformed himself
into a mighty king, set in an
incomparable palace. Witnessing the
Buddha in all his majesty, Jambupati
accepts the *dharma* and becomes a
monk.[204] This story seems to have been
very popular in Burma, as the number

of images illustrating it is considerable (see cat. 71 and 76).

The element of 'witness' in the story is perhaps linked with another part of the iconography, for the Buddha is here depicted with his right hand in the gesture of *bhumisparshamudra*, that is 'calling the Earth goddess to witness' that he has accrued sufficient merit in his previous lives to arrive, in the present life, at Enlightenment. While this gesture is one of the most popular in all Burmese sculptures of the Buddha (see cat. 74), it does here seem to have a special link with the story of Jambupati, as the Buddha, through this gesture, makes Jambupati witness the truth of the *dharma*, just as in the story of Mara.

On the reverse of the sculpture is a paper label, which unfortunately is no longer legible, other than the word 'Buddha'. The base has been repaired, probably before it entered the Museum in 1919.

201 For the method of producing dry-lacquer images, see cat. 39.
202 For use by king Thibaw, see Shway Yoe 1882: 474.
203 See Luce 1969, vol. 1: 184–7.
204 For a discussion and illustration of this legend, see Pal 1984: 241; Zwalf 1985: 165.

76
The Buddha, *minwut hpaya*
Burma, perhaps from the Moulmein region
Wood, lacquer, gold leaf; H 95.2 cm, W 30 cm
OA 1880-251 (probably ex-India Museum)

Just as the aesthetic of the Burmese court is summed up in the serene dry-lacquer Buddha image, cat. 74, so this image of the crowned Buddha represents a quite different ideal. Remarkably, the body is treated as if made up of a series of dramatically abutting planes – the smooth, svelte character of the sophisticated images of the court are far removed. The message of this Buddha image seems to be power and riotous pattern, not composure. In this respect, as also in a number of other features, the link between this sculpture and cat. 40 is most striking.[205]

The figure is set on a waisted plinth, which makes up a third of its total height. This plinth is a severe abstraction of the more usual lotus throne. The Buddha, who is shown crowned, sits bolt upright with his arms stiffly arranged, especially his right hand which displays the distinctive feature of a row of five rings, almost on the knuckle. The feet, which have an almost cubist aspect to them in their planal rigidity, are in the lotus position. The knees, remarkably, appear almost as bolsters, the ends beautifully decorated with geometric design. He is robed in royal attire, especially pronounced being the pointed epaulettes, the jewellery on the chest, the large barrel-shaped ear-plugs and the tall crown. The crown combines the notion of headdress (the tiered element) with *ushnisha* (the pointed element at the top). The dramatic scrollwork features attached to the sides of the crown are seen on Buddha images from the late Pagan period onwards.[206]

The whole sculpture has been lacquered prior to the application of gold leaf; this provides the maroon colouring. In a few places the surface of the lacquer has cracked to expose the wood beneath. The lips alone have a lacquer coating of a brighter colour.

It cannot be proved now, but this sculpture probably entered the British Museum from the India Museum of the East India Company which was disbanded in 1880.[207] There is a certain internal logic to this suggestion as Lower Burma came under British control earliest, Tenasserim in 1826 and the delta region in 1853. A provenance from the Moulmein/Martaban area would thus be compatible with an East India Company acquisition.[208]

205 Although much more sophisticated, an ivory sculpture in the British Museum, OA 1993.7-24.1, is iconographically very close to these two sculptures. It is currently on display in the Sir Joseph Hotung Gallery.
206 For wooden sculpture from Pagan with this feature, see Zwalf 1985: cat. 225 and 228.
207 For other items from the India Museum, and for bibliography, see cat. 50.
208 Upper Burma only fell to the British in 1885, after the closure of the India Museum.

77
The Buddha, *hpaya*
Burma, probably Mandalay
Wood, lacquer, gold leaf, glass, coloured glass spangles; H 147 cm, W 68 cm
OA 1923.1-9.1, bought from the collection of Sir Richard Carnac Temple

The serene face of this standing Buddha image is typical of the last school of sculpture in royal Burma. It is associated especially with Mandalay, the capital of the last two kings, Mindon (1853–78)[209] and Thibaw (1878–85). Indeed, this style is still in use for marble sculptures of the Buddha in the workshops of Tampawaddy, in the southern outskirts of the city. The distinct features of this style include the full, oval face with downward-gazing eyes (here inlaid with glass); the curving and elongated ear-lobes; the robe covering both shoulders; the cascade of folds of the robe over the chest, dextrously and exquisitely carved and so different from eighteenth-century sculpture (see cat. 39 and 74); the robe held apart by the outstretched arms, and the run of rippling pleats along the bottom edge, a *tour de force* of carving; the use of gold spangles set in lacquer; the broad fillet that separates the hairline from the face; and the large dome-shaped *ushnisha*.

Many of these features are of exceptional quality in this example, especially notable being the decoration of the robe edges (including where it descends down the back) with scrollwork made of small rolled out threads of *thayo*, among which are set

green and white glass spangles arranged in flower shapes. These designs in *thayo* with added glass spangles – *hmanzi shwe cha* – are the same as those seen on the covers of *parabaik* (see cat. 84–6). Both the sculpture and the *parabaik* are thought to have been produced in Mandalay in the second half of the nineteenth century. Also most unusual is the mass of green glass spangles set into the lacquer covering of the hair, which take the place of the points or snail-shells made from *thayo* found in earlier sculpture (see cat. 73). Originally this sculpture must have been covered in gold leaf which would have been laid on to the surface using lacquer. Fragments of the gilding still remain all over, but particularly on the edge of the robe. The Buddha holds, in his right hand, a myrobalan fruit, perhaps with the same medicinal connotation as that in the massive dry-lacquer Buddha image, cat. 72.

A large number of sculptures of this type have survived in museum collections, though few as fine as this.[210] Intriguingly, this sculpture once belonged to Sir Richard Carnac Temple before it entered the collections of the Museum in 1923.[211] How this great scholar/administrator came by it is unknown, other than that it was acquired in Hsenwi in the northern Shan States.[212] Temple's remarkable collection, which was located in his family house, The Nash, in Kempsey, Worcestershire, was sold in December 1922.[213] The sale included material not only from Burma but also from India and the Andaman and Nicobar Islands where he also served. The collections were regrettably dispersed, although a few items can still be identified in museum collections.[214] This sculpture of the Buddha may have been bought at The Nash sale by the British Museum, as from its museum registration number we know that it was in Bloomsbury in

January 1923 (i.e. the next month). The Museum's records only state that it was purchased from Knight, Frank and Rutley in London, though it was these auctioneers who carried out the sale at The Nash.[215]

209 It was king Mindon who moved the capital to Mandalay in 1857.
210 See Zwalf 1985: 163 and 168; also Chester Beatty Library 1991, cover photograph.
211 For biographical details on Temple, see Herbert 1991. Much of this paragraph is based on Herbert's essay.
212 The disparity between Mandalay – where the sculpture was surely made – and Hsenwi – where it was acquired – is not as remarkable as it sounds. Mandalay, throughout the second half of the nineteenth century, was the royal centre, and all tributary chiefs, such as those in the Shan States, would have travelled there and been in contact with it. The acquisition of a large Buddha image from Mandalay, in the latest style and for transport back to the remote hills on the Burmese-Chinese border, is entirely understandable within this context. Mandalay, to this day, remains the religious and cultural centre of Burma.
213 See Herbert 1991: IX for a photograph of Temple's museum at The Nash.
214 For instance, Temple's collection of wooden sculptures of the Thirty-Seven Nats are in the Ashmolean Museum, Oxford.
215 I am grateful to Sara Pimpaneau (Department of Ethnography) for the information linking this sculpture with Temple.

78

Leaf from a manuscript of *Abhidamma Pitaka* texts in Pali

Burma, 19th century
Ivory, with script of lacquer ink; each leaf: L 54.5 cm, w 8 cm
British Library Board, Or. 12010/K

This leaf comes from an incomplete manuscript of sections of the *Tika-Patthana* and the *Dhammasangani*, works of metaphysics from the *Abhidhamma Pitaka*. There are seven leaves in total. The finished manuscript must have been an object of *de luxe* quality, given the cost of the material and the difficulty of ensuring that the ink adheres to the ivory surface.[216] This type of script is known as *magyi zi*, 'tamarind seed', so called because the thick lustrous brown ink resembles the

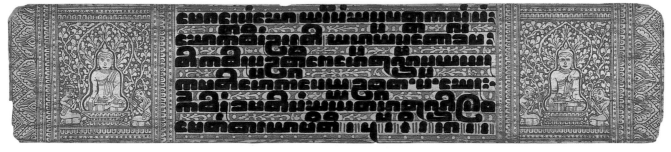

79a–c

seeds of this tree in their colour and glossiness. To produce ink of this consistency, lacquer sap is boiled and then thickened before it can be used to write with. While the letters of the text are written in dark brown lacquer, punctuation marks and some of the vowel markers are of red lacquer (made by the addition of cinnabar); this has subsequently been gilded.

The leaf is from the end of the manuscript (the reverse is now badly rubbed). The decoration here is made up of lotus petals at the edges (a common feature), and cruciforms within a stepped design, as well as other geometric motifs. This decoration is executed in the red-and-gold, *shwe zawa* technique[217].

216 Recorded in Herbert 1985: 173, cat. 244, describing another British Library manuscript with ivory leaves, Or. 14008.
217 For other examples of the red *shwe zawa*, see cat. 10 and 35.

79
Kammavaca manuscript in Pali, with coverboards

Burma, 19th century
Palm leaf, lacquer, wood (coverboards); L 56 cm, W 11.5 cm
British Library Board, Or. 12010/B

Burmese manuscripts generally follow their Indian prototypes in shape (long and rectangular), in material (palm leaf)[218] and in being kept together within wooden coverboards. This example illustrates all of these features,

80

81

82

with fine coverboards (a) decorated in the red-and-gold *shwe zawa* technique. The design is of five linked medallions containing *karaweik* birds; at the end of each are stylized lotus petals. The birds are arranged so that four of the five birds face each other while the central one faces upwards.

Kammavaca are manuscripts containing rules for correct performance of monastic ritual. These cover higher ordination (*upasampada*), admonitions to the newly ordained monk (*ovada*) and bestowal of new robes (*kathina*). These are the commonest, but others are concerned with electing elders, founding monasteries, and release from monastic vows. Depending upon which sections are included, the length of the manuscript increases or lessens.[219]

The first manuscript leaf (b) is decorated with a row of ten images of the Buddha seated beneath the Bodhi tree and in the posture of *bhumisparshamudra*, 'calling the Earth Goddess to witness that the merit gained in previous lives allows of Enlightenment'. This posture is the most frequently seen in Burma, and perhaps encapsulates the insistence on merit and its accumulation over many lives, which is at the base of so much popular Buddhism in Burma. The panels closest to the edges are again decorated with lotus petals, though here in the attenuated form well known from the stucco decoration on Pagan temples.

The next leaf (c) is the text proper and is written in the common nineteenth- and twentieth-century combination of five or six lines to the leaf in the square, Burmese 'tamarind seed' script usual for manuscripts of the *Kammavaca* (see cat. 78). Again there are panels at each end which show the seated Buddha beneath the Bodhi tree, but here attended by his disciples Sariputta and Moggalana, a figural assemblage also popular in Burmese sculpture.[220]

218 Made from the talipot palm, *Corypha umbraculifera*. For the method of production, see Zwalf 1985: 160.
219 See Zwalf 1985: 172, cat. 240; also Singer 1993.
220 For an example, see Zwalf 1985: 164–5, cat. 227.

80

***Kammavaca* manuscript in Pali**
Lower Burma, 18th century
Palm leaf, lacquer; L 53.5 cm, W 8.5 cm
British Library Board, Or. 1608, presented by Captain Conway Poole on 5 April 1878

These two folios are from a finely decorated palm-leaf manuscript made up of sixteen leaves. The opening leaf begins with the higher ordination text of the *Kammavaca*, the *upasampada*, and is followed by the admonitions to the newly ordained monk, the *ovada*, and the gift of robes, the *kathina*. There is lavish use of gold and the combination of this with red lacquer (they are applied using the *shwe zawa* technique) as well as the rich brown of the 'tamarind seed' lettering make a highly satisfactory visual scheme. As in cat. 79, use is made of the *karaweik* bird motif; here it appears in the margins in a near-mandala design of circles and stepped designs set within an overall square. Foreshadowing what is to come in the main body of the manuscript, the lines of text are divided from each other by vegetal scrollwork (not illustrated).

The main body of the text is made up of four lines per leaf, with intertextual decoration of small birds and foliage between the lines of script (illustrated). Each leaf is numbered on one side only in round script, using red lacquer.[221] This manuscript is notable for the richness of the decoration and the particular way in which the descenders (the small lines which hang down from certain letters) are drawn; the scribe is here exercising an element of individuality.

[221] In Burmese manuscripts folio numbers are indicated by a letter in conjunction with a vowel, starting with the first letter and running through each vowel, before moving to the second letter, and so on.

81
Kammavaca manuscript in Pali
Burma, 19th century
Palm leaf, lacquer; L 54 cm, W 9 cm
British Library Board, Or. 1609, presented by Captain Conway Poole on 5 April 1878

This unusual and striking manuscript depends for its success on the opposite effect to cat. 80: it is austere and unambiguous, whereas the earlier one is the epitome of complexity and luxury. Here the leaves have been covered with

a ground of deep red lacquer, on which the four lines of text have been written using black lacquer. Each leaf, of which seventeen survive, is numbered in black in the margin. As is customary, there are openings at the beginning and the end of manuscript where there is text only in the centre of the leaf. The thickness of the lacquer ink, the 'tamarind seed' script, provides an almost sculptural quality to the lines of text. The lack of coverboards probably explains the worn edges to all the leaves.

The fact that this manuscript came from the same source, Captain Conway Poole, as cat. 80 would suggest that they both came, originally, from the same part of Burma; certainly in both manuscripts there are the same distinctive descenders to some of the letters.[222] Whether the very unusual arrangement of black lettering on plain red leaves with no use of gold is a regional indicator is unknown.

[222] This manuscript and the previous one were perhaps acquired by Staff Surgeon Matthew Poole (1802–55), Madras Infantry, who fought in the Second Anglo-Burmese War (he was in Pegu in 1852). They were then probably donated by his son Lieutenant Matthew Conway Poole (born 1841).

82
Leaf from a *Kammavaca* manuscript in Pali
Probably southern Burma, 18th century
Cloth, lacquer paste, mother-of-pearl, gold; L 54.5 cm, W 10 cm
British Library Board, Add. Ms. 23939

Only three leaves of this visually startling manuscript written in Burmese ornamental square script survive. Both the mother-of-pearl inlay technique and the type of decorative motifs are Thai and include decoration to some of the individual letters as well as to the margins.[223] The flame motif can be found frequently in Thai decorative art. This combination of Thai forms with Burmese script could perhaps suggest an eighteenth-century date after the

sack of Ayutthaya in 1767, when Thai craftsmen of all kinds were brought back as captives to the Burmese capital.[224]

The method of production is distinctive: strips of cloth[225] are impregnated with a thick *thayo*, which gives the cloth a thickness and substance to carry the decoration. While the paste is still tacky, the mother-of-pearl letters can be set into it. The use of cloth in manuscript production is well known in the Burmese tradition (see cat. 10); what is unusual is the addition of mother-of-pearl. The three leaves survive in a wrapper of Chinese silk brocade. Five folios from a very similar manuscript are in the Chester Beatty Library in Dublin.[226]

[223] See Pothisoonthorn and Vorasart 1981. Among the examples of mother-of-pearl inlay illustrated are many items from a religious context, including manuscript boxes and chests – and even manuscript coverboards – but no example of a manuscript leaf. The use of cloth impregnated with lacquer sap for leaves may be a specifically Burmese trait.
[224] See Luang Phraison Salarak 1959: 50–51.
[225] This leaf has been published by P.M. Herbert in Zwalf 1985: 172, where the cloth is specifically described as 'discarded monastic robes'.
[226] See Chester Beatty Library 1991: 10–11, cat. 12 (ill.).

83
Leaf from a *Kammavaca* manuscript in Pali
Lower Burma, late 18th/early 19th century
Palm leaf, gold, lacquer; L 52.8 cm, W 7.4 cm
British Library Board, Add. 15290

This manuscript, of which six leaves survive, is unusual for several reasons. Firstly, the cursive round Burmese script is used, rather than the 'tamarind seed' script seen in other *Kammavaca* manuscripts (see cat. 10 and 81); secondly, the folios are numbered in black Burmese numerals, instead of Burmese letters; and thirdly, the marginal decorations of the Buddha seated in the earth-touching position,

83

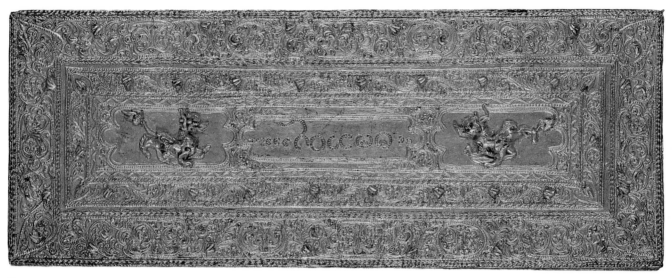

84

bhumisparshamudra, which appear on three faces of the six leaves, are executed in the black-and-gold lacquer *shwe zawa* technique, rather than the red and gold more often seen on manuscripts. These depictions of the Buddha are relatively crude, though lively, and the comparative size of the feet and hands links these images with sculptures of the Buddha.[227] The manuscript is kept within wooden coverboards, which are decorated in the red-and-gold lacquer *shwe zawa* technique.

Of importance for the dating of this manuscript is the fact that it was acquired by the British Museum in 1844 from the sale of the immense library of the Duke of Sussex.[228] Sussex in his turn had been given it by Captain Frederick Marryat who took part in the First Anglo-Burmese War.[229] This therefore provides a *terminus ad quem* for the manuscript, before 1826.

227 Although hugely larger, it may be significant that the dry-lacquer sculpture, cat. 72, which also came originally from Marryat and thus probably from the same part of Burma, also features very large hands and feet.
228 Lot 361. See Herbert 1989: 59–70 and especially 61–2 for the history of Marryat's manuscripts and the competition between London and Berlin to secure them.
229 For Marryat, see pp. 27–8 and cat. 72.

84

Paper book, *parabaik*, of a *Dhammathat* text in Burmese script and language: *Manugye Dhammathat* (abridged), part 1[230]

Burma, probably Mandalay, 19th century
Hand-made paper, lacquer, gold; L 43.6 cm, W 16.6 cm
British Library Board, Phayre Collection,[231] Or. 3447A

The *Dhammathat* of Burma is broadly based on the *Dharmashastra* literature of India, and deals with all manner of legal and prescriptive material.[232] The two examples, cat. 84 and 85, are

remarkable on account of the raised decoration made of *thayo*, which is found on the covers. In this example an effect of sumptuousness is produced by combining densely packed scrollwork, seen in the two bands around the central section, with a lavish use of gold. In the centre are three cartouches, the outer of which contain flying lions made of *thayo*, while in the centre is the word *Dhammathat*, written in raised and dotted lacquer putty; this indicates the type of work contained within the book, as if to provide information for a librarian.[233] The reverse cover is similar except that the central cartouche contains a cockerel rather than the word *Dhammathat*. The leaves of the *parabaik* are also gilded, indicating that this is a royal manuscript.

Decoration of this type is very fragile, and the near-pristine condition of both these manuscripts suggests that they were never used. Sir Arthur Phayre, to whom they both belonged, visited

Amarapura in 1855 and Mandalay in 1862 and 1866. Certainly on the first occasion he was presented with manuscripts by king Mindon.[234] On the actual occasion of the gift there is mention of 'other works' and a *Tipitaka* in the India Office Collection of the British Library was acquired from that source.[235] It is thus possible that these two very fine manuscripts with their juridical subject matter so suitable for a royal library – and indeed for the study of a colonial administrator – may have entered Phayre's possession at this time. There is almost a feeling to them that they were never meant to be used, as the decorative work on the covers would have so very quickly become cracked and broken. Perhaps they were prepared in the Burmese capital merely for presentation.

230 See also cat. 85, Or. 3447B, the second part of the same abridged law manuscript. This *parabaik* does not contain the full text of the *Manugye Dhammathat*, only some sections, but including some of the twelve decisions of Maha Thamada.
231 See cat. 85, note 2, for the Phayre Collection.
232 For early discussion of *Dhammathat*, see Sangermano 1995, ch. XXIV: 221–76. For a modern discussion of the code, see Okudaira 1986.
233 The actual title of the book is given at the head of the first page in gilded letters: *Manu manaw Dhaamma wilatha shwei myin dhammathat. Manu Akye pathama dwe.*
234 These included a copy of the 550 Jataka Tales (this copy is now in the Bibliothèque Nationale in

Paris), as well as chronicles; see Yule 1968: 107 and 111.
235 See Herbert 1989: 59–70.

85

Paper book, *parabaik*, of a *Dhammathat* text in Burmese script and language: *Manugye Dhammathat* (abridged), part 2[236]

Burma, probably Mandalay, 19th century
Hand-made paper, lacquer putty, gold, silver; L 44 cm, w 16.7 cm
British Library Board, Phayre Collection,[237] Or. 3447B

This concertina book or *parabaik*, along with its pair, cat. 84, illustrate the extraordinary virtuosity of the lacquerworkers' skill. All of the decoration on the two covers of this manuscript is made of *thayo*, which has subsequently been silvered and gilded. The scrollwork in the two bands around the central cartouches is made of tiny threads of *thayo*, which have been individually laid on to the cover surface. The cartouches in the centre contain four cranes (perhaps the birds known in Burma as 'paddy birds' or small egrets, *byaing*) which, like the lions and cockerel in the accompanying manuscript (cat. 84), are built up high above the surface of the cover. At the edges of the manuscript the silver has

become tarnished. A wooden panel with raised lacquer decoration now in the collection of the Victoria and Albert Museum shares with this manuscript the same use of bud-shaped motifs in the corner.[238]

The text of the manuscript is written in a fine round script using a steatite pencil which shows up clearly on the black paper.[239] This manuscript only has writing on one side of the concertina, and then, at each opening, only on one face.[240]

236 See also Or. 3447A (cat. 84), part of the same text.
237 For the Phayre Collection, see Herbert 1975: 62–70.
238 See Lowry 1974, pl. 39.
239 For the production of paper in Burma, see Scott and Hardiman 1900: 411. For other types of paper, see Fraser-Lu 1994: 289–90; also Koretsky 1991. For the use of *parabaik* in the Pagan period, see Than Tun 1988: 32.
240 Or. 3447A (cat. 84) has an almost identical layout, except that there are three openings on the reverse of the *parabaik*, which are lettered in large format.

85

86

86

Paper book, *parabaik*, of the *Mya Pakhet Daw Egyin hnint Luda Hlwegyin zon*

Burma, late 19th century
Burmese paper, lacquer, gold and glass spangles; L 40 cm, H 18.2 cm
British Library Board, Or. 14957

The back and front covers of this manuscript are a *tour de force* of the *hmanzi shwe cha* technique, lacquer relief decoration with small inset spangles of green and white reflective glass.[241] The central panel gives the title of the text in dotted raised *thayo* with vowel and final markers of great exuberance appearing above and below the consonants. Whether the near-roccoco scrollwork is a product of European influence or is of an indigenous type is not clear. However, the overall effect is one of great sophistication, an impression enhanced by the beautifully clear calligraphy of the manuscript itself, which is in Burmese, written in black ink surrounded by borders of gold scrollwork. This is a royal manuscript with fully gilded edges containing royal cradle songs and verse lullabies.

A *parabaik* with decorated covers of a very similar design is in the collections of the Victoria and Albert Museum.[242]

241 For other examples of this technique, see cat. 77 (sculpture) and 156 (vessel).
242 See Lowry 1974, pl. 45. It is dated 1881 and is said to be from Mandalay. It is described as a presentation volume of verses to be sung to the eldest daughter of king Thibaw and queen Suhpayalat, and thus very similar in content to this *parabaik*. It bears the registration number I.M. 127-1918.

87

Paper book, *parabaik*, of the Donations of King Mindon

Burma, probably Mandalay, 1857 (or immediately after)
Burmese paper, paint, red leather (covers); fully extended: L 683 cm, W 53.5 cm
British Library Board, Or. 13681

King Mindon ruled between 1853 and 1878 and this wonderfully illustrated folding manuscript records his acts of generosity to the monkhood in the first five years of his reign. Many of these gifts are made with, or decorated using, lacquer. The manuscript has recently been the subject of a study by Patricia

Herbert and the brief description that follows is based on that longer study.[243] The openings are divided into sequences of varying length, with each sequence illustrating one of the gifts as follows:

a) The gift of a monastery and a rest-house along with much else, including '50 offering trees', the wooden stands on which offerings to the monks were placed; these are in the background and include many lacquer-covered items – fans, umbrellas and offering vessels.
b) The offering of 100,000 oil lamps on the Irrawaddy. The royal set of golden betel vessels is placed in front of the king who sits on a European chair. Details of architecture and the helms of the boats would all have been decorated with lacquer and then gilded.
c) The king and queen offer a rich cloth to the Mahamuni pagoda. Rows of monks shield their faces with fans, while behind them are rows of 'offering trees' and in front of them many open stands, *daung baung kalat*, for holding further offerings. All the musical instruments as well as the helmets of the soldiers would have been decorated using lacquer (see cat. 126–8 for

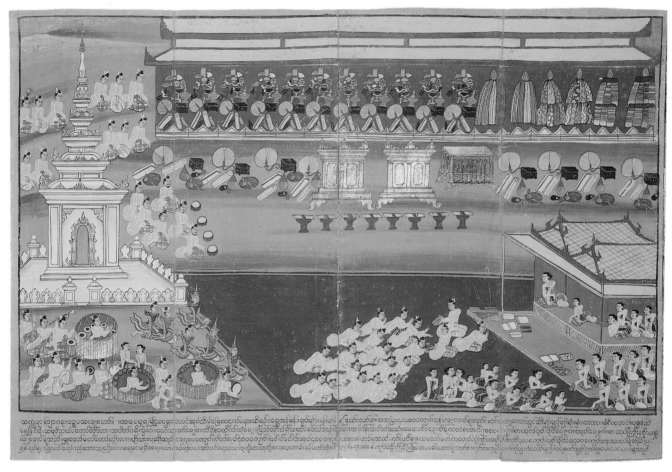

87

musical instruments and cat. 103 for lacquered helmet). In the final folio are rows of red-lacquered offering vessels.

d) The king makes offerings to the monks. Again, note the array of offering vessels.

e) The king offers a gilded and glass-set vane, presumably similar to the one depicted on the shrine. He offers cloth in the foreground, and is entertained by musicians and dancers, the latter wearing lacquer-decorated headdresses (see cat. 129). Behind are not only the usual 'offering trees', but also two cupboards specially for storing manuscripts, which would have been lacquered prior to gilding. Red-lacquered offering and food dishes abound (see illustration above and cat. 89–97).

f) The king offers a monastery and an assembly hall; the latter is specifically described as being decorated and coated with gold; these are seen to the left of the sequence. To the right, the royal party receive homage and an orchestra plays, while behind are the 'offering trees' with their mass of gold and red-lacquered objects – fan, umbrella, offering vessel, food container, betel-box.

g) The king offers two tanks with poles decorated with glass mosaic, and later donates six ponds 'on condition of no deaths', i.e. that all animal life is safe there – a reserve.

243 See Herbert 1998. Patricia Herbert has recently retired from the British Library where she was the Head of the Southeast Asia section of Oriental and India Office Collections. The authors are especially indebted to her for help with the manuscript catalogue entries.

88

Stand, *kalat*

Burma, early 20th century
Teak, lacquer; H 22.3 cm, D 23.2 cm
OA 1998.7-23.49, gift of Mr and Mrs R. Isaacs

These stands were used to place gifts, usually food, at an acceptable height above the ground in presentation ceremonies to the monkhood. They were once very common, and their use is depicted in nineteenth-century folding books (*parabaik*), in which royal donors had their donations recorded. One such book is cat. 87, which shows rows of similar *kalat*, each placed before an individual recipient monk. In 1797 Hiram Cox, sent to Burma as British Resident in Rangoon, noted the trays of sweetmeats were 'of wood painted red and gilt; they were about eighteen inches in height, the side supports little

the bowl are left plain smooth red.

Below the downturned ridge at the foot of the bowl, the piece is ringed with many bands or hoops of two distinct kinds. Some are moulded in *thayo* using a stone mould such as cat. 31. Long strips are lifted from the mould and wrapped round the vessel to stick in place while the last coat of lacquer is still tacky or they may be stuck down using lacquer sap as glue. These moulded strips derive their shape from the 'little turned balustrades' (*put lon*), which were part of the stand on which all offerings were placed, secular as well as devotional (see cat. 88). Long after stand and bowl were joined in a single complex vessel, the moulded bands persisted, simulating pegs or balusters of turned wood. The second sort of decorative bands are very narrow hoops of yellow bamboo. When the vessel was acquired, these hoops were covered by a thin layer of red lacquer – the article was unfinished. By gentle chipping, the lacquer was removed and the bright glossy yellow hoops were revealed, making a pleasant contrast with the red of the vessel.

88

turned balustrades, united at the bottom by a circular rim.'[244]

The top of the stand is formed of a single plate of teak, with a saucer-shaped depression to hold steady gifts contained in round-bottomed receptacles. It is joined to the solid hoop-shaped base by individually turned balusters (*put lon*). Lacquer is used as a glue, and the whole covered with black lacquer. There is an old repair to the top of the stand, which was collected from a large heap of discarded rubbish, deep in dust, in a corner of a village monastery in Pagan.

244 Cox 1821: 91.

89
Offering vessel, *hsun ok*
Burma, Shan States, Inle Lake, mid-20th century
Bamboo, wood, lacquer; H 60.5 cm, D 37.6 cm
OA 1998.7-23.150, gift of Mr and Mrs R. Isaacs

The rather flattened main bowl and moderately short spire are both typical of Shan *hsun ok*, vessels for carrying offerings, mostly cooked food, to the monastery. This vessel and its single internal tray are lacquered red. Beneath the finial knob of turned wood, the upper part of the lid is decorated with eighteen or more closely packed sharp ridges, each constructed from a narrow hoop of bamboo built up with lacquer before being coated red. The sides of

90
Offering vessel, *hsun ok*
Burma, Laihka, Shan States, early 20th century
Bamboo, lacquer, gold leaf; H 55.3 cm, D 38.2 cm
OA 1998.7-23.241, gift of Mr and Mrs R. Isaacs

This vessel, also from the Shan region, shares a similar shape with the previous example but has a different decorative scheme. The decoration includes a series of sharp ridges at the top of the lid below the finial knob of turned wood, and then, on the upper surface of the lid, a band of *yun* in black and silver (now tarnished). Broader bands of *yun* decoration, gilt and silvered, embellish the lower part of the lid and the bowl itself. Here some of the gold and silver colour has survived. Around the waist of the stem are two bands of

opposite: 89

90

91
Offering vessel, *hsun ok*
Burma, Shan States, early 20th century
Bamboo, wood, lacquer, gold leaf; H 557 mm, D 395 mm
OA 1998.7-23.170, gift of Mr and Mrs R. Isaacs

The broad, flat-topped body of this vessel and its moderately short spire are typical of Shan *hsun ok*, as is the gilded relief decoration. This consists of floral scrolling and flower heads formed from tiny strands of *thayo*. This is rolled out into little 'worms', which are cut to the length required, lifted with a tool of bone or horn and stuck in place on the still tacky lacquered surface of the vessel. When dry, the whole is given a thin coat of lacquer, usually red, as a foundation for gilding. The finial of the spire is of turned wood, stuck in place with *thayo*.

Such vessels were owned by well-to-do families and used for taking gifts of cooked food to the monastery.[245]

245 A similar example, in the Taunggyi Museum in the southern Shan States, is illustrated in Fraser-Lu 1985: 126, fig. 148.

92
Offering vessel, *hsun ok*
Burma, late 18th or early 19th century
Wood, lacquer; H 51 cm, D 32.5 cm
OL 4-262, courtesy of the Missorten Foundation

The origin of vessels of this distinctive shape is not clear, though an example in the Mandalay Museum suggests, though does not absolutely prove, central Burma. The function is, however, the same as other *hsun ok*.

The base is very low compared to other, later and more common *hsun ok*. This shape is a characteristic feature of the second Ava period (1763–83), as also are the large globes in the spire.[246] The application of black lacquer has been overlaid with several further layers of lacquer which have been coloured with vermilion. Where this has worn away a 'negoro' effect has

low relief made of moulded *thayo*. The lower band is of stylized stars or flower heads, while the upper band simulates the little turned wood pillars or balustrades which in the eighteenth and nineteenth centuries used to support

the tray top of gift stands (see cat. 88). The combinations of gold and silver work point to Laihka as the place of manufacture (see cat. 161).

92

93
Offering vessel, *hsun ok*
Burma, probably Kyaukka near Monywa, early 20th century
Bamboo, wood, lacquer; H 68.5 cm, D 29 cm
OA 1998.7-23.118, gift of Mr and Mrs R. Isaacs

This vessel is made of six parts, which fit neatly into each other. All are lacquered black outside and red inside. The point of the spired lid is made of turned wood. Such plain blackware was made in the large village of Kyaukka near Monywa in Upper Burma.[248] Most Kyaukka ware is robust (see cat. 155), but there is a slender *hsun ok* similar to this, acquired in 1900, in the collection of the Cambridge University Museum of Archaeology and Anthropology.[249]

Such vessels would be used by well-to-do families on festival days to carry offerings of cooked food to the monastery. In Burmese they are known as *mingala ok*, festive vessels.

248 For a description of the lacquer workshops at Kyaukka, see *Burma Gazetteer, Lower Chindwin District, 1912*.
249 Fraser-Lu 1985: 117, fig. 133.

94
Offering vessel, *hsun ok*
Burma, probably from Kyaukka, late 19th century
Bamboo, lacquer; H 73.2 cm, D 36.3 cm
OA 1998.7-23.89, gift of Mr and Mrs R. Isaacs

This imposing vessel has a finial knob of turned wood, but is otherwise made entirely of coiled bamboo, lacquered black. It lacks an internal tray but has a rich cinnabar red interior. Externally, narrow hoops or bands of split bamboo are the only decoration. There are nineteen of these which have been minutely notched to produce repeating patterns like poker-work, in chequers, chevrons or zigzags. There are also bands of plain, unnotched bamboo, which dramatically set off the notched decoration, the whole a *tour de force* of decorative art.[250] Each of the notched

been produced.[247] The vessel is of teak and has been made using a *put khon*, or lathe of the type still commonly used in Burma. Working wood on a lathe is a technique that has been known in Burma since at least the Pagan period, and the skills are now well honed (see Fraser-Lu 1994: 12, 13, 103).

246 The authors are grateful to U Win Maung (Tampawaddy) for this information.
247 A further example of this effect of chance differential wear is seen at cat. 4. The term 'negoro' is borrowed from the Japanese lacquer tradition.

Alain Missorten

93 (exploded view to show assembly)

bands must have been prepared before being fixed in place using lacquer sap as a glue. The whole process was incredibly time-consuming, but the overall effect is enviably rich and restrained. The lower part of the vessel, the stand, is further decorated in thick moulded panels, imitating individual pegs of wood, *put lon*.

The hoops or bands of plain unlacquered or notched bamboo must long ago have been the only technique for decorating unicoloured lacquer vessels. Even today in Karen areas and in Laos bands or little slivers of bare bamboo or palm leaf mid-rib are inlaid in black lacquer boxes.[251] With the introduction of the technique of colour-filled engraved patterns, *yun*, from Thailand some three or four hundred years ago, the old plain and notched bamboo hoops were simulated by the *yun* engraver (see cat. 5, 45 and 70).

250 For an example of a *hsun ok* of similar, though less grand type, also thought to be from Kyaukka, see cat. 94 and note 249. The present example combines the plain black and exposed bamboo of more usual Kyaukka vessels with the rarer notched decoration.
251 Examples in the Isaacs collection (British Museum) are OA 1998.7–23.155 (Karen) and cat. 154 (Lao).

95
Offering vessel, *hsun ok*
Burma, Pagan, mid-20th century
Bamboo, lacquer; H 39 cm, D 19.5 cm
OA 1998.7-23.16, gift of Mr and Mrs R. Isaacs

Four parts make up this vessel: the stand, which is integral with the lower part of the bowl; the lid with its spire; an internal tray within the bowl; and a detachable finial in the shape of a cup. The whole vessel is lacquered red, and the decoration consists of colour-filled *yun* in a simple floral pattern, *pabwa*, in green on the red ground. Bands of *pabwa* ring the bowl, with narrower bands on the spire and foot.

Such vessels were made for families to carry offerings of food to the monastery. Smaller ones were placed in the domestic shrine or 'Buddha shelf', *payazin*, on the eastern wall of the home. The present vessel, intermediate in size, could have served both purposes. A group of miniature *hsun ok* (cat. 98) shows the types made expressly for the domestic shrine.

94

95

96

Offering vessel, *hsun ok*, with a betel-box in the base

Burma, southern Shan States, early 20th century
Bamboo, lacquer; H 47 cm, D 23 cm
OL 2-320, courtesy of the Missorten Foundation

Uniquely this vessel combines a two-tray betel-box within the lower stand, along with a sub-spherical *ok khwet* or round *hsun ok* above. The whole of the exterior is covered in moulded *thayo*. Around the base and on the stem are thin strips of *thayo*; those around the stem imitate the individual pegs of wood, *put lon,* often seen on *hsun ok* and which hold the structure firm. Separating these two areas of vertical moulded *thayo* is a sloping surface covered with a different pattern, as if imitating rice grains. This decoration also covers the bowl and lid, higher up. The hidden container is elegantly decorated with a 'wave' design. Further up the structure, the offering bowl itself has a single tray.

The bowl shows traces of decay similar to an example in the Isaacs

96a

96b

collection,[252] where this effect is believed to have been caused by a chemical reaction from something stored in the vessel, perhaps sesame seeds which would leave a pattern similar to the ones seen. In the case of this vessel, in the collection of the Missorten Foundation, there is also the possibility that this is insect damage; only laboratory tests will decide this. However, lacquer has traditionally been used to protect against such damage. The protective property of lacquer sap was commented on from the time of the earliest contacts between Europe and this part of Southeast Asia. The seventeenth-century Jesuit, Father Tachart, when living at the Thai court at Ayutthaya described how white ants were a threat to the bibles and other manuscripts of the mission. In order to protect them, he coated the books with lacquer.[253] Later, another missionary, Father Sangermano, who was resident in Ava, refers to a tree called *chien* from which a varnish is extracted and which, besides giving a beautiful lustre or vividness to wood or paintings, especially when mixed with colours, also preserves from decay.[254]

252 OA 1998.7-23.55.
253 See Tachart, *Reis van Siam door de Vaders Jesuieten en in't Frans beschreeven door den Vader Tachart*, Utrecht 1687. For the same reason Burmese manuscript chests (see cat. 99–102) are also coated with protective lacquer.
254 See William 1883: 159.

Alain Missorten

97
Offering vessel, *hsun ok*
Burma, Shan States, Inle Lake, early 20th century
Wood, lacquer; H 22 cm, D 9.8 cm
OA 1998.7-23.259, gift of Mr and Mrs R. Isaacs

This Intha vessel of turned wood has a tightly fitting cover or lid, also of turned wood, which is shaped like a tall cone. The decoration consists of notches cut in the ridges of the wood turnery to produce a saw-tooth effect. This contrasts pleasingly with the smooth sides of the conical cover. The whole vessel is lacquered red, except for a band of black round the waist or stem.

The function of such vessels in Intha homes is not known for certain, but the stupa-like shape is evidence for devotional rather than merely domestic use. Most probably it was made for the home shrine, where the image or images of the Buddha sat.

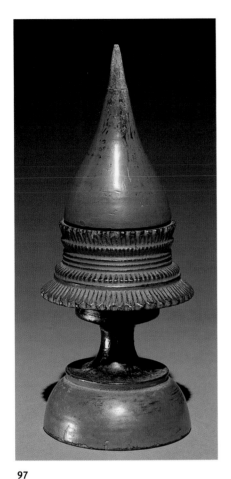

98
Group of miniature offering vessels, *hsun ok*

Burma, early 20th century
Wood, lacquer, gold leaf; H (average) 21.5 cm, D (average) 9.5 cm
OL 1-A-I, courtesy of the Missorten Foundation

Miniature *hsun ok* are traditionally used in Burmese domestic shrines for holding items that are offered to the Buddha image invariably located there (see also cat. 97). Other offerings may include flowers and fruit. These containers may also double up to hold small items of value that can safely be placed inside them. Domestic shrines are usually built into the side wall of the house and are the focus of daily devotions.

This group demonstrates the remarkable sense of design that the Burmese wood-carver brought to his task. Some of them replicate exactly the shape of the larger *hsun ok*, while others such as the gilded example are completely different.

Alain Missorten

99
Manuscript chest, *sadaik*

Burma, probably Pagan, early 19th century
Wood, lacquer, metal hinges and lock; H 60 cm, L 121 cm, W 59.5 cm
OL 5-74, courtesy of the Missorten Foundation

It is most unusual for a manuscript chest to be decorated in the *yun* technique, as is this one, and for the decoration to be on the top as well as on the four sides. The chest is made of six pieces of solid hardwood, which still bear traces of the saw. The four side panels have been nailed to the bottom panel and at a later stage glued with a tarry substance that may perhaps be lacquer mixed with sawdust. The cover hinges and square nails without heads are made of wrought iron and are tooled in a way similar to those found on seventeenth-century European chests,[255] but when they were fitted is unclear. 'V'-shaped staples with rings that still survive in the lid of the chest may also have once operated as hinges. There is a copper lock, which clearly replaced an earlier one. The chest

97

99

contains the usual small box (top right-hand side) for storing items linked with manuscript reading, such as the wooden spatula for turning the manuscript leaves. The inside has been protected from insect incursion with a coating of red lacquer, while the outside decoration has a brown lacquer base.

The story of Rama, known in Burma as the *Yama Zat Daw*,[256] is used as decoration for the box, and is executed with distinct Amarapura features.[257] The small elements depicting different scenes that are typical of the Ava period are replaced here by one big scene similar to the compositions of the Ratnakosin period of neighbouring Thailand.[258] Every possible space has been used. The wooden palace constructions sometimes appear three-dimensional, creating the illusion of perspective, and human figures are elegant and refined in their costumes

and expressions rather than stereotypes. Hair fashions of the women reflect an Amarapura date for the chest, as perhaps also does the device of using jungle animals and bending palm trees to separate different scenes. Certainly the lack of any inscriptions telling us who made it or providing captions for the story indicates a pre-1900 date. Also seen are slightly *risqué* elements such as the monkey-lieutenant of Rama, Hanuman, inspecting the breasts of a lady in the palace of Ravana, while he searches for kidnapped Sita.

The story starts on the cover of the chest where Rama is depicted as he arrives in the realm of king Janaka. He is shown participating in the archery contest and then winning the hand of Sita. On the front panel of the chest Rama goes into exile, along with Sita and his younger brother Lakshmana.

Also shown here are their wanderings in the forest and the approach by the ogress, Shurpanakha. Rama is unimpressed by Shurpanakha and does not respond to her declaration of love. She demands revenge and soldiers are sent to teach Rama a lesson. Rama destroys the thugs but is diverted by the appearance of the Golden Deer. The story continues on the right-hand panel where Rama and Lakshmana are depicted with the Golden Deer. This is followed by the encounter with the monkey-king Sugriva and the fight between Rama and Bali.[259] In the meantime Ravana, the brother of Shurpanakha, kidnaps Rama's wife Sita and carries her off in his aerial chariot. The panel on the back of the chest shows the monkey-king Sugriva sending out his monkey army and Hanuman penetrating Ravana's palace in his search for Sita. The left-hand side shows Hanuman finding Sita in the palace garden where he tells her that Rama will come with an army to rescue her. Interestingly, the final scenes of the epic – the defeat of Ravana by Rama and his army, and the triumphant return to Ayodhya where he is crowned king – are not depicted.

Yun embellished *sadaik* are exceptionally unusual, as most manuscript chests are decorated using the *shwe zawa* or *thayo* techniques (see cat. 102 and 100–101 respectively). The subject matter is also extremely rare as most monastery manuscript chests are decorated – understandably – with scenes from the Life of the Buddha or scenes from the *jatakas*. Could this chest perhaps have had a secular rather than a monastic context originally? Might it have been commissioned especially to hold manuscripts of the *Ramayana* and have stood in a royal, rather than a monastic library? Also very unusual is the fact that the chest has been decorated on all four sides a well as on the top; clearly it was to be seen from all sides. Iron rings on the left and right sides of the chest facilitated carrying.

255 See Hoffman 1990: 30–31.
256 For the Burmese version of the *Ramayana*, see *Myanmar Encyclopedia* 1970: 75–8. See also Singer 1989; Singer 1995: 23. For a discussion of the *Ramayana* in Burma, see cat. 65.
257 The style associated with the city of Amarapura only flourished for a short period at the end of the eighteenth and the beginning of the nineteenth century. It was a period of considerable external warfare, both with Thailand and the emerging power of the British. The styles of this period are still little known, but see Chew 1999.
258 See Boisselier 1976.
259 Why this later episode is shown here is unclear. In the Indian original the scenes in the monkey kingdom are part of the journey to Lanka to find captive Sita. The inscription of this important item is only an initial one. The chest will surely benefit from greater study in the future.

Alain Missorten

100

Manuscript chest, *sadaik*
Burma, 19th century
Wood, metal hinges and lock, lacquer; H (including stand) 111 cm, L 108 cm, depth 72 cm
National Trust, Curzon Collection at Kedleston Hall, Derbyshire

This manuscript chest, which is one of three at Kedleston, is of particular interest, as it is still united with its base. In Burma such chests invariably stand high up off the ground, away from the harm of insects or water.[260] However, the stand and the chest are made separately and they frequently do not survive together, especially among those that came to Britain in the luggage of returning Burma-hands.[261] After all, a chest is useful for packing, but a stand only gets in the way. One other example exists in the Victoria and Albert Museum, but these three in Derbyshire, acquired by Curzon during his viceroyalty (1898–1906) either from the Indian Art Exhibition at Delhi[262] or from his tour of Burma in 1901, represent rare examples outside Burma.

The chest is decorated in plain red lacquer at top and bottom. The panels of the chest itself are covered in relief work, *thayo*, which has then been gilded. Considering the use of these chests, it is not surprising that side panels illustrate episodes from the Life of the Buddha. On the long front panel is the Great Departure, when prince Siddhartha (the future Buddha) abandons his life of palace luxury and determines to seek Enlightenment. The three spires of the palace building are shown clearly in the centre of the panel, the riderless horse at bottom right, and the prince, seated on his faithful horse, leaving the palace at upper left.[263] The

100

101

panel to the right continues the story and we see the prince riding through the forest, jumping the Anoma river and then finally renouncing the world by cutting off his tresses of long hair indicative of his secular life. From now on he will live the life of a shaven-headed ascetic. The third panel (to the left as you face the chest) shows the culminating moment in the Buddha story and the one most frequently depicted in Burmese art, the Enlightenment. Although no Bodhi tree is shown, the hand-posture of the seated Buddha, *bhumisparshamudra*, is clear.[264] Within an architectural setting monks stand on either side of him,

while all around celestials acknowledge him, some with offerings of flowers which they shower down upon him. Around all three of these panels are bands of scrolling vegetation.

260 See Ferrars 1901: 209 for a very grand example on a large and impressive stand.
261 For an example that has lost its stand, see cat. 101. British soldiers called these chests 'pongyi [i.e. monk] boxes'.
262 See cat. 52.
263 Clearly visible in both these depictions of the Buddha's horse are the saddle panels that are exhibited at cat. 104.
264 See cat. 75 for further discussion of this hand position and the story it evokes.

101
Manuscript chest, *sadaik*
Burma, early 20th century
Teak, lacquer, traces of gold leaf; H 64.5 cm, L 121 cm, depth 66.5 cm
OA 1998.7-23.67, gift of Mr and Mrs R. Isaacs

Manuscript chests were used to store palm-leaf manuscripts in monasteries, and were often elaborately decorated in lacquer relief-work and gilt (cat. 100). This example is strongly constructed of teak, which has been lacquered black and retains traces of the original gilding on the *thayo* relief decoration. The scenes depicted cover the front and sides of the chest. They are from the Life of the Buddha: on the front of the chest, top left, the Great Departure, prince Sidhartha leaves the palace to become an ascetic. In the centre his wife, the princess Yashodhara, lies asleep with their baby son Rahula; the future Buddha takes a last look at them, peeping through the bed curtains. On the right are shown three of the 'four sights' that prompted Siddhartha's decision to renounce royal luxury – an old man, a sick man and an ascetic mendicant. The fourth sight – a dead man – is not shown. On the left side of the chest, as you face it, is the *shinbyu*, the cutting of the topknot of hair. At the top right Sakka, king of the *nats*, and his consort are shown collecting the Buddha's hair as it floats up into the air. Below, waves represent the river that the Buddha's faithful horse Kanthaka is not allowed to cross. At the bottom right the horse goes sadly off (to die of a broken heart).

The scene on the right side is less obvious to interpret, but probably shows, upper left, the seated Buddha with an alms bowl in his lap, preaching to his five former ascetic companions; they honour him with hands held in the posture of adoration. In the centre, and taking up most of the space of the panel, is a palace set within a fortification wall. The palace is depicted using the traditional convention of three tiered towers, *pyathat*, where a dancer and harpist perform. However, at bottom left people leave the city through a gate and do homage before the Buddha, seated at bottom left. The palace scene and the scene of adoration at the bottom left perhaps illustrate the story of the conversion of Yasa, which follows on immediately after the scene of preaching to the five companions.

This interpretation has the advantage of continuing the sequence of scenes from the Life of the Buddha seen on the other two panels, but the lack of *ushnisha* on the monk figure with the

alms bowl, must throw some doubt on this.

A comparison between this *sadaik* and cat. 100 is instructive, for although certain elements repeat, the actual scenes from the Life of the Buddha which are chosen for illustration are not always the same (the Great Departure and Renunciation are shown on both, but there is no common third scene).[265]

[265] For a general discussion of *sadaik*, see Fraser-Lu 1984.

102
Panel from a manuscript chest, *sadaik*
Burma, probably Pegu, late 18th or early 19th century
Wood, lacquer, gold leaf; H 74 cm, L 163 cm (both excluding European wooden frame)
OA 1995.4-5.1, Brooke Sewell Fund

This panel is decorated in the *shwe zawa* technique[266] and is a rare and magnificent example of the type. Set within a border of open lotus blossoms, it is decorated with scenes from the *Mahosadha Jataka* which are placed in a contemporary Burmese setting, thus providing the viewer with a palimpsest of Burmese life prior to 1850. As a single panel from what must once have been a most impressive and remarkable chest, one can only wonder at the overall effect of the complete item.

The identification of this panel as the front element of a manuscript chest, *sadaik*, is based on its shape, its inscription and also on the presence in the back surface of the panel, at the top right-hand corner, of a rectangular slot cut into the wood. This surely marks where the small rectangular box was located in which page-turning spatulas and other manuscript equipment were kept. This would have been attached to the front panel and its presence helps confirm the function of the object. Such boxes are common in manuscript chests, and there is an

example in the Isaacs collection (see cat. 101).

Monastic life is dependent on the possession of manuscripts, so that chests to contain them are essential items of monastery furniture. They are made of heavily lacquered teak and consequently the manuscripts stored inside are protected both from the humid climate and from insects. Typically, they are set on stands, raised up above the floor, as is appropriate for chests containing scriptures.[267] Many chests survive,[268] but few bear decoration of this grandeur, especially as *thayo* decoration on the exterior, rather than *shwe zawa*, is more common; this may, however, be partly explained by the robustness of *thayo* decoration compared to the fragility of *shwe zawa*, which is easily rubbed and damaged. An example of a chest with *shwe zawa* decoration in the British Museum, Department of Ethnography, is much smaller and of lesser quality.[269]

The date of the production of the panel is unknown. However, its history in this country indicates a date of at least pre-1850, as it has descended through the same Scottish family since it was acquired by their forebear during the Second Anglo-Burmese War (1852). Considering its function and the Buddhist nature of the decoration, it is very unlikely to have been made for him, so a date some time earlier than 1852 is most likely. The serviceman from whose family the panel came, was stationed at Pegu and it is for this reason that we have suggested that it was produced there. Given the geographical theatre of the Second Anglo-Burmese War, a provenance in Lower Burma, if not actually Pegu itself, is most likely.[270]

The panel is remarkable not only on account of the large number of scenes shown on it and the quality of the *shwe zawa* lacquerwork, but because of the inscriptions it bears. These are of two

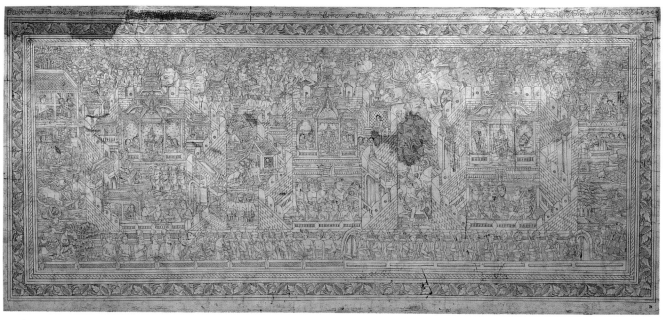

102 (see also pp. 8–9 and back cover)

types: the inscription along the top of
the panel in large characters; and the
more than fifty captions in more cursive
script that accompany the different
scenes. The inscription at the top deals
with the donation of the panel.
Unfortunately, it has been damaged
(this is clear at the top left-hand corner)
and the position where one would
expect information about the date of
the *sadaik* is lost. This damaged section
has been repaired with lettering that
just repeats what appears immediately
following the break. The fact of the
copying to make it seem intact and the
inexact quality of the copying itself
make it likely that the repair was done
after the panel came to Britain. The
inscription following the break reads:

> The lacquerwork has been completed
> by the lady wife of library donor Ko
> Tha Kaung of Hpo Thein Tan village.
> This deed of merit is done by library
> donor Ko Tha Kaung of Hpo Thein
> Tan village, his wife Ma Hpu,
> daughter and all their family with the
> aim of attaining Nirvana. We share
> the merit with all celestial and
> human beings and may this good
> deed cause them to call out in

approval 'Well done' [*thadu*].[271] May
we, on account of our deeds of
merit, attain Nirvana where all
defilements are extinct. May we
obtain the celestial eye by which we
can see the cycle of rebirth, the
destiny of beings and the process of
extinction of all the defilements.'[272]
The *jataka* illustrated here is the
Mahosadha Jataka, the fifth of the
Mahanipata, the Ten Last Great Jatakas
of the *Jatakatthakatha*.[273] These ten are
enormously popular in Southeast Asia
and are both more widely known and
more frequently represented in the
decorative arts than any of the other
Jataka Tales.[274] *Mahosadha Jataka* is
no. 546 in the standard Pali listing of
the Jatakas, but is 542 in the sequence
found in Burma, both in antiquity and
today.[275] As the narrative depicted on
the panel begins part way through the
jataka, we may speculate that the first
part (the prophetic dream of king
Vedeha, the miraculous birth of
Mahosadha [the Bodhisattva] and his
early wisdom demonstrated in a series
of judgements) was shown on one of
the side panels of the chest, while the
other side panel would have shown the

final scenes in the story (the
confrontation between king Culani and
the Bodhisattva, and the triumph of the
latter).[276] The backs of manuscript
chests were, almost without exception,
not decorated,[277] though it is possible,
with such a magnificent example as
this, that there were also scenes
depicted on the lid.

The narrative of the *jataka*, briefly
told, is as follows. (Text in brackets
refers to elements in the panel that can
be identified either from knowledge of
the story or from the inscriptions on the
panel. The Burmese convention whereby
scenes in the same locale are depicted
together irrespective of their
chronological place within the narrative
creates some problems of identification.
For ease of identification, the reader
should note that three palace buildings
are depicted in the panel: left, that of
king Vedeha at Mithila; centre, that of
king Culani at Uttarapancala; right, the
magical palace of Mahosadha.)

Mahosadha is tested by the king
who tells him to find a jewel, which
is seen in a lake (shown as a square
tank at top left). In fact the jewel is
hidden in an over-hanging palm-tree

and is merely reflected in the lake; the Bodhisattva quickly understands this and the jewel is recovered (figure climbing in the palm-tree above the water). The Bodhisattva encounters the four sages at the court of king Vedeha of Mithila where riddles are asked by the king (palace building at left of panel). He then meets Amara, later his wife (far left of panel where they are shown asking each other riddles both verbally and using hand gestures). The evil sage Kevatta brings the armies of India against Mithila, but is defeated through the cunning of the Bodhisattva (armies with elephants at top, centre). The wicked brahmin Kevatta sets out to lure Vedeha to the city, Uttarapancala, of his king, Culani; this he does by inflaming Vedeha's desire for the daughter of Culani, Pancalacandi (the palace is seen at the centre, Culani is shown in council and Pancalacandi appears in the small pavilion above and to the right of her father). Mahosadha erects a magical palace filled with magnificent rooms (palace building on right side of panel) and linked by a tunnel to the Ganges via the palace of Culani (exit from the tunnel shown as an arched doorway at the bottom of panel beneath the palace of Culani, and the entrance at bottom right beneath the magical palace of Mahosadha). Vedeha enters the magical palace on his arrival from Mithila and is threatened by the army of Culani (horses and elephants massing around the left side of the magical palace of Mahosadha). King Vedeha is terrified and realizes he is trapped. At first he requests the aid of the four sages who only suggest suicide (four figures in lower section of magic palace of Mahosadha); the king then consults Mahosadha who tells him of the existence of the tunnel, down which he escapes to

the Ganges. Meanwhile the troops of Mahosadha capture the princess who is also smuggled down the tunnel. She then meets Vedeha and they are married (scene at top right above expanse of water and up against the border of the panel). They leave for Mithila by elephant and by boat (expanse of water on far right-hand side up against border and beneath the 'marriage scene'). They are then enthroned back in the palace at Mithila (couple in pavilion at far top right-hand corner).

The final scenes of the story in which Culani is defeated and acknowledges the Bodhisattva probably appeared on the side panel of the chest. This is an outline of the story with many of the episodes only briefly identified, but it does show the way in which narrative scenes from either the Life of the Buddha or as here from his previous lives – the *jatakas* – were used to great effect in the decoration of monastic equipment. Such a remarkable example of the lacquerworker's skill will certainly repay much further study.

266 For description of this technique, see pp. 38–9.
267 See cat. 100 from Kedleston, a chest given to Lord Curzon.
268 Many examples are found in Britain, since they were brought back during the colonial period as items that were both decorative and useful – they made ideal blanket or linen chests. In this guise, however, they invariably exist without the stand. The example from Kedleston, cat. 100, is thus of great interest as this element is still intact. A further example exists at the Victoria and Albert Museum.
269 Illustrated in Fraser-Lu 1985: 98, pl. 112. See also p. 139 where the scene shown on the front of the box is identified as 'The Conversion of Minister Kaluda' and the interesting suggestion made that it could be the work of the famed Prome *shwe zawa* exponent, Hsaya Pa.
270 The Glasgow Museum at Kelvingrove possesses a palm-leaf manuscript which is labelled 'Taken at the fall of Taung Oo' during the same Second Anglo-Burmese War. For the very substantial contribution of the Scots to the British control of Burma in the colonial period, see McCrae 1990.
271 Although the whole inscription is in Burmese script, there is a break and change in language at this point from Burmese to Pali. The word *thadu*, translated here as 'well done', is frequently found

at the end of inscriptions to record the merit that is being acquired through a pious gift.
272 The authors are grateful to Patricia Herbert for her help in the translation of this inscription.
273 This text is the fifth-century AD compilation of the entire series of Jataka Tales in Pali. The bringing together of all the *jataka* material into a single text, all in Pali, is believed, traditionally, to have been undertaken by the great Indian scholar, Buddhaghosa, using earlier material then still preserved in Sri Lanka. It is made up of elements of verse (the Jataka Tales) and prose (commentaries). Only the verse element, the *gatha*, which linguistically is substantially earlier than the prose part, is considered canonical.
274 The special character of the Last Ten goes back at least to the pre-Pagan era. G. H. Luce (1956: 292) says, 'The earliest Mon descriptions of the ten great Jatakas occur in Makuta's *pandit* inscription at the Shwezayan pagoda, Thaton; in the glazed terracottas of the middle terrace of the Thagya pagoda, Thaton; and in the stone carvings of the boundary pillars of the *baddhasima* (ordination hall) at the Kalyani Thein, Thaton.' In the same article he lists the temples at Pagan – the Ananda and the Mingalazeidi – where the *Mahanipata* has a special place in the decorative scheme. For examples of the Ten Last Great Jatakas in this volume, see cat. 69 and 177.
275 See Cowell 1895, vol. VI: 156–246, where it is listed under its Pali name, the 'Maha-ummagga [Great Tunnel] Jataka'. Luce (1956) says that in Burma, both in antiquity and in the present, *Mahosadha* appears as 542, immediately after the *Nimi Jataka*, rather than as in the Sinhalese Pali version, where it appears as 546, immediately before the final, *Vessantara Jataka*.
276 In the Cowell edition the *jataka* begins on p. 156, but the first scenes on the panel relate to the story from p. 172 and continue to p. 231; the scenes narrated in pp 232–46 do not appear on the panel.
277 For a rare exception, see cat 99.

103

Shield and helmet, *daing and maukto*
Burma, perhaps of Shan manufacture, 19th/early 20th century
Shield: leather, lacquer, gold leaf, cane, wood; D 54.3 cm
Helmet: cloth, lacquer, gold leaf, wood, textile; H 30.3 cm, D 34.8 cm
Ipswich Museum, 1947-207.1 (shield), 1947-207.2 (helmet), gift of the Earl of Cranbrook

Both these items come from the same donor, the 4th Earl of Cranbrook,[278] and were acquired in the far north of Burma, at Khamti Long, near Fort Hertz (also known as Putao). According to Ipswich Museum records, shields and helmets of

this type were in use among Shan tribesmen settled in this remote area, far from the Shan States, so they may rather represent traditional Shan, or even lowland Burmese, styles rather than those prevalent in the area of Fort Hertz.[279] Engagingly, the reverse of the shield bears luggage labels for Cabin Class on the *SS Staffordshire*, a ship of the Bibby Line which, according to the labels, was due to travel to Colombo via Rangoon, and then onwards to London.[280]

The shield and the helmet illustrate the use of leather as a substrate for lacquer, which was common throughout Burma, as the lacquer provided both a protective and a waterproof coating.[281] Several layers of lacquer – red and black – appear to have been applied in the covering of the shield; the gold leaf has then been added on top, probably using lacquer as an adhesive. Depictions of the Burmese army in the nineteenth century folding illustrated books, *parabaik*, show soldiers wearing shields and helmets of exactly this type.[282] The helmet, although brilliant in colour, is the type used for general army wear; the grander the position within the army, the more highly decorated became the spire of the helmet. In this publication soldiers wearing helmets like this can be seen on the *shwe zawa* panel at cat. 102. Whether they are in mythological time (the *Mahosadha Jataka* of the panel) or historical time (the donations of King Mindon), the artist uses the conventions of the day.

278 The seat of the Earl of Cranbrook was at Great Glemham, near Saxmundham, which in its turn is not far from Ipswich.
279 The transplanting of captive populations far from their place of origin was a distinctive feature of the policy of Burmese kings from at least the Pagan period. The majority population were Kachins.
280 I am grateful to David Jones of Ipswich Museum for information about these two objects. A third item in Cranbrook's gift was a Kachin sword in a red lacquered wooden scabbard.

281 Another example of the use of leather as a substrate for lacquer can be seen at cat. 128 where the belly of the harp is formed of leather which has subsequently been lacquered. See also Harvey 1925: 230.

282 See *parabaik* in the collection of the British Library, one of which is illustrated at cat. 87. Others can be seen in Herbert 1999: 9 (Procession of King Mindon of 1867).

104

Saddle flap, *kadaung*

Burma, 19th or early 20th century
Leather, lacquer, gold leaf; L 74 cm, W 62 cm
Ethno As. 1972.Q.1931a

Produced in pairs, these near oval elements of horse-furniture act as an extension of the saddle down the side of the horse's flank. Horse-riders are frequently depicted in *parabaik* using them,[283] and they can also be seen on the magnificent *shwe zawa* panel of the *Mahosadha Jataka* (cat. 102).

The whole surface of the saddle has been lacquered red and then the outer face has been further decorated in the red-and-gold *shwe zawa* technique. In

105

the centre is a large leaf-edged cartouche containing a horned mythical animal with flowing foliage issuing from its mouth. Both this example and its

pair[284] have been well used and the lacquer decoration has been badly scuffed, presumably by the repeated rubbing across it of the rider's leg.

283 For examples, see Herbert 1993: 29, 30 (one horseman carries his saddle on a lance), 31, 33 and 53.

284 Ethno As. 1972.Q.1931b.

105

Alms bowl, *thabeik*

Burma, Ava, factory of U Kyaw Sein and Daw Than Than and Sons, 1993
Aluminium, bamboo, lacquer, plastic, cotton string;
H 12.5 cm, D 25.5 cm
OA 1998.7-23.249, gift of Mr and Mrs R. Isaacs

Purchased in 1993 from the Hsaya Ngwe Monk Shop on the eastern approach stairway to the Shwedagon Pagoda in Rangoon, this is a mass-produced alms bowl for use by monks on the daily alms-round. It is one of the 'eight chattels', the permissible personal possession for monks: three cloths (lower, upper and wrapper), a waist girdle or belt in cotton webbing, a needle, a water filter, a razor and a

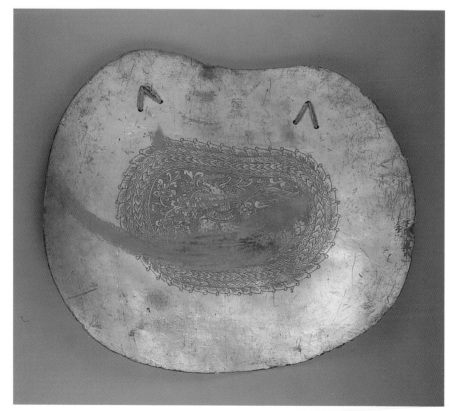

104

106

bowl. In 1900 Ferrars reported that monks customarily received in addition sandals, a deerskin to sit and sleep on, a broom and a fan.[285] Well-to-do supporting families supplemented the necessaries with offerings of 'books and writing materials, mats, carpets, cushions, handkerchiefs, tables, chairs, betel-boxes and spittoons, glassware and crockery, lamps, chandeliers, clocks, knicknacks and furniture'.[286]

This set comprises an aluminium bowl lacquered black, a lid of bamboo basketry or matting also lacquered black, a stand in greyish injection-moulded plastic, and a carrying sling in

cotton netting. The bowl is slung from the shoulder.

Amongst their necessities, already described, Ferrars noted the common *thabeik*, or alms bowl, was 'a hard-baked black earthen pot'. One very old bowl in the Museum of the Archaeology Department in Rangoon is of iron, lacquered black and with the rim encrusted with *thayo* relief decoration. The modern bowl and cover are stencilled in gold with the brand name of the product 'Burmese Branching Vine'.

285 Ferrars 1900: 15.
286 Ibid: 23.

106
Alms bowl with lid, *thabeik*
Burma, Mandalay, mid-20th century
Bamboo, lacquer, relief work, glass inlay; D 36.5 cm. H 25.5 cm
OA 1998.7-23.68, gift of Mr and Mrs R. Isaacs

This elaborate ceremonial bowl is decorated with scenes from one of the 547 *jatakas*, the stories of the Buddha's former lives. There are four elegantly shaped frames, each with an episode from a story in which the future Buddha, born as an ascetic mendicant, mediates to end conflict between men and *nagas* (serpent-dragons). Two scenes depict the conflict in the water,

opposite: 107

where the *naga* seems to have the advantage, and on land, where the man holds his own. Two further scenes show the Bodhisattva as a hermit, begging the human king to desist from fighting, and begging the *naga* king likewise to cease hostilities. In each case the Bodhisattva's persuasion is successful, for both the human king and the *naga* king bow their head in compliance.

Such a vessel, though shaped like a monk's alms bowl (*thabeik*), was not, of course, for use on the daily alms round. The bowl was originally gilded and would be a very splendid vessel. It would have been owned by a very wealthy person to hold the food cooked early in the morning and shared, one spoonful for each monk, among the procession as it filed past the house of the owner.

The *jataka* scenes would have been chosen by the owner, and the theme of conciliation and peacemaking may have pointed to the dangers of strife between contemporary factions of monks.

107
Offering stand, *kalat*

Burma, Shan States, Inle Lake, mid-20th century
Bamboo, lacquer; H 25.8 cm, D 41 cm
OA 1998.7-23.202, gift of Mr and Mrs R. Isaacs

This stand is typical of Intha manufacture in the villages around Ywama, the town on the western shore of Inle Lake in the southern Shan States. It is made of woven split bamboo thickly lacquered red on all visible surfaces, but black underneath. The wide shallow plate is joined to the cylindrical flared foot with a very broad band of moulded *thayo*. This represents turned rails or little balustrades of wood, *put lon*. Just below it a second much narrower band of moulded *thayo* completes the decoration of the piece.

Such stands are owned by families who use them for carrying offerings of food and other gifts to the monastery; they are thus similar in function to the *hsun ok* seen elsewhere in this publication (see cat. 89–96). Intha people crochet white cotton lace cloths, and one of these is first spread on the upper dish, with its corners hanging

down over the rim. On this are arranged open bowls and canisters of silver or white metal, each containing a dainty such as buffalo-skin crisps, roasted garlic or fried fish. Often flowers are scattered over all. The whole confection is carried on the head of a woman donor – a pretty sight.

The monastic communities that such gifts would sustain are visible around the edges of Inle Lake, a long and picturesque stretch of water, south of Taunggyi. In religious terms the area is renowned for the annual festival of the Hpaung Daw U which takes place in October. At this time, especially, vessels such as this one would have been used to bring offerings to the monastery.

108

Carrying pole, *kyizi dabo*

Burma, probably Mandalay, early 20th century
Wood, gold leaf, glass inlay, iron hook; L 230 cm
Gift of Mr and Mrs R. Isaacs

This pole of carved wood has a central

hook of iron from which a flat triangular bronze gong or bell (Burmese *kyizi* – see cat. 109) is suspended by a cord threaded through a hole in its apex. The pole is shouldered by two men, and the man walking behind has a short stick, its end wound with cloth, for striking the gong. The carved wood of the pole has been lacquered red and decorated with rings of relief moulding set with coloured glass. It is also partly gilded.

109

Triangular gong, *kyizi*

Burma, Pakkoku district, 1954
Bell metal, inscribed; L 36 cm, H 24.5 cm,
weight 5 kg
OA 1996.5–1.49

These flat triangular gongs or bells are made exclusively for religious use, either hung from a pagoda on a pair of posts with a crossbar or from·a pole shouldered by two men for street processions (see cat. 108).[287] Struck sharply on one of its lower points the

gong spins rapidly and this motion imparts a vibrato to the note emitted (in a musical demonstration of the Doppler effect). Captain Michael Symes noted in Amarapura in 1795 that 'the triangular gong (peculiar I believe to Burma) which the people strike on holidays as they pass along the streets to worship at the pagodas, is quite remarkable for its musical, prolonged and surging vibrations' (Symes 1800: 157 and fig. 29).

A long inscription on this gong records that it was made in the year 1316 of the Burmese Era (1954) on the 15th day of the waxing moon in the month of Kason, and donated by U Ba Tin, his wife Daw Shwe Yu and their family of Khway Hmway (Scented Dog?) village in Myaing Township in Pakkoku District, who call on Nats and humans to applaud their deed of merit. The weight of the bronze was 3 viss (almost 5 kilos) and the cost 39 kyats. The person who on behalf of the donors negotiated the casting of the bell and also nine small Buddha images and reverently carried them back to the donors was Ko Hpo Thaung, helped by U Than Kyi and his son Ko Thu Daw of Kaing Daw Hmi village.

287 For one collected by Andreino in Mandalay pre-1885, see Mazzeo (ed.) 1998: 75, cat. 112.

110

Acolyte's alms bowl, *kyok*

Burma, Shan States, Inle Lake, 1916
Bamboo, lacquer, cord, metal; H 25.7 cm,
D 27.8 cm
OA 1998.7-23.266, gift of Mr and Mrs R. Isaacs

This deep bowl with its domed lid is lacquered black on the outside, while the integral stepped stand and interior are lacquered red; there is one internal

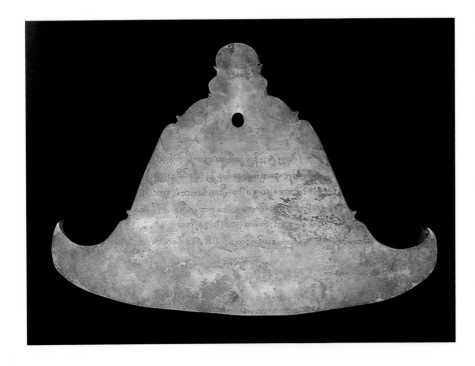

tray. Small eyelets of metal are set in the upper rim of the bowl to hold the carrying cord and allow the vessel to be hung from a yoke.

Such bowls have a special name, *kyok*, and purpose. They were used by *hpothudaw*, white-robed acolytes, who frequent the rest-halls, *zayat*, around pagodas, where they often offer fortune-telling by palm-reading. They are respected as possessing powers. In 1900 Ferrars noted: 'They make their appeal with a gong of triangular shape, *kyizi*,[288] which spins on the string it hangs by, and emits a high and sustained throbbing note. *Hpothudaw* eat in the forenoon only. They accept alms in money and in kind, for which they carry baskets with a shoulder-yoke. They wear a white robe, shave their heads and pluck out their beards. *Hpothudaw* shift for themselves in *zayat* about the temples and seldom remain long in one place.'[289] Nowadays, white-jacketed fortune-tellers with a rosary of large brown wooden beads are still seen on the platform of the Shwedagon in Rangoon, and other large pagodas.[290] In Pegu, on the platform of the Shwemawdaw pagoda, one enterprising *hypothudaw* advertised 'Predictions in English and Italian'.

This vessel is inscribed on the base with a date in English, 1916, and in Burmese 1278, and also in Burmese script, 'bowl of the donor of a thein (prayer hall)'. It was used by, and very likely gifted to, a white-robed acolyte who had prospered sufficiently to found a prayer hall.

288 For an example, see cat. 109.
289 See Ferrars 1901: 40 and pl. 85, where a *hpothudaw* is shown carrying such a basket on a yoke over his shoulder.
290 Palm-reading, astrology and horoscopes have always been popular in Burma, despite the fact that they are officially outside the realm of Buddhism. These techniques flourish, however, in exactly the same way as do the cults of the *nats*. For horoscopes, see Shway Yoe 1882: 9ff.

110

111
Nun's alms tray, *thi la shin ban*
Burma, early 20th century
Bamboo, lacquer; H 6.5 cm, D 39.5 cm
OA 1998.7-23.192, gift of Mr and Mrs R. Isaacs

This peculiar form of circular basket-tray was used only by Buddhist nuns in the past to collect alms. It was not carried in the hands nor slung from the shoulder like the monk's alms bowl, or *thabeik* (cat. 105), but was balanced on top of a folded cloth on the nun's shaven head. So characteristic was this tray that nuns were sometimes referred to as 'tray-carrying ladies'. The more general term for nuns still used today is *thi la shin* 'those who possess the precepts'. In the early days of Buddhism in India nuns were officially recognized as part of the *sasana*,[291] and there have recently been some moves in the West to revive this official status of Buddhist nuns. In Burma, though nuns are not part of the *sasana*, they are numerous and well respected. They wear robes of pale pink and folded

111

stoles of brown, and follow a quasi-monastic life. But the bowls they carry are nowadays of aluminium.

This basket has its rim sharply turned inwards, to form a ridge. The underside is reinforced and decorated with straps of basketry. Four long straps run across from the ridge to the opposite side, crossing in the centre where they overlap. There are eight short feet in the spaces between, and a further basketry strap joins all the feet, forming an octagon. Eight shorter straps run from each foot to just below the ridge. The whole underside is lacquered in reddish brown, the colour of red ochre (*myay ni*). The interior of the tray has been very lightly lacquered.

291 Gombrich 1988.

112
Stem bowl, *yay khwet gyi*
Burma, Pagan, late 19th or early 20th century
Bamboo, lacquer; H 27.3 cm, D 20.6 cm
OA 1998.7-23.207, gift of Mr and Mrs R. Isaacs

A detachable base raises this water bowl above the ordinary shape, and inscriptions around the rim record that it was donated to a monastery by a couple living in the Yun Tan (lacquer traders') quarter of Pagan. The donors, Ko Aung Ba and Ma Aung, would have commissioned the piece specially. No maker's name appears, so the date could be very early in the twentieth century or earlier.

The *yun* decoration uses a range of colours – green, yellow, pink and red on a black ground – and is of exceptional delicacy. The pattern is composed of

tiny figures of dancing people and men on horseback, among floral scrolls and palm trees, all rendered with great vivacity. This pattern is known as *pabwa yok lat*. The donors' dedication is inscribed in two cartouches in a frieze near the rim.

113
Standard, *dagon daing*
Burma, probably from Lower Burma, 18th or early 19th century
Wood, metal, lacquer, gold leaf, ?leather; H 265 cm
OA 1880-3534, from the Stuart Collection

Standards such as these are frequently found at the entrance to monasteries or on pagoda platforms. Sometimes they are referred to as 'prayer posts'. This one is made up of two parts, which are assembled separately: the pole with its hanging banner, and the figure of the *kinnara*, half-man, half-bird, fitting on top.[292]

The pole is of special interest because the flat banner hanging in front is decorated on the outer face with gilded threads of *thayo*; the banner itself seems to be made of stiffened leather. Lacquer has probably also been used in the preparation of the entire wooden assemblage, before the application of the gold leaf, and red lacquer has been used on the top surface of the *kinnara*. The *kinnara* itself is depicted bearded and crowned and with hands held palm together in the gesture of adoration. The upper part of the *kinnara* is in human form, while

the body and feet are those of a bird. As is usual in Burma, the upward-sweeping tail of the *kinnara* has become an important decorative element.

The link between these standards and the free-standing pillars and posts of ancient Indian shrines is unknown. However, the frequent presence crowning these wooden posts in Burma of bird elements such as the *hamsa* or *kinnara* may connect them with the ancient Indian pillars with their *garuda* finials.[293] Standing pillars are also known from early south Indian Buddhist shrines such as Amaravati, and the link established by Buddhist missionaries between the Andhra coast and southern Burma may have been a means for this form to have reached Burma.

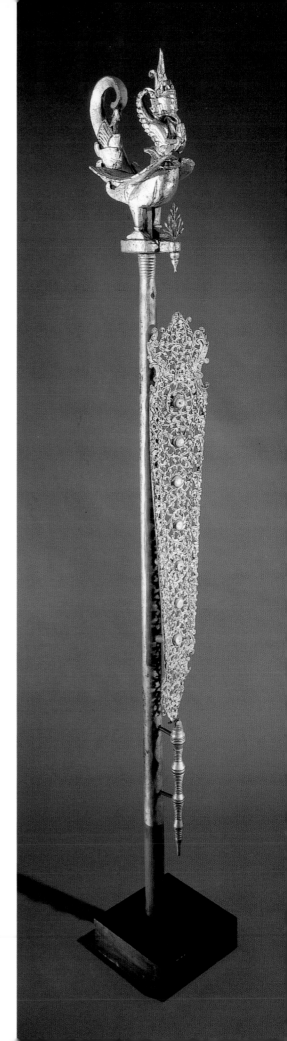

The presence of a small paper label (now removed) with 'Lot 108' on the front of the banner, indicates that this object was part of the auction of the collection of Major-General Charles Stuart in 1830.[294] Stuart died in Calcutta in 1828, so the date of this standard must precede that event and may perhaps be a late addition to his collection in the wake of the First Anglo-Burmese War (1824).[295]

292 The Museum records call the bird *garuda* rather than *kinnara*.
293 Perhaps the most ancient of these is the one at Besnagar, near Sanchi. The inscription on it describes it as a *garuda* pillar; see Harle 1986: 31. In Nepal the building of pillars topped with *garuda* images is also well documented; see Slusser 1982.
294 For Stuart, see cat. 39.
295 As it does not bear a British Museum number in the sequence allotted to the Bridge Collection (John Bridge bought much of Stuart's collection at the 1830 auction), it is assumed to have come to the British Museum via the India Museum which was disbanded in 1879. For the India Museum, see cat. 50.

114

Attendant figure, *nat yok*

Burma, 19th century
Wood, lacquer, paint, gold leaf; H 186 cm, W 37 cm
OA 1985.1-28.1, gift of Mr Derek Weeks

The gesture of adoration, with the two hands held palm to palm, is the classic position for an attendant figure.[296] The identification is, in this instance, emphasized by the large staring eyes that are clearly focused on an image, presumably of the Buddha, which is the reason for the hand gesture. This rudely carved sculpture, on its rough lotus pedestal and with the chip of the chisel still fresh upon it, has a considerable charm not least on account of its wildly flounced costume, the terminals of which provide an opportunity for the considerable skills of the village carpenter. The upper costume is decorated with flowers picked out in gold leaf, set upon the lacquered and painted surface, while the tiered crown – a rural version of the magisterial crowns seen on royal figures, such as those on the *shwe zawa* panel, cat. 102 – gives an excuse for scrollwork decoration around the ears. This last feature links this sculpture with a long line of post-Pagan sculptures where floral, vegetal and ribbon-like efflorescence around the ears complements the crowns of the so-called Jambupati Buddha images (see cat. 75 and 76).

296 Ferrars (1901: 171) illustrates a very similar wooden image which he calls *nat*. Such a generalized image certainly doesn't seem to be one of the 'Thirty-Seven Nats' as illustrated by Temple. However, used in a loose way, this may be an appropriate title for such a sculpture.

115

115

Set of four small baskets, *taung*

Burma, mid-20th century
Bamboo, lacquer; H 3.3 cm, D 4.7 cm
OA 1998.7-23.64 (a–d), gift of Mr and Mrs R. Isaacs

These four little baskets have been lightly lacquered red-brown, though all are more or less splashed with lime. They were made to hold some of the spices that make up the chewing quid of sliced areca nut wrapped in a betel-leaf smeared with lime. The lime would have been kept in a small round or oval covered box of brass or copper. The individual baskets may have held such condiments as cutch resin, cloves, cardamom pods and dried citrus peel. The set of four baskets and the lime-box would sit together on the upper tray under the deep cover of a lacquered betel-box. The lower held tobacco leaf, and the deep box itself fresh betel-leaf.

118

116

Miniature box, *it*

Burma, Shan States, mid- to late 19th century
Bamboo, lacquer; H 3.5 cm, D 9.2 cm
OA 1998.7-23.235, gift of Mr and Mrs R. Isaacs

This little box of bamboo basketry lacquered black and red has been decorated in the *yun* technique with equal care and skill on the cover and on the base. Both show in a roundel a highly stylized figure of an animal: on the lid possibly a horse, on the base perhaps an ox. Such boxes were far too small for betel and were used instead for holding cosmetics or a lucky talisman. A similar, but smaller box – OA 1998.7–23.127 – depicts on the lid a man richly dressed, one hand raised to his face, the other arm akimbo, and on the base a vigorously stylized lion.

It is not known which lacquer manufacturing centre or centres in the Shan States produced these little boxes.

The smaller has been tentatively been dated to the 1830s on the grounds of costume.[297]

[297] Noel Singer, personal communication.

117

Miniature box, *it*

Burma, Shan States, early 20th century
Bamboo, lacquer; H 4 cm, D 8.3 cm
OA 1998.7-23.82, gift of Mr and Mrs R. Isaacs

The lid and box are of woven split bamboo, lacquered red and black. The lid bears a design of simple flower heads. The sides are bright red with black rings, while the base has a design of fine radiating rays, each composed of minute black lines, with yellow flecks at intervals in between. This design clearly imitates basketry.

For the use, data and provenance of this box, see cat. 116. All recorded examples are at least sixty years old.

116

117

118

Medicine mixing box, *hsay daung*
Burma, probably Kyaukka, early 20th century
Bamboo, lacquer; H 18 cm, D 36.5 cm
OA 1998.7-23.222, gift of Mr and Mrs R. Isaacs

The base of this deep cylindrical box
has stout ridges at the foot and midline
and a shallower hoop at the top rim, all
for reinforcement. It is lacquered black
outside and red inside. A tray fits neatly
into the top of the box. This has a
square of openwork woven bamboo in
the centre to act as a sieve or strainer
for sifting foods or medicines; it is also
possible that it was used to prepare
cheroots.

119

Cigarette case, *hsayleik te*
Burma, Pagan, workshop of Hsaya Ba, mid-20th
century
Cotton, lacquer; H 10.7 cm, W 8 cm, depth 2 cm
OA 1995.10-5.2

This small slip case, ideally suited to fit
in the trouser pocket of a European or
Westernized Burmese, is decorated in
the *yun* technique with a scene
advertising its use. On each of the four
faces is depicted a Burmese belle
smoking, probably not a cigarette but a
typically large Burmese cheroot. The

119

120

case is pliable and almost certainly
made of cloth, which has then been
impregnated with lacquer paste prior to
its decoration. The background colour is
black while the design is executed in
yellow, orange and green.

Although this case was certainly
designed for cigarettes, the more robust
Burmese habit of smoking cheroots is
one of the most oft-repeated items of
folklore about traditional Burma. Even
today in travel books it is not
uncommon to see illustrations of people
smoking huge cheroots,[298] which bring
to mind Kipling's famous lines:

> An' I seed her first a-smokin' of a
> wackin' white cheroot,
> An' a-wastin' Christian kisses on an
> 'eathen idol's foot.[299]

The habit of smoking cheroots was a
frequent cause of fires in Burma,
especially as houses were built of
wood, bamboo and thatch. The colonial
literature is full of descriptions of such
blazes.[300]

The four short inscriptions on the
case read, 'Upper Burma, Pagan Town',
'Pyizu Ward, product of Hsaya Ba's

workshop', 'Genuine quality article' and
'Cigar or cheroot case in lacquer-ware'.

298 See Courtauld 1984: 99 or Everarda 1994: 36.
299 Rudyard Kipling, 'Mandalay', 1892.
300 In a letter to his wife in 1886, Brigadier George
White said, 'The [Mandalay] palace is all built of
wood and there are now nearly 2000 Burmese
carpenters at work inside it. They all smoke and
throw their cheroots about in the most
promiscuous fashion. I expect to be burnt out
before the season is over.' Quoted in Stewart 1972:
161. See also, Kelly 1905: 181.

120

Medicine phials/gourds, *hsay bu*
Burma, Shan States, Inle Lake; mid-20th century
Basketry, lacquer; (a) D 3.2 cm, H 5.5 cm; (b) D 6.4
cm, 9.5 cm; (c) D 4.8 cm, 6.6 cm
OA 1998.7-23.215, 262, 263, gift of Mr and Mrs R.
Isaacs

Though gourd-shaped, these little
bottles are all of basketry, lightly
lacquered inside and more thickly on
the outside. All now lack their stoppers
of wood or bunched grass. The largest
(262) has a typical Intha decorative
motif painted in pink lacquer at the
neck and on the base.

The Burmese word *hsay* denotes
tobacco and snuff as well as medicine,

paint or dye (such as tattoo dyes), narcotic drugs, poison, and magic potions or philtres. These bottles probably all held medicine, and one, the larger of the two plain black bottles (215) certainly did. It has an inscription scratched into the surface with a needle or other sharp point, which seems to have been composed by the doctor, or *hsay hsaya*, for it names the contents, 'yellow medicine'; the complaint, 'plague'; and the *hsay hsaya* who prescribed and sold the preparation, Ba Win. Deep inside the container some traces of a yellowish substance remain. Medicines were classified by their colour and by the ailment for which they were a specific. Plague, carried by rodents which live in the thatch of houses, is endemic in several parts of Burma, some of which experience annual outbreaks. The Burmese word used here for plague is transliterated from the English.

121

Water carafe, *yay tagaung*
Burma, probably Kyaukka, mid-20th century
Bamboo, lacquer; H 25.2 cm, D 21.5 cm
OA 1998.7-23.245, gift of Mr and Mrs R. Isaacs

Though shaped in imitation of a bottle gourd fruit (Burmese *bu ga*), this vessel is actually constructed of coiled

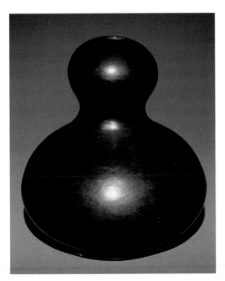

121

122

bamboo strips. Several coats of black lacquer have been applied to the exterior surface, and red lacquer shows inside the aperture. The base of the bottle is formed from a shallow ring. Kyaukka near Monywa in the dry country of Upper Burma is a likely place of manufacture.

122

Water bowl, *yay khwet gyi*
Burma, Pagan, mid- to late 19th century
Bamboo, lacquer; H 18.8 cm, D 23.8 cm
OA 1998.7-23.206, gift of Mr and Mrs R. Isaacs

This bowl is solidly constructed with thick walls on a comparatively heavy base. Its surface is covered with *yun* work of exquisite quality. There is no standard pattern but the many individual figures show exceptionally fine draughtsmanship. They include, on opposite sides of the bowl, two chariots drawn by horses and preceded by circular standards born aloft on tall poles. One depicts the rabbit, the emblem of the moon, and the other the displaying peacock, the symbol of the sun.

There are no inscriptions, which on work of this quality would indicate a date before *yun* artists took to signing their work, that is, before the colonial exhibitions such as the Delhi art exhibition of 1902. The solid construction also fits a date in the middle of the nineteenth century, before thin walls and the flexibility of weaving with horsehair became fashionable.

123

123

Flower basket, *pan daung*
Burma, Kyaukka, early 20th century
Bamboo, lacquer; H 39.5 cm, D 37 cm
OA 1998.7-23.48, gift of Mr and Mrs R. Isaacs

The manufacture of these flower baskets is a speciality of the lacquer masters of Kyaukka (see Fraser-Lu 1985: 12 for a photograph of this work). The base and bowl of the basket are oval and made of thin strips of split bamboo bent to shape and glued with lacquer sap. The floor of the basket is a piece of matting, which has been cut to fit. The handle is formed of thicker pieces of bamboo, bent to shape and strengthened where they are atached to the top rim of the basket with four little rings of coiled bamboo. The whole piece is lacquered black outside and red inside. There are traces of decoration in raised lacquer paste around the drum of the basket, which may originally have been gilded. One medallion has a barely legible inscription, the name of the owner Ma Chit Ohn.

Such baskets were used for carrying tightly tied bunches of flowers to the pagoda as offerings to be placed in flower vases, *pan o* (cat. 181), in front of Buddha shrines.

124

Box, perhaps for clothes, *bi-it*
Burma, ?late 18th/19th century
Bamboo, lacquer; H 25 cm, D 31.4 cm
OA 1996.2-19.1

This box has an odd shape: the top of the cover projects in a sharp keel beyond its walls. Its large size and lack of an internal tray suggest that it may have been used to store clothes, certainly not betel materials. Both box and cover are deep red within, while the outside of the box is orange. The top and sides of the cover carry *yun* decoration in both style and subject matter.

The top of the box features five *pyathat*, tiered roof spires, one with a seated figure in the base. Long-tailed peacocks fly between the spires. In front of the buildings is a serried row of highly stylized figures, with a second row at right-angles to the first. Around the sides of the cover are depicted further rows of figures, some of whom appear to be pulling on ropes to draw along a large structure on wheels. The front of this structure bears, like a figurehead, a large rearing bird like a *karaweik*. If this vehicle is indeed a *karaweik* car or float pulled in procession, then the occasion depicted would be a *hypongyibyan*, the funeral of a very senior monk, possibly even of the *thathanabaing*, the most senior *hsayadaw*, recognised by the royal government as the supreme head of the *sasana*. This interpretation of a *hpongyibyan* is supported by the participation in the procession of a long file of men carrying stout tubular objects, which may represent the *don* or rockets used for setting alight the funeral pyre. Shway Yoe (1882: 587) describes these rockets as follows: 'Scores of these *don* have been prepared for weeks beforehand and many have been carried round triumphantly in procession by the people who have made them.'

124

At the end of the float is a winged figure, perhaps a *kinnara*, with a large flag. This in its turn is followed by another sequence of spires, like those shown on the cover. Here there are ten, in front of which is a row of figures; one of the figures sits on a dais. This then brings the viewer to a tall spreading tree, and the figures pulling the *karaweik* float seen at the beginning.

This box may therefore depict the cremation ceremony of a major ecclesiastical figure. This is a memorable occasion for rejoicing, for when they die saintly *hsayadaws* are thought to approach nearer to nirvana.

It is even possible that the box was made for presentation to the monastery of the deceased *hsayadaw*.[301]

301 We are grateful to Noel Singer his very helpful suggestions concerning the box.

125
Circular clothes box, *bi it*
Burma, ?Pagan, late 19th/early 20th century
Bamboo, lacquer; H 46 cm, D 56 cm
Ethno As. 1928.3-5.3a&b; gift of W.D. Campbell

This large clothes box has one internal tray and is made almost entirely of pieces of matting of split bamboo which have been cut to make the parts of the

box and have then been formed into shape using lacquer as an adhesive. The exceptions are the base of the vessel and the point at the lid where there is a break in the outline; these sections are made of coiled split bamboo.

The box is decorated both on the outside of the lid and on the outer face of the inner drum with the Chinese 'cloud collar' design in the *yun* technique, in black and yellow on red. Although it is crude in comparison with other examples,[302] the size and bravura of the elements provide a very striking composition. Further, it shares with more refined examples the idea of

173

125

filling the clouds with cross-hatching. The 'cloud collar' design on the outer face of the drum (i.e. that part which is hidden by the lid) is much brighter than the design on the outer face of the lid, having been protected from the dulling effects of both light and dust. This is a common feature of both *bi it* and *kun it*. At the base of the box there is a crudely rolled out section of moulded lacquer putty decoration, *put lon*.[303] The main field of the underside of the box is decorated in *yun* with concentric compass-drawn lines in yellow. At the centre is a figure, perhaps set within a group of stylized trees; the details are not now clear.

A similar cloud-collar pattern is depicted in a Burmese painted manuscript of the Life of the Buddha, now in the British Library (Or. 14297, fold 10; see Herbert 1993: 28). The same colours – yellow on red – are used, but for a textile. The manuscript was acquired by Henry Burney during his period as British Resident at the court of Ava between 1830 and 1837, so the pattern was certainly in the repertoire of Burmese artists by that date. In her description of this imposing *bi it,* Sylvia Fraser-Lu says of the Chinese 'cloud collar' design: 'This type of decoration has been seen on Burmese *lon-gyi* in seventeenth and eighteenth century frescoes'; she also describes the vessel as being of Shan manufacture.[304]

Boxes such as these are recorded as being used not only in the home for storing clothing, but also for holding the more elaborate costume and cosmetics of travelling players.[305]

302 See cat. 50 and 51.
303 For a stone mould from which such decoration is made, see cat. 31.
304 Fraser-Lu 1985: 139.
305 Shway Yoe 1882: 291.

126

Drum, *ozi*

Burma, late 19th/early 20th century
Wood, leather, lacquer, coloured glass spangles;
H 70.5 cm, D 27 cm
1993.7-26.1, gift of the Hon. Mrs Marten

Although a standard shape, this drum is finely decorated with threads of gilded *thayo*, and inset colour glass fragments in the *hmanzi shwe cha* technique. Despite what appears to be a base for it, the drum is actually played slung diagonally across the chest, so that the player can walk while playing it. This means that the end farthest from the skin membrane is visible and is thus decorated – here with the same lacquer scheme as the outer surface. The tautness of the drum is controlled by the leather straps which are fastened on the outer side.

Noel Singer in his book *Burmese Dance and Theatre* describes their use: 'At festival times, groups of young men roamed the streets, with their leader playing on an *ozi* (goblet-shaped drum), accompanied by a dancer. Emphasis was on the skill of the drummer and his dancing partner, and there was no attempt to perform a play...'[306] This instrument was acquired by the grandparents of the donor when they attended the Delhi Durbar when in Waiting to George V and Queen Mary in 1911. Burmese and Shan dignitaries attended the Durbar – Burma was administered as a part of India until 1937 – and the drum was one of the gifts exchanged during the celebrations.

306 See Singer 1995: 41 and col. pl. 9.

127

Metallophone, with two strikers, *than pattala*

Burma, 19th century
Wood, iron, lacquer, gold leaf, green glass and coloured glass spangles; leather and wood strikers;
H 51 cm, L 100 cm, depth 25 cm
The National Trust, Curzon Collection at Kedleston Hall, Derbyshire, no. 643

The Burmese orchestra has circles of tuned drums and tuned gongs, augmented by wind instruments, little cymbals and bamboo clappers. Instruments associated with solo music-making include the elegant harp (cat. 128) and the *pattala*.[307] The latter has tuned bars of metal, as in this one – a *than pattala* – or bamboo. It is made up of an open box, high at each end and low in the middle, with cords slung between the two high points, on which

128

metal plates of graded thickness are strung, the difference in thickness producing notes of different pitch when struck by the small beaters.

This magnificently decorated example has delicately carved wooden panels at each end, with green glass backing and lavish use of gilding and small spangles of glass set in *thayo*. The carved and gilded figures at each end depict *thungedaw*, little naked page-boys of the royal court. This strongly indicates that the instrument is a palace piece. Singer (1998) has described the role of these gilded statuettes of *thungedaw* in the palace, where each of the thrones had a set of such figures facing it with hands raised in homage.

In this context Singer's reference to the royal character of instruments decorated with gilding and glass mosaic following the royal decree of 1787 is relevant,[308] and it is entirely appropriate that at the turn of the nineteenth century Lord Curzon, the most powerful man in Asia, should have been presented with an instrument such as this.

More humdrum were the undecorated examples recorded in use by itinerant musicians.[309]

307 See Shway Yoe: 318.
308 Singer 1995: 20.
309 See Moore *et al.* 1999: 154.

128

Harp, *saung gauk*

Lower Burma, said to be from Prome, 19th century
Wood, skin, lacquer, coloured glass spangles, cotton tuning cords with tassles and originally with varnished silk strings;[310] H 61 cm, L 72.5 cm
Published in Lowry 1974: 38
Victoria and Albert Museum IM 234-1927; bequeathed by the Marquess Curzon of Kedleston[311]

The thirteen-stringed, boat-shaped harp has had an important role in Burmese society, and its longevity is attested by twelfth-century depictions at Pagan: in relief at the Ananda temple and in mural form at the Payathonzu and the Kondawgyi pagodas.[312] It continues to be an instrument that is played as well as displayed or presented. This example may have been given to Lord Curzon during his viceregal visit to Burma in 1901. However, there is another explanation of its acquisition by Curzon. This would link it with the Indian Art Exhibition held in Delhi in 1902, of which Curzon, as viceroy, was the patron.[313] At the exhibition *shwe zawa* decorated lacquer items produced by the well-known mastercraftsman, Hsaya Pa of Prome, were exhibited; indeed one item won a prize in 'Division 27 – Lacquer-work of Burma'.[314] It is not impossible that Curzon acquired the harp on this occasion.

The ceremonial importance of the instrument is compounded by its very fine black-and-gold lacquer decoration, *shwe zawa*, which runs all the way around the sound box. This is decorated with six scenes from the *Ramayana*[315] and bears five kite-shaped panels of inscription commenting on the action (two on one side, three on the other). The inscriptions on the first side read (descriptions of the action are given in square brackets):

1. 'Prince Rama pursues Kambi disguised as a hind, shoots an arrow and hits her.' [A male hunter comes upon the Golden Deer who is shown as a human-faced quadruped, with no bestial features or ogre headdress.]
2. 'The royal younger brother Lakshmana goes off (?to help) Prince Rama.' [Lakshmana draws a line in the ground with his bow and heads off into the forest.]
3. 'Ravana disguised as a mendicant accepts a gift of fruit offered by Lady Sita.' [Ravana disguised as a beggar with an alms bowl approaches Sita who, kneeling, offers him fruit piled on a *daung lan* stand.[316] Ravana's aerial chariot is parked, ready for escape, at the far end of this panel.]
On the other side:
4. 'Prince Rama, his younger brother Lakshmana and Lady Sita are attacked by the ogres, the elder and younger

brothers, Duthagara' [A male figure, Lakshmana (?), brandishes a bow, or instructs in its use; a male and a female figure close by.]
5. No inscription. [The two ogres are attacked.]
6. 'Shot by prince Rama's arrows, the Duthagara brothers lie dead. The lady Meme Kambi having followed, comes up to the place.' [The two ogres lie dead in a pit with arrows through their chests; a female figure comes upon them.]

A peacock, the national symbol of Burma, is depicted in *shwe zawa* decoration at the end farthest from the neck, between the two long strips of decoration. There are also threads of gilded *thayo* decorating the top side of the sounding board, as well as inset glass spangles. The decoration is thus a combination of *hmanzi shwe cha* and *shwe zawa*, producing a scheme of considerable opulence, entirely suitable for the viceroy, however he came by it.

Such harps are still used in Burma as instruments of genteel and professional accomplishment, especially to accompany vocal presentations. When not in use, it is placed on a stand and never allowed to lie on its belly.

310 Yule: 1858: 14 and 15 describes the way the tassles function: ' Tasselled cords attached to the ends of the strings and twisted round the curved head, serve for tuning. This is done by pushing them up and down, so that the curvature of the head increases or diminishes the tension.'
311 For other items from Curzon's collection, see cat. 100 and 127.
312 See 'K' [U Khin Zaw] 1981: 72.
313 For the Indian Art Exhibition, see Watt 1904 and cat. 17 and 18.
314 Watt 1904: 223–4, 'Third Prize with bronze medal to Saya [*sic*] Pa of Prome for a gilt lacquered tray.'
315 For the use of the Ramayana as a design on Burmese lacquerware, see cat. 65.
316 For such a stand, see cat. 140.

129

Headdress, *si bon*

Burma, late 19th century
Wood, lacquer, metal, coloured inset glass; H 36.8 cm, D 21.6 cm
Victoria and Albert Museum, IS 06207

Theatrical performances have been popular in Burma, at all levels of society, for many centuries.[317] This magnificent headdress, used for dance or the theatre, is probably a product of the court, rather than the itinerant troupes who performed in the countryside. This assumption is based on the high quality of decoration of the headdress, most of which involves the use of lacquer. A rich effect is caused by the combination of flashing 'jewels' (actually fragments of coloured glass) on the gold background. For the gold leaf to adhere to the surface of the crown, a coating of lacquer was first applied over the wooden base of the headdress to anchor the gold leaf in place. Later, the fragments of glass were embedded into *thayo*, which was subsequently gilded. Each of the tiers of the headdress, which are made of sheet metal, has been separately made and slotted down on to the frame of the crown.[318]

The shape of the crown recalls that worn by certain Buddha images where his royal character is being emphasized. Another link with images of the Buddha, especially of the Mandalay period, is the fillet seen separating the crown from the forehead of the wearer (see cat. 77). This feature substantiates the date suggested for this item.

The links between the Burmese and the Thai theatre are numerous and have frequently been commented upon.[319] The similarity between this type of Burmese headdress and those found in the Thai royal theatre is further proof of this link.

317 The most recent study of the Burmese theatre, including history of the genre and bibliography, is Singer 1995.
318 For further discussion of this headdress, see Lowry 1974: 48.
319 See Singer 1995.

130

130
Betel-box, *kun it*
Burma, Pagan, *c.*1900
Bamboo, lacquer; H 22.1 cm, D 24.2 cm
OA 1998.7-23.28, gift of Mr and Mrs R. Isaacs

The fine *yun* decoration is in red,
orange and green on black. The scenes
depicted on the side of the cover and
on the box beneath are from the
gruesome folk tale of Maung Htilat
which, as a stage play, was popular
around 1900.[320] Maung Htilat, obsessed
with attaining immortality, cuts the
foetus from his lover's womb to make a
magic potion. His father-in-law pursues
him and has him killed.

Around the top edge of the cover
and the bottom edge of the box,
narrow friezes depict each sign of the
zodiac followed by a phrase for each
month, such as 'The figure of the goat
is for [the month of] *Tagu*'.[321] The
lacquer artist, having completed the
series on the top edge of the cover has
next turned the box and repeated the
series around the edge – with the result
that the whole frieze is upside down!
Further evidence of carelessness is that
the two cartouches on the side of the
lid have been left blank, and in the
zodiac series at the foot of the box the
month *Natdaw* (December) appears
twice and the month *Tawthalin*
(September) is omitted. The lettering is
tiny and very neat and could be the
work of Hsaya Nyunt (cat. 18 and 60).

320 See Singer 1995: 66 and fig. 23.
321 This is for the month of April.

131
Betel-box, *kun it*
Burma, Shan States, Laihka, late 19th century
Bamboo, lacquer, gold leaf; H 21.5 cm, D 28.9 cm
National Trust, Curzon Collection at Kedleston Hall,
Derbyshire, no. 425

Lord Curzon acquired this superb box
and another very similar to it (now in
the Victoria and Albert Museum)[322]
while he was Viceroy of India, probably
during his visit to Burma in 1901, but
possibly while he was patron of the
Indian Art Exhibition at Delhi in 1902–3
where lacquerwares were exhibited. The
yun decoration is of great quality, and
the lavish use of gold and the subject
matter and style of draughtsmanship
are all typical of the work for which the
lacquer masters of Laihka were
renowned. Examples of their best work
were customarily included in gifts
presented by Burmese kings to visiting
dignitaries and to the Emperor of China.

In this box the top of the lid shows
six figures dancing, and a seventh in
the centre of the circle. All are in lively
motion rather than static poses. They
wear their waist cloths girt high
between the legs in Shan style to form
baggy breeches. Between these figures
the infill of swirling stylized foliage
shows off the gilding against the red
background. The drum of the cover has
two registers of similar running and
dancing figures, all with very elaborate
coiffures, again with an infill of foliage
in gold and black on the red ground.
The artist who made this box has kept
his dramatic masterpiece for the bottom
of the base (see illustration opposite
below). A demon or ogre rides a horse,
and bites off the head of his startled
steed. This extraordinary feat possibly
features in a Shan legend, for it is also
depicted on the possible pair to this
box which Lord Curzon bequeathed to
the Victoria and Albert Museum when
he decided to keep the present box for
his own museum at Kedleston.

The interior is a fine cinnabar red.

There are two internal trays so that the box is in all respects fitted for betel-leaf use and for the ingredients to be wrapped in it. But such a box would have been made more for show than for daily use.

322 Reg. no. I.M. 199-1927. The example at the V&A is much larger than the one from Kedleston: height 32.5 cm, diameter of base 43.8 cm.

132
Betel-box, *kun-it*
Burma, central Upper Burma, perhaps Pagan, mid-19th century
Bamboo, lacquer; H 27.5 cm, D 28.8 cm
OA 1998.7-23.23, gift of Mr and Mrs R. Isaacs

In terms of overall shape this box resembles one in the Hamburgisches Museum für Völkerkunde und Vorgeschichte that is decorated with scenes from the *Maha-ummaga Jataka*[323] and numerous captions to the story in Burmese. It was obtained in 1899 by T.H. Thomann.[324] However, even closer, both in shape and in *yun* decoration, is a box published by Singer which has a scene of the *Ramayana* performed at court on the top of the box, and further scenes from the *Ramayana* around the drum of the lid.[325] All three boxes are similarly constructed. On this example the lid or cover is shallow and slightly domed, and the foot is flared and decorated with two bands of moulded *thayo* in *put lon* form. There are also traces of bare bamboo strips let into the surface to act as plain decoration; most of these have, however, been lacquered over fully or in part at a later period. The profile of the box is rather tall, the height only slightly less than the diameter – the *Ramayana* box illustrated by Singer is nearly the same size as this, while Prunner does not give the dimensions of the Hamburg box. The likely Burmese court provenance for depictions of theatre performances of the *Ramayana* and the

131 (above and right)

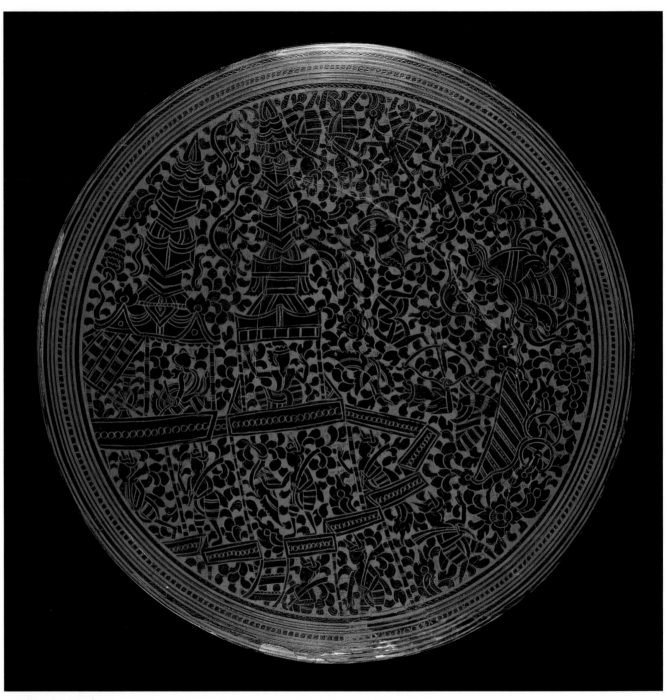

132 (top of the box)

fact that the Hamburg box probably came from Pagan indicate a production centre in Burma, not the Shan States. A date in the mid-nineteenth century, given the difference in style to the Hamburg example, seems likely.

This box has one internal tray just below the shallow cover, and another tray between the main box and the foot; both are red inside and toffee-brown outside. The foot itself is in two parts, each capable of functioning as a plate or tray. There are thus no less than six separate parts to the box, instead of the four usual in the later Pagan type.

The *yun* decoration is in black, silver (now tarnished) or perhaps green,[326] and gold – all on a red ground. There are two major areas of decoration: the circular top of the cover and a frieze running around the outer face of the cover. On the lid the decoration is dominated by two towers, *pyathat*.[327] Women are depicted in the upper stories, one with her hands thrown in the air. At the level below are four male, turbanned figures, all with swords over their shoulders. On the ground level are further warriors, one of whom turns towards the next element in the decoration, a royal figure in a horse-drawn chariot, aiming with a bow and arrow. A variety of animals and a figure (birds, ?mongooses, a goat and a goggle-eyed ogre-figure with hands in a position of adoration and legs akimbo) appear around, perhaps as filling devices, though this is not clear. Comparisons for this type of decorative arrangement can be found in Singer's already mentioned article, where three other boxes with similar arrays of figures in architectural settings are depicted; two of them also have surviving bases which show similar use of *put lon* and ridges of inset bamboo strips, coloured with red lacquer, forming the flared base.

These nineteenth-century boxes follow a different lay-out scheme for the decoration than do the later ones. Here the viewer's gaze is first held by the tall towers of the *pyathat*, which are placed off-centre and to the left; they fill that part of the circular area. The figures connected with the towers are 'read' from top to bottom. However, to continue the sequence, the box has to be turned, following the decoration that proceeds to the right and continues until the procession of activity is completed around the rim of the lid and ending up close to the top of the tower of the *pyathat*. This is seen in the current example, as well as in Singer's box with the court performance of the *Ramayana*.[328] This arrangement is in clear contrast to the later boxes where the field of decoration on the lids is divided from top to bottom and is read that way; twentieth-century *nandwin* designs on betel-boxes from Pagan are typical of this arrangement (see cat. 158).

Around the drum of this box is a further procession of martial activity. As with the scenes on the lid, the exact narrative – if there is one – is not known to the authors, though elements could be interpreted as from the *Ramayana* (in the description that follows, the possible *Ramayana* interpretation is given in brackets, and begins with a question mark). The frieze of decoration can be divided into six sections: (1) rows of warriors, both on foot and on horseback; (2) a figure protected by a royal umbrella in a horse-drawn chariot, with ogre-faced figures around (?Rama attended by the monkey army); (3) two rows of soldiers with Burmese swords, *da,* over their shoulders are accompanied by horsemen; (4) a conventional design for a water-crossing with ogres beyond, behind which are two female figures, one seated on the ground and one with her hands thrown up in horror – beyond them are further ogres and conventional designs which may be forest and a further water-crossing (?Sita under guard on the island of Lanka); (5) three wild animals precede an important male figure, who aims with bow and arrow towards the ogres, with a less-important male figure below (?Rama and Lakshmana); (6) two rows of warriors with dead animals, including an elephant.

There are two further elements of decoration on the box: firstly, around the lower drum, i.e. covered by the lid of the box, is an engraved and gilded 'fish-scale' or 'wave' pattern; secondly, on the underside of the base, in silver and gold but now cracked and damaged, is a highly stylized ogre brandishing a *da* in his right hand and a disc weapon in his left.

323 This is the *jataka* known in Burma as the *Mahosadha Jataka*. See cat. 102 for further discussion of this *jataka*.
324 Prunner 1966: 45–9, pl. IV (right) and folding plate at end of book.
325 Singer 1996: 96; the box illustrated in the same article is also close to the current one.
326 It is difficult now to differentiate between tarnished silver and darkened green.
327 In later work the palace is always indicated by three spires, symmetrically arranged with the central one being the tallest. The *pyathat* in this example are remarkable for the delightfully crooked arrangement of one tiered layer of the structure above the other. In this respect they are different from the well-arranged architecture of the Hamburg box.
328 Singer 1996: 96, bottom right.

133

133
Bowl, *khwet*
Burma, mid-20th century
Bamboo, lacquer, brass tacks; H 10.3 cm, D 17.5 cm
OA 1998.7-23.121, gift of Mr and Mrs R. Isaacs

This bowl is made of split bamboo basketry, which shows in places through the coating of red lacquer. It stands on four short feet shod with brass tacks. Vessels such as this are common throughout Burma to hold the curry accompanying the staple food of boiled rice. The cuisine of everyday life in Burma relies heavily on small dishes of meat or fish cooked in spiced gravies which, when taken with rice, enable the

consumption of large quantities of the latter. The (in)famous fish sauce, *ngapi*, is also widely used to enliven the plain boiled rice.

Ferrars in 1900 records how for most daily and communal meals the boiled rice was placed on 'a *byat* – a large, deep, wooden platter, lacquered red ... In the middle of the rice is set a bowl with the curry and the spoon.'[329] Each person seated around the *byat* can thus help themselves.

329 See Ferrars 1901: 64.

134
Bowl, *khwet*
Burma, perhaps Shan States, Inle Lake, early 20th century
Bamboo, lacquer; H 20.2 cm, D 29 cm
OA 1998.7-23.122, gift of Mr and Mrs R. Isaacs

This plain but elegantly shaped bowl stands on four claw feet and has deeply fluted sides. The ridges and the feet are made of *thayo*, and the whole vessel is lacquered red inside and out. The only other decoration is the narrow bands or hoops of bare bamboo at the lip and at the ridge above the fluted sides; these are left plain, unlacquered. When fresh, these bamboo hoops would have

134

135

provided a glossy golden yellow contrast to the red of the rest of the vessel.

Minor damage to the base and the feet has been recently repaired. A similar bowl seen for sale in Rangoon a few years ago had a medallion on the base made up of a central disc surrounded by fig leaves familiar in Burma from those of the sacred Bodhi tree.[330] This is a typical feature of some Shan bowls. The present example may thus have been made by Intha craftsmen near Ywama on the Inle

Lake.[331] Other Intha work features bare bamboo hoops contrasting with solid red (see cat. 89). This is probably a domestic vessel for cooked rice.[332]

330 *Ficus religiosa*, known throughout Buddhist Asia as the tree beneath which the Buddha sat when he achieved enlightenment. The leaves of the tree frequently appear in Burma as a decorative motif.
331 A similarly shaped, though less fine example is illustrated in Inglis 1998: 170, where it is described as Shan.
332 For another vessel for cooked rice, see cat. 137.

135
Rice pail, *htamin bon*

Burma, Shan States, Inle Lake, early 20th century
Wood, bamboo, lacquer, brass; H 25 cm, D 26.5 cm
OA 1998.7-23.267, gift of Mr and Mrs R. Isaacs

This vessel is a good example of the art of the Intha people who live around Inle Lake in the southern Shan States. Traditionally, their houses are built on stilts over the lake waters and they are renowned both as fishers and as agriculturalists, building up distinctive floating gardens along the swampy edges of the lake. They speak a dialect of Burmese related to that found in the Tavoy region in the far south and have traditions that date their settlement in the Inle region back to the twelfth century.[333] Their decorative art is quite distinct from that of the Irrawaddy valley and shows affinities with that of the Lan-na of northern Thailand.

The vessel is built of two elements joined together: a deep bowl of stout bamboo basketry and a square battered foot of wood. Both bowl and base have a black lacquered ground which has then been elaborately decorated with red lacquered relief work, and bands and slivers of bare, yellow bamboo. Two moulded bands of *thayo* ring the upper part of the bowl and the same two appear round the square foot. In each pair of moulded bands the upper one is broader and has finer 'pegs'; the lower is more coarsely beaded. On the foot the red lacquered moulded bands are separated by a broad, flat black-lacquered area, and this is itself edged with narrow strips of bare bamboo which, when fresh, would have been bright golden yellow. On the bowl the broader and finer band of *put ton*, imitation wooden peg-work, is edged above and below with narrow bands of bare bamboo minutely notched in two different patterns.

Yet a third pattern of notching is used on the hoop of bare bamboo just beneath the lower and coarser band of *put lon*. Below this is the most striking part of the decorative scheme. A row of bold pendent triangles stands out in red against the black lacquer of the bowl. Each triangle is formed of double lines of notched bamboo, lacquered red in the centre and inset with tiny squares of bamboo set in a diamond pattern.

The rim of the bowl is inverted and lacquered red, as is the interior of the pail. Handles of thick brass wire are set in the rim. These would have served to suspend the pail from a yoke or pole when it was being used to carry cooked rice to the monastery as a donation by the family which owned it.

The bold aesthetic of this and other wares from the environs of Inle Lake strikes the modern viewer as impressive. However, almost no art-historical work has so far been carried out on the lacquerwares of this region and few examples are found in public collections. Dating them is consequently extremely difficult. *Yun* wares are not popular in this part of the Shan States, though elsewhere the technique is practised (see cat. 131).

333 Dr D. Richardson (1836) describes how he 'saw … many Tavoyers today, who form the principal part of the inhabitants of En-lay, Enma, four villages of the lake (though they are not now confined to four); their dialect is so similar to that spoken at Tavoy at this day, that I could immediately detect a Tavoyer, though they must have been here about 662 years, if the tradition be correct that they accompanied Narapadi Say Thoo or Shoo, King of Pagan, as he reigned there about 1175 AD.'

136

Bowl, *ko kaw tee*

Burma, Kentung, Shan States, made by Hsaya Tay Ya in 1938
Bamboo, lacquer, gold leaf; H 11.8 cm, D 17.2 cm
OA 1998.7-23.164, gift of Mr and Mrs R. Isaacs

This bowl of bamboo basketry stands on four short feet. It is lacquered black inside and out, and decorated in relief with bands formed of delicate scrolling. Each little strand of *thayo* has been rolled out, cut to length and individually laid in position, and all this relief work is gilded. Four little birds – crows – ornament the legs. More elaborate high relief decorates other examples, which have models of couples in the costume of ethnic groups living near Kentung (cat. 36 and 169). Singer has traced the increasing elaboration of these bowls, called *ko kaw tee*.[334] This example is signed by the maker Hsaya Tay Ya and dated 1300 Burmese era, or 1938.

334 Singer 1991.

136

137

137
Food dish with cover, *htamin ok*
Burma, probably Prome, early 20th century
Bamboo, lacquer; H 25 cm, D (max.) 41 cm
OA 1998.7-23.227, gift of Mr and Mrs R. Isaacs

This deep bowl of bamboo basketry
stands on six short feet, each with a
pin-hole below where a brass thumb-
tack would have provided protection
against wear. The bowl is reinforced by
twelve sharp ribs, which also enhance
its decorative effect; they appear to be
composed of *thayo*. The lightly domed
cover fits closely. Bowl and cover are
lacquered red outside and in, but an
area on the bottom between the feet
has been left black. It is inscribed

'Hsaya Pya, workshop owner in Hkway
Dan'. This may have been a ward of a
town, probably Prome where similar
red-lacquered domestic wares were
made and signed in the first decades of
the twentieth century.

The vessel is a *htamin ok*, a food
dish or (literally) a cooked rice dish,
and would have held sufficient for a
sizeable family.[335] The two elements of
this vessel – bowl and lid – frequently
become separated,[336] so this set is
somewhat more unusual than its
mundane use would suggest. It is
further attractive on account of having
been well looked after and because of
its silky patina.

[335] Rice is the staple food in the Burmese diet,
and appears in practically every meal. Much of the
agricultural activity of the country is given over to
its cultivation. The annual cycle for those who work
on the land is dominated by the sequence from
planting of rice through to the gathering in and
threshing of the crop. Traditionally in Burma, all
economic and thus social activity revolved around
this cycle. The link between rice cultivation and the
spread of civilization throughout Southeast Asia is
a profound one.
[336] Elsewhere in the Isaacs Collection there is a
vessel of this type without a lid (1998.7-23.100),
and a lid which has become separated from its
vessel (1998.7-23.77).

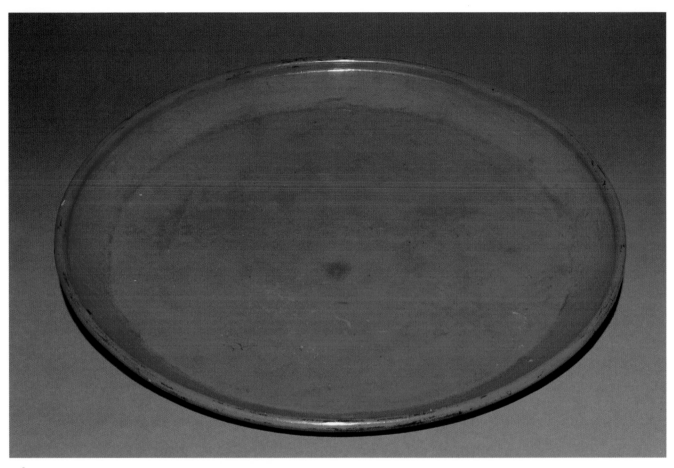

138

138
Tray, *pagan bya*

Burma, 1925–50
Bamboo, lacquer; D 41.7 cm
OA 1998.7-23.61, gift of Mr and Mrs R. Isaacs

This shallow circular tray made of bamboo basketry has been lacquered with good quality cinnabar lacquer and has a fine silky gloss. Wear has exposed the black undercoat in places, especially on the underside of the tray. Such trays were commonly used in Burmese households for serving food, but were quickly replaced by tin, which was more durable and almost as cheap.

This example is much finer in colour and finish than another of similar size (cat. 41). It also differs in being equally smooth on upper and lower surfaces, which have been carefully filled in with *thayo* before the coats of lacquer were applied.

139
Platter, *byat*

Burma; mid-20th century
Bamboo, lacquer, pearl buttons; H 6 cm, D 62.5 cm
OA 1998.7-23.111, gift of Mr and Mrs R. Isaacs

Large deep platters, lacquered red, were the usual, common eating dish and table in the past. Shway Yoe in 1882 noted the *byats*, 'platters of all sizes, up to the gigantic circular tray as big as a small table, used for dishing up the family dinner...'337 Most were made of wood when planks of great breadth were plentiful. This example is of strong split bamboo basketry, first smoothed with *thayo* to fill all the interstices of the basketry on the upper surface, then given several coats of red lacquer. The base still shows the pattern of the basketry weave and has nine short feet made of lumps of *thayo*. Four of them retain the pearl shirt buttons with which

they were shod to make them hard-wearing. Sometimes chips of broken glazed pottery were used for this purpose, and in later days brass-headed upholstery tacks.

Daily use meant inevitable wear of the lacquer surface, and when this became cracked or flaked it had to be renewed. Before the Second World War there used to be lacquer-repair men walking the streets of Rangoon. They cried 'Fix your lacquer, black or red', and carried on a shoulder yoke two bamboo tubes, one of raw lacquer sap for the black and the other of sap mixed with cinnabar, *hinthabada*, for the red. Called upstairs by the housewife, the lacquer man would soon stroke on a fresh coat of lacquer. An elderly man recalled in the 1990s how as a small child he could not resist touching the gleaming new lacquer surface, leaving a

139

small hand print on it. He learnt in this
sticky way that lacquer needs several
days to set dry (or, as the Burmese say,
'settle to sleep').338

337 Shway Yoe 1882: 276.
338 Hsaya Aung Thin, personal communication.

140

Stand, *daung lan*

Burma; early 20th century
Bamboo, lacquer; H 13 cm, D 26 cm
OA 1998.7-23.220, gift of Mr and Mrs R. Isaacs

This stand, or *daung lan*, consists of a
tray made of woven bamboo matting
joined by many little splints of bamboo
to a foot-ring of coiled bamboo. The

140

141

apparently been gnawed by a rat which must have become trapped inside.

Such stands were used to present gifts to foreign guests, and early European travellers needed stands like these for return presentations. Hiram Cox at the capital Amarapura in 1820 noted:

> I should have mentioned that the sandogans brought to my bungalow several stands or wooden waiters, about eighteen inches high, painted red and gilt, to carry the presents on; these I had covered with red silk, and placed the Governor-General's letter to the king on one; the shanscrit [sic] books on five others; my own present to his majesty, a pair of right-handed chank[339] on a sixth, and the Governor General's letters to the whoonghees[340] on a seventh; and when I left my house, they were carried down to the boat before me.[341]

and, speaking of Burmese trays of sweetmeats:

> These trays were of wood, painted red and gilt; they were about 18 inches in height, the side supporters little turned balustrades, united at the bottom by a circular rim.[342]

While this example is clearly not of the same quality as those used by Cox in high diplomacy, the shape and function are near identical.

339 i.e. conch, from the Sanskrit, *shankha*. Those with a right-handed spiral are auspicious for religious and royal ceremonies.
340 i.e. ministers.
341 Cox 1821: 83.
342 Cox 1821: 91.

tray is lacquered red above and brown below. Red lacquer is also used on the row of splints and on the outer surface of the foot-ring. The inner side is black.

There were many varieties of this kind of stand. Some were quite grand with 'balustrading' of turned wood, and were used to hold gifts both secular and monastic (cat. 141). But the present stand is for purely domestic use, and would have held a dish or bowl of food at the family meal.

141
Table stand, *daung baung*
Burma, 19th century
Teak, lacquer; H 38.4 cm, D 38.5 cm
OA 1998.7-23.128, gift of Mr and Mrs R. Isaacs

This stand of lacquered teak is built of a plate at the top, joined to a wooden ring base by a set of twenty-three turned wooden legs. The plate and base are lacquered brownish red, and the legs blackish-brown. One leg is a replacement and two more legs have

142

Steamer, *paung o*
Burma, mid-20th century
Bamboo, lacquer; H (with lid) 18 cm, D 22 cm
OA 1998.7-23.44, gift of Mr and Mrs R. Isaacs

When basketry is soaked in liquid lacquer (*thit si*), it is strengthened, hardened and made rot-proof and, most importantly, waterproof. This lidded basket has been lightly lacquered in dark red-brown to fit it for its purpose, that of a food steamer. Holes have been left in the centre of the base and lid to allow steam to rise through the contents when the basket is placed on top of a clay pot of boiling water over a charcoal fire. The basket has been skilfully woven in imitation of the earthenware pots commonly used all over Burma. Good pots are made near Pegu in the village of Bhan-dagon. The contents would be leaf-wrapped packets of rice or spiced fish (*ngabaung dok*). Nowadays Chinese steamers of bamboo strips, bent into flat cylinders, are in general use. They stack one above another.

143

Cup, *khwet*
Burma, probably Kyaukka, early 20th century
Bamboo, lacquer; H 7.2 cm, D 8.8 cm
OA 1998.7-23.183, gift of Mr and Mrs R. Isaacs

This simple cup is formed from bamboo basketry, lacquered black outside and brown inside. It was probably made in Kyaukka, a large village near Monywa, whose plain black red or brown wares were renowned for their durability. The owner of this cup, Maung Nyunt, must have been anxious not to lose it, since

142

143

144

cheapness.[343] If they lasted only a few months in use, they could be discarded and easily replaced.

343 Symes in 1795 noted that 'the coarser work is amazingly cheap. Ten or twelve half-pint mugs may be had for one rupee, whilst a single mug of good finish will cost the same sum.' (Symes 1800) Crawfurd remarked in 1827: 'neat, tasteful and comparatively very cheap ... 100 cups approximately one pint for about 15 shillings ... these last six months.' (Crawfurd 1834)

145

Covered dish, *lahpet ok*
Burma, Kyaukka, early 20th century
Bamboo, lacquer; H (with lid) 12.7 cm, D (inc. handles) 25.5 cm
OA 1998.7-23.204, gift of Mr and Mrs R. Isaacs

he has pecked his name on the base with a pin or needle, filling the dots with white lime.

144

Cup, *khwet*
Burma, Pagan, mid-20th century
Bamboo, lacquer; H 7.5 cm, D 10.4 cm
OA 1998.7-23.98, gift of Mr and Mrs R. Isaacs

This drinking cup of bamboo basketry lacquered black has been decorated in yellow with the *yun* technique. The motifs are floral swags and birds. Such cups were produced in huge numbers in Pagan for export mainly by river steamer to markets in the cities and towns of Burma. Early travellers remarked on their amazing

This shallow oval dish and its lightly domed cover are lacquered black outside and red inside, typical of the sober domestic wares made in Kyaukka near Monywa, on the lower Chindwin

145

146

river. The dish has two handles set horizontally and a third, identically shaped, is set vertically on the cover.

In use this dish would have held pickled tea-leaf, *lahpet*, an essential accompaniment to Burmese social intercourse.344 *Lahpet* is offered after meals with crispy garlic slices, roast beans, tiny dried shrimps and toasted sesame seeds; '*lepet* clears the palate into sweetnesss'.345 It is also used at certain ceremonies and in the past was made up into little packets and sent out as invitations to family celebrations such as the ear-boring ceremony for a young girl.346 Mi Mi Khaing also records the use of *lahpet* as a stimulant:

Card players need it to be served every hour through their day-long sessions. Theatregoers rely on it to sit through dramas lasting from dusk to dawn. Students apt to doze over exam books pause ... to make *lepet*

salad and keep awake on its pep, added to chili's sting and lime's piercing sour.

She goes on to say:

The rhyme which chooses for excellence:

Of leaves the tea, or *lapet*,

Of meat, chicken or *kyet*,

Of fruits the mango or *thayet*

must have been composed to extol *lepet*, naming the other two for the sake of the rhyme.347

Also from the same source, we learn that 'the tea-leaf, plucked tender, is pressed into bamboo containers which acts like a silo'. She continues with a recipe for all the dainties that can accompany the taking of *lahpet*.348

344 Tea is grown in the northern hills. See Ferrars 1901: 65.
345 See Mi MI Khaing 1975: 156.
346 See Daw Khin Myo Chit 1988: 136–7. Ferrars 1901: 70 and 72 records the traditional link

between taking pickled tea and the marriage ceremony (and with the much rarer divorce).
347 See note 345.
348 See note 345.

146

Box, *thitta*

Burma, probably Pagan, early/mid-20th century
Wood, lacquer; H 8.5 cm, L 23 cm, W 22 cm
OA 1998.6-13.4

The vivid depiction of the prowling feline on the base of this box marks it out as the work of a considerable artist. It is executed in the *yun* technique in red, yellow and black.

It comes from the same group as the two plates at cat. 166 and is thus an indicator of the type of container acquired by Chettiar families to bring back to India from Burma.

147

Instrument cases, *tauk*
Burma, mid-20th century
Bamboo, lacquer; L 19.5 cm and 21 cm
OA 1998.7-23.173 and 257, gift of Mr and Mrs R. Isaacs

These tubes of woven bamboo have been lacquered to protect the basketry from fraying and to render it rot-proof and waterproof. They have close-fitting caps. Such tubes were used to hold tools or instruments such as a tattooing needle or a chisel-like fingernail cutter. One has been lacquered red and has a patina of greasy black dirt, giving a chequered appearance. The other, lacquered black, has a patch repair at one end effected with a small piece of cloth affixed with lacquer.

149

Snack carrier, *jaint*
Burma, Shan States, Inle Lake, early 20th century
Bamboo, wood, lacquer; H 24 cm, W 15 cm
OA 1998.7-23.175, gift of Mr and Mrs R. Isaacs

147

Box in the shape of a ?frog
Burma, early 20th century
Palm nut, lacquer; H 10.8 cm, L 15.1 cm
OA 1998.7-23.197, gift of Mr and Mrs R. Isaacs

The two elements of this box are made up of the split nut of the toddy, or palmyra palm (*Borassus flabellifer*); it was probably used to hold sweetmeats. Such confectionery was made from boiling down the sweet sap of the palm which produced palm sugar, 'jaggery'.[349]

Thayo has been used to build up the shape of the beast, so that the nut origin is almost completely lost, at least from the outside. The interior of the box and the full lips and face of the animal are lacquered red, the rest of the object black. The eyes were originally beads of glass, now missing.

The precise identity of the beast portrayed is a matter of conjecture. It is said to be a frog, but may actually be a very junior *makara*, or sea-monster.[350] Such boxes are still being made today but this one dates from the first half of the twentieth century. Cat. 26 is also formed from the split fruit of a toddy palm, but has been modelled into a more readily recognized animal – a chicken.

[349] See Yule and Burnell 1886: 446, for the various palms from which jaggery can be made.
[350] Of Indian origin, the *makara*, is a mythical water monster, a cross between a crocodile and a water serpent. It made its entry into Burma along with Buddhism and has remained an important element in the decorative vocabulary of artists. For *makara* in Burmese art, see Aye Myint 1993: 95 and 98–100.

This stacked container consists of four parts, all made of woven split bamboo and fitting one above the other. The largest is mounted on an integral rectangular base of lightweight wood, and the uppermost forms a lightly convex lid to the whole. All four parts have eyelets set into the lacquered basketry to hold a carrying cord. The individual containers are lacquered black inside and out, and all are decorated with a narrow band of pink at the rim. The lid has pink lines along the folds of the basketry forming a shallow St Andrew's cross.

Though far too small to hold a full meal, such containers might be used for tasty and sustaining snacks to carry on a journey. Very similar examples are in the Ethnography collections of the British Museum.[351] One of them, exhibited at the Paris Exhibition in 1900, was collected in Shwebo district. However, the present example displays

148

the pink and black colouring favoured
by the Intha people who live around
Inle Lake in the southern Shan States.
Provenances over as wide an area as
Shwebo and Inle Lake imply that such
stacked containers were probably widely
used throughout Burma – and indeed
probably in parts of northern Thailand
and Laos.

351 Reg. nos: Ethno 1901.6-5.20 and 1919.7-17.156.
One is also illustrated in Fraser-Lu 1994: 297, fig.
57, where it is described as being 'Woven by the
Intha people of Inle Lake'.

150

Two basketry boxes, *pachok*
Burma, probably from the Shan States, mid-20th
century
Bamboo, lacquer; (a) H 5.3 cm, L 9.4 cm; (b) h. 8.5
cm, L 16.1 cm
OA 1998.7-23.264 (a) and 268 (b), gift of Mr and
Mrs R. Isaacs

These small boxes of woven bamboo
have close-fitting lids reinforced with
diagonal splints. Several coats of
lacquer inside and out serve to stiffen
the whole and make it waterproof. Both
are lacquered black outside as is the
inside of the larger box; that of the
smaller one is brown. Such boxes, with

149

150

or without a coating of lacquer waterproofing were, until the advent of plastic, the common storage containers in Burmese houses. The largest were woven from strips of toddy-palm leaf-stalk, sometimes in chequered weave of white with dark brown or black.[352]

These little boxes would have held almost any small item, including lucky charms or talismans.[353]

352 For a general discussion of Burmese baskets, see Fraser-Lu 1994, pp. 295–302.
353 Such talismans might even include a lump of nickel-iron meteorite, constantly carried around to provide protection from thunder and lightning (Hkam Hpa Tu Sadan, personal communication).

151

151

Tea-plate, *pagan bya*

Burma, Pagan, made by Hsaya Hsaing, *c.*1930
Bamboo, lacquer; D 19.5 cm
OA 1998.7-23.169, gift of Mr and Mrs R. Isaacs

This tea-plate was probably one of a
matching set made to order, complete
with tea-pot and cups.354 Lacquer
resists hot water and is quite suitable
for serving hot liquids. The maker,
Hsaya Hsaing of the Glass Melter's Ward
of Pagan Town, has put his name and
address in two cartouches on the lip.
The *yun* decoration, mainly in green
and red on black is in the *pabwa* floral
pattern with little figures reserved
within it – *yok let pagya*. On the back
of the plate the owner has daubed the
letter 'ta'. In the late 1930s new shapes
introduced at the Lacquer School in
Pagan included portable folding picnic
tables, ice-cream cups, saucers and
spoons, and plain yellow and green
dessert plates.

354 A tea-pot whose shape exactly copies that of
enamelled metal tea-pots, so common in early- and
mid-twentieth-century Britain, but made of split
bamboo, lacquered black, is in the British Museum,
OA 1996.5-1.56.

152

Tiffin box, *htamin jaint*

Burma, Kyaukka, Lower Chindwin District, pre-1940
Wood, bamboo, lacquer; H 32.6 cm, D 14 cm
OA 1998.7-23.221, gift of Mr and Mrs R. Isaacs

This vessel is not a traditional Burmese
shape, though it was quickly
assimilated into Burmese life. It was
brought to Burma from India in the first
decade of the twentieth century.355
Though smaller than many examples,
this tiffin box is typical. A handle of
turned wood holds in place three bowls
and a lid; the latter could be turned
over and used as a cup. Each part of
the vessel is lacquered black outside,
and a good cinnabar red inside. The
box was made in Kyaukka, near
Monywa on the lower Chindwin.

Kyaukka plain black, red or brown wares were famous for their solid construction and durability in daily use. The maker, Ko Hpo Yu, has signed his name on the top of the lid.

These boxes were used as lunch-boxes to contain home-cooked meals eaten at the place of work, frequently by civil servants at government offices. Each of the bowls would have held a separate dish. The importance of such vessels among the large Indian population brought into Burma during the late nineteenth and early twentieth centuries can hardly be overestimated, since it was necessary for different Indian groups to ensure ritual purity as regards food consumed. This is underlined by the survival of the tiffin box today in Indian cities such as Bombay, where it continues to fulfil the requirement that food cooked at home can be carried or delivered to the desk of an individual without contamination.

355 Other examples imported from India include octagonal and hexagonal tables on stands. These have an Indo-Persian origin.

153
Tumbler, *khwet*
Burma, Kentung, Shan States, made by Hsaya Nanda in 1935
Bamboo, lacquer; H 11.1 cm, D 8.2 cm
OA 1998.7-23.237, gift of Mr and Mrs R. Isaacs

This tumbler, most probably made in a set of half a dozen for an Englishman's whisky peg, is decorated in typical Kentung style.356 Bands of low relief decoration are formed of individual strands of *thayo*. This mixture can be rolled out into fine strands which are cut to the required length, lifted with a little tool of wood or horn, and with a deft twist laid in place on the still tacky lacquer surface of the vessel. The pattern is built up strand by strand, and gilded when complete. Here both red and black lacquer have been used on the exterior, but the inside is red. On

153

154

the base in a small circular medallion the maker, Hsaya Nanda, has used the black and gold *shwe zawa* technique to sign his name, adding 'Kentung Town' and the date 1297 in the Burmese era, equivalent to 1935.[357]

356 For other examples, see cat. 136 and 165. Shway Yoe in 1882 mentions the production of 'peg' tumblers and cigar cases as examples of non-Burmese forms, and bemoans the non-development of 'national forms' (p.276).
357 For lacquer work at Kentung generally, see Singer 1991: 154–8. For Burmese eras, see Shway Yoe 1882, ch. LIX: 549–59.

154
Tumbler, *khwet*
Burma, Pagan, at the approach to the Ananda Temple, 1991
Bamboo, lacquer, acrylic paints; H 8.6 cm, D 7.6 cm
OA 1998.7-23.99, gift of Mr and Mrs R. Isaacs

These tumbler-shaped cups are made of bamboo basketry, lacquered black and painted with decorative patterns using acrylic paints. This technique is very new, and much quicker to execute than *yun* designs. It is also faster to dry. Although the lacquered surface is rough and gritty, the painted patterns are gay and lively. One of the cups has a design of green network, filled alternately with ochre and magenta dots, and crossed by diagonal wavy lines in white. The design even includes an inscription, which reads 'Pagan, Number One Hundred'.

These are cheap and cheerful tourist ware, sold for less than 5 pence each.

155
Offering vessel, *hsun gwet*
Burma, Kyaukka near Monywa, made by Ko Htun Aye, mid-20th century
Bamboo, lacquer; H 39.7 cm, D 47.8 cm
OA 1998.7-23.190, gift of Mr and Mrs R. Isaacs

Well-off Burmese families owned such vessels, and used them to carry cooked food to the monastery. This example shows no sign of use and is in exceptionally fine condition.
It was made by lacquer master Ko Htun Aye of Tanaung-Wun, part of the village of Kyaukka near Monywa in the dry country of Upper Burma. Kyaukka wares were for long famed for their sturdiness and quality. The best examples attain dignified proportions.

The vessel is assembled from six parts, all lacquered black outside and red inside. The deep bowl stands on six feet and, with two deep trays, can hold a considerable quantity of food in several separate dishes at once. The

155

main bowl is fluted, the ribs having been built up separately in *thayo* and stuck to the sides of the bowl using lacquer as glue.

In a roundel on the bottom of the base the lacquer master has put his name, engraved and filled with red.

156

Offering vessel, *hsun ok*

Burma, Mandalay, late 19th or early 20th century
Bamboo, wood, metal sheet, laquer, gold leaf, coloured glass spangles and prisms; H 102 cm, D 46 cm
OA 1993.11-17.1

Spired offering vessels frequently come in pairs so that they can be placed in a shrine on either side of a Buddha

image, and this example is one of such a pair.358 Both the shape and embellishment of this vessel represent the Mandalay style of decorating lacquer vessels and objects, which are typically elaborated with gilded relief work made of *thayo*, and inlay of coloured glass. The heyday of producing such items was the last years of the independent kingdom of Burma (the fall

of Mandalay took place in 1885) and
the next couple of decades; another of
the finest pairs of Mandalay *hsun ok*
now in Britain was acquired there in
1895.[359] It is a happy accident of
history that this type of florid and
highly coloured decoration was popular
not only with the Burmese at this time,
but also in Europe, for such a style was
entirely in keeping with the aesthetic of
late Victorian and Edwardian Britain.

Three elements make up the
standard offering vessel: the stand
including the bowl, the lid including the
spire, and an internal tray. The first two
elements of this *hsun ok* are mostly
made of coiled split bamboo, the
exceptions being the upper part of the
spire which is of wood, the filigree
wings of the *hintha* bird which are of
metal, and the bottom of the bowl
which is of split bamboo matting. The
tray is also made of a piece of matting
cut to the requisite shape and then
lacquered. The lacquer surfaces inside
are all a good red colour: lacquer sap
mixed with cinnabar, the mixture known
in Burma as *hinthabada*. The external
decoration is made up of *thayo* work,
mainly scrolls set with coloured glass
spangles, mostly green and white.
However, the two registers on either
side of the opening – the most visible
parts – bear more elaborate *thayo*
decoration. Here, lion-like animals
charge around the belly of the vessel
amidst higher relief scrollwork. Here
also, the glass decoration is added to,
as not only are there spangles but
larger octagonal pyramids set into the
floral designs. The spire of the vessel is
topped with a *hintha* bird, the body of
wood and the wings of metal sheet set
with glass spangles.

358 The other one is OA 1993.1-17.2.
359 See cat. 1.

157

157
Basin, *hpala*
Burma, Ava, workshop of Hsaya Maung Za, 1930s
Bamboo, lacquer; H 11.1 cm, D 38.8 cm
OA 1998.7-23.239, gift of Mr and Mrs R. Isaacs

This large basin, lacquered glossy black
outside and a good cinnabar red inside,
has the flared mouth characteristic of
Ava wares. The industry did not survive
the Second World War, though one
workshop still turns out plain black
alms bowls for monks (*thabeik*) but on
a metal, not coiled bamboo, foundation
and with plastic stands. This basin was
made to order by Hsaya Maung Za in
his workshop in the Lacquerware
Quarter of Ava for a customer in
Rangoon, U Maung Galay of the
Produce Market District, as inscriptions
on the base of the vessel tell us. These
are inscribed in yellow *yun*; the maker
adds the same claim for the high
quality of his wares as do all the Ava
lacquer masters: 'Number One'. While it
is true that no piece of 'Number Two'
quality has yet been found, we can

admit the truth of Hsaya Maung Za's
claim for this fine basin.

It may have been ordered for a
special occasion and could have held
cooked rice. But it may instead have
contained a *kadawbwe*, an offering 'so
characteristic of Burmese cultural life
and so popular that it is almost a
symbol of the national culture'.[360] The
basic components of this ancient
arrangement are a green coconut with
long stalk attached, several hands of
green bananas, and sprigs of eugenia
leaves. Optional are flowers such as
gladioli, rice cakes, money notes held in
sticks, paper flags and ribbons. The
kadawbwe appears at all *nat*
ceremonies, but also in rows in prayer
halls on pagoda platforms. At weddings,
celebrations of examination success,
and football and sports competitions it
is often seen.

360 Rodrigues 1992: 19.

158
Betel-box, *kun it*
Burma, Pagan, workshop of Hsaya Than in Market
Ward, 1910–20
Bamboo, lacquer; H 23 cm, D 26.5 cm
OA 1999.3-1.5, Brooke Sewell Fund

This fine box is typical of wares made
at Pagan during this century, with a lid
without mouldings or domed top, and
with two internal trays. *Yun* design, in
orange and green on black and using
the *nandwin* 'king at court' pattern, has
become the very trademark of Pagan
workshops. One of the internal trays
has been clumsily repaired, producing a
poor fit inside the drum. The interiors
of the trays, the drum and the lid are of
a fine cinnabar colour – this, in
combination with the design, is a
further indicator of Pagan manufacture.

However, it is the vibrancy of the
nandwin design that marks out this
large betel-box from among so many
others of similar type. The three areas
of decoration with this design are the
top of the lid, the sides of the lid and

the sides of the drum. As often happens, the decoration on the last of these areas is slightly cruder than on the lid; it will, after all, not be seen for most of the lifetime of the vessel.

1. The layout on the top of the lid displays both standard and non-standard features. The king is clearly seen in the centre and located beneath the tallest of the three spires, which always indicate the palace, while behind is a zigzag wall with gates let into it; these are all standard. Less standard are the five figures behind the wall, three of whom brandish weapons – two have Burmese swords, *da*, while the third waves a spear above his head.

2. Here there are four divisions of the decoration, two of conventional *nandwin*. The other two panels are

clearly narrative with the space divided into registers and with captions for the different scenes. On one side there is an elephant carrying a *hsun ok* in its howdah – is this the arrival of the Tooth Relic in Pagan?[361] The other narrative panel, on the other side of the lid, is also densely figured and inscribed. The inscriptions record the narrative of Byatta, the twisted henchman of Anawrahta, and Meh Wunna, the flower-eating forest nymph, and their two sons 'Gold Pot the Elder' and 'Gold Pot the Younger' (Khin Myo Chit 1984: 79–81). Bands of imitation bare bamboo in *yun* appear above the narrative.

3. The sides of the drum also display four panels, two of them *nandwin*. The other two panels are again more narrative than the *nandwin* sections:

here we even see a figure in a European-style chair, as well as – once more – figures with *da*. At the base of the drum are further inscriptions mentioning that the story illustrated is that of Ambassador Wayluthaya.

361 For a depiction of this scene, see cat. 61.

159
Bowl, khwet
Burma, Pagan, 1920
Bamboo, horsehair, gold leaf, lacquer; H 7.5 cm, D 15.2 cm
OA 1996.5-8.1, gift of Colleen Beresford, in memory of Mrs Gretta Golledge

This engaging bowl is of a type produced in very large numbers – and indeed still made today – in the lacquer manufactories of Pagan. The split bamboo woven with horsehair gives it the distinctive flexible frame so admired by visitors to Pagan. It is decorated both inside and out in the black-and-gold, *shwe zawa*, technique.[362] Inside the bowl a galloping horse stands out in gold leaf, brilliant still, despite wear, against the glossy black of the rest of the interior. Around the outside is a figured scene, perhaps drawn from the *Ramayana*.[363] There are four episodes, all of which take place in the forest: (1) a female figure seated on a rock with a kneeling male figure in the foreground; (2) a running male figure with upraised staff advancing on two masked ogres, *balu*; (3) as (1), but the male now has a staff; (4) a different male figure attacking a quadruped with human head and mask appearing from the beast's neck.[364] On the broad base of the bowl is a hybrid bird/lion beast amidst swirling foliage.

As so often happens with items decorated in the *shwe zawa* technique, the gold surface has become very worn, because the gold leaf used is very thin.

The purchase of this bowl at Nyaung-U in 1920 by Mrs Golledge recalls the fact that visitors to Pagan in the first

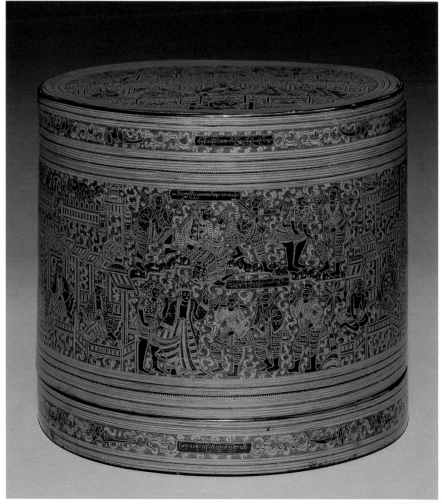

159

A painted inscription on the top of the largest cover has been deliberately rubbed off by a later owner, but remains legible and clearly indicates the original use of the vessel. It reads, 'The deed of merit of the deceased U Hliang Win Yi'. The family of the deceased, whose name suggests Chinese descent, used this vessel to hold cooked food, which was offered to monks on the day of his death as a final deed of merit, in a custom called *thet pyauk hsun*. It is also customary to offer food to monks for seven consecutive days following the death, in a custom called *hsun zin*. The monks invited to the bereaved family's home would recite the *paritta* daily.367

Prome was an important place of lacquer manufacture, though not during most of this century. It is still, however, remembered as the town of the *shwe zawa* master, Hsaya Pa (see cat. 128), and was also a centre for the production of *hmanzi shwe cha* furniture at the beginning of this century.368

decades of this century arrived there rather than at Pagan because it had the best landing station. This small town immediately to the north-west was where lacquerwares made at Pagan were sold to passengers on the passing steamers.365

362 For a description of this technique, see pp. 38–9.
363 For the use of the Indian epic as a source for scenes on lacquer vessels, see cat. 65.
364 It is this scene that suggests a *Ramayana* identification, as it could be interpreted as Rama shooting the Golden Deer. In Burma this scene is shown with the mask of the ogre tipped back off the head, just as here, to show that this is a disguise (another example of this is seen at cat. 65). If this is a correct identification, 1) could be the scene of Sita being left in the care of Lakshmana while Rama goes into the forest to hunt the Golden Deer, and 3) could be Sita approached by Ravana. However, 2) with the ogres would still be difficult to understand, unless the ogres are actually to be taken for monkeys and thus represent Hanuman and his army.
365 See Talbot Kelly 1905: 143. For information on the famous Irrawaddy Flotilla Company which ran the steamer service on the river, see McRae and Prentice 1978 and McRae 1990.

160

Offering vessel, *hsun gwet*

Burma, Prome, made by Hsaya Hpyu, 1925–50
Bamboo, lacquer; H 44 cm, D 48 cm
OA 1992.7-28.3

This large vessel, made in Prome by Hsaya Hpyu, is signed by the maker using a seal to impress the lettering on to a roundel on the base. For this signature, see photograph on p. 47. It is constructed of bamboo basketry, which has been purposely left apparent on the main bowl between the ribs. There are twelve ribs, six short feet and five separate parts to the vessel, including a deep internal tray. The four stages of the vessel are all ridged and decorated above the ridge with a band of applied *thayo* pressed from a mould. The first three stages have a band of twisted orchid sprays – *thazin gway* – while the topmost vessel has a dog-tooth design, or *acheik*. Covering the vessel is a cinnabar red lacquer of good quality.366

366 Compare shape and decoration with cat. 32.
367 'The Paritta or Mahaparitta, a small collection of texts gathered from the Suttapitaka [the discourses of the Buddha], is, to this day, more widely known by the Burmese laity of all classes than any other Pali book. The Paritta, learnt by heart and recited on appropriate occasions, is to conjure various evils physical and moral.' (Bode 1909: 3.)
368 A photograph of an elaborately decorated shrine on a plinth covered with a mass of relief decoration apppeared in the *Rangoon Gazette Pictorial Supplement*, n.d. [1930s?]. It is captioned 'carved lacquer industry at Prome'. I am grateful to Patricia Herbert for this reference.

161

Offering vessel, *hsun ok*

Burma, Laihka, Shan States, c.1900
Bamboo, wood, lacquer, gold; H 54 cm, D 32 cm
National Trust, Curzon Collection at Kedleston Hall, Derbyshire, no. 423

The rather flattened bowl and moderately short spire are typical of Shan *hsun ok*, the offertory vessels

used to carry gifts to the monastery, usually of cooked food. The lavish use of gold in the *yun* decoration round the walls of the bowl and on the lid and foot point to Laihka as the place of manufacture. This is confirmed by a paper label loose inside the vessel, on which is written in Curzon's hand:[369] 'Laihka. Big pinnacle shaped lacquer bowl.' A second label pasted to the bottom of the base is in Burmese script and reads: '2 colour traditional style Shan offerings box.' Another very similar but slightly smaller *hsun ok* is also in Curzon's Indian Museum at Kedleston Hall, but it has no label. It is surely the pair to this example, as these offering vessels invariably come in twos so that they can be placed one on either side of a Buddha image.

The whole vessel is in pristine condition having never, apparently, been used. The interior of the cover and bowl and the single internal tray are all covered with a layer of fine red lacquer – 'pigeon-blood' red as it is known in Burma. The outside of the tray is toffee-brown in colour.

369 We are grateful to Jill Banks, archivist at Kedleston, for confirming this. To have such certain provenance for wares from the Shan States is unusual, so the discovery of this label is of considerable importance.

162
Betel-box, *kun it*
Burma, probably from the Shan States, 19th century or earlier
Bamboo, lacquer; H 18 cm, D 19.3 cm
OA 1991.4-10.1, gift of Dr Jessica Rawson

This betel-box is made up of the following elements: (1) a densely decorated lid; (2) an internal tray with a heavy lip and red lacquer inside and orange/brown outside; (3) a lower drum with brownish red interior and an exterior that has been saved from fading by being covered by the lid; and (4), very distinctively, a small low base with an orange interior on which the

162 (top of lid)

drum is set. The use of this small base – an extra element compared with Burmese betel-boxes – as well as the colouring throughout, is characteristic of Shan manufacture.

The decoration on this box is in the *yun* technique in red and yellow lacquer, and is in a style that is not well known, though thought to be old. There is much use of cross-hatching and of tightly packed rows of parallel-engraved lines, both vertical and horizontal. The main field is on the top of the lid and is made up of figures in an architectural setting. In this respect it is similar to cat. 124, though the colouring is different and the abstraction – although severe here – is slightly less. Three tiered spires, perhaps representing palace buildings, dominate, with the central one being taller than the other two. Figures are

visible in the bottom storey of the structures, especially the central one, and other figures – mostly indicated by rows of heads – are depicted in front. Right at the front is a figure who appears to be carried on a litter. The tableau is framed by zigzag panels of fencing around the compound.

On the side of the lid is a frieze of birds, each with rounded wings and hooked beaks. Above this are rows of inlaid strips of bare bamboo. On the drum, and thus usually covered by the lid, is a poorly executed frieze of repeating triangular elements. Beneath this is a band of decoration made of moulded *thayo*, imitating small turned wood balusters. The base is decorated on the bottom with the same triangular motif seen on the drum; in the centre is a hole, perhaps the seating for a now lost repair.

opposite: 161

163

164

164
Ceremonial rice basket, *ko kaw tee*
Burma, Shan States, Kentung, *c.*1900
Bamboo, lacquer, gold, metal hoop handles; H 16
cm, D 24 cm
OA 1994.5·31.1, gift of Martin U.L. Williams and T.
Richard Blurton in memory of Richard Hough
(1959–93)

The organic shape of the *ko kaw tee*,
starting from a square base and ending
with a circular lip, makes them
especially attractive. Noel Singer and
Sylvia Fraser-Lu have elucidated the
history of these rice baskets from
Kentung, both the type with panels of
lacquer putty figures in high relief on
each of the four sides and those – such
as this example – with no figured
decoration.[371] Singer has convincingly
suggested that the non-figured type is
the precursor of the figured variety, and
that baskets, such as this one, with a
plain red interior are to be dated to
before the first decade of the last
century.[372]

The exterior decoration is made
using tiny threads of *thayo*, which are
teased into tendrils and scrolls on the
lacquered surface of the basket and
then gilded. On this example there is
such a scroll around the rim, while at
the four corners and set above each of
the four feet are triangular elements
with scalloped edges filled with further
thayo decoration. In each of these
elements is a vase (just above the foot)
from which springs a scrolling tree that
Singer calls a 'karabuk or wish-fulfilling
tree'. Along the middle of each side of
the basket are pendent triangular
elements also filled with *thayo*
scrollwork, though without the vases.
Metal handles on the circular rim, which
were used for attaching a carrying strap,
suggest an early date in the sequence,
consistent with the red interior. Once
the baskets were made as curios, these
last vestiges of their original usefulness
gradually disappear. One of the authors
has seen in a private collection in Delhi
a *ko kaw tee* with its original carrying

163
Stem bowl, *khwet*
Burma, Shan States, Inle Lake, early 20th century
Bamboo, lacquer; H 20.5 cm, D 22.5 cm
OA 1998. 7-23. 219, gift of Mr and Mrs R. Isaacs

The body of this bowl is of unlacquered
basketry in a fancy diamond pattern of
brown and white. The rim, stem and
foot are lacquered red and decorated
with narrow hoops of bare yellow
bamboo. Though rare today, the
juxtaposing of smooth lacquered
surfaces with bare basketry is an old
decorative technique. In 1827 Burney

considered Shan boxes superior to
those made in Pagan. He noted 'In
some Shan boxes parts of the
basketwork are left plain, and are not
covered with *theet-see* [lacquer], and of
these the basket work is very fine and
delicate.'[370] Boldness rather than
delicacy is the effect of this bowl.
Indeed, the diamond pattern used,
kyudayan gwet, is popular for the large
panels of bamboo matting for the walls
of houses.

370 Burney 1832: 175

165

cord intact. This is of thick braided silk with tassels of silver wire thread.

On the base is a fine inscription in the form of a gilded cartouche with letters in *thayo*; it records that the vessel was made in Kentung Town by Hsaya Gyi.

371 Singer 1991: 154–8, and Fraser-Lu 1985: 126–7.
372 Singer 1991: 154, n. 1. However, an example dated 1920 has been recorded by one of the authors. Singer's dating therefore probably needs to be slightly adjusted.

165
Bowl, *ko kaw tee*

Burma, Shan States, Kentung, made by Hsaya Tay Ya in 1936
Bamboo, lacquer, gold leaf; H 12.8 cm, D 19.2 cm
OA 1998.7-23.65, gift of Mr and Mrs R. Isaacs

This bowl of bamboo basketry stands on four short feet. It is lacquered black inside and out, and decorated with bands of scrolling, formed of strands of *thayo* and all gilded. The effect is both rich and sober. Some *ko kaw tees* are even more elaborately decorated with little birds on each foot, and high relief models of tribal couples on each of the four sides (cat. 36, 169). This example is signed by the maker, Hsaya Tay Ya, in a *shwe zawa* gold-leaf rectangular cartouche on the base. It is also dated year 1298 of the Burmese era (1936). Another piece by the same maker is cat. 136. In the 1990s one family claiming descent from this master is still making black and gold *ko kaw tees* in Kentung.

166
Two plates, *pan gan*

Burma (larger of the two probably from Meiktila or
perhaps Pyinmana), late 19th/early 20th century
Bamboo, lacquer; H 3 cm, D 26 cm; H 2.5 cm,
D 14.5 cm
OA 1998.6-13.1 & 2

Both of these plates are undistinguished
functionally or aesthetically but are
illustrated here because they bear, on
the reverse, two- and three-letter
inscriptions in Tamil.373 These plates
were used by members of the Tamil
community who during the colonial
period settled in Burma in large
numbers, especially in Lower Burma and
in the cities.374 Many were engaged in
trade, above all in money-lending. This
last activity produced a small class of
enormously wealthy families, known
collectively as 'Chettiar' from the region
in Tamil Nadu, Chettinad, where their
ancestral lands are located.375 These
banking families, although based in
Burma for several generations,376
maintained their links with Chettinad,
returning there for family events such as
weddings. The family houses were kept
up for this purpose and were filled with
fine materials from Burma, including
lacquer vessels, some of excellent
quality. In India today lacquerware from
Chettiar houses is often described as
'Madras lacquer', for most people in
India are now unaware of the historic
link between Chettinad and Burma.

The larger of these two plates is
decorated on the front face with a
design in yellow, using the *yun*
technique, and is of a type believed to
have been made in Meiktila or possibly
Pyinmana. The vessels are distinctively
constructed of woven cane, which has
then been lacquered thickly in red. On
the base is a circular seal with a
signature.377 Another distinguishing
feature is the use of chips of broken
pottery set into the five stubby feet.

373 These very short inscriptions are probably
initials, perhaps of the owners. They read as

follows: 'si mu [?]tu' and 'nu mu'. Neither make
sense as words, so are presumably abbreviations.
Could the 'mu' statement in both refer to the
common Tamil name Mudaliyar? Our thanks to Dr
Stuart Blackburn, School of Oriental and African
Studies, London, for his assistance with this entry.
374 Although the largest Chettiar community was in
Burma in the late nineteenth century and in the
first half of the twentieth century, Chettiar financiers
were found throughout colonial Southeast Asia.
375 For the Chettiars in general, see Rudner 1994;
for their mansions in Chettinad and specifically for
the extraordinary wood-carving to be found in
these houses – much of it of Burmese teak – see
Thiagarajan 1992. We are grateful to Grace

Krishnaswami for her help with this entry.
376 Following Independence in 1948, the lot of
Indians in Burma was not easy and many left. As
money-lenders, they were not greatly liked among
the Burmese population. Even in 1882 their
reputation was not enviable: according to Shway
Yoe, 'hapless is the man, Burman or Englishman,
who has dealings with the fat, shaven-headed
Madras money-lender' (p. 250). Indians who remain
in Burma today are much reduced in wealth and
influence; many have taken Burmese names.
377 Other examples exist in the British Museum as
well as in the Museum of Archaeology and
Anthropology, Cambridge. For a further discussion
of this group, see the Appendix, p. 228.

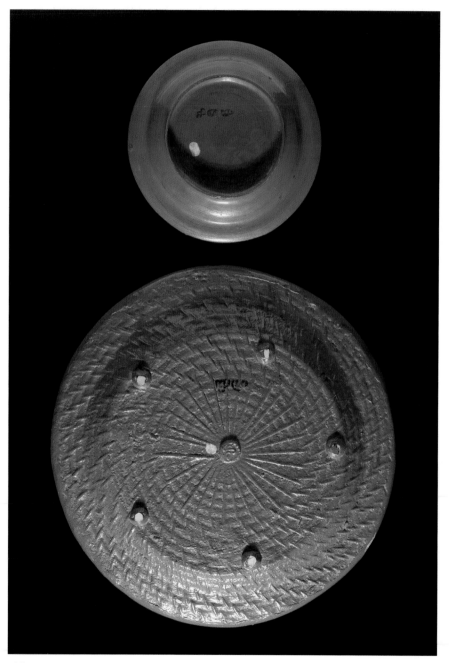

166

167

167

Betel-box, *kun it*

Burma, Pagan, made by Hsaya Ban in the Pyizu Quarter, 1920s
Bamboo, lacquer; H 15.4 cm, D 15.8 cm
OA 1998.7-23.133, gift of Mr and Mrs R. Isaacs

This betel-box, one of Hsaya Ban's 'Royal Peacock Brand' as signified by the peacock depicted on the box, has *yun* decoration in red, green and yellow on black (see photograph, p. 52). The inscriptions are a fine example of the range to be found on a betel-box and include the maker's signature, claims of excellence for his wares, and good wishes to the buyers and users. The couple who purchased the box did so in order to gain spiritual merit by donating it to the monks of a monastery.[378]

The top of the lid has the original inscription by the maker: 'Hsaya Ban of Pyizu Quarter, Pagan, finest quality lacquerware'. This is followed by another added by the male donor: 'This is the deed of merit of Monastery Founder U Gyin Dok'. In two cartouches in the narrow frieze around the upper side of the cover the female donor adds: 'This is the deed of merit of Ma Khant Kyi, who waters the sacred Bo tree (on her frequent visits to the pagoda).'[379] On the left and right of the displaying peacock on the sides of the cover are the good wishes of the maker for both purchaser and user: 'Goodwill, fidelity, health and wealth'. In a narrow frieze at the base of the box, the maker praises his wares: 'The pinnacle of lacquerware' and 'Simply the best'.

378 Despite the addictive quality of betel, the habit of chewing betel quid was not something that was frowned upon in most monasteries, quite unlike the consumption of alcohol.
379 Many pagodas have examples of the *Ficus religiosa* growing in their precincts. It was beneath a tree of this type that the Buddha achieved Enlightenment at Bodh Gaya in eastern India. The link between the tree and this sacred event has lead to a substantial cult devoted to the propagation and nurturing of the *Bodhi* tree; indeed many trees at major pilgrimage sites are thought to descend linearly from the ancient one beneath which the Buddha sat.

168

168
Betel-box, *kun it*
Burma, Pagan, workshop of Maung Wa Kyi of Pyizu Ward, mid-20th century
Bamboo, lacquer; H 8.4 cm, D 15.9 cm
OA 1998.7-23.213, gift of Mr and Mrs R. Isaacs

This flat cylindrical box has several features of particular interest. The sharp ridges on the rim of the cover and on the top and foot of the box are most unusual, and suggest that from the earliest stage, long before it was ready to be decorated, the box was intended to become an exceptional piece. The *yun* decoration is in only one colour, pink, and of fine quality. Even the border edgings are minute, while the splendid roundel on the top of the lid depicts the *nat* ogre Ponnaka riding on a horse and holding in his hand an object which may represent the heart of the wise minister Vidura. The inscriptions include not only the name and address of the lacquer master (Maung Wa Kyi of Pyizu Ward, Pagan) in whose workshop the box was made but uniquely the signature, in fancy script, of the actual craftsman who drew the *yun* decorations – lacquer master Maung San Aye. He adds good wishes to the buyer or recipient of the box: 'prosperity, and many friends'.

169
Ceremonial bowl, *ko kaw tee*
Burma, Shan States, Kentung, *c.*1910
Bamboo, lacquer, gold leaf; H 15.2 cm, D 18.8 cm
OA 1998.7-23.8, gift of Mr and Mrs R. Isaacs

These black and gold basket bowls with gilded relief decoration are unique to Kentung, which is close to the Chinese border in the eastern part of southern Shan States. Cat. 36, 136, 164 and 165 show the variety of low- and high-relief decoration lavished on these four-footed baskets, called *ko kaw tee*. *Thayo* can be moulded like plasticine; it can also be rolled out into thin strands, cut to length, lifted on a little tool of

169

170

wood or horn, and curled as it is laid into place. Relief patterns of scrolling can be laboriously built up strand by strand, as can script.

Here the maker has reserved a large medallion, 7 cm in diameter, on the base of the bowl for the inscription: 'In South Shan country, Kentung Town, the Ahlawga Master made this, finishing it on the 12th day of the waning moon of Natdaw.' *Natdaw* is usually December, but unfortunately there was no space left on the base for the year. It may have been as early as 1910, for the little figures of tribal couples modelled in light relief on the sides of the bowl are all identical. In later *ko kaw tee* the four couples can be distinguished by their costume, headgear and musical instruments, each typical of one of four ethnic groups living around Kentung:

the Khun, Kaw, Khamu and Lahu.[380]

[380] Singer 1991.

170
Rectangular tray, *kahpi sabweh*
Burma, Pagan, workshop of Hsaya Ko Aye Hpay, 1920s
Wood, lacquer; L 56 cm, W 37 cm
OA 1996.5-1.50

The rectangular tray is not a traditional Burmese shape, but was made for Europeans and Westernized Burmese. This example was fashioned by the *yun* artist Ba Htet in the workshop of Ko Aye Hpay in the Market Quarter of Pagan, and the maker calls it a 'coffee table' in his inscription. It is decorated in the *yun* technique with yellow, orange and green on a black ground and illustrates a scene from the

Vessantara Jataka,[381] the most favoured in Burma of all the *jataka* stories and the last before the birth of the historical Buddha. The *jataka* tells of the unbounded generosity of the future Buddha which culminates in his giving away treasures, his royal white elephant[382] and even his own two children. Indeed, this scene is shown on the tray, where – in a summation of all that is generous – Vessantara hands over the children to the brahmin Jujaka (seen as a bent old man, to right).

The large lettering to the left and right above the figures is the title of the *jataka*. The theme of generosity was most apt for objects purchased as gifts for friends and the maker surely had this in mind when he wrote his own good wishes for the buyers and users in the form of rhyming verse:

I, Maung Aye Hpay, who made this
    tray
With all my heart and soul I pray
That those who buy and use it may
Meet more auspiciousness each day
And treasure rain down in their way!

381 No. 547 in the standard Pali listing translated
into English in Cowell 1907, vol. VI: 246–305.
382 White elephants were considered the absolute
epitome of kingship in Burma, as elsewhere in
Southeast Asia. In Burma much effort and money
was spent on finding and then taming them so that
they could be an auspicious ornament to the court
of the king. Many European travellers mention the
importance of the animal and the royal conditions
in which they were held – see Sangermano 1995:
76–80; also Yule 1858: 133–5. For white elephants
in the neighbouring country of Thailand, see
Ginsburg 1989: 33.

171
Bowl with lid, *bu*

Burma, probably Pagan, late 19th century
Bamboo, wood, lacquer; H 24.5 cm, D 35.7 cm
OA 1998.7-23.90, gift of Mr and Mrs R. Isaacs

This large covered bowl is made of
coiled and woven split bamboo,
lacquered black. The knob has been
restored and may originally have had a
few lines of yellow *yun* decoration. The
lid is deep and reaches below the mid-
point, which is marked by a series of
close-set parallel lines in yellow. Below
these, on the body of the bowl, are
three Burmese lions, *chinthe*, drawn in
the classic style. Above, on the sides of
the cover are three classically drawn

hintha birds.[383] Between these is an
inscription repeated three times and
forming part of the whole decorative
scheme. Written in a beautiful
calligraphic script, in the form of a
garland or horseshoe, it reads: 'For use
by U Ohn Sein and Daw Lon Yun of
Acacia Grove Ward, Myitche Town.' This
couple most probably commissioned the
bowl themselves, but it is also possible
that friends ordered it and had it
inscribed for them as a gift. Such bowls
were used for serving food such as
cooked rice or fruit.

    Myitche lies on the west bank of the
Irrawaddy river, opposite Nyaung-U, and
thus only a few miles from Pagan. The

172

style of the artwork – yellow on black *yun* decoration – and lack of a maker's signature all suggest a date before 1900.

383 See note 7, cat. 1.

172
Kammavaca manuscript with binding ribbon, *sa si gyo*
Burma, possibly Mandalay, 1930
Wood, cloth, lacquer, gold leaf; leaves: L 61.5 cm, W 16 cm
OA 1998.7-23.246, gift of Mr and Mrs R. Isaacs

This manuscript is a *Kammavaca*, a selection of texts from the *Vinaya*, the rules of conduct for members of the community of monks, the *sangha*. It was made in 1929 for the donors U Shwe Dun, his wife Daw Hta, their daughter Ma Mya Yi and her husband Maung Po Meik, who lived in Minhla township near Mandalay. In a brief inscription on the inner face of the lacquered and gilt wooden cover of the manuscript the donors call on *nats* and humans to applaud their deed of merit by calling out *thadu*, 'well done'. The long text woven into the cotton binding ribbon, *sa si gyo*, in eighty-six high-flown verses praises the munificence of the main donor and the virtue of his wife. It also reveals the immediate motive for the donation: 'Their beautiful and intelligent daughter, Ma Mya Yi and her husband Maung Po Meik, have bestowed on them a lovely baby grand-daughter, Ma Thein Nyunt. Inspired by the impulse to donate, they have commissioned the writing of this *Kammavaca* manuscript, paying the scribe and providing a fine gilded and glass-inlaid box to hold the manuscript in its own wrapping cloth and specially woven binding ribbon, a complete set.'[384]

The covers are of wood, lacquered and gilt in *shwe zawa* work, and the leaves of thickly lacquered cloth also with gold-leaf decoration. The dark red-

opposite: 174

brown ink is made of boiled lacquer and the script is the special one reserved for *Kammavaca* manuscripts, known as *magyi zi*, or 'tamarind seed'.

384 For binding ribbons, see Zwalf 1985: 170 (cat. 235); also Singer: 1993.

173
Funeral salver, *matha ban*
Burma, Ava, made by U Hpo Ya, 1930
Bamboo, lacquer; L 36.3 cm, W 29.8 cm
OA 1998.7-23.184, gift of Mr and Mrs R. Isaacs

This oval tray has been lacquered black over a red undercoat and bears interesting inscriptions. The maker was U Hpo Ya whose workshop was in the Fan Makers Quarter of Ava town, and the tray was presented to the village monastery by Ko Hpo Khin and his family, who call on *nats* and humans to applaud their act of merit. A later inscription on the underside of the tray was probably added by the lay attendant (*kappiya*) of the monastery, and designates the tray for use in the village's 'royal' street.

Such trays were funeral salvers for carrying cooked food, often in banana-leaf parcels, from the house of the dead person to the burial ground. The food was ostensibly for the sustenance of the deceased on his journey, but in practice was consumed by indigent cemetery dwellers.

174
Gun case, *thanat thitta*
Burma, Pagan, workshop of U Salway, *c*.1915
Wood, lacquer; H 10 cm, L 80.7 cm, W 20 cm
Ethno 1966.As.10.2a

This interesting box illustrates the way

173

175

in which traditional techniques were adapted to produce items for twentieth-century use. The internal compartments of the box would hold the dismantled parts of a shot-gun of the type used in the colonial period for hunting game.

The decoration is in the *yun* technique with red, green and yellow on a black ground; the many inscriptions are all in yellow. The use, on the top face of the box, of elephants in the decorative scheme is typical of *yun* work of this period.[385] They advance with riders towards the centre of the panel to what appears to be a stage occupied by acrobats and a central figure with a wand; he also wears a mask. The decoration on the sides and the base is less elaborate, and is limited to birds and foliage.

The many inscriptions on the box are as follows: 'Your honour, the Inspector',[386] 'May you get promotion in your job and may you be free from danger', 'Pagan Town, Bazaar Ward, Superintendent of the Principal Produce Market', 'U Salway's workshop, authentic traditional lacquer box', 'This box is meant (or made) for the use of U Hpo Kyaung', 'Superior quality, the very best, the real thing, resistant to hot water'. The user who probably also commissioned the box, was a police inspector and the maker's wishes in the inscriptions are thus very appropriate. The maker, U Salway, uses his local government title, 'Market Head Official', so he was clearly an important and comparatively wealthy citizen. Both maker and owner were enjoying advancement under the colonial government.

The box is a European shape, *par excellence*, as well as a very appropriate use of lacquer, since it waterproofs the contents, as described in the inscription.

385 Trays or boxes with similarly arranged elephants are common. Elephants were (like modern luxury cars) a symbol of wealth and rank. 'May you get to ride on an elephant' was to wish a person in civil or police service promotion to high rank, with an entitlement to elephant transport. Thus, if one could not afford a real elephant, one could nevertheless enjoy a lacquer representation of one.
386 The Burmese letters spell 'Inspeiktaw'.

175

Teak chest, *yun thitta*

Burma, Pagan, *c.*1900
Wood, lacquer, metal hinges and lock; H 23.5 cm, L
60 cm, W 27.5 cm
National Trust, Curzon Collection at Kedleston Hall,
Derbyshire, no. 198

This box has fifty captions to the *yun*
scenes from the legendary exploits of
the heroes of Pagan, king Anawrahta
and his successor, Kyanzittha.[387] The
story scenes are crowded tightly on to
the surfaces of the front, back and
sides of the box, as well as the top of
the lid. Most of the space and over half
the captions are devoted to the military
expedition to Yunnan in western China
to seek the Sacred Tooth relic of the
Buddha.[388] Other scenes are from
Anawrahta's mission to the Mon capital
Thaton, this time for an authentic set of
Theravada Buddhist scriptures. Both
missions took place in the eleventh
century and can be regarded as
essentially wars of expansion justified
on religious pretexts.[389] The borders
around all five rectangular spaces are at
least three times as deep as the
cartouches used for the story captions.
However, all 3.5 metres of these
borders are filled with floral scrolling
and small birds, and are devoid of
script. The maker of this box has
nowhere put his name to his work.

Similar lacquered wooden chests of
only ten years later are invariably
signed and one in a private collection,
made by Hsaya To of Pagan, has twelve
cartouches, of which only two are
captions for the story scenes depicted:
the remaining ten give the maker's
name, address, claims for the quality of
his wares and his good wishes to the
buyer. The Kedleston box may thus be
confidently dated internally to before
1902 on the grounds of its high quality
and lack of signature. This argument is
based on the assumption that signed
wares, along with advertisements on
vessels, became common practice in
Pagan as a direct result of the 1902

exhibition in Delhi (see pp. 42-3). This
dating is corroborated by the fact that
Lord Curzon visited Burma as viceroy in
1901 and that the chest was probably
new when it was presented to him.

387 For a similar epic sequence, see cat. 87.
388 See *Glass Palace Chronicle* 1922, pt IV: 80–82,
paras 133–4.
389 Aung-Thwin 1985: 57–9.

176

Betel-box, *kun it*

Burma, Pagan, mid-1920s
Bamboo, lacquer; H 20 cm, D 21 cm
OA 1998.7-23.76, gift of Mr and Mrs R. Isaacs

The maker of this box, Hsaya Kyon of
Tangyi Ward in Pagan, has decorated it
in *yun* designs using red, green and

yellow on a black background. The
scene repeated in four lobed frames on
the sides of the cover is perhaps a
conventional reference to the
Ramayana: a prince with a bow pursues
a deer which is an ogress in disguise.
In complete contrast the picture on the
top of the lid dates the box to the mid-
1920s by its uniquely political content.
A proud 'Mother Burma' figure wears a
helmet with a peacock crest, and the
national bird and emblem of the
Burmese kings stands by her side. This
is in effect an anti-Britannia, for the
banner on the end of her spear bears a
motto written in Burmese script but
using the then topical English words:
'Home Rule will be achieved!' Burma
was a province of the British Indian
Empire, and the Congress agitation

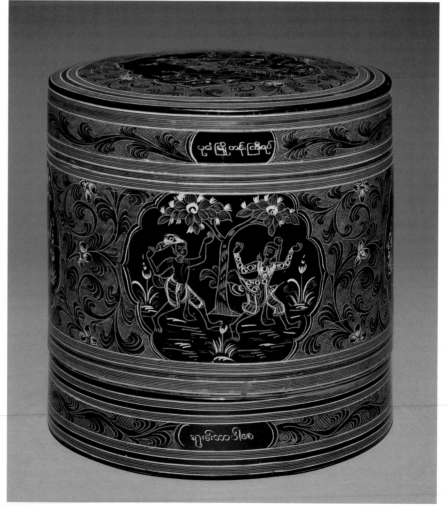

176

177

against the Raj enthused Burmese activists. Protests spread into school boycotts and refusal to pay poll-tax. Home rule associations were outlawed in 1924. Above the banner the lacquer artist has started to engrave the words 'HOME RULE' but has stopped, leaving only 'HO'. Perhaps the purchaser wanted no English on his betel-box.

177
Tray, *byat*
Burma, Pagan, 1920s
Bamboo, lacquer; D 46 cm
OA 1999.3-1.2, Brooke Sewell Fund

The *yun* decoration on the upper surface of this circular tray is executed in the typical Pagan colours of red,

orange, green and yellow. The scene depicted is often shown on lacquer vessels, especially on trays, which offer a large space. We see the two brothers Polajanaka and Aritthajanaka in combat, mounted on elephants and brandishing spears. This is an incident from the *Mahajanaka Jataka*, one of the previous life stories of the Buddha.390

178

The fine inscription in semi-circular form on the under surface dates the tray to the 1920s, the *wunthanu* period.[391] This is an appeal to the patriotic purchaser to buy local produce rather than imported British goods. It reads: 'The silver gong is struck to proclaim that using this product will safeguard the race and the national identity.' Whether the use of imagery from the *Mahajanaka Jataka* with its story of brotherly conflict is linked with the political message is unclear.

390 The *Mahajanaka Jataka* is the second of the Mahanipata, the ten last *jatakas*. It is no 539. See Cowell 1907 (reprint 1957), vol. VI: 19–37.
391 For the *wunthanu* period, see pp. 61–2 and Aung San Suu Kyi 1991: 143. The authors are indebted to Andrew Robinson for directing us to the links between the *swadeshi* movement in India and *wunthanu* in Burma.

178

Set of three bowls, *khwet*
Burma, Ava, workshop of U Hpo Ya, 1950s
Bamboo, lacquer; H 10 cm, D 20.7 cm
OA 1998.7-23.161 a, b, c, gift of Mr and Mrs R. Isaacs

These bowls of coiled bamboo have a flared rim typical of the mid-twentieth-century wares of Ava, where they were made by U Hpo Ya. The interior is

lacquered red, and the exterior a toffee-brown, with a decorative band of simple scrolling and wavy lines in yellow *yun* which incorporate the maker's name. They were owned by a lady called Ma Hpwa May, who has added her name on the base of the bowls, using neat dots from her pink nail varnish brush to form the letters (see photograph, p. 52).

These bowls are good quality domestic ware made for holding soup or curries.

179

Cover for dish, *htamin ok ahpon*
Burma, early 20th century
Bamboo, lacquer; D 41 cm
OA 1998.7-23.77, gift of Mr and Mrs R. Isaacs

This is the cover of a now lost rice container (see cat. 137 for a complete bowl and cover). The cover is evenly convex, formed of bamboo basketry with a rim made of a hoop of split bamboo. The vessel has been smoothed with *thayo* both inside and out before being lacquered red. On the concave

179

180

inside of the cover the owner marked her name, Ma Aye, in the still-wet lacquer (see photograph, p. 52).

The marking of vessels with the name of the owner is often seen on food containers. This is so that they can be easily recognized by their owners following a *hsun*, or feast prepared for monks as a donation. This may take place on a special day in the religious calendar or to mark a family occasion (for further discussion, see p. 52).

180

Five-fold screen, *yun khanzi*

Burma, Pagan, workshop of U Aung Myint in Myinkaba village, 1998

Wood, metal hinges, lacquer; each fold: H 181 cm, W 46.5 cm

OA 1996.8-6.1, Brooke Sewell Fund

The workshop of U Aung Myint in the village of Myinkaba, between Old and New Pagan, is well known for the production of furniture decorated in the *yun* style. They also make chests of drawers, tables and trays. This screen was commissioned by the British Museum and took two years to complete.[392] The idea of a folding screen is not Burmese in origin, and was probably introduced into the repertoire of the Burmese lacquer workshops by the British, drawing on similar screens used in north India.

Each side is decorated with scenes from the *jatakas*, one side from the *Vessantara Jataka* and the other from the *Mahosadha Jataka*.[393] All of the scenes are captioned in Burmese script

180 (detail)

181

Two flower vases, *pan o*
Burma, Pagan, Myat Mon Workshop, 1993
Bamboo, lacquer; H 36 cm, D 30 cm
OA 2000.3-30.2 & 3

These two vases use a shape traditionally reserved for altar vessels that held flowers offered to the Buddha; the lacquer makes them completely waterproof. Bought specifically for the collections of the British Museum, they represent work of the highest quality still being made today. They come from a well-known workshop in Pagan, and bear its name on the base in Roman script, thus perhaps indicating the expected international clientele for them. They both have good red lacquer at the lips and glossy black interiors.

They are made of strips of bamboo coiled in overlapping sequence. The interstices of the basketry have subsequently been filled in, smoothed, lacquered and eventually engraved to take the colour scheme seen here. Both use red, green and yellow lacquer – one on a black and one on a brown ground. The figured example is especially interesting as it very consciously uses scenes and motifs from the wall-paintings of the ancient pagodas and temples of Pagan, the ruined city in which the lacquer workshops are based. Elsewhere we have noticed the use of this rich visual source (see cat. 58), but here it is not just motifs but whole figured scenes that have been copied.[394] Of special interest are the scenes that show Bodhisattvas with their distinctive pointed crowns, figures who find no canonical existence in the Theravada Buddhism of Burma today. The conservation at Pagan in recent years of temples such as the Myinkaba Kubyauk-gyi with its breathtaking array of brilliantly coloured twelfth-century paintings[395] has only enhanced the interest in using motifs such as those seen here. The other vessel uses a non-figured scheme with animals on a

and executed in a style common today in Pagan in which lacquer artists draw on the surviving murals of the twelfth-century temples for inspiration. The ancient conventions are followed in, for instance, depicting trees, water, buildings and indeed human figures. These are all highly stylized and filled with pattern; not even the human figures escape attention and are shown with textiles of great variety and complexity. These conventions can, eventually, be traced back to Indian notions of narrative presentation.

The inscription in the detail shown above reads: 'While still a child of seven years, Vessantara gives with great generosity.'

392 The Museum is grateful to Mr Robert Gordon, British Ambassador in Rangoon, and Mrs Gordon for their assistance with the transport of this item to Rangoon.
393 For other items decorated with these *jatakas*, see cat. 69 and 170 for the *Vessantara Jataka* and cat. 102 for the *Mahosadha Jataka*.

background of scrollwork and cross-hatching.

394 In Fraser-Lu 1986: 104 there is also mention of black-and-gold, *shwe zawa* panels produced today which draw on the same imagery.
395 See Strachan 1989 for recent colour photographs.

182
Pumpkin box, *shwe hpayonthi it*
Burma, perhaps from Pagan, late 19th century
Bamboo, lacquer, wood, metal; H 32 cm, D 28 cm
OA 1998.7-23.163, gift of Mr and Mrs R. Isaacs

The swollen ribs are moulded separately from a thick putty of raw lacquer and teak sawdust coated with ash for ease of handling. Each is then glued with lacquer into place on a basketry foundation. When the whole assembly is set dry, several further coats of lacquer are applied. Before the final coat is fully dry, red and yellow lacquer 'paint' is applied to give the naturalistic blotched effect shown here.

The stem handle of carved wood, realistically grooved and twisted, is detachable. It locks into place with a metal tang and socket, which must have been handmade by a blacksmith. There is one internal tray. Although these pieces have been called wedding dowry boxes by dealers, they were in fact used like a special sort of *hsun ok* for carrying cooked food to a monastery. For a modern version of this type of vessel, see cat. 183.

183
Large pumpkin box, *shwe hpayonthi it*
Burma, probably Pagan, late 20th century
Bamboo, lacquer paste, lacquer, gold leaf, wood; H 45 cm, D 50 cm
OA 1993.10-22.1; previously published: Blurton 1999

Boxes of this form were used as offering vessels, *hsun ok*, as the presence of fine examples in pagoda treasuries substantiates.[396] This example has a single tray inside and a

182

deep lower part for holding gifts. Today such vessels are made as a gift either to a monastery or perhaps to an important official. With its dazzling decoration, it is certainly an object to be displayed and admired.

The construction is remarkable as it is mostly made of coiled split bamboo. The ribbing of the fruit is of *thayo*, which is modelled on top of the coiled bamboo to make the undulating design. The handle of carved wood has been locked into the lid and then lacquered. The waisted base is separate.

The decoration is in the *shwe zawa* technique, which, although primarily associated with Prome at the beginning of the twentieth century, is now practised in Pagan, where it was introduced in the 1920s when the

governor, Sir Harcourt Butler, ordered some tables from Hsaya Khant; this vessel was almost certainly produced there. In this technique the black background is painted with a mixture of yellow orpiment and gum, leaving the design (here the leaf motifs) reserved. The whole surface is then covered with lacquer and gold leaf and left to dry. Before completely drying, the vessel is washed and the gold leaf covering the area coated with the orpiment mixture comes away, leaving a glistening black surface. The area where no mixture was applied retains the gold leaf.

396 For instance at the Mahamuni Pagoda in Mandalay (all-over gold decoration with raised *thayo* inscription; donated in 1960) and at the Shwe Dagon Museum, Rangoon (all-over *shwe zawa* floral decoration).

183

185

Betel-box, *kun it*

Burma, Pagan, Royal Golden Tortoise Workshop, 1991
Bamboo, lacquer, gold leaf; H 8.3 cm, D 7.7 cm
OA 1998.7-23.143, gift of Mr and Mrs R. Isaacs

This box is one of a series commissioned in 1991 to illustrate a selection of traditional *yun* designs for lacquerware decoration. Though shaped like a betel-box – it even has an internal tray – it is far too small to be useful for betel. Such miniatures are used for cosmetics or merely for display. In the past they were made as children's toys (cat. 52), so rather few have survived.

The foundation of coiled bamboo is smoothed on a lathe before receiving several coats of lacquer. This sets jet black, and must be kept free of dust and grit to provide a smooth glossy surface for the *shwe zawa* gold-leaf decoration, a technique described and illustrated on pp. 38–9. Here the traditional vegetal scrolling, *chu pan*, forms the decorative background in which cells of *balu gwin* shape are reserved. These hold Burmese lions, or *chinthe*. A band of a toothed motif, *acheik*, rings the lower part of the box.

The bottom of the base bears in *yun* engraving the tortoise logo of the workshop: Royal Golden Tortoise Myanma Traditional Lacquerware Enterprise.

184

Two plates, *pagan bya*

Burma, Pagan, from the Royal Golden Tortoise Workshop,[397] 1991
Bamboo, lacquer; D 23.4 cm
OA 1991.10-23.27 and 28[398]

As with the flower vases, cat. 181, these two plates draw on the rich reservoir of designs and motifs to be found in the murals of the ruined medieval temples of Pagan. In the first a crowned Bodhisattva is shown seated on a double lotus throne.[399] This is presumably Avalokiteshvara on account of his compassionate posture of 'stepping down to his devotee'. On the other plate is a *hintha* bird,[400] set within an elaborate circular design. This is the type of motif seen in the vaults of twelfth-century shrines at Pagan. On both plates the decoration is in the *yun* technique, and uses yellow, red and green on black.

In the early 1990s the Royal Golden Tortoise Workshop was producing some of the finest modern lacquerwares in Pagan.

397 For Royal Golden Tortoise, see cat. 21 and 185.
398 1991.10-23.28 has been previously published: see Blurton 1999.
399 Murals with Bodhisattvas of this type are to be found in the Abeyadana temple. See Luce 1970, vol. III, pls 227 and 230.
400 For the *hintha* bird, see note 7, cat. 1.

185

Appendix: Lacquerware Makers and Workshops

The following lists of makers' names, arranged by place of manufacture, are intended to act as a nucleus for further research. For Pagan, which has been the principal centre for lacquer production for over two centuries, only some seventy names are listed of the many hundreds of makers active since the beginning of the twentieth century when the practice started of inscribing the maker's name on lacquer pieces. The names that appear on Pagan lacquerware are usually those of the *taik hsaya*, or owner of the workshop. He, or she, may well have started out as a craftsman or *yun* artist, a *yun hsaya*. The earliest signatures are those of the makers whose handiwork won prizes at the Delhi exhibition of 1902–3. But by the 1920s the owners of lacquer workshops were employers of lacquer craftsmen and women – referred to by the Government Superintendent of Cottage Industry as 'capitalists' – and it is the owner's name that appears on the bowl or box.

Workshop owners prefix their name with the title 'Hsaya'. Frequently another prefix, *pahtama*, or 'first', is adopted, such as 'Pahtama Hsaya Chin'. The ward or quarter of Pagan where the *taik* is situated is given to ensure future orders. Prizes won in competitions are also incorporated in the title, for example 'First prize winner, first Hsaya Chin'. The dates appearing in the lists are mostly estimations based on stylistic grounds, but some (those without a '*c*.') are firm dates that are actually inscribed on the object or otherwise documented. In Kentung in the Shan States makers very often dated their pieces.

Kyaukka and Ava makers' signatures are less conspicuous than those of Pagan makers, and usually appear on the underside of a vessel. They often call themselves 'U', 'Ko' or 'Maung', thus 'Hsaya Ko Ba Yu'. After their name, many masters add 'Number 1' using the English word, which for them may have meant 'first-class'. Makers in Ava sometimes add the address of their retail outlet in Mandalay or Rangoon.

In Prome votive and domestic rice bowls were signed on the base in relief, perhaps impressed with a mould or seal. A group of rather distinctive bowls and trays of strong cane basketry, lacquered red and with the weave left prominent outside, have also apparently been stamped on the base with a seal. An impressed seal-like medallion about 2 cm in diameter and ringed with raised beads contains the maker's name. Two such pieces by Hsaya Thin were purchased in Pyinmana in 1898 (now in the Cambridge University Museum of Archaeology and Anthropology). They may have been made in Meiktila, mentioned by Sylvia Fraser-Lu as the place of manufacture of a tiered *hsun ok*, which however is more refined in shape and finish than the seal-impressed vessels in Cambridge (Fraser-Lu 1985: 88, fig. 91).

Mandalay gilt relief, glass-inlaid wares (*hmanzi shwe cha*) are unsigned. The tasks of making the vessels, applying the *thayo* relief decoration, glass inlay and gilding probably involve many different craftsmen, none of them using a tool exactly adapted to writing.

On the Inle Lake, Intha lacquer makers may occasionally have signed their work. A square betel-box (cat. 38) has a name Ko Hteik, and an address, Yaymale quarter of Ywama village painted on the base. This could be either the maker or the owner.

In other lacquer manufacturing centres in the Shan States, apart from Kentung, the makers neither signed their wares nor put the place of manufacture on them.

Finally, Kentung in the eastern Shan States has produced richly ornamented gilded basket-bowls for perhaps centuries. Since the early twentieth century makers have signed and dated these pieces on the base. Early pieces are signed in raised lettering formed of tiny strands of *thayo*. From the 1930s the signature medallions are in *shwe zawa* gold-leaf work.

For each lacquer maker, the lists show the piece or pieces bearing his or her name. Some of these are in public museums, and others in private collections. A few were noted on display in shops and their inscriptions recorded.

Collection abbreviations
(in addition to those listed on p.8)

BEN	Erik Bentsen
BER	Colleen Beresford
CUMAA	Cambridge University Museum of Archaeology and Anthropology
EHB	Elephant House, Bangkok
EHR	Elephant House, Rangoon
HI	Hilary Isaacs
KEN	Babs and Sheldon Kent
MIS	The Missorten Foundation
NFS	Noel Singer
TW	Tom White

TITLE (OR STYLE) AND NAME	WARD / VILLAGE	DATE	INSCRIBED LACQUER PIECE
PAGAN			
1 Hsaya **Hmi**	Pyizu Ward	1930s	water pot: OA 1998.7-23.1
2 Hsaya **Kaing**		c.1910	bowl: OA 1998.7-23.2 (cat. 70)
3 Hsaya **Htat**, 'Tiger Brand'	Yondan	c.1940	betel-box: OA 1998.7-23.4 (cat. 7)
			betel-box: OA 1998.7-23.119 (cat. 9)
4 First Hsaya **Ban**, 'Peacock Brand'	Pyizu Ward	c.1950	betel-box: OA 1998.7-23.6
			betel-box: OA 1998.7-23.133 (cat. 167)
5 U **Ba Kywe**	Pyizu Ward	c.1920	betel-box: OA 1998.7-23.21
6 **Aung/Aung Hsa**	Myin-Kaba Village	c.1950	betel-box: OA 1998.7-23.27
7 Hsaya **Yon**	Bazaar Ward	c.1920	betel-box: OA 1998.7-23.32
8 First Hsaya **Kyaw**/Hsaya **Kyaw**	Taik-Kon Ward	c.1925	betel-box: OA 1998.7-23.34
			betel-box: MIS 172
			betel-box: British Museum: OA
9 Hsaya **Htway**		c.1960	betel-box: OA 1998.7-23.8
			betel-box: OA 1998.7-23.70 (cat. 48), 71
			betel-box: Ethno 1966 AS 10-1
10 Hsaya **Kyi**, 'Golden Moonlight Lacquerware'	Myin-Kaba Village South Ward	1990	betel-box: OA 1998.7-23.52
U **Ba Kyi** (see also Pagan 39)			betel-box: OA 1998.7-23.14
11 Hsaya **Sein**	Town: Taik-Su Ward	c.1910	betel-box: OA 1998.7-23.55 (cat. 47)
First prize certificate-holder Hsaya Sein			screen: V&A IS 78-1990
Certificate-holder Hsaya Sein			tray: OA 1993.3-1.1
12 Hsaya **Tha**		c.1950	betel-box: OA 1998.7-23.56
13 Hsaya **Pu**		c.1940	betel-box: OA 1998.7-23.66
14 Hsaya **Kyon**	Tangyi Ward	c.1920	betel-box: OA 1998.7-23.76 (cat. 176)
First Hsaya Kyon			betel-box: MIS 275 (cat. 56)
15 Hsaya **Htu**	Tangyi Ward	c.1930	betel-box: OA 1998.7-23.75
16 Hsaya **Chin**		c.1930	
17 First Hsaya **Sein**	Kyauk-hmaw Ward	c.1940	betel-box: OA 1998.7-23.85
			dish and lid: HI
18 Hsaya **Maung**	Taik-Su Town	c.1950	bowl: OA 1998.7-23.92
19 Maung **Waing**	Myin-Kaba Central Ward	c.1930	dish and lid: OA 1998.7-23.96
20 U Aung **Ban** (perhaps the same as Pagan 4)	First Hsaya Ban	c.1950	betel-box: OA 1998.7-23.104
21 First Hsaya **Min**, 'Hawk Brand'	Town: Hsandan Ward	c.1960	betel-box: OA 1998.7-23.112 (cat. 64)
22 Hsaya **Min**	Town: Yondan Ward	c.1910	tray: OA 1998.7-23.113
23 Hsaya **Nyunt**		1902	letter canister: OA 1998.7-23.130 (cat. 18)
Certificate-holder Hsaya Nyunt			flat betel-box: private collection
24 Hsaya **Hlaing**, 'Parrot Brand'	Pyizu Ward	c.1950	betel-box lid: OA 1998.7-23.134
			betel-box: MIS
25 Hsaya **Khant**		c.1960	letter tube OA 1998.7-23.152 (cat. 25)
Certificate and medal winner			octagonal table: V&A
			betel-box: Ethno As 1952.04.5a, b & c
			betel-box: EHB
26 Hsaya **Myo**	Town: Taik-Su Ward	c.1910	betel-box: OA 1998.7-23.159
27 Hsaya **Thu**	Taik-Kon Ward	c.1920	betel-box: OA 1998.7-23.166 (cat. 65)

#	TITLE (OR STYLE) AND **NAME**	WARD / VILLAGE	DATE	INSCRIBED LACQUER PIECE
28	Hsaya **Hsaing** Prize certificate holder 'Certificate can be shown'	Town: Hman-gyo Ward	c.1930	tea-plate OA 1998.7-23.169 (cat. 151) water bowl: V&A IM57-1932 water bowl: Ethno AS 4.2.1952 *bi it*: private collection
29	Hsaya **Pyay**	Town: Pyizu Ward	c.1910	oval tray: OA 1998.7-23.189
30	U Thet **Shay**	Town: Bazaar Ward	1963	betel-box: OA 1998.7-23.196 (cat. 58)
31	Hsaya **Man**		c.1930	miniature betel-box: OA 1998.7-23.212
32	First Lacquer Master Maung **Wa Gyi**	Town: Pyizu Ward, South Division	c.1920	flat betel-box: OA 1998.7-23.213
33	Royal Golden Tortoise Traditional Myanmar Lacquer Enterprise	'New Town'	1990	bowl: OA 1998.7-23.123 (cat. 21), betel-box: OA 1998.7-23.143 (cat. 185)
34	Everstand Doll Lacquer Enterprise	Wet Kyi-in Village	1993	*hsun gwet*: OA 1998.7-23.248
35	Hsaya **Ka**	Town: Taik-Su Ward	c.1910	green and gold betel-box: TW
36	U **Tha Shein** Grand prize winner	Town: Taik-Su Ward	c.1905	betel-box: TW rectangular box: TW
37	Hsaya **Aye**	Town: Taik-Su Ward	c.1910	betel-box: TW
38	Hsaya **Hset**	Town: Pyizu Ward	c.1910	flat betel-box: OA 1998.6-13.5
39	U **Kyi**	Town: Tan-byo Ward	c.1920	betel-box: OA 1998.6-13.3
40	Hsaya Ba (perhaps the same as Pagan 62)	Town: Pyizu Ward	c.1920	cigarette case: OA 1995.10-5.2 (cat. 119)
41	Bazaar Superintendent U **Salwe**	Town: Bazaar Ward	c.1910	gun box: Ethno As 1966.10.2 (cat. 174)
42	Hsaya **Khin**	Town: Pyizu Ward	c.1920	flat betel-box (seen in a shop)
43	Hsaya Ko **Aye Hpay**	Town: Bazaar Division	c.1920	rectangular tray: OA 1996.5-1.50 (cat. 170)
44	Hsaya **Dun**	Town: Pyizu Ward	c.1910	bowl: British Museum: OA
45	Hsaya **Ka**	Lay ya Ward		stem cup: OA 1969.5-1.69
46	Hsaya **Lin**	Town: Taik-Su Ward	c.1920	*bi it*: EHB no. 8553
47	Ma **Thit** Hsayama Ma Ma Thit	Town: Yundan Ward	c.1930 c.1945	collar box: BER set of plates: Liverpool Museum 50.4.189
48	Hsaya **To**	Town: Pyizu Ward	1911	teak box: BER
49	Hsaya **Thant**	Myin-Kaba Trade Ward	c.1910	betel-box: OA 1998.7-23.3
50	Ko **Yin Maung**'s brick-built shop	Town	c.1920	betel-box: OA 1998.3-1.6
51	Hsaya **Thant** (perhaps same as 49)	Town: Bazaar Ward	c.1910	betel-box with many inscriptions: OA 1998.3-1.5
52	Maung **Ba Chit**, workshop owner	Town: Pyizu Ward	c.1920	octagonal table: OA 1999.8-4.1
53	Hsaya **Tin**		c.1910	green and gold betel-box: NFS
54	Hsaya **Kyaw**'s 6-man team		c.1920	betel-box: MIS 78
55	Hsaya **Pyant** Tiger Brand		c.1950	betel-box: MIS 18
56	Ko **Kyawt Hmu** (dated 10th day of waning moon, *Wagaung* BE 1264, 'Price 20 Kyats')		1902	betel-box: MIS 251A
57	Hsaya **Daw**	Town: Tangyi Ward	c.1910	betel-box: MIS 293
58	Ma **Nyunt**	Town	c.1940	flat betel-box: OA 2000.3-30.14
59	Hsaya **Khan**	Town: Pyizu Ward	c.1910	flat betel-box: OA 2000.3-30.13
60	Hsaya **San**	Kyauk-hmaw Ward	c.1922	rectangular tray: Asian Arts Museum, San Francisco (seen at)
61	Hsaya **Khin** (not the same as 42)	Bazaar Ward	c.1930	rectangular wood box: private collection

	TITLE (OR STYLE) AND **NAME**	WARD / VILLAGE	DATE	INSCRIBED LACQUER PIECE
62	Maung **Aung Ba**	Yundan Ward	1934	sewing box: OA 2000.2-3.1
	(perhaps the same as Pagan 40)			
	Prize certificate-holder Hsaya Ba			
63	First prize winner Maung **Hla Aye**	Hmangyo Ward	c.1930	tray: OA 2000.2-3.6
64	Hsaya **Hpay**		c.1930	small box: private collection
65	Hsaya **Gaung**		c.1930	flat betel-box: private collection

Pagan makers selected to exhibit at the Delhi Exhibition 1902–3 (Watt 1903: 220 pl.44A, 221, 224)

66	Maung **Kywe**		1902	box 'chief exhibit'
	(probably the same as Pagan 5)			
67	Ma **Gyan Yi**		1902	round box 'chief exhibit'
68	Maung **Twa**		1902	vase with dishes
69	Maung **Tha Shein**		1902	table (Commended) and collection of
	(surely the same as Pagan 36)			lacquered work (3rd Prize and Bronze Medal)
70	Nyain, Saya **Nyain** (sic)		1902	betel-boxes (Commended)
	(surely the same as Hsaya **Nyunt**, Pagan			
	23, whose certificate survives – cat. 17)			

SALAY

1	Hsaya **Ba** and Ma **Ma Aung**	Taikkon (Lacquer Works) Ward	1920	bowl: OA 1991.10-23.66 (cat. 62)

KYAUKKA

1	U **Hpo Thant**, Kyaukka Taik Hsaya		c.1910	*hsun ok*: KEN
2	U **Kyin**, 'Number 1'		c.1920	betel-box: MIS
3	Ko **Aung Hpay**		c.1920	betel-box: OA 1998.7-23.115
4	U **Htun Ba**/Ko **Htun Ba**		c.1920	covered bowl: OA 1998 7-23.141
5	Ko **Htun Aye**,		c.1910	*hsun gwet*: OA 1998.7-23.190 (cat. 155)
	'Acacia Tree Circle Lacquer Master'			
6	U **Htun Paw**, 'younger brother'		c.1910	flat betel-box (seen in shop)
	of Kyaukka 5			tiffin box: Fraser-Lu 1985: 118, fig 152
7	Ko **Ba Yin**, Kyaukka Lacquer Master		c.1920	cup: OA 1998.7-23.203
8	Ko **Hpo Yu**, Hsaya Ko Hpo Yu		c.1930	tiffin box: OA 1998.7-23.221 (cat. 152)
9	U **Chan Za**, Kyaukka Lacquer Master		c.1960	*kalat*: OA 1991.10-23.22
10	U **Hpo So**		c.1920	betel-box: BEN
11	Ko **Htway**		c.1930	*hsun ok*: EHB
12	Hsaya **Nyunt**		c.1930	tiffin carrier: EHB
13	Ko **Sein Maung**		c.1910	betel-box: MIS 270
14	Hsaya **Htun**		c.1920	tray: Fraser-Lu 1985: 117, fig. 134 (CUMAA)
15	Hsaya **Tin**		1984	painted tray on stand: Fraser-Lu 1985: 119, fig. 138

AVA (Burmese: INWA)

1	Taik hsaya **Maung Za**	Yundan Ward	c.1930	basin: OA 1998.7-23.239 (cat. 157)
2	U **Hpo Ya**	Yattan Ward	c.1930	three soup bowls: OA 1998.7-23.161 (cat. 178)
				funeral salver: OA 1998.7-23.184 (cat. 173)

TITLE (OR STYLE) AND **NAME**	WARD / VILLAGE	DATE	INSCRIBED LACQUER PIECE
3	Hsaya **Ngway**	Beiktan	*c.*1930	cup: OA 1998.7-23.187
4	Ko **Mya**		*c.*1910	cup: TW
				plate (seen in sale)
5	Hsaya **Tin**, Number 1		*c.*1910	deep plate: TW
6	Hsaya **Kywe**	Beiktan	*c.*1900	brown cup: CUMAA
7	U **Htun**		*c.*1930	tray: EHR
8	U **Hmin** & Co.	Kaing-ma Ward	*c.*1930	bowl (seen in shop)
9	U Kyaw Sein, Daw Than Than and Sons, 'Myan-ma vine'		1993	*thabeik*: OA 1998.7-23.249 (cat. 105)

PROME (Burmese: PYAY)

1	Hsaya **Pyu**		*c.*1920	*hsun gwet*: OA 1992.7-28.3 (cat. 160)
			*c.*1920	rice bowl with lid: MIS
2	Hsaya **Po**		*c.*1920	rice bowl with lid: MIS
3	Hsaya **Pya**, Taikhsaya	Kway-dan (ward or village?)	*c.*1920	offering vessel: OA 1998.7-23.227

MEIKTILA (or PYINMANA)?

1	Hsaya **Kyi**			bowl: OA 1991.10-23.95
2	**Kyaw**			bowl: OA 1992.7-28.1
3	Hsaya **Thin**		1898	bowl: CUMAA tray: CUMAA

KENTUNG TOWN

1	**Alawga** Hsaya		*c.*1910	*ko kaw tee*: OA 1998.7-23.8 (cat. 169)
				ko kaw tee: Singer 1991, fig. 5
2	Hsaya **Tay Ya**		1936	*ko kaw tee*: OA 1998.7-23.9
			1938	*ko kaw tee*: OA 1998.7-23.65 (cat. 165)
				ko kaw tee: OA 1998.7-23.164 (cat. 136)
3	Hsaya **Nanda**		1935	tumbler: OA 1998.7-23.237 (cat. 153)
			1930	*ko kaw tee*: Liverpool Museum 50.4.121
4	Hsaya **Gyi**		*c.*1920	*ko kaw tee* (entirely gilded): OA 1994.5-31.1 (cat. 164)
5	NO NAME		1923	*ko kaw tee* (entirely gilded): Brighton Art Gallery
6	Hsaya **Taw-na**		1931	*ko kaw tee*: private collection
7	**Thin Hsein**		*c.*1910	*ko kaw tee*: EHB
8	**Khan Htun** Hsaya		*c.*1950	*ko kaw tee*: EHB
9	Hsaya **Hsan Maung**		*c.*1930	*ko kaw tee*: OA 1992.7-18.4
10	Hsaya **Maung Htun**		1940s	*ko kaw tee*: OA 1998.7-23.232 & 157 and numerous examples in private houses in Burma
11	Hsaya **Kahtika**			*ko kaw tee*: MIS 80
12	U **Muleinda** and Nan **Pok Pyu**	Khun Mung Village	1990	*ko kaw tee*: OA 1998.7-23.42 & 43
			1996	*ko kaw tee*: Brighton Art Gallery, no. 507496

Glossary

Each entry is followed by a letter, (B), (P) or (S), indicating whether the word is Burmese, Pali or Sanskrit.

Abhidhamma (P), *Abhidharma* (S): one of the 'three baskets' of the *Tipitaka*; the philosophical exegesis of the Buddhist doctrine.

acheik (B): wavy or zig-zag lines forming a border.

acheik chu pan (B): design of undulating lines of vegetal scrolling.

avatara (S): lit. 'descent'; incarnation of the divine in the phenomenal world, often in series.

bagan khit (B): Pagan era, name of patterns derived by recent lacquer makers from decoration of 11th and 12th century temples.

balu (B): ogre, usually malevolent. Female is *baluma*.

balu gwin (B): lobed frame in gold-leaf designs, usually holding figures of Burmese lions or story scenes.

balu pan gaik (B): ornamental motif in stucco depicting an ogre disgorging flowers and foliage. See also, *kirttimukha*.

bhumisparshamudra (S): the hand gesture, *mudra*, of the Buddha when he touches the earth with the fingers of his right hand, palm inwards, calling the earth to witness his potential for enlightenment.

bi it (B): lit. comb-box: box to hold ladies' hairpieces, comb, cosmetics and toiletries; the largest held clothes.

bodhi (S): lit. 'enlightenment', but coupled with 'tree' refers to the banyan tree, *Ficus religiosa*, beneath which the Buddha sat at the time of his Enlightenment.

byaing (B): paddy bird, little egret.

byat (B): platter or tray or plate of turned wood or of strong basketry, usually lacquered red or black. It serves as the Burmese family meal table.

chinthe (B): mythical Burmese lion; pairs guard the approaches to *stupas*.

chu pan (B): design of spiral fronds of fern-like foliage used in gold-leaf work.

da (B): sword.

dagon daing (B): standard, usually topped with a mythical bird; from a monastery or pagoda.

daing (B): shield.

damma zaydi (B): pagoda enshrining scriptures; the scripture itself.

daung baung (B): votive stand, a tray with lid, on small feet.

daung lan (B): stand for food or gifts, a tray supported by numerous small rails or balusters.

dhammathat (P): the code governing mundane life; law code.

Dharma (S): in the Buddhist context, the teachings of the Buddha; one of the Triple Gems. See also, *Sangha*.

dharmashastra (S): see *dhammathat*.

don (B): rocket, for setting alight funeral pyre of a senior monk.

galon (B), *garuda* (S and P): mythical giant bird, half-bird, half-man. Mortal enemy of *naga*, snake-dragons; the 'day of the week' beast for Sunday.

gatha (P): verse element in Pali Jataka Tales.

gwin shet (B): lit. 'twisted fields'. Design of interlocking frames.

gyo shit lon (B): eight planets; each governs a day of the week; design of the eight beasts.

gyo shit myo (B): the eight planets.

hamsa (S and P), *hintha* (B): auspicious mythical bird, like a duck or goose; associated with the city of Pegu.

hinthabada (B): cinnabar, vermillion; mercuric sulphide.

hmanzi shwe cha (B): gilded relief work set with coloured glass.

hpala (B): basin.

hpaya (B): pagoda; also a term for the Buddha.

hpaya zin (B): Buddha shelf, domestic shrine.

hpongyibyan (B): funeral of a senior monk.

hpothudaw (B): acolyte, white robed, shaven headed; thought to possess powers of prediction. They often read horoscopes.

hsaing waing (B): orchestra, drum circle (also *pat waing*).

hsay (B): medicine, drug, dye, paint.

hsay bu (B): gourd, phial or box for medicine.

hsay daung (B): box with a sieve for sifting and mixing herbal medicines, and tobacco fillings for cheroots.

hsay hsaya (B) traditional healer and seller of charms and medicines.

hsaya (B): teacher, master craftsman, owner of a business, head of an office: boss.

hsayadaw (B): senior-most monk in a monastery: 'abbot'.

hsun (B): donations to monks, usually of cooked food, a meal offered to monks.

hsun gwet (B): tiered, round topped vessel for offering food to monks.

hsun ok (B): spire-lidded vessel for offering food to monks.

hsun zin (B): custom of inviting monks for a meal at the home of a deceased person, who gains merit thereby.

htamein (B): woman's wrapped skirt of silk.

htamin bon (B): pail for cooked rice.

htamin jaint (B): tiffin carrier of tiered trays or boxes, each holding a different dish.

htamin ok (B): capacious bowl with cover for domestic use, to hold cooked rice.

htanaung (B): acacia tree.

hti (B): umbrella, finial of a *stupa* or pagoda.

hton bu (B): lime box: usually of brass or silver, holds the lime for smearing on betel leaves.

it (B): box.

jaint (B): snack carrier/box.

jataka (S and P): the previous life stories of the Buddha. In the Pali tradition there are 547.

kadaung (B): saddle flap (lit. 'wing').

kadaw (B): reverential greeting, by prostration.

kadawbwe (B): traditional arrangement in a wide basin or on a stand of one or more hands of bananas, a green coconut with its stem, and paper flags or umbrellas or a 'money tree'.

kahpi sabweh (B): lit. 'coffee table'; thus a round or rectangular tray.

kahtein (B): ceremony before building or completing a house at which monks read from *Kammavaca* texts.

kalat (B): a receptacle of lacquered wood or bamboo raised on a pedestal or on feet. Gifts are placed on it in ceremonies of presentation or donation.

Kammavaca (P): manuscripts used for monastic ritual, most commonly for ordination; see also *kathina, ovada* and *upasampada*.

kanok (B): general term for floral designs.

karaweik (B): mythical bird supposed to have a melodious cry. Its shape is seen in royal barges and in the floats used to carry the coffin of a senior monk at his funeral.

kathina (B): gift of robes to monks; *Kammavaca* texts used for this.

khit (B): age, era; thus, *bagan khit*: Pagan era.

khwet (B): cup or bowl; also tumbler.

kinnara (S and P); *keinara* (B): mythical creature with human face, arms and torso, and legs and wings of a bird; symbol of constancy in love. Female is *kinnari*.

kirttimukha (S): the ancient Indian motif of a lion face and front paws, from the mouth of which vegetal scrollwork issues. See, *balu pan gaik*.

ko kaw tee (Khun language): decorative basket on four short feet made in Kentung, Shan state.

kunan kanbyat (B): lit. 'Yunnan semi-circles'; design of lobed frames formed of arcs. There are many variants.

kun hnyat (B): betel cutter, tool for slicing the areca nut.

kun it (B): betel-box.

kya hmauk (B): design for a border of downward-pointing lotus petals.

kyay wygn (B): early attempt at transcription of *kyi waing*: gong circle.

kyet (B): chicken.

kyet pon ok (B): box in the shape of a chicken.

kyi waing (B): gong circle.

kyizi (B): flat triangular gong; emits a surging tone.

kyizi dabo (B): pole for suspending a flat bronze gong, carried on the shoulders of two men.

kyok (B): covered bowl for alms, carried by white-robed acolyte.

kyudayan gwet (B): diamond pattern, in woven cloth and woven bamboo matting.

lahpet (B): pickled tea-leaf, a condiment and snack.

lahpet bu (B): a small box for carrying personal supplies of pickled tea.

lahpet ok (B): box for pickled tea and its crispy accompaniments.

leik (B): tortoise, turtle.

let hmat (B): certificate, ticket.

let taik let kya (B): lacquer design of alternate buildings and human figures.

longyi (B): skirt-like waist cloth or sarong worn by either sex.

lut ngan (B): commercial enterprise.

magyi zi (B): 'tamarind seed', a special square script for *Kammavaca* manuscripts written with thick brown lacquer.

makara (S): auspicious mythical sea monster.

manbaya (B): hollow, dry-lacquer image of the Buddha.

matha ban (B): funeral tray placed on the coffin. The food in it is consumed by the burial or cremation workers.

maukto (B): helmet.

mingala ok (B): lit. 'auspicious box'; a high-spired *hsun-ok*, votive receptacle.

minwut hpaya (B): lit. 'kingly clothed Buddha image'; crowned Buddha, Jambupati type.

myay ni (B): lit. 'red earth'; red ochre, mixed with lacquer sap to coat cheap wares; brick coloured rather than scarlet.

myin mo (B): lit. 'Mount Meru'; the centre of the Theravada Buddhist cosmos. A lacquer design of interlocking rectangular frames.

myitta (B): kindness, benevolence.

naga (S, P, and B): mythological serpent-dragon; the planetary beast for Saturday.

nandwin (B): lit. 'inside the palace walls'; a design of generalized palace scenes.

nat (B): spirit beings derived from pre-Buddhist animistic beliefs; they all require propitiation. The Thirty Seven *Nats* are most prominent but there are thousands of minor and local *nats*.

ngabaung dok (B): steamed packets of spiced fish wrapped in banana leaf.

ngapi (B): fish sauce; a pungent and strong smelling condiment of fermented prawns or fish.

ngayok si (B): lit. 'chilli seed'; all-over design of squarish yellow flecks on red.

ok khwet (B): votive vessel in form of a deep bowl with a round topped cover.

ovada (P): reprimand of newly ordained monk; *Kammavaca* texts used for this.

ozi (B): a long, waisted drum carried slung over the shoulder.

pabwa (B): all-over design of stylized foliage and blossom.

pabwa yok let (B) an all-over design of many small human and animal figures on a background of *pabwa*.

pachok (B): box of lightly lacquered bamboo basketry with a deep close-fitting lid; usually rectangular.

padmasana (S): the 'lotus position'. Seated cross-legged, in meditation, with the soles of both feet turned upwards.

pagan bya (B): shallow bowl or deep plate.

palin (B): throne on which a Buddha image is placed.

pan daung (B): flower basket.

pan o (B): flower vase.

ponzangwet (B): mould.

pandita (S and P): exponent, teacher.

parabaik (B): book of paper folded in concertina form.

paritta (P and B): selection of *suttas* from scripture recited to ward off evil or harm.

pattala (B): xylophone of a tuned set of bamboo bars; *than pattala* (B): the same with metal bars.

paung o (B): basket vessel for steaming food.

ponna (B): a Brahmin or court astrologer.

punna (P): merit.

put khon (B): lathe for turning wood, or shaping coiled bamboo vessels.

put lon (B): little rails or balusters of turned wood, or imitation ones moulded in lacquer putty.

pwe (B): festival or theatrical and dance performance event, usually all night long.

pyathat (B): many-tiered, spire-like roof.

pyi daung (B): basket for rice, votive or domestic.

pyinsa yupa (B): mythical beast composed of bird wings, fish tail, snake's body, deer antlers and head, elephant's tusks and trunk. Many variants. The mount of Katay, king of the planets.

pyittaing daung (B): tumbling kelly, billiken: a round-based, bottom-heavy doll, hard to upset.

sa dauk or *sakyi dauk* (B): tube or canister of lacquered cloth or bamboo for holding documents or letters.

sa si gyo (B): specially woven tape or ribbon for binding palm-leaf manuscripts in their wrappers.

sadaik (B): chest to hold manuscripts, of teak, lacquered and decorated.

sale (B): measure of capacity, approx. 0.567 litres.

salwe (B): royal official's chain of office worn over one shoulder, the number of strands between the buckles indicates rank.

Sangha (S and P): the brotherhood of monks, third of the Three Gems (others are the Buddha and the Dharma).

sasana (P and B): religious teaching or dispensation.

saung gauk (B): Burmese harp, boat-shaped with a long swan-like neck. The national instrument.

seik (B): a measure of capacity, approx. 9 litres.

shankha (S): conch shell.

shanzi (B): lit. 'Shan oil'; a wood oil from the trees of the *Aleurites* genus.

shauk (B) (but probably local to the Pagan region, and technical): small gouge, a tool for making broad lines in *yun* engraving.

shinbyu (B): ceremony of cutting off the top knot or entirely shaving the head prior to taking monastic vows.

shwe cha (B): gilded relief moulded decoration on lacquer.

shwe zawa (B): gold leaf decoration on black (or, uncommonly, red) lacquer.

shwe hpayonthi it (B): pumpkin-shaped box.

si bon (B): ceremonial headdress.

simhasana (S): lion throne on which the Buddha is frequently depicted.

stupa (S): hemispherical, or later, bell-shaped solid structure within which a relic is placed; the focus of Buddhist veneration, symbolizing the triumph of the Buddha over rebirth; in Burma called *zaydi*, and by the British, pagoda: eg. Shwe Dagon, in Rangoon.

Sutta (P), *Sutra* (S): one of the 'three baskets' of the *Tipitaka*; the sayings of the Buddha.

swadeshi (Hindi): nationalist campaign in early 20th century India to encourage purchase of locally-produced goods, rather than imported British items; see also, *wunthanu*.

tagaywet (B): door-leaves, doors.

taik (B): any brick-built structure; a brick walled compound; a workshop or factory in such a compound; a cellar for drying lacquerware.

taw lay wa (B): four paragons of virtuous womanhood.

thabeik (B): monk's alms bowl.

thadu (B): lit. 'well done!' A formula used by witnesses to deed of merit which they share by thus applauding it.

thalun (B): couch or reclining throne for royalty or senior monks.

thanahka (B): cosmetic made from powdered bark of a tree; mixed to a cream with water and applied to the face and body; mildly astringent, faintly scented.

thanahka bu (B): small box to hold *thanahka*.

thanat thitta (B): box or case to hold a gun.

than pattala (B), see *pattala*.

thayet (B): mango.

thayo (B): lit. 'flesh and bones'; a putty of lacquer sap mixed with clay or sawdust or for the best quality, with ash. This can then be moulded or sculpted.

thazin gway (B): lit. 'twisted orchid'; a design for borders in gold-leaf work.

thein (B) (from Pali, *sima*): ordination hall, also used for regular meetings of monks.

thein hnok (B): ceremony for 'erasing' trace of a *thein* before building on a site.

thet pyauk hsun (B): special form of *hsun* given by a recently bereaved family.

thila shin (B): lit. 'one who has taken the precepts'; a nun.

thila shin ban (B): alms tray carried on the head by nuns.

Thingyan (B): New Year water festival.

thissa (P): loyalty, constancy, fidelity.

thit si (B): lacquer tree (*Gluta usitata*); the sap or oleo-resin obtained from it, i.e. raw liquid lacquer sap.

thitta (B): chest or casket of wood; thus, *yun thitta*, a lacquered chest.

tinwa (B): variety of bamboo with nodes far apart, the best bamboo for splitting for weaving and for the basketry foundations of lacquer vessels.

Tipitaka (P), *Tripitaka* (S): lit. 'three baskets'; the Theravada Buddhist scriptures made up of the Suttas, the Vinaya and the Abidhamma.

tont (B – but probably local to the Pagan region, and technical): needle-like tool for engraving designs on lacquer.

tont yun (B): lacquerware decorated with fine lines, using a *tont*.

t'sehnit yathi (B): twelve zodiac signs.

ushnisha (S): the protuberance on the head of the Buddha indicating his supreme wisdom.

upasampada (P): monastic ordination; *Kammavaca* text used for this.

Vinaya (S) and (P): one of the 'three baskets' of the *Tipitaka*; the rules of monastic life.

wunthanu (B): preservation of one's lineage; of the national identity.

ya thi (B): the zodiac.

yathi yok (B): figures or signs of the zodiac.

yay gyan zin (B): public drinking-water shelf, usually donated by charitable persons.

yay khwet gyi (B): large water bowl for display or for donation to a monastery.

yay tagaung (B): water carafe.

yok let pan gya (B): all-over design of tiny animal and human figures.

yun (B): lacquerware, especially if decorated with colour-engraved work, also called *yun*.

yun khanzi (B): partition, folding screen, decorated with *yun* work.

yun thitta (B): chest or box lacquered and decorated in *yun*.

yunto (B): decorated in *yun* engraving.

yunto ok (B): box decorated with *yun* designs.

ywe dan (B): beaded design often used in borders on lacquerware.

za yun (B): lace or netting design in chequers or rosettes.

zawgyi (B): alchemist, wizard; they can fly.

zayat (B): hall near a pagoda containing Buddha images.

zaydi (B): pagoda. See *stupa*.

zaydi pon (B): vessel with lid shaped like the 'bell' of a pagoda, *zaydi*.

zin me (B): Chiang Mai, city in northern Thailand; name of a design of Thai origin consisting of lotus stems and flower- or seed-heads.

Bibliography

Entries of Burmese names appear under the first letter of the first name element, with 'U', 'Daw', 'Ma', etc. appearing at the end of the name: thus, U Thein Han appears under 'Thein'. The only exception is where there is a Christian name: thus, Michael Aung-Thwin appears as, 'Aung-Thwin, Michael', not as 'Michael Aung-Thwin'. In multiple entries, books are listed before articles; otherwise entries appear in chronological sequence.

Allcroft, H.J. *A Trip to the Delhi Durbar, Burmah, Ceylon, 1902–3*. Ms in Stokesay Archives, Stokesay Court, Staffordshire. See Sotheby's: 1994.

Archer, Mildred. *Natural History Drawings in the India Office Library*. London. 1962.

Aung San Suu Kyi, Daw (ed. Michael Aris). 'Literature and Nationalism in Burma' in *Freedom from Fear and Other Writings*. pp. 140–64. London. 1991.

Aung Thaw, U. *Report on the Excavations at Beikthano*. Rangoon. 1968.

Aung-Thwin, Michael. *Pagan. The Origins of Modern Burma*. Honolulu. 1985.

Aye Myint, U. (ed. Sone Simatrang). *Burmese Design through Drawings*. Bangkok. 1993.

Barley, Nigel. *The Golden Sword. Stamford Raffles and the East*. London. 1998.

Beurdeley Matthews & Co. *Burmese Art and its Influences*, exh. cat. London. 1981.

Bechert, Heinz. '"To be a Burmese is to be a Buddhist": Buddhism in Burma', pp. 147–158 in (eds) Bechert, Heinz and Richard Gombrich. *The World of Buddhism*. London. 1984.

Bharadwaja, L. *History of Burma*. Rangoon. 1959.

Bhirasri, S. *Thai Lacquer Works*. Thai Culture Series No. 5. Bangkok. 1995.

Blackburn, Terence R. *A Report on the Location of Burmese Artifacts in Museums*. Kiscadale Asia Research Series No. 2. Gartmore. 1994.

Blurton, T. Richard. 'Scarlet, Gold and Black: the Lacquer Traditions of Burma' in (ed.) Stadtner, Donald, M. *The Art of Burma. New Studies*. Marg Publications. Vol. 50. pp. 103–16. Bombay. 1999.

Bode, Mabel Haynes. *The Pali Literature of Burma*. Royal Asiatic Society, Prize Publication Fund, Vol. II. London 1909. Reprinted by the Burma Research Society. Rangoon. 1965.

Boisselier, J. *La peinture en Thaïlande*. Fribourg. 1976.

Brac de la Perrière, Bénédicte. 'La fête de Taunbyon: le grand rituel du culte des naq de Birmanie.' in *Bulletin de l'École française d'Extrême-Orient*. Vol. 79. No. 2. pp. 201–231. Paris. 1992.

Brownrigg, Henry. *Betel Cutters from the Samuel Eilenberg Collection*. Stuttgart and London. 1991.

Burma Gazetteer. Lower Chindwin District, Upper Burma. Rangoon. 1912.

Burma, Government of. *Burma Handbook*. Simla. 1944.

Burney, Henry. Some Account of the Lacquered or Japanned Ware of Ava. *Journal of the Asiatic Society of Bengal*. No. 5. pp. 169–82. May 1832.

Cadet, J. M. *The Ramakien. The Stone Rubbings of the Thai Epic*. Tokyo. 1975.

Catalogue of Curiosities in the Museum of the Asiatic Society, Calcutta, prepared by the Librarian. Calcutta. 1849.

Chester Beatty Library, exh. cat. *The Noble Path. Treasures of Buddhism at the Chester Beatty Library*. Dublin. 1991.

Chew, A. M. *Les temples excavés de la colline de Po Win en Birmanie centrale: architecture, sculptures et peintures murales*. Unpublished doctoral thesis for Université Paris III, Sorbonne Nouvelle U.F.R. Orient et Monde Arabes. 1999.

Collis, Maurice. *Trials in Burma*. London. 1938.

Conze, Edward (trans.). *Buddhist Scriptures*. Harmondsworth. 1959.

Courtauld, Caroline. *In Search of Burma*. London. 1984.

Cowell, E. B. (ed.). *The Jataka or Stories of the Buddha's Former Births*. Vols I–VI. Cambridge. 1895–1907. Reprinted by the Pali Text Society, London, 1957 and for UNESCO, in 1981.

Cox, Hiram *Journal of a Residence in the Burmhan Empire and more particularly at the court of Amarapoorah*. London. 1821.

Crawfurd, John. *Journal of an Embassy from the Governor-General of India to the Court of Ava in the year 1827*. London. 1829. 2nd edition 1834.

Curzon, George Nathaniel. 'Journeys in French Indo-China'. Part 2. *Geographical Journal*. Vol. II. No. 3. September 1893.

Desai, W. S. *The History of the British Residency in Burma 1826–1840*. Rangoon. 1939; reprinted, Farnham. 1972.

Desmond, Ray. *The India Museum 1801–1879*. London. 1982.

Desmond, Ray. *Kew. The History of the Royal Botanic Gardens*. London. 1995.

Dhamma Yok son. No. 2. Rangoon. pp. 108–13. February 1995.

Di Crocco, V. McK. 'Arts and Crafts: Shan Lacquerware' in (ed.) Inglis, Kim. *Myanmar Style. Art, Architecture and Design of Burma*. pp. 170–71. Bangkok. 1998.

Dictionary of National Biography (ed.) Sidney Lee. For Marryat, see vol. XXXVI. pp. 201–3. 1893; for Wallich, see Vol. LIX. pp. 135–6. 1899.

Donkers, J. and M. Nijhuis (ed.). *Burma behind the Mask*. Amsterdam. 1996.

Dowleans, A. M. *Catalogue of East India Productions collected in the Presidency of Bengal and forwarded to the Exhibition of Works of Art and Industry to be held in London in 1851*. 1851.

East India Company (publ.). *A Catalogue of the Highly Important and by far the greater Portion of the Valuable and Interesting Collection as Exhibited by the Honourable the East India Company at the Great Exhibition in 1851 . . .* nd. [1852]. National Art Library, Victoria and Albert Museum, London. Pressmark – General Collections. 23. L.

Edinburgh Journal of Science. Vol VIII. pp. 96–100. Edinburgh. 1828.

Everarda, Ellis. *Burma. Encountering the Land of the Buddhas*. Gartmore. 1994.

Fernald, Helen E. 'A Chinese Buddhistic Statue in Dry Lacquer' in *The Museum Journal*. Vol. XVIII. No. 3. pp. 284–94. The Museum of the University of Pennsylvania, Philadelphia. September 1927.

Ferrars, Max and Bertha. *Burma*. London. 1901. Reprinted, Bangkok. 1996.

Fraser-Lu, Sylvia. *Burmese Lacquerware*. Bangkok. 1985. New edition forthcoming.

Fraser-Lu, Sylvia. *Burmese Crafts Past and Present*. Oxford University Press. Kuala Lumpur. 1994.

Fraser-Lu, Sylvia. 'Sadaik – Burmese Manuscript Chests' in *Arts of Asia*. Vol. 14. No. 3. pp. 68–74. May–June 1984.

Fraser-Lu, Sylvia. 'The Government Lacquer School and Museum of Pagan.' in *Arts of Asia*. Vol. 16. No. 4. pp. 104–11. July–August 1986.

Garner, Henry. *Chinese and Associated Lacquer from the Garner Collection*. British Museum, London. 1973.

Garner, Henry. *Chinese Lacquer*. London. 1979.

Ginsburg, Henry. *Thai Manuscript Painting*. British Library, London. 1989.

Glass Palace Chronicle of the Kings of Burma, The. (trans.) Pe Maung Tin, U and Gordon H. Luce. Burma Research Society. Rangoon. 1922. Reprinted by Rangoon University Press. Rangoon. 1960.

Gombrich, Richard. *Theravada Buddhism: a Social History*. London. 1988.

Greenhalgh, Paul. *Ephemeral Vistas. The 'Expositions Universelles', Great Exhibitions and World's Fairs 1851–1939*. Manchester. 1988.

Guy, John. 'The Art of the Pyu and Mon' in (ed.) Stadtner, Donald M. *The Art of Burma. New Studies*. Marg Publications. Vol. 50. pp. 13–28. Bombay. 1999.

Guy, John and Deborah Swallow (eds). *Arts of India 1550–1900*. London. 1990.

Hall, D. G. E. *Burma*. London. 1950.

Hall, D. G. E. *Henry Burney, a Political Biography*. London. 1974.

Harle, J. C. *The Art and Architecture of the Indian Subcontinent*. Harmondsworth. 1987.

Harvey, G. E. *History of Burma. From the Earliest Times to 10 March 1824, the Beginning of the English Conquest*. London. 1925. New impression 1967.

Herbert, Patricia, M. (compiler). *Burma*. World Bibliographical Series. Vol. 132. Oxford. 1991.

Herbert, Patricia M. *The Life of the Buddha*. London. 1993.

Herbert, Patricia M. 'The Sir Arthur Phayre Collection of Burmese Manuscripts', in *The British Library Journal*. Vol I. pp. 62–70. 1975.

Herbert, Patricia M. 'The Making of a Collection: Burmese Manuscripts in the British Library', in *The British Library Journal*. Vol. 15. Number 1. pp. 59–70. Spring 1989.

Herbert, Patricia M. 'Sir Richard Carnac Temple and the Thirty-Seven Nats' in London 1991 reprint of Temple, R. C: 1906 (see Temple for reference).

Herbert, Patricia M. 'An Illustrated Record of Royal Donations' in *Études birmanes en hommage à Denise Bernot*. Réunies par Pierre Pichard et François Robinne. pp. 90–100. École française d'Extrême-Orient. Paris. 1998.

Herbert, Patricia M. 'Burmese Court Manuscripts' in (ed.) Stadtner, Donald M. *The Art of Burma. New Studies*. Marg Publications. Vol. 50. pp. 89–102. Bombay. 1999.

Hla Pe, U. See Pok Ni.

Hoffman, J. *Die Konstruktion alter Möbel*. 1990.

Htin Aung, U. *Folk Elements in Burmese Buddhism*. Oxford. 1962.

Htoon Chan, U. *The Arakanese Calendar with the Corresponding Dates in Burmese and English 1820–1918*. Arakan. 1905.

Hu Shin-chang, see Lee King-Tsi.

Imperial Gazetteer, The. 'Pegu District'. Vol XX. Oxford. 1908.

Inglis, Kim (ed.). *Myanmar Style. Art, Architecture and Design of Burma*. Bangkok. 1998.

'K', see Khin Zaw, U.

Kan Gyi, U. *Shwesettaw Thamaing Pya Zat*. Burma Herald Steam Press, Rangoon. 1881.

Kelly, Robert Talbot. *Burma Painted and Described*. London. 1905.

Khin Maung Gyi, Pagan U. *Memoirs of Oil Industry in Burma 905 AD–1980 AD*. Rangoon. 1989.

Khin Myo Chit, Daw. *Wonderland of Burmese Legends*. Bangkok. 1984.

Khin Myo Chit, Daw. *Colourful Burma*. 2 vols. Rangoon. 1988.

Khin Zaw, U. *Burmese Culture. General and Particular*. Rangoon. 1981. (Appeared under his *nom de plume*, 'K'.)

Khin Zaw, U. See also Thein Han, U.

King, J. C. H. 'Franks and Ethnography' in (eds) Caygill, Marjorie and John Cherry. *A. W. Franks. Nineteenth-Century Collecting and the British Museum*. London. 1997.

Kipling, Rudyard. 'Mandalay'. 1892.

Koretsky, Elaine and Donna Keretsky. *The Goldbeaters of Mandalay*. Brookline. 1991.

Lee King-Tsi and Hu Shih-Chang. 'Chinese Lacquer: Three Important Pieces at the Royal Museum of Scotland' in *Oriental Art*. Vol. XLII. No. 2. pp. 33–8. 1996.

Lowry, John. *Burmese Art*. London. 1974.

Lowry, John. 'A Burmese Buddhist Shrine', in *Victoria and Albert Museum Yearbook 1972*. pp. 117–32. London. 1972.

Luang Phraison Salarak. 'Intercourse between Burma and Siam, as recorded in the Hmannan Yazawindawgyi (Glass Palace Chronicle of the Kings of Burma), trans. U Aung Thein, selected articles from the *Journal of the Siam Society*. Vol. VI. 'Relationship with Burma: Part II'. Bangkok. 1959.

Lubeigt, G. *Civilisations et Société Pagan. Histoire et Légendes*. Paris. 1998.

Luce, Gordon H. *Old Burma-Early Pagan*. 3 vols. Artibus Asiae Supplementum 25. New York. 1969 (Vol. 1), 1970 (Vols. 2 and 3).

Luce, Gordon H. 'The Ancient Pyu', in *Journal of the Burma Research Society*. Vol. XXVII. Part III. pp. 239–53. 1937.

Luce, Gordon H. 'The 550 Jatakas in Old Burma' in *Artibus Asiae*. Vol XIX, 3/4. pp. 291–307. Ascona. 1956.

Luce, Gordon H. and U Pe Maung Tin (trans.), see *Glass Palace Chronicle ...., The*.

Mabberley, D. J. *The Plant Book*. Cambridge. 1997.

McRae, Alister and Alan Prentice. *Irrawaddy Flotilla*. Paisley. 1978.

McRae, Alister. *Scots in Burma. Golden Times in a Golden Land*. Edinburgh. 1990.

Marryat, Frederick. *Olla Podrida*. London. 1840.

Mazzeo, Donatella (ed.). *Suvannabhumi. La Terra dell'Oro. Giovanni Andreino, un Italiano in Birmania*. Rome. 1998.

Metcalf, Thomas R. *Ideologies of the Raj*. Vol. III.4. *New Cambridge History of India*. Cambridge. 1994.

Mi Mi Khaing, Daw. *Cook and Entertain the Burmese Way*. Rangoon. 1975.

Moore, Elizabeth, Hansjörg Mayer and U Win Pe. *Shwe Dagon. Golden Pagoda of Myanmar*. London. 1999.

Morris, A. P. 'Lacquer Ware Industry of Burma' in *Journal of the Burma Research Society*. Vol. IX. Part 1. April 1919.

Mya Sein, Ma. *Burma*. Oxford Pamphlets on Indian Affairs No. 17. London. 1943.

Myanmar Encyclopedia. Published by Sapay Beikman. Rangoon. 1970.

Nay Myo, Pan-chi (*nom de plume* of Noel Singer; see also Singer), 'In-ga-lan yauk nan-si nat-yoke-mya' (Images of nat spirits from the palace which are now in England), in *Ngwe-tar-yi*. No. 391. Rangoon. 1993.

Okudaira, Ryuji. 'The Burmese Dhammathat' in (ed.) Hooker, Michael Barry. *The Laws of South-East Asia*. Vol I. *The pre-modern texts*. Singapore. 1986.

Orwell, George. 'Shooting an Elephant' in *Shooting an Elephant and Other Essays*. pp. 1–10. London. 1950.

Oshegowa, Nina and Sergej Oshegow. *Kunst in Burma: 2000 Jahre Architektur, Malerei und Plastik im Zeichen des Buddhismus und Animismus.* Translated from the Russian by Christian Heidemann. Leipzig. 1988.

Pal, Pratapaditya (ed.). *Light of Asia.* Los Angeles. 1984.

Pe Maung Tin, U. and Gordon H. Luce (trans.), see *Glass Palace Chronicle ..., The.*

Pichard, Pierre. *Inventory of Monuments at Pagan. Monuments 256–552.* Vol. 2. Paris and Gartmore. 1993.

Pok Ni, U. *Konmara Pya Zat (An Example of Popular Burmese Drama in the XIX Century).* Vol. 1. Introduction and translation by U Hla Pe. London. 1952.

Pothisoonthorn, Visantanee and Somchai Vorasart. *The Art of Mother of Pearl Inlay.* Bangkok. 1981.

Prunner, G. *Meisterwerke Burmanischer Lackkunst.* Hamburg. 1966.

Rangoon Gazette Pictorial Supplement. Rangoon. nd. 1930s.

Raven-Hart, R. *Canoe to Mandalay.* London. 1939.

Rawson, Jessica (ed.). *Chinese Ornament. The Lotus and the Dragon.* London. 1984 & 1990.

Rawson, Jessica (ed.). *The British Museum Book of Chinese Art.* London. 1992.

Reichart, P. A. and H. P. Philipsen. *Betel and Miang: Vanishing Thai Habits.* Bangkok. 1996.

Richardson, D. 'Journey to Chiengmai' in *Journal of the Asiatic Society of Bengal.* October 1836.

Rodrigues, Yves. *Nat-Pwe: Burma's Supernatural Sub-Culture.* Gartmore. 1992.

Rooney, Dawn. *Betel Chewing Traditions in South East Asia.* Images of Asia Series. Oxford University Press. Kuala Lumpur. 1993.

Royle, J. Forbes. *Papers referring to the proposed contributions from India to the Industrial Exhibition of 1851.* London. 1851.

Rudner, David W. *Caste and Capitalism in Colonial India: the Nattukottai Chettiars.* London. 1994.

Sangermano, Father Vincenzo. *The Burmese Empire a Hundred Years Ago. With an Introduction and Notes by John Jardine.* (Many editions). Reprinted Bangkok. 1995. See also, Tandy, William.

Satow, Ernest. *A Diplomat in Siam.* Reprinted as Kiscadale Research Series No 4. Gartmore. 1994.

Scott, James George. See Shway Yoe: 1882, and below.

Scott, James George. *Burma. A Handbook of Practical Information.* London. 1906 and further editions.

Scott, James George and J. P. Hardiman *Gazeteer of Upper Burma and the Shan States.* 5 vols. Rangoon. 1900.

Shway Yoe (*nom de plume* of Sir George Scott, see above). *The Burman. His Life and Notions.* London. 1882; revised 1910; many later editions.

Singer, Noel F. See, Nay Myo, Pan-chi: 1993, and below.

Singer, Noel F. *Burmese Dance and Theatre.* Images of Asia Series. Oxford University Press. Kuala Lumpur. 1995.

Singer, Noel F. 'The Ramayana at the Burmese Court' in *Arts of Asia.* Vol 19. No. 6. pp. 90–103. November–December 1989.

Singer, Noel F. 'Survivors from a Burmese Palace' in *Arts of Asia.* Vol. 18. No 1. pp. 94–102. January–February 1988.

Singer, Noel F. 'Jengtung Lacquerware' in *Arts of Asia.* Vol. 21. No 5. pp. 154– 8. September–October 1991.

Singer, Noel F. 'Kammavaca Texts, their Covers and Binding Ribbons' in *Arts of Asia.* Vol. 23. No. 3. pp. 97–106. May–June 1993.

Singer, Noel F. 'Nineteenth Century Court Lacquerware from Myanmar and the Box of "The Sorceress"' in *Arts of Asia.* Vol. 26. No. 4. pp. 91–101. July–August 1996.

Singer, Noel F. 'Felice Beato's "Burmese Days"' in *Arts of Asia.* Vol. 28. No. 5. pp. 96–107. September–October 1998.

Skinner, the Reverend John. Unpublished journal in British Library. Western Mss. Add. Ms. 33697.

Slusser, Mary. *Nepal Mandala.* 2 vols. Princeton. 1982.

Smith, Martin. *Burma: insurgency and the politics of ethnicity.* London. 1991.

Soni, R. L. *A Cultural Study of the Burmese Era.* Mandalay. 1955.

Sotheby's – catalogue for sale at Stokesay Court, Shropshire, 29 September– 1 October 1994.

Sparling, T. A. *The Great Exhibition. A Question of Taste.* New Haven. 1982.

Stadtner, Donald M. (ed. and contributor). *The Art of Burma. New Studies.* Marg Publications. Vol. 50. Bombay. 1999.

Stargardt, Janice. *The Ancient Pyu of Burma.* Vol. 1. *Early Pyu Cities in a Man-made Landscape.* Cambridge and Singapore. 1990.

Stewart, Anthony Terence Quincey *The Pagoda War. Lord Dufferin and the fall of the Kingdom of Ava 1885–6.* London. 1972.

Strachan, Paul. *Pagan. Art and Architecture of Old Burma.* Whiting Bay. 1989.

Strachan, Paul (ed.). 1988, see Than Tun, U. 1988.

Swain, M. *Ayrshire and other Whitework.* Shire Albums 88. Aylesbury. 1982.

Symes, Michael. *An Account of an Embassy to the Kingdom of Ava Sent by the Governor-General of India in the Year 1795.* London. 1800.

Tachart *Reis van Siam door de Vaders Jesuieten en in't Frans beschreeven door den vader Tachart.* Utrecht. 1687.

Tandy, William (trans.). *A Description of the Burmese empire, compiled chiefly from Burmese documents by the Rev. Father Sangermano.* Rome. 1833. (This is an earlier version of the work listed above, under 'Sangermano'.)

Taw Sein Ko, U. 'A Preliminary Study of the Kalyani Inscriptions of Dhammaceti, 1476 AD.' *Indian Antiquary* XXII. Calcutta. January–February. 1893.

Temple, Richard Carnac. *The Thirty-Seven Nats, a Phase of Spirit Worship Prevailing in Burma.* London. 1906. Reprinted with additions (see Herbert, Patricia M.). London. 1991.

Temple, Richard Carnac. 'Notes on a collection of royal regalia of the Kings of Burma.' *Indian Antiquary.* Vol. 31. November 1902. pp. 442–4. Reprinted in Bombay, 1903.

Than Tun, U. *The Royal Orders of Burma. AD 1598–1885. Part III 1751–1781.* Kyoto. 1985.

Than Tun, U. 'Religion in Burma 1000–1300' in (ed.) Paul Strachan. *Essays on the History and Buddhism of Burma by Professor Than Tun.* Arran. 1988.

Thein Han, U and Khin Zaw, U. 'Ramayana in Burmese Literature and Arts' in *Journal of the Burma Research Society.* Vol LIX. Parts I & II. 1976.

Thiagarajan, Deborah. 'Doors and Woodcrafts of Chettinad' in (ed.) Michell, George. *Living Wood.* pp. 53–72. Marg Publications. Bombay. 1992.

Thierry, Solange. *Le Bétel. 1. Inde et Asie du Sud-Est.* Catalogues du Musée de L'Homme. Série K. Paris. 1969.

Tilly, Harry L. *Woodcarving of Burma.* Rangoon. 1903.

Treasures from the National Museum, Bangkok. Bangkok. 1987.

Wallich, Nathaniel. *A Numerical List of Dried Specimens of Plants in the East India Company's Museum collected under the Superintendence of Dr Wallich.* London. 1828.

Wallich, Nathaniel. *Plantae Asiaticae Rariores*. 3 vols. London. 1830, 1831 and 1832.

Warren, William and Luca Invernizzi Tettoni. *Arts and Crafts of Thailand*. London. 1994.

Watt, George. *Indian Art at Delhi 1903, being the Official Catalogue of the Delhi Exhibition 1902–3*. London. 1904.

Wheeler, J. Talboys. *Journal of a Voyage up the Irrawaddy to Mandalay and Bhamo*. Rangoon. 1871. Reprinted in Bangkok as Vol. III Burma, *Itineraria Asiatica*. 1996.

Williamson, A. *Burma Gazetteer: Shwebo District*. Vol A. Rangoon. 1929.

Willis, Michael. 'Sculpture from India' in (eds) Caygill, Marjorie and John Cherry. *A. W. Franks. Nineteenth Century Collecting and the British Museum*. London. 1997.

Win Pe, U. *Shwe Dagon*. Rangoon. 1972.

Yule, Henry. *A Narrative of the Mission Sent by the Governor-General of India to the Court of Ava in 1855*. London. 1858. Reprinted with additions and an Introduction by Hugh Tinker. Kuala Lumpur. 1968.

Yule, Henry and A C Burnell. *Hobson-Jobson. A Glossary of Anglo-Indian colloquial words and phrases*. London. 1886. Many later editions and reprints.